MW00788287

Asian Traditions

of Meditation

EDITED BY HALVOR EIFRING

 University of Hawai'i Press ◈ Honolulu

Printed in the United States of America

23 22 21 20 19 18   6 5 4 3 2 1

Library of Congress Cataloging-in-Publication Data

Names: Eifring, Halvor, editor.
Title: Asian traditions of meditation / edited by Halvor
     Eifring.
Description: Honolulu : University of Hawai'i Press,
     [2016] | Includes index.
Identifiers: LCCN 2016015383 | ISBN 9780824855680
     (cloth ; alk. paper)
Subjects: LCSH: Meditation—Asia—Cross-cultural studies.
Classification: LCC BL627 .A85 2016 | DDC 204/.35095—dc23
LC record available at https://lccn.loc.gov/2016015383

ISBN 978-0-8248-7667-8 (pbk.)

University of Hawai'i Press books are printed on acid-free
paper and meet the guidelines for permanence and
durability of the Council on Library Resources.

CONTENTS

Acknowledgments vii

Introduction ix

1 What Is Meditation? 1
HALVOR EIFRING

2 Types of Meditation 27
HALVOR EIFRING

3 *Samādhi* in the *Yoga Sūtras* 48
EDWIN F. BRYANT

4 *Yantra* and *Cakra* in Tantric Meditation 71
MADHU KHANNA

5 The History of Jaina Meditation 93
JOHANNES BRONKHORST

6 *Nām Simran* in the Sikh Religion 103
KRISTINA MYRVOLD

7 Meditation Objects in Pāli Buddhist Texts 122
SARAH SHAW

8 Tibetan Longevity Meditation 145
GEOFFREY SAMUEL

9 *Kànhuà* Meditation in Chinese Zen 165
MORTEN SCHLÜTTER

10 Meditation in the Classical Daoist Tradition 185
HAROLD D. ROTH

11 "Quiet Sitting" in Neo-Confucianism 207
MASAYA MABUCHI

12 The Science of Meditation 227
ARE HOLEN

List of Contributors 245

Index 247

ACKNOWLEDGMENTS

The starting point for this book was a conference made possible by generous support from the Chiang Ching-kuo Foundation for International Scholarly Exchange, Taipei; the Department of Culture Studies and Oriental Languages, University of Oslo; PluRel, University of Oslo; Kultrans, University of Oslo; and the Institute for Comparative Research in Human Culture, Oslo. The initial planning of the conference and the book took place during the five months the editor spent as a guest researcher at the Research Center for Monsoon Asia, National Tsing Hua University, Hsinchu, Taiwan, in 2009. The conference took place at the Acem International Retreat Centre Halvorsbøle, Oslo, Norway, in May 2010. In addition to the editor, the organizing committee included Svend Davanger and Terje Stordalen, both from the University of Oslo.

The following persons helped in the organization of the conference or assisted in the work with the book: Wubshet Dagne, Yue Bao, Regina Cinduringtias Pasiasti, Torbjørn Hobbel, Stig Inge Skogseth, Alexander Lundberg, and—last, but not least—the editor's patient and loving wife, Joy Chun-hsi Lu, who along the way has provided much food both for thought and for the belly. The long and winding process from initial proposal to finished book was much helped by the patient guidance of Patricia Crosby and, later, by Stephanie Chun at the University of Hawai'i Press. The editor would hereby like to express his deep-felt gratitude for the many kinds of support given by these persons and institutions, as well as by others who have offered help along the way. This includes the anonymous reviewers who have given their feedback on earlier versions of the book.

Halvor Eifring
Oslo, October 2015

Meditative practices have flourished since the founding of the great civilizations in Eurasia. For the first time, this volume brings together studies of the major traditions of Asian meditation, including Yoga, Tantra, Jainism, Sikhism, Buddhism, Daoism, and Confucianism, as well as modern secular and scientific approaches to meditation.

Few if any scholarly attempts have been made at cross-cultural comparison of meditative practices. This is in contrast to the cross-cultural study of mystical experience that has been thoroughly addressed in the debates pitting the constructivist approach of Steven T. Katz against the perennial approach of Robert K. C. Forman.[1] It is also in contrast to the comparative issues raised in scientific rather than cultural studies of meditation, as in Maria Ospina et al.'s impressive report "Meditation Practices for Health: State of the Research." Finally, while scholarly studies of meditation have tended to shy away from cross-cultural comparison, more popular works seldom have the same qualms, including Claudio Naranjo and Robert E. Ornstein's *On the Psychology of Meditation* and Daniel Goleman's *The Meditative Mind*, both of which were first published in the 1970s, as well as Livia Kohn's more recent *Meditation Works*.

Scholars studying meditation have typically stayed within one specific tradition and stuck to culture-specific modes of explanation with limited general relevance. This includes excellent monographs, such as Sarah Shaw's *Buddhist Meditation*, Isabelle Robinet's *Taoist Meditation*, and Rodney L. Taylor's *The Confucian Way of Contemplation*. To the extent that scholars have ventured beyond the bounds of a single tradition, they have mostly limited themselves to traditions that are historically related, as in Geoffrey Samuel's *The Origins of Yoga and Tantra*. Scholars have usually avoided the comparison of traditions that have no obvious historical relation but may have generic features in common or may, for that matter, differ from each other in interesting ways.

This collection of essays brings together different Asian traditions and compares them not only with each other but also with the traditions studied in another recent volume I edited, *Meditation in Judaism, Christianity and Islam.*[2] In addition to delving deeply into the individual traditions, this book places each tradition in a global perspective, looking at both historical and generic connections between meditative practices from different historical periods and different parts of the Eurasian continent.

The aim of this book is twofold. On the one hand, it seeks to identify the cultural and historical peculiarities of various Asian schools of meditation, both for their own sake and as a basis for further comparison. On the other hand, it seeks to identify basic features of meditative practices across cultures, and thereby to take a first step toward a framework for the comparative study of meditation.

◈

Asian forms of meditation have two main historical sources: Indian and Chinese. In the course of their development, both forms have ventured far beyond their places of origin to eventually cover most of Asia. They have also mixed with one another, and with meditative, devotional, ritual, and shamanistic practices in the various localities to which they have traveled. More recently, they have become global phenomena on a larger scale, and have exerted substantial influence on the cultures of America, Europe, Australia, and other parts of the world, often in combination with Western medicine, physical exercise, psychotherapy, and various forms of modern spirituality. The resulting practices have in turn exerted an equally substantial influence on Asian meditation.

The notion of Asian traditions of meditation is in contrast to the Judaic, Christian, Islamic, and ancient Greco-Roman traditions stemming from Europe, the Middle East, and North Africa. There is no absolute line of division between the two. For instance, it has been persuasively argued that Indian impulses have strongly influenced the Kabbalah of Judaism, the Orthodox Christian Jesus Prayer, and the recitative and sometimes musical practices of *dhikr* and *samā'* of Islamic Sufism. It can also easily be argued that the exclusively devotional practices of the Sikh *nām simran* (discussed by Kristina Myrvold in this volume) are generically more similar to the corresponding European, Middle Eastern, and North African practices than to most Asian forms of meditation. The recitative practices of the Jesus Prayer and the Islamic *dhikr* display many parallels not only to *nām simran* but also to the Indian repetition of *mantras* and to the East Asian recitation of Buddha names (Ch. *niàn fó*; Jap. *nen butsu*). Similar cross-cultural parallels can be found in the realm of visualization practices. Thus, distinguishing the Asian traditions from European, Middle Eastern, and North African practices is done mainly for practical and heuristic reasons, not because they are typologically distinct.

Nevertheless, there are some general tendencies that distinguish the two groups. While meditation practices originating in Europe, the Middle East, and North Africa typically center on devotional, thematic, and scripture-based forms of recitation and visualization, Asian forms of meditation cover a much greater range of methods, including body and breath techniques, awareness training, and other methods involving a high degree of technical sophistication. In Asian traditions, even some of the recitative and visual practices have a technical rather than a content-oriented emphasis, as in some uses of *mantras* and *yantras*. Of course, European, Middle Eastern, and North African meditation also have their technical features, but the main focus lies on the devotional, thematic, and scriptural content.[3] And while devotion-, theme-, and scripture-based forms of recitation and visualization are by no means uncommon in Asia, most Asian traditions also include a number of practices that tend to emphasize technical practice over semantic, affective, thematic, or symbolic content.

About the spiritual exercises of the Greco-Roman philosophers of antiquity, the French historian of philosophy Pierre Hadot says, "In all the schools, for various reasons, philosophy will be especially a meditation upon death and an attentive concentration on the present moment in order to enjoy it or live it in full consciousness" (*Philosophy as a Way of Life*, 39). This could almost have been said about Asian schools of meditation as well. However, the following characterization contrasts the Asian and the Greco-Roman practices: "Unlike the Buddhist meditation practices of the Far East, Greco-Roman philosophical meditation is not linked to a corporeal attitude but is a purely rational, imaginative, or intuitive exercise that can take extremely varied forms. First of all it is the memorization and assimilation of the fundamental dogmas and rules of life of the school" (59). Several Buddhist and other Asian forms of meditation also involve "rational, imaginative, or intuitive" activities. However, Hadot is right in pointing to the "corporeal" or in other ways technical and prelogical aspect of meditation as something more typical of Asian schools.

In spite of these differences, all forms of meditation share a number of elements. By definition, meditation always has technical elements, and always seeks to modify the use of attention and to bring about some form of long-term inner transformation. At a technical level, meditation methods are built from a large number of elements, including a wide variety of meditation objects, a few more or less well-defined mental attitudes, and spatial, temporal, social, ritual, interpretive, and other settings. The choice of technical features influences the meditative process and its effects. Again, however, the range of variety is larger in the Asian traditions than in the traditions originating in Europe, the Middle East, and North Africa.

In modern Western culture, the meaning of the term "meditation" has changed radically to accommodate the enormous influx of Asian practices, and the modern scientific and popular interest in meditation is directed almost entirely toward techniques originating in Asia. The technical and often body-oriented nature of Asian practices allows them to fit more neatly into modern Western secular and scientific thinking than the typical devotional and scripture-based practices of European, Middle Eastern, and North African traditions. In the process, Asian methods have often been detached from their cultural and religious backgrounds and placed within secular and scientific contexts. Many of them have then found their way back to their places of origin, and this has in turn influenced modern Asian cultures of meditation.

This book consists of twelve chapters written by scholars from various fields. Although all of the chapters have a scholarly ambition, they are written for interested readers with a general academic background.

Comparative issues are most strongly present in my opening chapters, one of which explores a generic definition of meditation, and the other, the classification of meditative practices into directive and nondirective types.

The part of the book addressing individual meditative traditions begins with two chapters dealing with traditions usually subsumed under the broad label of Hinduism: Edwin F. Bryant's account of the inner transformations associated with the term *samādhi* in the highly diverse Indian tradition of Yoga, and Madhu Khanna's chapter discussing the Indian tradition of Tantra and its meditative use of *yantras*, simple linear diagrams of concentric configurations used for visualization, and their correlation with the bodily energy centers known as *cakra*.

Next come chapters on two traditions that are not often explored in the context of meditation: Johannes Bronkhorst looks into the historical discontinuity and innovation of Jaina meditation, and Kristina Myrvold examines the many varieties of *nām simran*, the Sikh recitative practice of remembering the divine name.

Three chapters discuss various Buddhist approaches to meditation: Sarah Shaw's study of various meditation objects suitable for different stages and individuals in Southeast Asian Buddhism; Geoffrey Samuel's exploration of how Tibetan Buddhist longevity practice highlights the complex relation between the inner transformation that meditation is thought to bring about and its other more "worldly" goals; and Morten Schlütter's account of keyword (*kànhuà*) meditation in Chinese Zen, which works toward a final transformative experience of enlightenment, with no regard for states of calm or quietude.

Two other chapters discuss indigenous Chinese traditions: Harold D. Roth's argument that the early Daoist tradition was based not primarily on philosophical ideas and scriptures but on a common set of meditative practices that would ultimately reveal a deeper reality known as the Way (Dào), with which the actions of the individual would be made to spontaneously resonate; and Masaya Mabuchi's account of the ambivalent attitude toward meditation, referred to as "quiet sitting," in Neo-Confucianism, in which the wish to achieve an intuitive grasp of one's "original nature" or a "universal principle" was tempered by the fear that the experience of quietude could undermine traditional teachings and norms, and draw the meditator away from external action and social relationships.

In the final chapter, Are Holen discusses two waves in the recent scientific interest in meditation, one focusing on the physiology of relaxation, the other on the neuroscience of attention. The purpose of his chapter is not to assess the scientific validity of such studies but to see them as part of a cultural history of modern meditation practices. While science is typically associated with modern Western concerns, and most of the studies under scrutiny are written in English and have been published in European and American journals, almost all of the meditation techniques studied hail from the Asian traditions explored in the rest of the volume.

◆

Cultural historians typically study meditation as a function of its linguistic and historical situatedness, and the focus of this volume is on some of the world's major meditative traditions. In addition to such cultural and symbolic contexts, this volume also seeks to take into account the specific impact and importance of the technical features of meditation. More specifically, it aims to squeeze out from the limited source material we have whatever information there is about specific technical practices within the traditions studied.

This is not unproblematic. As any cultural historian knows, and as should be clear from most of the contributions in this volume, meditation is usually tightly interwoven with the context in which it takes place, often making purely technical descriptions appear inadequate. For instance, the *yantra* and *cakra* practices presented by Khanna, the Tibetan practices described by Samuel, and the Chinese Zen practices discussed by Schlütter would be hard to envisage in a culturally neutral setting. Furthermore, the early sources are typically more interested in the doctrine behind meditation, or the states of mind it is supposed to produce, than in the technical practice itself, prompting Bryant to proclaim that his contribution to this volume is merely concerned with the metaphysical presuppositions of Yoga, not its actual practice. Even to the extent that early sources do account for meditative practice, these accounts are often prescriptive rather than descriptive, idealized rather than realistic, and determined by doctrinal rather than practical concerns, as Bronkhorst shows with particular clarity in the case of Jaina meditation. Meditative practice is also sometimes surrounded by taboo, as something to be discussed only with one's teacher or master, to the extent that Buddhist monks who have been meditating together for years still may not know which technique their fellow monks are practicing.[4]

Despite such problems, however, many sources do provide at least some information regarding actual, or at least ideal, meditative practice, and they usually presuppose that practice is more important than doctrine. The major obstacle for the study of practice has perhaps been not the lack of source material but a scholarly orientation that has prioritized doctrinal issues and sociocultural contexts over actual practice. To varying degrees, the contributions in this volume seek to counter this bias. For instance, Bronkhorst shows how the tension between practical and doctrinal concerns produced challenges for any meditator attempting to take seriously traditional Jaina accounts of meditation. Myrvold combines the study of historical texts with her own ethnographic material on modern Sikh practices, providing life to the former and depth to the latter. Shaw uses early narrative texts, supplemented with ethnographic material from Southeast Asia, to get closer to the reality of Buddhist meditative practice and teacher-student interactions. Roth shows how the purely textual material of early Daoist scriptures can provide a basis for conjectures regarding actual meditative practice. Mabuchi presents an indirect piece of evidence for the importance of practice when discussing the Neo-Confucian fear that meditative practice, even if it takes place in a Confucian context, may draw the adept away from Confucian norms and action. Holen argues that one of the determining factors behind the scientific approach employed in the study of meditation is the type of meditative practice under scrutiny.

In other words, the crux of meditation lies only partly in its symbolic meaning within a larger sociocultural and interpretive context. Just as important are the effects of what a practitioner actually does while meditating. This volume aims to combine the study of meditative practice with an interest in the cultural contexts in which such practice takes place.

Notes

1. See, for example, Katz, *Mysticism and Philosophical Analysis*; and Forman, *Problem of Pure Consciousness*.

2. Both books may be profitably read along with two other volumes I edited: *Hindu, Buddhist and Daoist Meditation: Cultural Histories* and *Meditation and Culture: The Interplay of Practice and Context*.

3. See Eifring, "Meditation in Judaism, Christianity and Islam," which includes several forms of prayer in the notion of meditation.

4. Cf. Shaw, *Buddhist Meditation*, 11. On the problems regarding historical sources for meditative practice, see also Eifring and Holen, "The Uses of Attention," 2–6; and Bielefeldt, *Dōgen's Manuals of Zen Meditation*, 11–12.

Glossary

nen butsu 念佛
niàn fó 念佛

Bibliography

Bielefeldt. *Dōgen's Manuals of Zen Meditation*. Berkeley: University of California Press, 1990.

Eifring, Halvor, ed. *Hindu, Buddhist and Daoist Meditation: Cultural Histories*. Oslo: Hermes, 2014.

———, ed., *Meditation and Culture: The Interplay of Practice and Context*. London: Bloomsbury Academic, 2015.

———, ed., *Meditation in Judaism, Christianity and Islam: Cultural Histories*. London: Bloomsbury Academic, 2013.

———. "Meditation in Judaism, Christianity and Islam: Technical Aspects of Devotional Practices." in Eifring, *Meditation in Judaism, Christianity and Islam*, 3–13.

Eifring, Halvor, and Are Holen. "The Uses of Attention: Elements of Meditative Practice." In Eifring, *Hindu, Buddhist and Daoist Meditation*, 1–26.

Forman, Robert K. C., ed. *The Problem of Pure Consciousness: Mysticism and Philosophy*. New York: Oxford University Press, 1990.

Goleman, Daniel J. *The Meditative Mind: The Varieties of Meditative Experience*. Los Angeles CA: Jeremy P. Tarcher / Perigree Books, 1988. First published 1977.

Hadot, Pierre. *Philosophy as a Way of Life: Spiritual Exercises from Socrates to Foucault.* Edited by Arnold I. Davidson. Translated by Michael Chase. Malden, MA: Blackwell, 1995.

Katz, Steven T., ed. *Mysticism and Philosophical Analysis.* New York: Oxford University Press, 1978.

Kohn, Livia. *Meditation Works: In the Hindu, Buddhist and Daoist Traditions.* Magdalena, NM: Three Pines Press, 2008.

Naranjo, Claudio, and Robert E. Ornstein. *On the Psychology of Meditation.* New York: Viking Press, 1971.

Ospina, Maria B., Kenneth Bond, Mohammad Karkhaneh, Lisa Tjosvold, Ben Vandermeer, Yuanyuan Liang, Liza Bialy, Nicola Hooton, Nina Buscemi, Donna M. Dryden, and Terry P. Klassen. "Meditation Practices for Health: State of the Research." *Evidence Report/Technology Assessment,* no. 155. Rockville MD: Agency for Healthcare Research and Quality, 2007.

Robinet, Isabelle. *Taoist Meditation: The Mao-shan Tradition of Great Purity.* Translated by Julian F. Pas and Norman J. Girardot. Albany: State University of New York Press, 1993. First published 1979.

Samuel, Geoffrey. *The Origins of Yoga and Tantra: Indic Religions to the Thirteenth Century.* Cambridge: Cambridge University Press, 2008.

Shaw, Sarah. *Buddhist Meditation: An Anthology of Texts from the Pāli Canon.* London: Routledge, 2006.

Taylor, Rodney L. *The Confucian Way of Contemplation: Okada Takehiko and the Tradition of Quiet-Sitting.* Columbia: University of South Carolina Press, 1988.

What Is Meditation?

The term "meditation" has a long and complex history in the West, and it has no exact correspondent in the Asian traditions.[1] The modern usage of the term, however, is strongly influenced by encounters with Asian, and particularly Indian, spiritual practices. As a result, our current understanding of the notion reflects a mixture of Western and various Asian concerns.

In the West, the term "meditation," often in its Latin form *meditātiō*, has been related mostly to Christianity, but also to philosophy and the arts. In this multifaceted tradition, the term typically denotes an associative and nonlinear type of reflection that transcends purely rational thinking but still, as the *Oxford English Dictionary* puts it, "engages the intellectual or discursive faculties." Meditation is often based on scripture and seen as a special form of reading, prayer, or imaginative visualization.

When Western scholars began to translate Indian and other Asian classics, however, the term "meditation" often came to be used in a wider sense, referring to Buddhist and Yogic practices that are, according to the *Oxford English Dictionary*, "aimed at the eradication of rational or worldly mental activity." Such nondiscursive meanings of the term have been further strengthened by the technical orientation of the scientific investigation of these practices. As pointed out by Are Holen in this volume, almost all scientific meditation research examines technical (rather than content-oriented) practices of Asian origin, and these have also dominated the general popular interest in meditation in the past half century. As a result, the term "meditation" now more often refers to practices that do *not* primarily engage "the intellectual or discursive faculties."

The Asian traditions explored in this volume include a large variety of different practices—discursive and nondiscursive, content-oriented and more narrowly technical. As a starting point for these discussions, the present chapter attempts to define the term "meditation" in a way that poses questions of interest concerning the nature of meditation. The suggested definition is:

Meditation is an attention-based technique for inner transformation.[2]

This definition is broad and inclusive, but in some respects also quite radical. On the one hand, it includes practices that often go by other names, such as certain forms of ritual, prayer, and contemplation. On the other hand, it deliberately excludes a number of practices that are sometimes referred to as meditation, such as pure relaxation techniques. Moreover, the suggested definition refers to technical practices and does not cover spontaneously engendered states of mind. It also excludes artistic or philosophical products often referred to as "meditations" on a given topic.

This chapter will discuss in some detail the various elements of the definition of "meditation," as well as the borderlines between meditation and other phenomena. Moreover, by linking these elements to the history of meditation across the Eurasian continent, including material from other chapters in this volume, this chapter will attempt to show the cultural relevance of the definition. Before embarking on this discussion, however, some basic problems relating to definitions need to be addressed.

Generic Definitions

Cultural historians sometimes object to the use of generic, unitary definitions such as the one defining meditation as "an attention-based technique for inner transformation," since these are in some respects deliberately insensitive to cultural and historical features. Such a definition of meditation can easily be accused of the anachronistic and Eurocentric imposition of modern-day Western concepts on a predominantly premodern Asian material, in contrast to the historical, cultural, and social "situatedness" reflected in most of the chapters in this volume. This is easily seen as what cultural historians disparagingly call "essentialism," referring in this case to a mode of thinking that ascribes a stable and often abstract "essence" to social, cultural, or otherwise human phenomena. Generic definitions, therefore, are often looked upon as tools for natural scientists, who tend to look away from cultural and historical distinctions and to view actual language use and local conceptual schemes as being of limited relevance to their research. Indeed, most earlier generic definitions of meditation have been suggested by scientists working within biomedical research or psychology.[3]

Furthermore, while generic definitions avoid explicit reference to cultural and historical features, they are hardly neutral in the sense of not being influenced by their context. The definition of meditation suggested above is linked to theoretical concerns, and these concerns are also situated in culture and history. For instance, some might argue that the definition's reference to "technique" reflects a strong Asian influence, since European and Middle Eastern forms of meditation are typically less technical and more devotional than many Indian and Chinese forms, while others might suggest that the reference to "technique" is a product of modern scientific and technological concerns and thus in reality linked to Western thinking. There may be some truth in both suggestions.

However, the fact that the theoretical implications of a definition are bound to reflect some cultural and historical concerns simply means that these concerns should also be explicated and made the objects of critical reflection, which is indeed what this chapter is trying to do. Our definition points not to the unchanging "essence" of a "thing" called "meditation" but to some features that may, for the moment at least, be seen as useful and interesting to explore and debate.

In any case, it is not clear what the alternative to a generic definition would be. As pointed out by the historian of religion Jonathan Z. Smith, we should not "rest content with reproducing native lexicography and, thereby, give in to the prevalent ethos of localism, branding every attempt at generalization a western imposition. . . . How 'they' use a word cannot substitute for the systematic stipulative and precising procedures by which the academy contests and seeks to control second-order, specialized usage."[4] In particular, it would be hard to see what a comparative study of meditation would be comparing if it were solely based on local concepts rather than a notion of meditation that supersedes each individual language and culture.

Smith's own suggestion of a "self-consciously *polythetic* mode of classification which surrender[s] the idea of perfect, unique, single differentia"[5] does not seem to solve the problem. Smith himself admits that he knows of "no examples of attempts at the polythetic classification of religions or religious phenomena,"[6] and a reviewer of Smith's work points out that "the reader who expects an exhaustive list of [the] characteristics [of a polythetic definition of religion] is in for a disappointment; Smith does not supply it."[7] While later scholars have made a few attempts in this direction,[8] the challenge has mostly proven to be too complex.

Polythetic definitions have been useful in biology, where they have helped to overcome problems left behind by traditional, monothetic definitions of species. In such cases, however, even polythetic definitions have a monothetic core, since they presuppose a common evolutionary origin of species that are classified together. Social and personal phenomena such as meditation have no such monothetic core—no stable "essence," if you like. Furthermore, while a definition of biological species is usually built on features that have what Rodney Needham calls "a real, distinct, and independent character," definitions of social and personal phenomena "cannot be carried out by reference to discrete empirical particulars, but [entail] instead a reliance on further features of the same character which themselves are likewise polythetic." The immense complexity of polythetic classification of social and personal phenomena may in the end render it impracticable, since "comparative studies, whether morphological or functional or statistical, are rendered more daunting and perhaps even unfeasible."[9]

There is no a priori reason to assume that social and personal phenomena such as meditation that lack the monothetic core displayed by species in biology are in themselves naturally divided into classes. More probably, they do not constitute natural taxa, and beyond the conceptualizations forced upon them by different languages in different ways, any classification will have artificial elements. The purpose of defining meditation, therefore, is not primarily to suggest a natural class of meditative phenomena but to establish a single point of reference to which comparative studies of meditation may usefully refer. Being more distinct and less fuzzy, a monothetic definition serves this purpose better than a polythetic one, which is indeed why some scholars have found it "reasonable to ask whether a definition of a [polythetic] concept is after all a *definition*, since it is certainly imprecise."[10]

In spite of accusations to the contrary, a precise generic definition can easily be combined with a keen awareness of the historical and cultural situatedness of natural language concepts and the social and personal realities to which such concepts refer, as well as with the ambiguities, family resemblances, overlaps, and gradient distinctions underlying both language and reality. Natural language concepts such as the English "meditation"—or, for that matter, the Arabic *dhikr*, the Sanskrit *dhyāna*, and the Chinese *jìng-zuò*—are multivalent, mutable, and fuzzy, and this is also the case with the social and personal phenomena to which they refer. However, these concepts and phenomena may all be fruitfully related to a monothetic definition of meditation, though they diverge from it in different ways. If, for instance, meditation is defined as a practice, the states of mind covered by the English "meditation" and the Sanskrit *dhyāna* fall outside the definition, and so do the philosophical and artistic products referred to by the English term. However, the recitation implied by the Arabic *dhikr*, the visualization implied by some Tantric uses of the Sanskrit *dhyāna*, and the seated posture implied by Chinese *jìng-zuò* restrict these terms to a much narrower range of practices than our general notion of meditation. In a comparative study of meditation, a monothetic definition provides us with a common focus, against which the peculiarities of each tradition may be highlighted.

In an essay on the personal and social aspects of the Sufi practice of *dhikr*, Shahzad Bashir wrote, "Just as thinking about *dhikr* as meditation helps us understand the practice better, examining meditation in the light of presumptions coming from *dhikr* highlights meditation's connection to modern forms of human subjectivity that are ingrained in the way we think and act but are not always easily visible. . . . Thinking about their similarities and differences provides an excellent venue to deepen our understanding of both."[11] Bashir refers to meditation "in its most commonsensical English meaning," but his point is just as valid if we think of meditation as a monothetically defined technical term.

A weak version of a generic definition would be merely stipulative, without deeper theoretical aspirations, with only the practical goal of providing common ground for the comparative treatment of related phenomena across cultures and languages. A stronger version of a generic definition is a theoretical definition, which not only has practical implications but also purports to link the defined notion to larger theoretical issues. As we have seen, defining meditation as a *technique* (not a state, and not a nontechnical form of practice) implies a certain theoretical view of meditation, as does the notion of meditation being *attention-based* (excluding automatized ritualistic practice) and practiced in order to achieve long-term *inner transformation* (and not just passing changes of state or changes that affect only the body). Such theoretical implications make a discussion of the definition into much more than a simple terminological question, touching as such a discussion does upon the nature of the phenomena to which the term in question refers.

Technique

According to our definition, all forms of meditation are "techniques." A technique is a kind of practice that is *deliberately undertaken*, not simply taken for granted, unlike many of the everyday social practices typically studied by sociologists and anthropologists. A technique is *systematic* in the sense that its procedures are clearly specified, though this does not rule out spontaneous or even creative elements, as when random thoughts are made the object of meditation. It is *continuous*, meaning that the intentional activity undertaken is either durative (as when sustained attention is directed toward an image) or repetitive (as when a word or a sound combination is repeated over time), not sequential (as in the sequence of postures and movements involved in Hatha Yoga or Tàijí, the nonrepetitive chanting of the entire Lotus Sūtra in Buddhism[12] or the Book of Psalms in East Syrian Christianity,[13] or the nondurative and nonrepetitive visualizations of the Gospels in Christianity or the imaginative space travels of Shàngqīng Daoism[14]). A technique is *set aside* from other activities in time, often also with regard to posture and location, and by means of specific rituals.[15] And it is undertaken to achieve certain *effects*, to which we shall return below, and at least partly to do so indirectly by means of *universal mechanisms* inherent in the nature of the human body and mind.

Many meditative traditions have an ambivalent relation to the technical aspects of meditation. For instance, meditative prayer and visualization are often explicitly content-oriented, devotional traditions focus on a personal relation to God, and apophatic practices typically emphasize the "unmediated" contact with the divine or the "direct" realization of ultimate truth. In all cases, this sometimes leads to a negative attitude toward the technicality of meditation. However, this does not mean that content-oriented, devotional, and apophatic practices are excluded from our definition, only that our emphasis is placed on their technical aspects, in contrast to the emphases of the traditions themselves.[16]

Sometimes the ambivalence regarding the technicality of meditation is given direct expression in paradoxical statements, such as the thirteenth- to fourteenth-century German mystic Meister Eckhart's notion of a "pathless path,"[17] or the Zen Buddhist notion of a "gateless gate."[18] At other times, a strong skepticism toward meditative techniques is juxtaposed with exhortations to meditate, as when the "Platform Sūtra" presents the seventh- to eighth-century Chinese Zen master Huìnéng as claiming that he "has no techniques" (*wú jìliǎng*), but in the same work exhorting his disciples to continue practicing "straight sitting" (*duān-zuò*, i.e., meditation) after he has passed away. In the Christian context, the paradox is clearly explicated in "The Epistle of Prayer": "It is not possible for a man to attain perfection in this work unless these two means, or two other like them, come first. And yet perfection of this work is its suddenness, without means."[19] In modern times, Jiddu Krishnamurti has been famous for his opposition to meditation techniques ("the truth is a pathless land"), but others have interpreted his approach as a form of systematic meditative awareness training.[20] A modern collection of essays on the Zen practice of *shi-kan ta-za* (lit. "just sit") vacillates between insisting that the practice has no particular method and describing clearly technical elements such as attention to the lower abdomen, specific breathing practices, and a strong focus on correct bodily posture.[21] The Taiwan-based Buddhist master Sheng Yen describes one of his meditation techniques as "the method of no method."[22]

One reason for this skepticism or ambivalence is the strong goal-orientation inherent in the notion of a technique. Techniques are practiced to achieve certain effects, but the active pursuit of effects may, paradoxically, make it more difficult to achieve them. The pursuit of a goal may divert the mind away from the actual practice, and it may involve a mental focus so strong that it fails to perceive realities of a more fleeting and ephemeral nature. A technical orientation may also encourage passivity, as if the transformative effects of meditation will come automatically, almost machine-like or magically, rather than involve a strong sense of agency and personal participation. It may also stand in the way of the personal devotion required in some meditative traditions, as in the Sikh practices described by Kristina Myrvold in this volume. In the Christian tradition, a reliance on techniques is sometimes seen as standing in the way of God's grace, as in the following quotation concerning meditative prayer from Jacques Philippe's *Time for God:* "St. Jane Frances de Chantal used to say, 'The best method of prayer is not to have one, because prayer is not obtained by artifice'— by technique, we would say today—'but by grace.' There is no 'method' of praying, in the sense of a set of instructions or procedures that we merely have to apply in order to pray well" (9). In general, the technical orientation of meditation may be contrasted with the content-orientation of prayer. Both meditation and prayer may aim at achieving certain effects, but while prayer typically does so directly by means of its content, meditation typically does so indirectly, in a nonlinear way, by means of technical elements that build on universal mechanisms. For instance, prayer may aim at obtaining the forgiveness of sins by asking for it, or may try to achieve intimate contact with God through the expression of devotion, while meditation may seek to obtain its transformative effects at least partly by means of cross-cultural elements that go beyond such content, for example, by directing one's attention to the breath, by repeating certain sound combinations, by gazing at or visualizing geometrical figures, and so on. Such mechanisms typically lie beyond the individual's direct control, and the main effects of meditation result from the methodical practice of a technique rather than any purposeful striving. While the outcome of prayer may also lie beyond the individual's control, it is typically conceived of as being dependent on God's grace rather than any mechanisms inherent in the human mind or body.

In many traditions, even technical elements are given content-oriented interpretations, as when the breath is understood as an expression of the transience of existence in certain Buddhist contexts, or as a link to cosmic energy in Daoist and Yogic contexts, or the breath of life in Christian contexts. Only with an outsider's comparative perspective is it possible to observe the universal mechanisms involved in such elements, irrespective of the cultural context in which they are used.

Scientific definitions of meditation tend to focus on its technical aspects, since this makes it more easily available for standardized measurement. One much-quoted definition emphasizes that meditation makes "use of a specific technique (clearly defined)."[23] Some definitions use terms such as "[psychoactive] exercise,"[24] "[mental] training,"[25] and "[self-regulation/emotional and attentional regulatory] practice"[26] instead of or in addition to "technique." The technical orientation of meditation is sometimes contrasted with the content orientation of other practices by pointing out that meditation emphasizes "process rather than content,"[27] while nonmeditative practices such as self-hypnosis, visualization, and psychotherapy "aim primarily at changing mental contents . . . such as thoughts, images, and emotions."[28] In our definition, however, meaningful content is not excluded from the notion of meditation as long as there are also technical elements.

Individual agency is an important part of the practice orientation involved in defining meditation as a technique. Meditation is done *by* the practitioner, not *to* him or her. Our definition does not include so-called spontaneous or natural meditations occurring as inadvertent responses to a scenery or a situation, like the Buddha's famous childhood experience of meditative bliss: "I recall once, when my father the Sakyan was working, and I was sitting in the cool shade of a rose-apple tree, then—quite secluded from sensuality, secluded from unskillful mental qualities—I entered & remained in the first jhana [=Skt. *dhyāna*; usually translated as "meditation"]: rapture & pleasure born from seclusion, accompanied by directed thought & evaluation."[29] However, most traditions acknowledge that meditative practice always takes place in a context, and that elements of the context may be as important in triggering transformative change as the meditation technique itself, as Sarah Shaw argues for the Buddhist case in this volume. Meditation may be practiced individually or communally, and even communal meditation may involve a high degree of individual agency, nicely illustrated by the fact that monks who have been practicing meditation together for years still do not necessarily know the nature of one another's practice.[30] The degree of reliance on a teacher or master will also vary from no reliance beyond the initial instruction to so-called guided meditations, in which all stages of the practice rely on continuous instructions from a teacher or a tape recording, as in some of the Sikh practices discussed by Myrvold in this volume. The role of the master in the *kōan* practices discussed by Morten Schlütter is an in-between case, where in addition to the initial technical instructions the meditator is repeatedly given new *kōan*s to ponder.

Attention

According to the suggested definition, meditation is based on the use of attention. In one sense, this is stating the obvious fact that all forms of meditation involve directing the attention toward a specific meditation object. The object may be a static item, such as a geometrical figure in *yantra* meditation, or a dynamic element, such as the ever-changing reality sought to be included in *shi-kan ta-za* and similar Zen practices. In either case, the technique consists in directing the attention toward this object.

In addition to the focus of attention, meditation also involves the cultivation of the mode of attention. While many meditative traditions have elaborate discussions of what constitutes an effective meditation object, there are also traditions claiming that *any* external or internal object can have this function, and that the crucial difference lies in the mode of attention, the mental attitude, in *how* the attention is directed toward this object. In many cases, this implies the training of a one-pointed and fully absorbed, yet effortless, frame of mind. In other cases, the training involved is aimed at achieving an open and accepting mental attitude that includes spontaneous impulses and even distractive thoughts. Quite often a meditative attitude is seen as stimulating an element of distance or detachment from the objects of the world, in order to transcend worldly attachment and let the mind dwell in a dimension that goes beyond all things. At other times, or maybe even simultaneously, meditation is believed to foster a way of being that brings about a closer intimacy with the things of the world. In all cases, the mode of attention is of central importance, and any attempt at meditating in a mechanistic way, on autopilot, will fall outside our definition. Meditation is a form of awareness training.[31]

Quite a few scientific definitions agree that meditation techniques involve the training of attention (or awareness).[32] As mentioned, some of them even go to the lengths of excluding visualization techniques from the field of meditation on the grounds that they aim at changing the contents of attention rather than training the attention itself. By the same logic, they also exclude methods of "controlled breathing and body postures (yoga), or body movement and supposed energy manipulation (Tai Chi [Tài-jí] and Chi gong [Qì-gōng])."[33] In fact, this line of thinking would also leave out most forms of recitative meditation, which also involves the conscious alteration of mental content. The result would be a very narrow notion of meditation that would, for instance, exclude the visualization techniques described by Madhu Khanna, Geoffrey Samuel, and Sarah Shaw in this volume, as well as most forms of traditional Christian meditation. The fact is that the training of attention by no means excludes attempts at changing or modifying the contents of the mind. Many visualization exercises do both, and so do many body practices and recitative techniques. We shall return to a discussion of the uses of attention in the next chapter, which partly bases its classification of meditation techniques on the "focus of attention" and the "mode of attention."

Inner Transformation

According to the suggested definition, meditation is practiced with the aim of achieving "inner transformation." Traditionally, the changes involved are understood in religious or at least spiritual terms, though nothing in our definition excludes psychological, philosophical, or otherwise existential interpretations.

In the written sources of different schools and traditions, descriptions of transformative change are typically varied and vague. In the scientific literature, there also exist only a few scattered comparative studies of long-term trajectories of meditative processes, and these are limited in scope.[34] One scientific definition of meditation mentions "[mental] development," but has little to say about the nature of such development beyond simple statements about cultivating positive emotions and reducing negative emotions.[35]

I tentatively suggest the following definition: "Inner transformation consists in long-term fundamental changes affecting many aspects of the person, such as perceptual, emotional, intellectual, spiritual, or behavioral patterns, eventually bringing about the anchoring of the person in more fundamental aspects of existence." This definition allows for a wide variety of interpretations. In the monotheistic religions originating in the Middle East, such transformation usually involves getting closer to God, and the same may be true of the Sikh practice of nām simran described by Myrvold in this volume. In several Hindu schools, including the Yogic disciplines discussed by Edwin F. Bryant and the yantra and cakra practices analyzed by Khanna, the point is to realize the ultimate Self (puruṣa or ātman), which is also often equated with God (Īśvara or Brahman, or Śiva in union with Śakti). In the various Buddhist approaches, the aim is rather to become enlightened to the fundamental emptiness of the self or of all existence, though some have pointed to the similarities between the ultimate Self that Buddhism is supposed to deny and the "Buddha nature" (Ch. fó-xìng) prevalent in the meditative traditions of Tibet, as discussed by Samuel in this volume, and of East Asia, as discussed by Schlütter. In Daoism, described by Harold D. Roth, and Neo-Confucianism, described by Masaya Mabuchi, the aim is an increased proximity to the Way (Dào), which in Neo-Confucianism often has strong moralistic undertones. Modern schools of meditation often avoid the religious connotations of the traditional terminologies, though some of them imply a deeper spiritual realm to which the meditator gradually opens his or her mind. As shown by Holen's contribution, others are more strictly scientific in their interpretation of the processes involved. In all cases, however, the point is for the person to be more permanently grounded in aspects of existence that are, in the relevant cultural context, considered to be more fundamental than his or her starting point.

This view of inner transformation does not entail a commitment to the perennialist idea that all schools of meditation (or religion, mysticism, and so on) are at bottom attempts to reach toward the same ultimate reality, as most famously argued in the contemporary context by Robert K. C. Forman.[36] In some cases, the structural and linguistic parallels that obtain across different meditative traditions may reflect actual similarities of substance, whether that substance is linked to the notion of an ineffable experience of a nonphenomenal reality, as usually argued within the perennialist discourse, or to effable and phenomenal experiences, as Matthew T. Kapstein suggests for the widespread visions of light.[37] In other cases, formal and descriptive parallels between different traditions may be deceptive and may gloss over underlying differences, as has sometimes been argued regarding parallels between accounts of meditative and drug-induced mystical experiences. Even with such underlying differences, however, the various schools of meditation are bound together by the structure of their discourses.

David Shulman and Guy G. Stroumsa make a typological distinction between "models of gradual self-transformation, often built upon the active cultivation over years of ascesis or meditative practice, and those of sudden or even violent change in the composition of the self—for example, in religious conversion."[38] Thus formulated, the transformations induced by meditative practice seem to be securely located in the first category. However, although meditation is often looked upon as a lifetime pursuit, meditative transformation is sometimes seen as a sudden and, perhaps paradoxically, unpremeditated event. This is most famously true of the dominant schools of Zen Buddhism, as described by Schlütter in this volume. More surprisingly, perhaps, it is equally true of some Christian forms of contemplation, as in the quotation from "The Epistle of Prayer" cited above, indicating that the transformations involved are "sudden and without any means."[39]

The matter becomes even more complex when Shulman and Stroumsa suggest that in gradual self-transformation the self is "the active agent of its own evolution," while in sudden change the self is "a passive recipient of the process." This sounds logical enough. As argued above, however, the connection between the activities involved in meditative practice and the effects obtained is not linear, whether the effects come gradually or suddenly. In her chapter on southern Buddhism in this volume, Shaw points out how "meditation objects, chosen and engaged with intent, overlap with surprise objects, or external events, occurring at crucial and timely moments." Gradualness and individual agency are combined with suddenness and passive recipiency, or rather, in Shaw's words, "a willing openness to the fortuitous and the fortunate." Technical meditation is combined with the nontechnical features of everyday events.

Sudden religious conversion may also be argued to involve the anchoring of a person in more fundamental aspects of existence, at least if considered from within the worldview of the religion involved. Yet, Shulman and Stroumsa may be right in suggesting that such conversion is not typical of meditative processes. More often, at least in premodern contexts, meditation takes place *within* a specific tradition to which the adept already belongs, and the practice pursues long-term goals defined by this tradition. In addition to the technique itself, meditation depends on social settings as well as cultures of learning, transmission, and interpretation. Quite often, it is also practiced communally, and several schools of meditation believe that the effects of communal practice exceed those of individual practice. Many meditative traditions strongly emphasize the master-disciple relation, and place great authority in the hands of the *abba* of early Christianity, the *shaikh* of Sufism, the Indian guru or Chinese *shī-fu.* All of this prompts the question of the nature of the "person" or "self" that is being

transformed. Is this self primarily a subjective arena of individual agency spring-
ing from within, as in the nineteenth-century Western idealist view? Or is it
rather a tabula rasa that obtains its main features through impressions and influences from the environment, in a form of interior or interiorized sociality?[40]

One possible interpretation of the strong integration of meditation within its
sociocultural context is that the changes taking place are due to an outside-in
movement, in which socially defined expectations are interiorized and determine the shape of the transformation involved. In some cases, these expectations are inherent in the practice itself, as in the case of meditations on a
specific religious content; in other cases, the expectations may be part of the context surrounding the practice. Either way, this outside-in movement resembles
one of the possible working mechanisms of the placebo effect in psychology,
psychiatry, and somatic medicine, in which motivation and expectations have
been argued to be important factors behind the outcome of the treatment.[41] It
also has elements in common with autosuggestion and autohypnosis, which
will be further discussed in the next chapter. Finally, it is consistent with social
and cultural constructivist views on human cognition, which have long been
dominant in cultural and religious studies.

However, this is not the only possible interpretation of the strong integration
between meditation and its sociocultural context. As we saw, Shulman and
Stroumsa suggest that meditative transformation involves more, not less, active
agency than the passive recipiency of sudden religious conversion. Even in communal settings, meditation is often seen as primarily an individual endeavor, as
argued above. In traditions of meditation, the increased effect believed to arise
from communal practice is only partly attributed to straightforward social
factors such as motivation and encouragement; more often it is interpreted as
the effect of spiritual energies released during meditation. In most traditions,
guided meditations, in which practice takes place in direct response to continual instructions from a meditation guide (or a tape or compact disc, as in some
of the Sikh practices described by Myrvold in this volume), are at best peripheral to the field of meditation. The focus on individual agency is shared by modern scientific definitions, which typically describe meditation as a "self-regulation
practice"[42] making use of a "self-focus skill"[43] or a "self-observation attitude"[44]
to bring about a "self-induced state."[45] Furthermore, there often exists a strong
tension between meditative traditions and the expectations and ideals induced
by their general religious or cultural contexts, which meditation is often understood to transcend. In the "recorded sayings" (yǔ-lù) of Chinese Zen,
meditators are encouraged to "kill the Buddha when you see him, and kill the
patriarchs when you see them,"[46] expressing the need to let go of all inner ad-
herence to sacred authority. In Catholicism, the relationship between the organized church and its various contemplative orders has been uneasy, largely
because the contemplatives have insisted on their personal visions of truths
that the church has felt a need to control. In more subtle ways, the technical and
nonsemantic nature of some meditation objects—as in body and breath practices, "objectless" attention training, meaningless *mantras*, aniconic *yantras*,

desemanticized Zen *kōan*s, and the blurring of the recitative content in some Sufi *dhikr* practices—indicates that meditation may transcend the webs of meaning provided by the cultural and religious context. All of this points in the direction of increased autonomy rather than a pure adaptation to social expectations.

The importance of social contexts may go beyond the provision of external cultural norms, spiritual ideals, and interpretive webs of meaning. The motivation and encouragement received from the environment do not necessarily stimulate conformism, but may rather provide the sense of safety needed for the individual exploration of existential issues. Similarly, the guidance of teachers or masters may not always be geared toward the exertion of power, but may equally well seek to provide the student or disciple with opportunities for technical or existential clarification. In this view, meditative transformation is not only about the interiorization of external expectations or webs of meaning, but just as much about the triggering of internal and individual processes that may be physiological, psychological, or spiritual in nature, or all at once. Again, this view is compatible with perennialism but does not presuppose it, since the inner elements activated may or may not belong to what is considered the perennial "core" of meditation, mysticism, or religion. The next chapter in this collection will further discuss the interplay between outside-in and inside-out changes in various forms of meditative practice.

Some forms of what Shulman and Stroumsa call self-transformation do not usually imply the conceived long-term anchoring of a person in the more fundamental aspects of existence that both meditative transformation and religious conversion are understood to do. Demonic possession and spirit mediumship may refer to long- or short-term contact with beings that fall outside the everyday experience of most people but are seldom thought of as belonging to more fundamental layers of existence in the sense discussed above. In the case of spirit mediumship, the most obvious long-term transformation involved is not on the part of the spirit medium him- or herself but of the community or individual that the medium is serving. Finally, while madness may be long- or short-term, it is usually thought of as making the individual lose his or her grounding in the basics of everyday reality rather than become rooted in more fundamental aspects of existence. Nevertheless, a number of societies have had currents of thought treating certain forms of madness as gateways to or expressions of wisdom or insight that are sometimes even tied to meditative practice.[47] While none of these alterations—religious conversion, demonic possession, spirit mediumship, or madness—is typical of meditation, they do occur, such exceptions serving to prove the wide range of the changes associated with meditative practice.

In the term "inner transformation," the qualifying adjective "inner" indicates that the changes are implied to go beyond purely physical effects on the body. This contrasts with both gymnastic and some medical traditions, in which mental training regimes are subordinated to concerns with physical achievement or well-being. In between the two lies the traditional use of physical training for character building. In meditation, both body and mind are usually involved, but the "embodied" nature of meditation is not part of its definition. The body does play an important role in many meditative traditions, through postures and movements and bodily meditation objects, as well as various attempts to "liberate" the mind or spirit from the body. Most obviously, meditative practice is often connected to seated (and often cross-legged) posture, and in Chinese the verb *zuò* "to sit" is a constituent element in many terms for meditation: *jìng-zuò* (sit in quietude), *dǎ-zuò* (hit-sit), *chán-zuò* (sit in zen), *zuò-chán* (sit in zen), *jiā-fū-zuò* (sit cross-legged), *duān-zuò* (sit straight), and *zhèng-zuò* (sit straight). Nevertheless, while seated posture may be a prototypical element of meditation, a number of lying, standing, walking, and even dancing meditations also exist. Similarly, while closed eyes are part of the prototypical image of meditation, half-closed or open eyes are also quite common. And whatever role the body plays in the practice and process of meditation, the transformative changes it effects go beyond the narrow concerns of the physical body.

States of Mind

As we have seen in the case of seated position and closed eyes, some features often associated with meditation are not part of our definition. This most notably applies to so-called meditative states of mind. These play no role in the definition, which focuses on long-term changes of *trait*[48] rather than short-term changes of *state*.

In this respect, our technical usage of the term "meditation" contrasts with English everyday usage, which often refers to short-term changes of state, sometimes as a result of practice, and at other times as a spontaneous shift with no reference to practice whatsoever. This semantic ambiguity between practice and state of mind is found in terms for meditation in a number of languages across the Eurasian continent, such as Arabic *muraqaba*, *mushāhada*, and *mu'āyana*; Sanskrit *yoga*, *dhyāna*, and *samādhi*; and Chinese *chán* (borrowed from Sanskrit *dhyāna*). Transitory states of mind play an important role in quite a few meditative traditions, and the transient experiences referred to in the meditative literature are often understood to be transformative in the sense of redefining a person's relation to himself and his surroundings. This also applies to several practices discussed in this volume, such as the seven forms of *samādhi* in the Yoga tradition presented by Bryant. Meditation is often linked to specific states of mind, and is sometimes distinguished from other practices by the nature of such transitory states. Such states are also more easily defined and identified than long-term changes of trait, and most meditative traditions have terms that designate states or stages along the way.

The suggested definition does not exclude state-oriented practices but requires that they are intended to bring about long-term changes as well. Sufism, for instance, recognizes a number of typical transient states (*ahwāl*) but links them to various enduring stages (*maqāmāt*). Many traditions warn practitioners against the temptation posed by transient states that might lure them away from actual transformative change. In his contribution to this volume, Schlütter describes how the Chinese Zen master Dà-huì (1089–1163) criticizes those who try to attain quietness instead of "break[ing] [their] mind of birth and death." Another Chinese Zen master, Xū-yún (1840?–1959), warns against "greedily chasing after the realm of purity" and calls this "a Zen illness to be shunned by every practitioner."[49] In the Christian tradition, "The Cloud of Unknowing" warns against the experience of "a spurious warmth, engendered by the fiend" that the practitioner may falsely "imagine . . . to be the fire of love, lighted and fanned by the grace and goodness of the Holy Ghost,"[50] and "The Epistle of Prayer" advises the practitioner to "neither care nor consider whether you are in pain or in bliss."[51] In the modern context, the most prominent proponent of mindfulness meditation, Jon Kabat-Zinn, states plainly that "any state of mind is a meditative state,"[52] while the free mental attitude of Acem Meditation is described as "neither a feeling, nor a particular experience, nor a state of mind."[53]

The widespread focus on meditative states of mind also reflects the strong concern with "experience" that has dominated religious thought since the late eighteenth century, and modern religious studies since William James's classic book *The Varieties of Religious Experience*. The "experience" orientation of religious studies in general and studies of Asian religion in particular has been strongly denounced as a modern Western idea imposed on premodern and Asian religion. Modern exponents and scholars of Hinduism as well as Buddhism have been criticized for projecting the Western notion of "religious experience" onto texts that are in fact more often prescriptive and performative than descriptive and experience-oriented.[54]

Nevertheless, both the modern and the traditional discourse on meditation is often concerned not only with long-term inner transformation but also with the more immediate changes in mental state that meditation is often thought to bring about. Certain changes of state are prototypical elements of meditation, even if they are not universally present or part of the definition. The following list is an attempt at providing a summarized overview of physiological, mental, and spiritual states that are typically considered meditative:

1. arousal reduction
2. mental absorption
3. mental clarity
4. sense of contact with fundamental aspects of reality

The first point covers the traditional emphasis on silence, calmness, stillness, quietude, and tranquility, as well as the modern scientific interest in mental and physical relaxation.[55] Some scholars distinguish meditative from ecstatic and shamanic states on the basis of the degree of arousal, with ecstasy and shamanism implying an increase, and meditation a decrease.[56] The scientific focus on the temporary easing of logic and preconceived assumptions, called "logic relaxation," where "ego-related concerns and critical evaluations are suspended," also belongs here.[57]

The second point refers to the high degree of mental focus associated with meditative states. In the terminology used here, absorption is distinguished from concentration in being spontaneous rather than active, though the terms often overlap, so that, for instance, Sanskrit *dhyāna* and *samādhi* sometimes refer to the act of concentrating, and at other times to spontaneous mental absorption, which may or may not be the effect of meditation. The increase in mental absorption is often understood to imply a reduction or even absence of random thought activity, so-called mind wandering.

The third point refers to the subtle awareness and mindful presence often linked to meditation. In Buddhism, sleep, drowsiness, or sloth are looked upon as one of the five obstacles to meditative progress. Note, however, that this kind of awareness and presence is typically combined with relaxation and thus differs from the vigilance and watchfulness often associated with adjectives such as "alert" and "wakeful." In the scientific literature, this combination has been called a "wakeful hypometabolic physiologic state."[58]

The fourth point refers to transient experiences that are more clearly linked to our concern with the long-term anchoring of the person in more fundamental aspects of existence. The experiences in question are hardly available for intersubjective inquiry, and they are typically couched in metaphorical and strongly culture-dependent language, sometimes referring to a personified god, at other times to the self, and at yet other times to a way or path, or to more abstract notions such as emptiness or timelessness, or, in Kohn's definition of meditation, "a deeper, subtler, and possibly divine flow of consciousness."[59] Whether different accounts of such experiences refer to the same ultimate reality, as in the perennial view, is highly controversial, not only because of the oft-cited cultural situatedness of such descriptions, but also because the terms themselves are so ambiguous. Even within the same culture, descriptive similarities may conceal great experiential differences, ranging from the subtle visions of a transcendent reality to intoxicated hallucinations induced by psychedelic drugs.[60]

In the idealized image, arousal reduction paves the way for mental absorption, as the thoughts calm down, leading to increased mental clarity and ultimately closer contact with fundamental aspects of reality:

arousal reduction
↓
mental absorption
↓
mental clarity
↓
sense of contact with fundamental aspects of reality

This sense of contact becomes transformative when it redefines the person's long-term relation to himself and his surroundings. However, the simple beauty of this image is deceptive, and this is not only because of the obvious difficulties of defining the fundamental aspects of reality referred to in the fourth point. The first, second, and third points are also quite problematic.

As to the first point, some traditions link meditation to ecstatic states rather than any form of arousal reduction,[61] and Mircea Eliade's famous distinction between (high-arousal) *ecstasy* and (low-arousal) *enstasy* has been criticized by religious historians. One tradition within Zen Buddhism repeatedly refers to the frustrating and not particularly relaxing experience of doubt as a precondition for meditative progress.[62]

As to the second point, attempts at ridding the mind of random thoughts have been highly controversial throughout the history of meditation. In the Buddhist tradition, a separate category covers meditative practices that do not aim at mental absorption (*vipaśyanā*, often translated as "insight meditation"). The Chinese Zen master Hānshān Déqīng changed his original emphasis on ridding the mind of thoughts to a focus on seeing the illusory nature of the thoughts and thus no longer being attached to them.[63] Moreover, while modern science seems to corroborate the first point, about arousal reduction, the data concerning this second point are much more confusing. On the one hand, in two scientific studies,[64] self-reported mind wandering during meditation is reduced in experienced practitioners of breathing meditation, loving-kindness meditation, and "choiceless awareness," and in a third study,[65] self-reported time on task during breathing meditation increased, all seeming to confirm this point. On the other hand, yet another study,[66] which detected the occurrence of mind wandering during meditation by asking the participants to press a button every time they discovered that their mind had drifted, showed no difference between experienced and inexperienced meditators, the mind wandering occurring on average every eighty seconds over a twenty-minute session in both groups. Some effects of meditation have been shown to be more prominent in methods that allow mind wandering than in concentrative practices.[67]

As to the third point, some modern forms of meditation, such as Transcendental Meditation and Acem Meditation, look upon sleep as just one of many different states of mind that may appear during meditation. Mental clarity may feature among the effects of meditation, but sleep and drowsiness may also be important parts of the process. A monk with whom I spoke during a stay at a Chinese Zen monastery complained about his tendency to fall asleep as soon as he started meditating, but added that his mind became much clearer after such periods of meditation-engendered sleep. In the Yoga tradition, the kind of lucid sleep called Yoga Nidra is looked upon as a meditative state.

In conclusion, meditation is not always about specific states of mind, but is just as often about processes that may include a number of different moods or emotions. Thus, none of the physiological, psychological, or spiritual states commonly associated with meditative practice has been included in our definition of meditation.

Meditation and Other Practices

To sum up, our definition stipulates that meditation is a *technique* in the sense of a deliberately undertaken and systematic practice involving continuous (i.e., repetitive or durative) activity aimed at producing certain effects at least partly by means of universal mechanisms. It is *attention-based*, whether the use of attention is characterized by a narrow concentrative focus or an open and inclusive awareness. Its intended effects include long-term and fundamental *inner transformation* affecting many facets of the person, such as perceptual, emotional, intellectual, and behavioral patterns, and entailing a movement toward the more fundamental aspects of existence.

In addition, a number of other characteristics are often considered typical of meditation, without having found their way into our definition. We have seen that the popular view considers closed eyes and a seated posture as typical of meditation. With regard to effects, we have seen how short-term changes of state are often associated with meditation, in particular various forms of arousal reduction, mental absorption, mental clarity, and a sense of contact with fundamental aspects of reality. None of these characteristics has been included in our definition, but they are still prototypical features of meditation.

Thus defined, meditation may be distinguished from many other types of practice with which it shares certain features. However, the borderlines are often gradient rather than absolute, and there is considerable room for overlap. The following is only a provisional and rough sketch of some such distinctions.

Scientific discourse often lumps together meditation and pure *relaxation techniques.* In our terminology, only meditation has long-term transformative aspirations beyond the health and well-being that results from basic relaxation. With a few exceptions, methods such as progressive muscle relaxation and autogenic training are not presented as transformative practices. In principle, our definition of meditation excludes modern relaxation techniques that focus exclusively on momentary rest and recreation.

Medicine may overlap with meditation, and the two words are etymologically related. Both in modern and traditional contexts, meditation is often practiced for improved health, and inner practices may be supplemented by medicinal herbs, pills, and concoctions, as in the Tibetan practices described by Samuel in this volume. In early China, meditation was sometimes believed to have the power of driving away demons that could otherwise cause illness.[68] As Roth points out in this volume, however, the overlap between meditation and medicine in early China was by no means complete, and the two were considered separate fields. In our terminology, health-oriented techniques count as meditation only when they are also used for long-term inner transformation.

Like meditation, *prayer* is a deliberately undertaken practice that frequently follows more or less clearly specified procedures. It often aims at producing certain effects, such as the cleansing of sins, though it may also be motivated by a sense of obligation rather than the hope of future rewards. One of the crucial characteristics distinguishing meditation from prayer lies in the continuous activity involved in the former. The activities involved in prayer are typically much more complex, and often involve sequences of actions or utterances rather than one continuous activity; they are sequential rather than continuous. In the prototypical case, meditation differs from prayer in being a technical form of self-transformation rather than a communicative method of expressing devotion, petition, submission, or gratitude to a divine being. In practice, there is considerable overlap, as when an Orthodox Christian practices the Jesus Prayer, in which a short, formulaic, and strongly devotional prayer is repeated continuously, sometimes aided by breathing techniques. Related practices include the *dhikr* of Sufism, the *japa* of Hinduism, and the *niàn-fó* (Chinese) or *nen-butsu* (Japanese) of Buddhism. Similar considerations apply to devotional visualization practices. Like prayer, many forms of meditation aim at establishing contact with fundamental aspects of reality, and these aspects are often presented in anthropomorphic language, as divine beings with their own sense of agency. When prayer becomes wordless, as in some forms of Christian mysticism, it also comes close to meditation.

"Mysticism" is a wide and multifaceted term but typically focuses on experiences and states rather than technical issues. Meditation as a self-transformative technique may be part of a mystical orientation, but this is not necessarily the case.

Meditation differs from *ritual* in typically being more focused on the individual rather than the community, and in involving durative or repetitive action rather than the stepwise or sequential procedures of ritual behavior. However, meditation may take place in communal settings, and ritual in individual settings. Repetition also constitutes an important element in quite a few rituals. In many contexts, meditation is surrounded by ritual, rituals contain meditative elements, and the border between the two is quite blurry.

Shamanism and *spirit mediumship* involve entering a different state of mind and contacting gods or spirits not primarily for the sake of the shaman or medium but for some other person or for an entire community. While this differs from the self-transformative purpose of meditation, many traditions hold that meditation is not only good for the meditator but also for his environment, and communal meditation is sometimes practiced for the sake of a whole community.

What about *body practices* such as Hatha Yoga, Tài-jí, and Qì-gōng? Though focusing on the body, these also involve the use of attention and are concerned with inner transformation. However, in addition to static (and thus durative) postures, they involve sequential rather than repetitive movements and thus differ from the most typical forms of meditation.

Traditional *martial arts*, which are also sometimes claimed to contain meditative elements, have their main focus on external self-defense rather than internal change. Arguably, however, some of them pursue this goal partly by including techniques for bringing about inner transformation but, like body practices, often in a way based on sequential rather than repetitive movements.[69]

Psychotherapy, though also a transformative practice, differs from meditation in several respects. First, it presupposes the presence of a therapist, while meditation usually takes place without the active or intervening presence of another person. Second, psychotherapy hardly counts as a technique in our narrow sense, since it is seldom characterized by the durative or repetitive elements typical of meditation. Note, however, that the various forms of guidance often linked to meditation and sometimes considered indispensable for its effect share these and other features of psychotherapy.

Many practices have both meditative and nonmeditative usages. Where some practitioners seek long-term transformation, others go for short-term relaxation; some prefer inner development, others physical health; some have spiritual aims, while others seek to improve their performance in work or sports. This phenomenon is not restricted to modern uses of meditation. As shown in particular clarity by Myrvold and Samuel in this volume, traditional meditative practices may also be employed to achieve material wealth, bodily health, and other worldly benefits.

This discussion of the nature of meditation hardly solves all of the problems related to the term, and we may still be uncertain whether to include particular practices. At least, however, we have criteria to base our discussion on. Quite a lot of practices, whether they are called meditation or go by other names, may come close to our definition, but with one or two features missing, thus positioning themselves in the gray areas between meditation and other types of practice. For instance, some meditation-like practices resemble ritual and prayer in proceeding stepwise rather than in a durative or repetitive fashion.[70] Rather than identifying a natural class or taxon, our definition seeks to establish, on practical and theoretical grounds, a single point of reference for cross-cultural and comparative studies.

Notes

1. This essay has profited much from comments on earlier versions by Ole Gjems-Onstad.

2. Cf. Eifring and Holen, "Uses of Attention," 1.

3. In religious studies, Livia Kohn is an exception in suggesting the following generic definition: "Meditation is the inward focus of attention in a state of mind where ego-related concerns and critical evaluations are suspended in favor of perceiving a deeper, subtler, and possibly divine flow of consciousness. A method of communicating with hidden layers of the mind, it allows the subconscious to surface in memories, images, and thoughts while also influencing it with quietude, openness, and specific suggestions" (Kohn, *Meditation Works*, 1). Even in Kohn's case, however, generic definitions are mainly used in her popularized works, not her scholarly publications.

4. Smith, *Relating Religion*, 134.

5. Ibid., 4.

6. Ibid., 5, 8.

7. Van der Toorn, review of *Relating Religion*, 586.

8. See, for example, Satlow, "Defining Judaism."

9. Needham, "Polythetic Classification," 358, 364.

10. Beckner, *Biological Way of Thought*, 24.

11. Bashir, "Movement and Stillness," 211.

12. Cf. Eifring, "Meditative Pluralism in Hānshān Déqīng."

13. Cf. Seppälä, "Meditation."

14. Cf. Robinet, *Taoist Meditation.*

15. Sometimes, however, the same technique is practiced both in specified meditation periods and throughout the day (and even night) accompanying other activities; cf. Schlütter's discussion of Chinese keyword practice in this volume, and similar discussions of the Orthodox Jesus Prayer in Rydell-Johnsén, "Early Jesus Prayer."

16. Cf. Eifring, "Meditation in Judaism, Christianity and Islam."

17. *Der weglose Weg*; cf. Cooper, "*Pathless-Path* of Prayer."

18. Most famously in the title of the thirteenth-century *gōng-àn* (*kōan*) collection *Wú Mén Guān* (lit. "the gateless checkpoint"), but later also in the even more obviously paradoxical formulation *wú mén zhī mén* (gateless gate), sometimes co-occurring with the equally paradoxical *bú rù ér rù* (to enter without entering).

19. Wolters, *Cloud of Unknowing*, 231.

20. Goleman, *Meditative Mind*, 97ff.

21. Loori, *Art of Just Sitting.*

22. Sheng Yen, *Method of No Method.*

23. Cardoso et al., "Meditation in Health."

24. Ibid.; West, "Meditation"; Kokoszka, "Axiological Aspects."

25. Walsh and Shapiro, "Meeting of Meditative Disciplines," 227–228; West, "Meditation"; Kohn, *Meditation Works.*

26. Walsh and Shapiro, "Meeting of Meditative Disciplines," 228; Manna et al., "Neural Correlates."

27. Perez de Albeniz and Holmes, "Meditation."

28. Walsh and Shapiro, "Meeting of Meditative Disciplines," 229. Ospina et al., "Meditation Practices for Health," 10, excludes the same practices.

29. "Tassa mayhaṃ Aggivessana etad-ahosi: Abhijānāmi kho panāhaṃ pitu Sakkassa kammante sītāya jambucchāyāya nisinno vivicc' eva kāmehi vivicca akusalehi dhammehi savitakkaṃ savicāraṃ vivekajaṃ pītisukhaṃ paṭhamaṃ jhānaṃ upasampajja viharitā." Trenckner, *Majjhima-nikaya*, 246, lines 30–35. Nanamoli, *Middle Length Discourses.*

30. Cf. Shaw, *Buddhist Meditation*, 11.

31. An interesting attempt to deny the importance of attention is the late nineteenth-century Chinese Buddhist monk Yùfēng Gǔkūn, who argues that practicing his form of meditation in a "digressive and messy" (*sànluàn*) way is still full of effects; see Eifring, "Spontaneous Thoughts in Meditative Traditions."

32. Walsh and Shapiro, "Meeting of Meditative Disciplines," 228 ("focus on training attention and awareness"); Goleman, "Meditation and Consciousness" ("a consistent attempt to reach a specific attention position"); West, "Meditation" ("involves training the individual to focus the attention or consciousness in a single object, sound, concept or experience"); Perez de Albeniz and Holmes, "Meditation" ("training one's level of awareness").

33. Walsh and Shapiro, "Meeting of Meditative Disciplines," 229.

34. Brown, "Stages of Meditation," represents an initial attempt at investigating long-term trajectories of meditative processes.

35. Walsh and Shapiro, "Meeting of Meditative Disciplines."

36. See, for example, his and others' contributions in Forman, *Problem of Pure Consciousness.* The most prominent arguments against perennialism are presented by Steven T. Katz and others in Katz, *Mysticism and Philosophical Analysis*, as well as in other books on mysticism edited by Katz.

37. Kapstein, "Rethinking Religious Experience."

38. Shulman and Stroumsa, "Introduction," 5.

39. "Soudeyn withouten any menes"; Hodgson, *Deonise Hid Diuinite*, 58.

40. On interior sociality, see Handelman, "Postlude," and Du Bois, "Co-Opting Intersubjectivity," 59ff.

41. Kirsch, "Response Expectancy"; Geers et al., "Goal Activation"; Geers et al., "Expectations and Placebo Response"; Linde et al., "Effect of Patient Expectations"; Bausell et al., "Is Acupuncture Analgesia an Expectancy Effect?"

42. Walsh and Shapiro, "Meeting of Meditative Disciplines," 228.

43. That is, the direction of attention toward the meditation object, or "anchor"; Cardoso et al., "Meditation in Health."

44. Craven, "Meditation and Psychotherapy."

45. Cardoso et al., "Meditation in Health."

46. In Chinese, "Jiàn Fó shā Fó, jiàn zǔ shā zǔ."

47. Cf. McDaniel, *Madness of the Saints* (mainly concerned with passing states of ecstatic madness); Ivanov, *Holy Fools in Byzantium*; Larchet, *Mental Disorders and Spiritual Healing*; Feuerstein, *Holy Madness*; and Linrothe, *Holy Madness*.

48. See Roth's contribution to this volume, as well as Cahn and Polich, "Meditation States and Traits"; Davidson, "Empirical Explorations of Mindfulness."

49. "Zhǐ tān qīng-jìng jìng-jiè, zhè shì wǒ-men yòng-gōng zuì yào bù dé de chán-bìng," *Xū Yún lǎo héshàng niánpú fǎhuì zēngdìngběn*, 248.

50. Hodgson, *Cloud of Unknowing*, 86; Wolters, *Cloud of Unknowing*, 114.

51. Hodgson, *Deonise Hid Diuinite*, 55; Wolters, *Cloud of Unknowing*, 228.

52. Kabat-Zinn, *Coming to Our Senses*, 62.

53. Holen, *Inner Strength*, 13.

54. Halbfass, "Concept of Experience"; Sharf, "Buddhist Modernism."

55. Benson, *Relaxation Response*; Lazar, "Functional Brain Mapping."

56. Fischer, "Cartography"; cf. Komjathy, *Cultivating Perfection*, 94–95; Eliade, *Yoga*, 339.

57. Kohn, *Meditation Works*, 1 (including note 1); Cardoso et al., "Meditation in Health," 59 (defining "logic relaxation" as "(a) [n]ot 'to intend' to analyz[e] (not try to explain) the possible psychophysical effects; (b) [n]ot 'to intend' to judg[e] (good, bad, right, wrong) the possible psychophysical [effects;] (c) [n]ot 'to intend' to creat[e] any type of expectation regarding the process"); Ospina et al., "Meditation Practices for Health," 9.

58. Wallace et al., "Wakeful Hypometabolic Physiologic State."

59. Kohn, *Meditation Works*, 1.

60. Thus, the psychological study of altered states of consciousness typically includes meditative states as well as states resulting from fever, delirium, mental illness, machines, drugs, sleep deprivation, and so on. For one of many attempts at equating meditative states and states resulting from psychedelic drugs, see Ram Dass's preface to Goleman, *Meditative Mind*.

61. Cf. book titles such as *Meditation: The Art of Ecstasy* by Osho; *Tantra: The Path of Ecstasy* by Georg Feuerstein; and *Yoga: The Technology of Ecstasy* by Georg Feuerstein.

62. See Schlütter's contribution to this volume.

63. See Eifring, "Meditative Pluralism in Hānshān Déqīng."

64. Brewer et al., "Meditation Experience"; Hofmann et al., "Loving-Kindness and Compassion Meditation."

65. Holzel et al., "Differential Engagement."

66. Hasenkamp et al., "Mind Wandering and Attention."

67. Xu et al., "Nondirective Meditation."

68. Strickman, *Chinese Magical Medicine*.

69. Cf. Raposa, *Meditation and the Martial Arts*; Kennedy and Guo, *Chinese Martial Arts Training Manuals* (which argues against the premodern use of martial arts for other uses than combat); Shahar, *Shaolin Monastery*, 137ff.

70. Cf. Brill, "Meditative Prayer in Cordovero" (on Kabbalah), and Seppälä, "Meditation."

Glossary

bú rù ér rù 不入而入
chán 禪
chán-zuò 禪坐
Dào 道
Dà-huì 大慧
dǎ-zuò 打坐
duān-zuò 端坐
fó-xìng 佛性
gōng-àn 公案
Hānshān Déqīng 憨山德清
jiā-fū-zuò 跏趺坐
"Jiàn Fó shā Fó, jiàn zǔ shā zǔ" 見佛殺佛，見祖殺祖
jìng-zuò 靜坐
kōan 公案
nen-butsu 念佛
niàn-fó 念佛

Qì-gōng 氣功
shī-fu 師父
shi-kan ta-za 只管打坐
Tài-jí 太極
wú jì-liǎng 無伎倆
Wú Mén Guān 無門關
wú mén zhī mén 無門之門
Xū-yún 虛雲
yǔ-lù 語錄
Zen 禪
zhèng-zuò 正坐
"Zhǐ tān qīng-jìng jìng-jiè, zhè shì wǒ-men yòng-gōng zuì yào bù dé de chán-bìng" 只貪清淨境界，這是我們用功最要不得的禪病
zuò-chán 坐禪

Bibliography

Bashir, Shahzad. "Movement and Stillness: The Practice of Sufi Dhikr in Fourteenth-Century Central Asia." In Eifring, *Meditation in Judaism, Christianity and Islam*, 201–211.

Bausell, R. B., L. Lao, S. Bergman, W. L. Lee, and B. M. Berman. "Is Acupuncture Analgesia an Expectancy Effect? Preliminary Evidence Based on Participants' Perceived Assignments in Two Placebo-Controlled Trials." *Evaluation & the Health Professions* 28, no. 1 (2005): 9–26.

Beckner, Morton. *The Biological Way of Thought*. New York: Columbia University Press, 1959.

Benson, Herbert. With Miriam Z. Klipper. *The Relaxation Response*. Updated and expanded edition. 1975. Reprint, New York: HarperTorch, 2000.

Brewer, J. A., P. D. Worhunsky, J. R. Gray, Y. Y. Tang, J. Weber, and H. Kober. "Meditation Experience Is Associated with Differences in Default Mode Network Activity and Connectivity." *Proceedings of the National Academy of Sciences of the United States of America* 108 (2011): 20254–20259.

Brill, Alan. "Meditative Prayer in Cordovero." In Eifring, *Meditation in Judaism, Christianity and Islam*, 45–60.

Brown, Daniel P. "The Stages of Meditation in Cross-Cultural Perspective." In *Transformations of Consciousness: Conventional and Contemplative Perspectives on Development*, edited by Ken Wilber, Jack Engler, and Daniel P. Brown, 219–283. Boston: Shambhala, 1986.

Cahn, B. Rael, and John Polich. "Meditation States and Traits: EEG, ERP, and Neuroimaging Studies." *Psychological Bulletin* 132, no. 2 (2006): 180–211.

Cardoso, Roberto, Eduardo de Souza, Luiz Camano, and José Roberto Leite. "Meditation in Health: An Operational Definition." *Brain Research Protocols* 14 (2004): 58–60.

Cooper, Jeffrey. "The *Pathless-Path* of Prayer: Is There a Meditation Method in Meister Eckhart?" In Eifring, *Meditation in Judaism, Christianity and Islam*, 123–135.

Craven J. L. "Meditation and Psychotherapy." *Canadian Journal of Psychiatry* 34, no. 7 (1989): 648–653.

Davidson, Richard J. "Empirical Explorations of Mindfulness: Conceptual and Methodological Conundrums." *Emotion* 10, no. 1 (2010): 8–11.

Du Bois, John W. "Co-Opting Intersubjectivity: Dialogic Rhetoric of the Self." In *The Rhetorical Emergence of Culture*, edited by Christian Meyer and Felix Girke, 52–83. New York: Berghahn Books, 2011.

Eifring, Halvor, ed. *Hindu, Buddhist and Daoist Meditation: Cultural Histories*. Oslo: Hermes, 2014.

——, ed. *Meditation and Culture: The Interplay of Practice and Context*. London: Bloomsbury Academic, 2015.

——, ed. *Meditation in Judaism, Christianity and Islam: Cultural Histories*. London: Bloomsbury Academic, 2013.

——. "Meditation in Judaism, Christianity and Islam: Technical Aspects of Devotional Practices." In Eifring, *Meditation in Judaism, Christianity and Islam*, 3–13.

——. "Meditative Pluralism in Hānshān Déqīng." In Eifring, *Meditation and Culture*, 102–127.

——. "Spontaneous Thoughts in Meditative Traditions." In Eifring, *Meditation and Culture*, 200–215.

Eifring, Halvor, and Are Holen. "The Uses of Attention: Elements of Meditative Practice." In Eifring, *Hindu, Buddhist and Daoist Meditation*, 1–26.

Eliade, Mircea. *Yoga: Immortality and Freedom*. Princeton, NJ: Princeton University Press, 1969.

Feuerstein, Georg. *Holy Madness: Spirituality, Crazy-Wise Teachers, and Enlightenment*. Revised and expanded edition. Prescott, AZ: Hohm Press, 2006.

——. *Tantra: The Path of Ecstasy*. Boston: Shambhala Publications, 1998.

——. *Yoga: The Technology of Ecstasy*. Los Angeles: J. P. Tarcher, 1989.

Fischer, Roland. "A Cartography of the Ecstatic and Meditative States." *Science* 26 (1971): 897–904.

Forman, Robert K. C., ed. *The Problem of Pure Consciousness*. New York: Oxford University Press, 1990.

Geers, A. L., P. E. Weiland, K. Kosbab, S. J. Landry, and S. G. Helfer. "Goal Activation, Expectations, and the Placebo Effect." *Journal of Personality and Social Psychology* 89, no. 2 (2005): 143–159.

Geers, A. L., S. G. Helfer, P. E. Weiland, and K. Kosbab. "Expectations and Placebo Response: A Laboratory Investigation into the Role of Somatic Focus." *Journal of Behavioral Medicine* 29, no. 2 (2006): 171–178.

Goleman, Daniel J. "Meditation and Consciousness: An Asian Approach to Mental Health." *American Journal of Psychiatry* 30, no. 1 (1976): 41–54.

——. *The Meditative Mind: The Varieties of Meditative Experience*. Los Angeles: Jeremy P. Tarcher / Perigee Books, 1988.

Halbfass, Wilhelm. "The Concept of Experience in the Encounter between India and the West." In *India and Europe: An Essay in Understanding*, edited by Wilhelm Halbfass, 378–402. Albany, NY: SUNY Press, 1988.

Handelman, Don. "Postlude: The Interior Sociality of Self-Transformation." In Shulman and Stroumsa, *Self and Self-Transformation*, 236–253.

Hasenkamp, W., C. D. Wilson-Mendenhall, E. Duncan, and L. W. Barsalou. "Mind Wandering and Attention during Focused Meditation: A Fine-Grained Temporal Analysis of Fluctuating Cognitive States." *Neuroimage* 59 (2012): 750–760.

Hodgson, Phyllis, ed. *The Cloud of Unknowing and the Book of Privy Counselling*. London: Oxford University Press, 1973.

———, ed. *Deonise Hid Diuinite, and Other Treatises on Contemplative Prayer Related to "The Cloud of Unknowing."* London: Oxford University Press, 1958.

Hofmann, S. G., P. Grossman, and D. E. Hinton. "Loving-Kindness and Compassion Meditation: Potential for Psychological Interventions." *Clinical Psychology Review* 31 (2011): 1126–1132.

Holen, Are. *Inner Strength: The Free Mental Attitude in Acem Meditation*. 2nd ed. Oslo: Acem Publishing, 2006.

Holzel, Britta K., Ulrich Ott, Hannes Hempel, Andrea Hackl, Katharina Wolf, Rudolf Stark, and Dieter Vaitl. "Differential Engagement of Anterior Cingulate and Adjacent Medial Frontal Cortex in Adept Meditators and Non-Meditators." *Neuroscience Letters* 421 (2007): 16–21.

Ivanov, Sergey A. *Holy Fools in Byzantium and Beyond*. Oxford: Oxford University Press, 2006.

Kabat-Zinn, Jon. *Coming to Our Senses: Healing Ourselves and the World through Mindfulness*. New York: Hyperion, 2005.

Kapstein, Matthew T. "Rethinking Religious Experience: Seeing the Light in the History of Religions." In *The Presence of Light: Divine Radiance and Religious Experience*, edited by Matthew T. Kapstein, 265–299. Chicago, IL: University of Chicago Press, 2004.

Katz, Steven T., ed. *Mysticism and Philosophical Analysis*. New York: Oxford University Press, 1978.

Kennedy, Brian, and Elizabeth Guo. *Chinese Martial Arts Training Manuals: A Historical Survey*. Berkeley, CA: Blue Snake Books, 2005.

Kirsch, I. "Response Expectancy as a Determinant of Experience and Behavior." *American Psychologist* 40, no. 11 (1985): 1189–1202.

Kohn, Livia. *Meditation Works: In the Hindu, Buddhist and Daoist Traditions*. Magdalena, NM: Three Pines Press, 2008.

Kokoszka, A. "Axiological Aspects of Comparing Psychotherapy and Meditation." *International Journal of Psychosomatics* 37 (1990): 78–81.

Komjathy, Louis. *Cultivating Perfection: Mysticism and Self-Transformation in Early Quanzhen Daoism*. Leiden: Brill, 2007.

Larchet, Jean-Claude. *Mental Disorders and Spiritual Healing: Teachings from the Early Christian East*. Translated by G. John Champoux and Rama P. Coomaraswamy. San Rafael, CA: Angelico Press, 2011.

Lazar, Sara W., George Bush, Randy L. Gollub, Gregory L. Fricchione, Gurucharan Khalsa, and Herbert Benson. "Functional Brain Mapping of the Relaxation Response and Meditation." *NeuroReport* 11, no. 7 (2000): 1581–1585.

Linde, K., C. M. Witt, A. Streng, W. Weidenhammer, S. Wagenpfeil, B. Brinkhaus, S. N. Willich, and D. Melchart. "The Effect of Patient Expectations on Outcomes in Four Randomized Controlled Trials of Acupuncture in Patients with Chronic Pain." *Pain* 128, no. 3 (2007): 264–271.

Linrothe, Rob, ed. *Holy Madness: Portraits of Tantric Siddhas.* New York: Rubin Museum of Art.

Loori, John Daido, ed. *The Art of Just Sitting: Essential Writings on the Zen Practice of Shikantaza.* Boston: Wisdom Publications, 2002.

Manna, A., A. Raffone, M. G. Perrucci, D. Nardo, A. Ferretti, A. Tartaro, A. Londei, C. Del Gratta, M. O. Belardinelli, and G. L. Romani. "Neural Correlates of Focused Attention and Cognitive Monitoring in Meditation." *Brain Research Bulletin* 82, nos. 1–2 (March 2010): 46–56.

McDaniel, June. *The Madness of the Saints: Ecstatic Religion in Bengal.* Chicago: The University of Chicago Press, 1989.

Nanamoli, Bhikkhu, trans. *The Middle Length Discourses of the Buddha: A New Translation of the Majjhima Nikaya.* Edited by Bhikkhu Bodhi. Boston: Wisdom Publications, 1995.

Needham, Rodney. "Polythetic Classification: Convergence and Consequences." *Man: New Series* 10, no. 3 (1975): 349–369.

Osho. *Meditation: The Art of Ecstasy.* Pune, India: Tao Publishing, 2006.

Ospina, Maria B., Kenneth Bond, Mohammad Karkhaneh, Lisa Tjosvold, Ben Vandermeer, Yuanyuan Liang, Liza Bialy, Nicola Hooton, Nina Buscemi, Donna M. Dryden, and Terry P. Klassen. "Meditation Practices for Health: State of the Research." *Evidence Report/Technology Assessment*, no. 155. Rockville, MD: Agency for Healthcare Research and Quality.

Perez de Albeniz, A., and J. Holmes. "Meditation: Concepts, Effects and Uses in Therapy." *International Journal of Psychotherapy* 5, no. 1 (2000): 49–58.

Philippe, Jacques. *Time for God.* New York: Scepter Publishers, 2008.

Raposa, Michael J. *Meditation and the Martial Arts.* Charlottesville: University of Virginia Press, 2003.

Robinet, Isabelle. *Taoist Meditation: The Mao-Shan Tradition of Great Purity.* Translated by Julian F. Pas and Norman J. Girardot. New York: SUNY Press, 1993.

Rydell-Johnsén, Henrik. "The Early Jesus Prayer and Meditation in Greco-Roman Philosophy." In Eifring, *Meditation in Judaism, Christianity and Islam*, 93–106.

Satlow, Michael L. "Defining Judaism: Accounting for 'Religions' in the Study of Religion." *Journal of the American Academy of Religion* 74, no. 4 (2006): 837–860.

Seppälä, Serafim. "Meditation in the East Syrian Tradition." In Eifring, *Meditation in Judaism, Christianity and Islam*, 107–121.

Shahar, Meir. *The Shaolin Monastery: History, Religion, and the Martial Arts.* Honolulu: University of Hawai'i Press, 2008.

Sharf, Robert. "Buddhist Modernism and the Rhetoric of Meditative Experience." *Numen* 42, no. 3 (1995): 228–283.

Shaw, Sarah. *Buddhist Meditation: An Anthology of Texts form the Pāli Canon.* London: Routledge, 2006.

Sheng Yen. *The Method of No Method: The Chan Practice of Silent Illumination.* Boston: Shambhala, 2008.

Shulman, David, and Guy G. Stroumsa. "Introduction: Persons, Passages, and Shifting Cultural Space." In Shulman and Stroumsa, *Self and Self-Transformation*, 1–16.

———, eds. *Self and Self-Transformation in the History of Religions.* Oxford: Oxford University Press, 2002.

Smith, Jonathan Z. *Imagining Religion: From Babylon to Jonestown.* Chicago: University of Chicago Press, 1982.

———. *Relating Religion: Essays in the Study of Religion.* Chicago: University of Chicago Press, 2004.

Strickman, Michel. *Chinese Magical Medicine.* Edited by Bernard Faure. Stanford, CA: Stanford University Press, 2002.

Trenckner, V., ed. *The Majjhima-nikaya.* Vol. 1. London: Pali Text Society / Henry Frowde, 1888.

van der Toorn, Karel. Review of *Relating Religion*, by Jonathan Z. Smith. *Journal of Biblical Literature* 124, no. 3 (2005): 584–587.

Wallace, R. K., H. Benson, and A. F. Wilson. "A Wakeful Hypometabolic Physiologic State." *American Journal of Physiology* 221, no. 3 (1971): 795–799.

Walsh, Roger, and Shauna L. Shapiro. "The Meeting of Meditative Disciplines and Western Psychology: A Mutually Enriching Dialogue." *American Psychologist* 61, no. 3 (2006): 227–239.

West, M. "Meditation." *British Journal of Psychiatry* 135 (1979): 457–467.

Wolters, Clifton, trans. *The Cloud of Unknowing and Other Works.* London: Penguin Books, 1978.

Xu, Jian, Alexandra Vik, Inge R. Groote, Jim Lagopoulos, Are Holen, Øyvind Ellingsen, Asta K. Håberg, and Svend Davanger. "Nondirective Meditation Activates Default Mode Network and Areas Associated with Memory Retrieval and Emotional Processing." *Frontiers in Human Neuroscience* 8 (2014): article 86, 1–10.

Xūyún lǎo héshàng niánpǔ fǎhuì zēngdìngběn. Taipei: Shífāng dàjuésì, 1986.

Types of Meditation

S ince the 1970s, both scientific and popular literature in the West have tended to classify meditation techniques on the basis of the Buddhist dichotomy between *samatha* and *vipassanā*, often rendered in English as "concentration" and "insight" (or "mindfulness"),[1] and more recently termed "focused attention" and "open monitoring."[2] The interpretation of this distinction, however, varies from one writer to the next and has proven to be quite problematic. Before the twentieth century, the distinction had little impact outside Buddhism, apart from its early borrowing and transformation within Chinese Daoism.[3] Even within Buddhism, the distinction was always ambiguous and controversial. More importantly, quite a few scholars have pointed to modern forms of meditation that do not fall neatly within either category, and this problem is exacerbated when, as in this volume, we include a broader spectrum of traditional meditation practices.

This chapter will explore an alternative classification into "directive" and "nondirective" practices, which in recent years has been suggested by a number of scientists studying the effects of meditation. In our context, the distinction may be defined as follows:[4]

> Directive techniques seek to lead the mind and body toward preset goals embedded in culturally determined webs of meaning, while nondirective techniques are based on universal psychobiological working mechanisms bringing about reflexive effects on mind and body.

Unlike the Buddhist dichotomy, this classification does not purport to reflect traditional concepts. It is *etic* not *emic*, and thus transcends the division lines between various traditions. This chapter will attempt to explore the relevance of the distinction for both modern and traditional meditation practices across the Eurasian continent.

The chapter builds on three types of source material. First, it refers to other contributions in this volume and other volumes in the Cultural Histories of Meditation project. Second, it refers to modern discussions of the classification of meditative practices, including various scientific attempts. And third, it refers to a number of texts on meditation from various contemplative traditions, in particular the dharma texts (*fǎ-yǔ*) of the Chinese Buddhist meditation master Hānshān Déqīng (1546–1623) and "The Cloud of Unknowing" by an anonymous fourteenth-century English country parson.

Directive and Nondirective Elements

The extent to which meditation seeks to direct the person toward preset goals largely depends on the degree of active interference with the cognitive and emotional content of the mind. Such interference may lie in the context in which meditation is learned or practiced, with suggestive elements bringing about expectations of particular states of mind, visions of deities, healing effects, and so on. It may also lie in the mental attitude with which meditation is practiced, in the form of attempts at excluding peripheral or digressive thoughts, in order to concentrate fully on the meditation object. Or it may lie in the meditation object itself, as when the thematic content of the meditation object leads the cognitive or emotional content of the mind in predetermined directions. Conversely, nondirective meditation seeks to reduce suggestive elements in the context, to accept the presence of peripheral and digressive thoughts, and to use meditation objects without thematic content. See table 2.1.

The different elements may be freely combined, so that, for instance, a concentrative mental attitude may be combined with a nonthematic meditation object, or vice versa. The setting usually contains both suggestive and nonsuggestive elements. The contrast between directive and nondirective meditation, therefore, is a question of degrees, not of absolute opposites.

While the context is obviously important and needs to be studied, this chapter will focus on the role of the elements that are part of the meditation technique, that is, the mental attitude and the meditation object. The object of meditation is the *focus* of attention during meditation, the element toward which attention is intentionally directed, while the mental attitude is the *mode* of attention during meditation, characterized by the relation between the focal element (meditation object) and elements that are either peripheral (background thoughts or impressions) or unintentionally focal (digressions, as when the object of meditation is temporarily forgotten and random thoughts take over).

The distinction between directive and nondirective forms of meditation reflects two ways in which meditative practice may bring about inner transformation. On the one hand, such change may be an *outside-in* process in which the context plays a dominant role, as when the meditative effect of *mantras* comes from their place within the cosmologies surrounding them that endow them with symbolic if not literal meaning and thus help meditators to "'discover' the

Table 2.1. Directive and Nondirective Forms of Meditation

	Directive meditation	*Nondirective meditation*
Context	suggestive	nonsuggestive
Mental attitude	concentrative	nonconcentrative
Meditation object	thematic	nonthematic

knowledge already cultivated by their traditions."[5] On the other hand, meditative change may be an *inside-out* process that starts in the mind and body of the meditator, as when the effects of *mantra*-based meditation come from a psychobiological "relaxation response" triggered by the "repetition of a . . . sound . . . or muscular activity" combined with a mental attitude of "passively disregarding everyday thoughts that inevitably come to mind and returning to your repetition,"[6] without any conceptual or symbolic meaning being involved. Directive meditation fosters outside-in processes, while nondirective meditation fosters inside-out processes. Most often, the two are combined in various proportions.[7] Toward the end of this chapter, we shall return to the question of whether directive and nondirective forms of meditation constitute different paths toward the same goal or actually produce different effects.

The distinction between directive and nondirective forms of meditation is also reflected in the contrast between content and process orientation. As mentioned in the previous chapter in this volume, some scholars argue that all meditation emphasizes "process rather than content,"[8] in contrast to nonmeditative practices such as self-hypnosis and psychotherapy, which "aim primarily at changing mental contents . . . such as thoughts, images, and emotions."[9] While this may be true of nondirective meditation, and therefore to a large extent of the modern practices studied by scientists, many traditional forms of meditation are directive and aim at "changing mental contents."[10]

The Problems with *Samatha* and *Vipassanā*

At the outset, *samatha* and *vipassanā* (or "concentration" and "insight," etc.) are Buddhist terms. The modern discourse on the distinction between the two is largely a product of Western scientific attempts at interpreting these traditional terms, and their English near-equivalents, and applying them to the various meditation practices that figure prominently in scientific studies, or that have been popular in Europe and America in the last fifty years. Both the terms and the practices to which they have been applied have their origins in Asia, but have been largely dislodged from their original contexts. Furthermore, while the terms are rooted in Buddhism, many of the meditation methods to which they are applied hail from other Asian traditions.

The modern discourse on this distinction differs considerably from traditional Buddhist notions, according to which *samatha* seeks stillness and absorption, while *vipassanā* seeks insight and wisdom. In the modern context, the distinction is typically no longer based on the purpose of meditation but on its technical features. In brief, the mental attitude corresponding to *samatha* seeks an exclusive focus on the meditation object, while the attitude corresponding to *vipassanā* cultivates an open awareness toward all impressions, without any specific meditation object.[11] See table 2.2.

The most obvious problem with the distinction between *samatha* and *vipassanā* is where to place meditative practices that combine the use of

Table 2.2. *Samatha* and *Vipassanā*

	Samatha	Vipassanā
Specific meditation object	yes	no
Acceptance of random impressions	no	yes

specific meditation objects (as in *samatha*) with an acceptance of thoughts and other random impressions within the field of awareness (as in *vipassanā*). In reality, few meditation practices make no use of meditation objects at all, even the practices that go under names corresponding to *vipassanā*.

Some scholars solve the problem by routinely treating as concentrative any form of meditation that uses a specific meditation object, especially when this object is generated by the meditator (as opposed to spontaneous elements such as the natural breath or body sensations). Richard Davidson and Daniel Goleman, for instance, call Transcendental Meditation "a concentrative practice,"[12] since it is based on the mental repetition of a *mantra*, despite the fact that its basic instruction explicitly tells the practitioner not to concentrate on the *mantra* and to allow thoughts to come and go. Other scholars acknowledge the problems involved in using the term "concentrative" this way and admit that "this suggests the limitations of the classification scheme."[13]

Yet other scholars argue that meditation should be divided in three rather than two basic types. Thus, Deane Shapiro suggests a tripartite division based on the following "attentional strategies": "a focus on a specific object within the field" (corresponding to *samatha*), "a focus on the field" (corresponding to *vipassanā*), and "a shifting back and forth between the two."[14] Fred Travis and Jonathan Shear make a similar distinction between "focused attention" (*samatha*), "open monitoring" (*vipassanā*), and what they call "automatic self-transcendence," the latter covering "automatic or effortless" practices "marked by the absence of both (a) focus and (b) individual control or effort," primarily referring to their interpretation of advanced stages of Transcendental Meditation, arguing that the three types produce different brain-wave patterns.[15]

Antoine Lutz et al. instead suggest that the solution lies in a combination of the two basic types. The practice of "open monitoring" (*vipassanā*) starts with "focused attention" (*samatha*), after which "the practitioner gradually reduces the focus on an explicit object in F[ocused] A[ttention], and the monitoring faculty is correspondingly emphasized."[16] In effect, this makes the distinction between the two types a gradient one, but at the same time it seems to imply that meditative practice should eventually lead in the direction of a pure form of "open monitoring," in which the object of meditation is discarded. This ideal may exist within some traditions, particularly in some Buddhist practices, but is far from universal.

Other scholars have fewer qualms about acknowledging the use of specific meditation objects in forms of meditation that cultivate an open awareness.

This is most often mentioned in connection with breathing meditation, as when Maria Ospina et al. discuss techniques that "focus on the breath and cultivate an objective openness to whatever comes into awareness," or when Shapiro discusses techniques in which "the breath [is] used as an anchor (but not a focal point) to keep the meditator engaged with the present moment." Other spontaneous elements used as meditation objects, such as body sensations, emotions, and mental processes, are also often mentioned in connection with *vipassanā* meditation.

Ospina et al. go one step further and include not only spontaneous meditation objects but also objects actively generated by the practitioner, such as Zen *kōans* and the active counting of breath. They conclude that the decisive point characterizing *vipassanā* (which they call "mindfulness") is not the absence of a specific meditation object but the "acceptance of . . . other thoughts into the field of awareness."[17] Thus interpreted, the distinction between *samatha* and *vipassanā* resembles our distinction between a concentrative and nonconcentrative mental attitude, and thus comes close to the notion of directive versus nondirective meditation.

Concentrative versus Nonconcentrative Mental Attitude

A number of scholars maintain that it is the mental attitude that lies at the core of meditative practice.[18] Some argue that the mental attitude is both the "path" and the "goal" of meditation, reflecting the confluence of practice and effect that is so widespread in meditative traditions. Some even insist that the mental attitude is not necessarily tied to any specific technique at all, but may be practiced at all times, whether, as many Buddhist sources say, "walking, standing, sitting, or lying down." In many contexts, however, the mental attitude is also clearly treated as a technical tool for meditation, just like the meditation object with which it is combined.

Let us begin with some terminological clarifications. "Concentrative meditation" works to attain an exclusive focus on the meditation object, and seeks to avoid other elements, such as peripheral thoughts, digressions, and so on, while "nonconcentrative meditation" does not actively work to attain an exclusive focus on the meditation object but rather accepts the presence of both peripheral and digressive thoughts, in some cases even dispensing with the use of a specific meditation object altogether.

Concentrative practices are typically directive in that they often attempt to lead the mind toward specific states, sometimes tied to the thematic content of the object of meditation, and at other times to a state of one-pointed absorption in the object, or a combination of the two. The transformative power of meditation is at least partly seen as a product of such states. In contrast, nonconcentrative practices typically rely on technical working mechanisms, including nonthematic meditation objects, to open the mind and set in motion latent impulses at or beyond the peripheries of conscious awareness. The transformative power of meditation is seen, wholly or partly, as coming from whatever impulses are thereby brought into play, whether they are understood as obstacles to be overcome or as resources to be made use of.

This definition of concentrative meditation presupposes a distinction between *concentration* and *absorption*. Concentrative meditation involves an active effort to secure an exclusive focus on the meditation object by ridding the mind of peripheral thoughts and unintentional digressions. Nonconcentrative meditation may also include moments of complete absorption in the meditation object, without distracting thoughts, but not as the direct result of an active, goal-oriented effort, rather as a spontaneous effect of meditative practice. Much of the scholarly literature fails to distinguish between concentration and absorption, using the term "concentration" for both.[19] Technical practice (concentration) and resultant state (absorption) are thereby blended in a single term, as is commonly done in meditative traditions. In translations and explanations, this may be excusable, since it reflects the polysemy of the original terms. In a scholarly typology of meditation techniques, however, the difference between concentration and absorption is of vital importance for our understanding of the distinction between concentrative and nonconcentrative techniques.

In the following, I shall explore further some implications of the basic distinction between concentrative and nonconcentrative forms of meditation by applying the following three subcriteria to descriptions of meditation in traditional sources from different periods and different parts of the Eurasian continent:

1. forceful vs. effortless focus on the meditation object
2. narrow vs. open focus on the meditation object
3. suppression vs. acceptance of distracting thoughts

On all three points, the first item of the pair refers to a concentrative attitude, while the second item refers to a nonconcentrative attitude. In reality, the concentrative and nonconcentrative features of different pairs can hardly be combined freely, but actual descriptions—or prescriptions—of one and the same meditation technique often vacillate between concentrative and nonconcentrative features.

All three of the points regard the relation between the intended object of meditation and other contents of the mind. In the following, we shall illustrate this by quoting traditional discussions of meditation, in particular the Chinese Buddhist master Hānshān Déqīng and the English country parson who wrote "The Cloud of Unknowing."

First, if the meditation object is produced or focused in a forceful manner, this leaves less room for other elements. Sometimes this is done explicitly to keep random thoughts away, as when Hānshān Déqīng exhorts his disciples to produce the meditation object "forcefully [*jílì, jíjí, zhuólì*]," "as if exerting all the strength of the body pushing a heavy cart up the hill," so that "when deluded thoughts arise, you just press the keyword [the meditation object] forcibly and they are instantly crushed to pieces."[20] Similarly, the author of "The Cloud of Unknowing" tells his disciple to use the meditation object to "hammer the cloud and the darkness above you" in order to "suppress all thought under the cloud of forgetting."[21] Conversely, if the meditation object is produced or focused in an effortless manner, this may leave more room for other elements to intrude. In fact, Hānshān Déqīng also tells his disciples to produce the meditation object "gently [*huǎnhuǎn*]," and to avoid "clinging to the keyword [i.e., the meditation object; *sǐshǒu huàtóu*]." Similarly, the author of "The Cloud of Unknowing" also instructs his disciple to "work with eager enjoyment [*a list*] rather than with brute force [*liþer strengþe*]."[22] It may seem like a paradox that the same teachers produce what seem like opposite instructions in this regard. A possible explanation is that effortlessness comes only with experience. As "The Cloud of Unknowing" says, "What previously was very hard [*ful harde*] becomes much lighter [*ful restful & ful liȝt*], and you can relax [*haue ouþer litil trauaile or none*]."[23] This corresponds to the observation made in a modern scientific context by Lutz et al. that "progress in this form of meditation is measured in part by the degree of effort required to sustain the intended focus," and that "at the most advanced levels, ... the ability to sustain focus thus becomes progressively 'effortless.'"[24] In such cases, effortlessness may no longer leave room for other elements to intrude.

Second, if the attention is narrowly focused on the meditation object, peripheral thoughts and impressions tend to be excluded from the field of awareness, while an open focus allows the simultaneous perception of both focal and nonfocal elements. The many words for "concentration" in the various meditative traditions, such as the "naked intent [*nakid entente*]" of "The Cloud of Unknowing," the "one-pointedness [*ekāgrata, ekatānatā*]" of the Yogic and Buddhist traditions, or "guarding the one [*zhí yī, shǒu yī, bào yī*]" in early Daoism, may be interpreted as referring to a narrow focus in this sense. In "The Cloud of Unknowing," this focus is directed toward God himself: "Indeed, hate to think of anything but God himself, so that nothing occupies your mind or will but only God." It is hard to find texts that distinguish clearly between such avoidance of peripheral thoughts and the more often discussed avoidance of digressive thoughts, to which we shall return below. For the converse case, however, we do find texts that presuppose the presence of peripheral thoughts while the meditation object is kept in focus. In the Chinese context, the multiple meanings of the word *niàn*, which may mean "thought" (and "to think"), "mindfulness" (and "to be mindful of"), and "to recite," give rise to interesting forms of word play: "Just let thoughts [*niàn*] arise, while you recite [*niàn*] the Buddha['s name]."[25]

And in an even more playfully complex statement:

So the Tathāgata Buddha taught people to recite [*niàn*] the phrase "Amitābha Buddha," in order to assimilate all their hundreds or thousands or 850 million random thoughts [*zá-niàn*] into single-pointed mindful awareness [*yí niàn*], and recite [*niàn*] until not a single thought [*yí niàn*] arises and they spontaneously get a fully realized view of Amitābha Buddha, then knowing that all their hundreds or thousands or 850 million random thoughts [*zá-niàn*] are in fact the mindful awareness [*niàn*] of Amitābha Buddha.[26]

Both statements are used to counter the claim that random thoughts constitute an obstacle to meditation, and both argue for the possibility of combining the focus on the meditation object with the peripheral presence of random thoughts; the second statement does so by invoking the notion of mindful awareness. In the end, though, the second statement seems to revert to what in the Buddhist context is a more conventionally negative view of random thoughts by insisting that the meditation practitioner will reach a state where they no longer arise.

Third, while *peripheral* thoughts occur simultaneously with the meditation object, *distractive* thoughts are spontaneous interruptions, intermittently occupying the mental focus that was originally reserved for the object of meditation. Negative attitudes toward distractive thoughts are common in meditative traditions; in both Europe and Asia, they are often referred to as "evil" or "deluded." Tellingly, the Greek term *logismoí*, "thoughts," which is often used to refer to digressions in meditative prayer,[27] develops into a notion meaning "assaultive or tempting thoughts" and eventually forms the basis for the notion of the seven deadly sins. St. Hesychios the Priest (ca. eighth century) is a strong advocate of "watchfulness" against such thoughts or digressions: "If we have not attained prayer that is free from thoughts [*logismoí*], we have no weapon to fight with."[28] Within Buddhism, digressive thoughts are routinely referred to as *wàng-niàn* or *wàng-xiǎng* "deluded thoughts," and since delusion is considered one of humanity's primary problems, this is perhaps as negative as the sinful thoughts of a Christian. According to the Buddhist text "Atthasālinī," attributed to the influential meditation scholar Buddhaghosa (ca. fifth century), meditative absorption (*samādhi*) is characterized by a lack of digressive thoughts: "This concentration [*samādhi*], known as one-pointedness of mind [*ekaggatā*], has non-scattering (of itself) [*avisāra*] or non-distraction (of associated states) [*avikkhepa*] as characteristic."[29] On the basis of the English translation, one could be tempted to take *avisāra* to mean "no peripheral thoughts" and *avikkhepa*, "no digressive thoughts," but the Pali text hardly makes such a distinction, the direct meaning of the terms rather being "no floating aside" and "no casting away," respectively.

Rather than suppressing digressive thoughts, some forms of meditation have a more exploratory attitude. Hānshān Déqīng represents a long Buddhist tradition when he urges his disciples to "watch diligently the place where a deluded thought arises and disappears, to see from where it arises and to where it disappears."[30] Even the "watchfulness" propagated by St. Hesychios the Priest involves some degree of exploration, of "scrutinizing every mental image or provocation," though only in the name of "spiritual warfare" against "impassioned" or "evil" thoughts.[31]

Yet other forms of meditation attempt neither to suppress nor to actively explore digressive thoughts, but simply to go gently back to the meditation object once the meditator discovers that he or she has digressed, without any active attempt at stopping the flow of thoughts. This more accepting attitude may be reflected in the comparison of the wandering mind to a sexually aroused elephant made by the Jain scholar Hemacandra (1089–1172), who points out that the elephant will become calm and malleable if it is given what it seeks, while restrictions will make it stronger and more dangerous (see Johannes Bronk-horst's contribution to this volume). The nineteenth-century Chinese Buddhist monk Yùfēng Gǔkūn also argues strongly that a "scattered" (sànluàn) mind is no obstacle to the recitative practices that he advocates.[32] Acceptance of digressive thoughts is very widespread in modern approaches to meditation, such as the Taiwan-based Buddhist master Sheng Yen's breathing meditation, and in the large number of methods influenced by Transcendental Meditation (including Centering Prayer, which reads like an amalgamation of traditional Christian recitative meditation and the principles of Transcendental Meditation). Another sound-based meditation form, Acem Meditation, goes one step further in not only accepting digressive thoughts but arguing for their importance for the processing of physical and mental stress as well as deeper psychological issues.[33]

The simple acceptance of digressive thoughts, followed by a gentle return to the meditation object, is typically intended to set in motion latent impulses at or beyond the peripheries of conscious awareness, in a nonconcentrative way. This contrasts with some forms of "mindful" or "watchful" exploration of digressive thoughts, including *vipassanā*, which more often work to keep such thoughts at bay or to actively "let go" of them by including them within one's mental focus. This latter approach frequently involves various degrees of concentration, ranging from the active fight against digressions of St. Hesychios the Priest to the much subtler attempts at reaching beyond "deluded thoughts" or leashing the "monkey mind" of Hānshān Déqīng and modern mindfulness practices.

Thematic versus Nonthematic Meditation Objects

As discussed in the previous chapter, the traditional Latin term *meditātiō* usually refers to discursive practices, while the modern and scientific interest in meditation more often focuses on nondiscursive practices, mostly of Asian origin. This distinction can be redefined in terms of thematic versus nonthematic meditation objects.

A *thematic* meditation object implies a focus on semantic, cognitive, or devotional content, such as a sacred text or image, a holy person, a deity, a moral virtue, an idea, or a concept. A *nonthematic* meditation object makes use of universal working mechanisms usually involving body, breath, or sensory impressions rather than semantic, cognitive, or devotional content. Various meditative objects may be placed at different points along a scale, from the strongly thematic to the entirely nonthematic, depending on the degree to which they seek to replace the spontaneous activity of the mind with predetermined cognitive or devotional content.

Most thematic meditation objects are deeply embedded in the culture in which they are employed, to the extent that they lose their meaning if taken out of this context, while nonthematic meditation objects have at least a core element that transcends cultural differences. In other words, thematic meditation objects most obviously include directive elements, "planting concrete ideas of future states that manifest in reality over time."[34] Nonthematic meditation objects, however, are in themselves basically nondirective and instead trigger autonomic responses in body and mind, and practitioners are typically warned against goal orientation, because this reduces the openness to transformations that are meant to unfold naturally from within.

Scientists often include the "suspension of logical thought processes," also called "logic relaxation," as a part of their definition of meditation, reflecting a nonthematic rather than a thematic orientation, and they commonly assume that all forms of meditation aim to "discourage logical and conceptual thinking."[35] This is partly true even of thematic meditation objects, since discursive meditation often aims at a slow and associative reflection that goes beyond mere logical reasoning, which in the early Christian tradition is typically compared to the rumination of animals.[36] Still, the connection between a meditation object and its intended effect is closer and more logical in thematic than in nonthematic objects of meditation.

In the monotheistic religions originating in the Middle East, meditation objects are mostly thematic rather than purely technical, typically focusing on God (or His representations on Earth) or on sacred scripture or, in some traditions, on images. Similar thematic forms of meditation are also common in South and East Asian traditions, such as the chanting of *sūtras*, the visualization of buddhas, or the recitation of buddha names within Buddhism. In South and East Asian traditions, however, there also exists a large group of more clearly nonthematic meditation objects based on technical elements related to body, breath, and sensation. Some technical elements are found in Christian, Judaic, and Islamic forms of meditation too, including the role of the body in Sufi *dhikr*,[37] the uses of breath in Eastern Orthodox hesychasm and some of St. Ignatius of Loyola's spiritual exercises, and the suggestion in "The Cloud of Unknowing" that meditative prayer should be based on monosyllabic utterances. In these practices, however, the main object of meditation is almost always thematic.

The fact that modern scientists emphasize the technical rather than thematic aspects of meditation has led to an almost exclusive interest in methods originating in Asia. Among the 1,031 scientific studies of meditation referenced and reviewed by Ospina et al., we find only a single article dealing with any of the religions originating in the Middle East, a study comparing the effects of Catholic rosary prayer and Yogic *mantra* meditation.[38] Even among Asian practices, strongly thematic forms of meditation are seldom included in scientific studies. Science typically looks for general, universal mechanisms and attempts to look away from the cultural or religious features that thematic meditation objects often bring to the forefront. Ospina et al. observe that among the methods they have studied, "no meditation practice required the adoption of a specific religious framework."[39] This reflects a technical and nonthematic view of meditation, in which cultural or religious settings are not parts of the techniques as such, the way they are in thematic meditation objects.

The distinction between thematic and nonthematic meditation objects is much more complex than might be easily assumed. In the humanities, where a constructivist view of meditation is common, it is often assumed that meditation cannot be studied independently of its cultural or religious background, as scientists often do. The psychologist Michael A. West also argues that meditation may be "inextricably bound up with belief systems and expectations,"[40] and questions whether it makes sense to study meditation outside of its cultural context. From this point of view, the distinction between thematic and nonthematic meditation objects is of little relevance, since even nonthematic objects are so strongly imbued with cultural meaning and thematic content that they are just as strongly integrated in the setting in which they are learned and practiced as are thematic objects, and are just as suggestive. For instance, while the breath in itself is a neutral element, its use as a meditation object may be interpreted as an illustration of Buddhist ideas of transience, or may be tied to ideas about cosmic life energies such as Indian *prāṇa* or Chinese *qì*.[41] The "heart" or the chest, like other body parts, is in itself a neutral element, but it may be understood in terms of various notions of a "subtle" or "mystical" body, such as Indian *cakra*, Chinese *dāntián*, or Islamic *laṭā'if*, or as the location of spiritual love in Christianity.[42] Purely sensory meditation objects, like meaningless sound combinations (*mantra*, *śabda*) and geometrical figures (*yantra*) in Indian traditions, are also in and of themselves neutral but are typically associated with deities and suffused with cultural and metaphysical symbolism. Suggestive elements in the framework surrounding meditation may influence the practice even of techniques that are at the outset nonthematic.

However, thematic meditation objects also make use of technical elements. In terms of culture and religion, it clearly makes a difference whether one recites the name of the Virgin Mary, Allah, Krishna, or Amitābha Buddha. In terms of technical working mechanisms, however, these are more or less the same, and each allows for technical variations, for example, loud chanting, quiet murmuring, silent repetition, and so on. Similarly, visualizations of Jesus Christ, the Hindu goddess Kālī, the bodhisattva Avalokiteśvara, or the deified Daoist master Lǎozǐ are culturally and religiously different, but in many technical respects they resemble each other closely. Not only are the suggestive working mechanisms that lie at the heart of such practices in themselves universal and in a sense technical in nature, but the acts of repeated recitation and prolonged visualization are technical elements with effects that go beyond pure suggestion.

One particular type of thematic meditation object is the Zen keyword often referred to by the Japanese term *kōan*, with famous examples including "What is the sound of one hand clapping?" and "[Does even a dog have buddha nature?] No!" These *kōan*s clearly have thematic content but are designed to break down ordinary language and logic and bring the meditator beyond their semantic meaning. In the words of Hánshān Déqīng, "You should not seek to understand the keyword, but only use it to generate doubt and to chop off and block out all deluded thoughts."[43]

The equation between thematic meditation objects and directive working mechanisms is not absolute. Some thematic objects of meditation may be, in principle at least, quite independent of their cultural or religious settings. Meditations focusing on universal existential issues, such as death, do not have to be couched in cultural or religious language; on the contrary, they may seek to approach the naked reality of such issues *beyond* cultural and religious notions. In such cases, we have thematic meditation dealing with universal issues.[44]

Finally, it is not quite clear how to classify so-called apophatic practices, forms of meditation designed to restrict, eliminate, or look beyond cognitive, emotional, and sensory impressions in order to approach an ineffable reality beyond. Such practices are found in most religious traditions on the Eurasian continent, including the Christian *via negativa*, Buddhist approaches to *anātman*, "no self," and the Daoist methods called *zuò-wàng*, "sitting in oblivion."[45] As in the case of death, it is possible to look upon the ineffable reality beyond all cognition and sense perception as a universal existential issue, and to treat apophatic practices as thematic forms of meditation dealing with universal issues. In contrast to the case of death, however, the existence of such a reality is not universally accepted. All *ideas* about such a reality by necessity activate the cognitions and sensations that these methods are meant to go beyond. In the debates surrounding mysticism, cultural constructivists argue that the so-called reality beyond is inextricably tied to such ideas, in which case apophatic practices are simply directive forms of thematic meditation aimed at integrating cultural and religious notions of ultimate reality. Others, however, argue that the capacity to fathom such a reality is not primarily a question of instilling in the practitioner certain ideas, but of using nondirective practices to awaken a potential residing within human beings.[46] Under this latter interpretation, it is tempting to classify apophatic forms of meditation as technical and nonthematic. However, such practices are often accompanied by ideas refuting the value of "techniques" and "methods" and favoring a more "direct" approach. It is also possible, at least for practical purposes, to treat apophatic practices as a third category, in addition to directive and nondirective.

To sum up, thematic meditation objects fill the mind with semantic, cognitive, or devotional content and build on directive working mechanisms, while nonthematic meditation objects use instead nondirective technical elements to elicit autonomic responses in body and mind. Apophatic practices seek to approach directly a reality beyond all cognitive and sensory perception. As we have seen, however, thematic and nonthematic (and arguably also apophatic) elements are often mixed in one and the same practice, and few meditation practices belong exclusively to either type.

The Effects of Directive and Nondirective Meditation

This chapter has argued for a fundamental distinction between directive and nondirective forms of meditation, based on the ways they attempt to achieve their effects. The former seek to bring about transformative change by means of external influence, while the latter aim to activate internal reflexive mechanisms in the body and mind of the practitioner. The former attempt to manipulate the spontaneous contents of the mind in preset directions, by working toward specific experiences, feelings, or states of mind, while the latter typically leave the spontaneous activities of the mind to proceed of their own accord, without active external interference.

As discussed in this chapter, the basis for the distinction between directive and nondirective meditation lies in the contrast between suggestive versus nonsuggestive settings, concentrative versus nonconcentrative mental attitudes, and thematic versus technical meditation objects, of which the two latter pairs have been discussed in some detail. Other features may also influence the degree of directiveness. For instance, the multiplex contrast between guided and self-administered meditation practices may play an important role, guided practices typically being more directive, while self-administered practices at least leave more room for open, nondirective exploration.

While the distinction between directive and nondirective meditation is based on the ways in which the methods attempt to achieve their effects, it is an open question to what extent it also influences the effects themselves. Some meditative traditions have argued that the various forms of meditation merely constitute different paths toward the same goal or goals, while other traditions hold that the type of method also affects the eventual result.

In language sometimes resembling new age terminology, Claudio Naranjo suggests that directive and nondirective forms of meditation ultimately "converge upon a common end state."[47] According to him, even directive meditation techniques ultimately explore and awaken in the individual the same fundamental features that nondirective ones do. In the same spirit, Livia Kohn points out that even practitioners of hypnosis (which according to her provides the basis for the working mechanisms of meditation) "frequently speak about waking the inner wisdom, encouraging natural intuition, or even unfolding the true self in their clients."[48]

In a more scholarly context, Bettina Bäumer makes a similar, though more specific, argument for the Indian Tantric form of meditation called *bhāvanā*, or creative contemplation. This is a highly directive practice, in which the meditators are encouraged to create certain mental states and realizations by first imagining them and then gradually integrating them as genuine parts of themselves. For instance, by meditating on the void, one enters the state of the void; by imagining that one's body or the world is filled with bliss, one becomes united with a supreme bliss; and, somewhat paradoxically, by fixing one's mind on the external space, one is eventually absorbed in nonspace.[49] In the present volume, Madhu Khanna refers to techniques of the same type. In this view, the changes brought about by directive meditation are not simply imposed from the outside but exist as potentials in the practitioner, though they are helped to fruition by external and directive stimuli.

In contrast, Mircea Eliade argues strongly against the Swedish scholar Sigurd Lindquist's attempt to demonstrate "the hypnotic [≈ directive] nature of yogic experience,"[50] pointing out that ancient Indian sources clearly distinguished between hypnosis and meditative processes, as Surendranath Dasgupta had argued before him.[51] Eliade contends that hypnosis (and, by implication, directive meditation) leads only to a provisional "damming of the 'stream of consciousness'" and "paralysis . . . of the mental flux," comparable to the "easy extinction of consciousness" through "trances and ecstasies obtained from intoxicants, narcotics, and all the other elementary means of emptying consciousness." The "enstasy" (Skt. *samādhi*) brought about by meditation differs from this kind of "self-hypnosis" and "fetal preconsciousness" in providing reintegration and unity in a frame of mind characterized by "the utmost lucidity" and "superconsciousness" or "transconsciousness." Unlike hypnosis, it does not reach for a *"given* situation" but establishes "a new and paradoxical mode of being."[52]

Many scientists ignore the technical differences between meditation practices, simply providing the name of the method they study.[53] Others, however, attempt to show that directive and nondirective (or concentrative and nonconcentrative) forms of meditation actually produce different results. Daniel P. Brown argues that practitioners of directive meditation typically go through "distinct levels of practice" with a "logical order" and an "invariant sequence," whereas the types of nondirective meditation he studies "do not have well-defined levels" but lead, after many years of practice, to "a sudden and dramatic reorganization of cognition."[54] Several reports discuss how different mental attitudes lead to differences in brain-wave patterns,[55] neuroimaging patterns,[56] uses of attention,[57] and a number of psychological (short-term) states and (long-term) traits, including creativity.[58] One study finds that both directive and nondirective forms of meditation increase the activity of the brain's default mode network, which is associated with mind wandering, but that nondirective forms have the greatest effects, especially in areas associated with the processing of memories and emotions.[59] If these studies are correct, the distinction between directive and nondirective practices is not only technically important but may also be decisive for the eventual outcome of meditative practice.

Notes

This essay has been inspired by discussions among Acem instructors, as well as Holen, "Acem Meditation and Other Meditation Practices." It has profited much from comments on an earlier version by Mark Teeuwen and Øyvind Ellingsen.

1. On "concentration" versus "insight," see Goleman, "Meditation and Consciousness." On "concentration" versus "mindfulness," see Perez de Albeniz and Holmes, "Meditation"; and Davidson and Goleman, "Role of Attention." Historically and terminologically, the conflation of "insight" (*vipassanā*) and "mindfulness" (*sati*) is confusing, since the two are at the outset quite distinct notions. In the Buddhist tradition, "mindfulness" may be just as strongly linked to "concentration" as to "insight," and the common meditative practice "mindfulness of breathing" (*ānāpānasati*) is sometimes classified as a concentration technique, and at other times as an insight practice. In line with this, but in contrast to modern definitions, Edward Conze's early exposition of Buddhist meditation distinguishes between three mental (or, in his terminology, subjective) attitudes: concentration, insight, and mindfulness (Conze, *Buddhist Meditation*, 16ff.).

2. Lutz et al., "Attention Regulation"; Manna et al., "Neural Correlates"; Sperduti et al., "Neurocognitive Model."

3. Cf. Kohn, "Daoist Adaptation"; Kohn, "Taoist Insight Meditation."

4. Cf. Lagopoulos et al., "Increased Theta and Alpha EEG Activity"; Nesvold et al., "Increased Heart Rate Variability"; Xu et al., "Nondirective Meditation". The distinction between "directive" and "nondirective" meditation was first made in Naranjo, "Meditation," though with a slightly different distinction than the one made here.

5. Ferrer and Sherman, "Introduction."

6. Benson, *Relaxation Response*, 12; cf. Beary and Benson, "Simple Psychophysiologic Technique."

7. The distinction between directive and nondirective practices breaks with the social, cultural, and linguistic constructivism that has dominated cultural and religious studies for decades. While today no one seriously disputes the formative role of contextual factors, constructivism has more recently been challenged from a variety of angles, some arguing for the agency of the individual subject in the face of external influences, others for the centrality of the body and its energies, as well as affective, intuitive, and other prelogical aspects of consciousness, yet others opening up for spiritual and noumenal qualities beyond materialist or naturalist visions of reality. The present chapter may be seen as a modest contribution to this debate, mainly by contrasting working mechanisms that correspond to a constructivist view of meditation with more purely technical ones. For a summary of trends that break with social, cultural, and linguistic constructivism, see Ferrer and Sherman, "Introduction."

8. Perez de Albeniz and Holmes, "Meditation."

9. Walsh and Shapiro, "Meeting of Meditative Disciplines," 229.

10. Most probably, a similar distinction applies to psychotherapy, with cognitive therapies leaning toward a directive content orientation, and psychodynamic therapies leaning toward a nondirective process orientation.

11. The following are descriptions of "concentration" or "focused attention": "focus attention on a singular external object" (Shapiro, "Overview"); "sustaining the attention directly to a single object, point or focus" (Goleman, "Meditation and Consciousness"); "focusing attention on a single-target percept" (Davidson and Goleman, "Role of Attention"); "attention . . . focused on an intended object in a sustained fashion" (Manna et al., "Neural Correlates"); "the concentration of attention on a particular external, corporal or mental object while ignoring all irrelevant stimuli" (Sperduti et al., "Neurocognitive Model"); "sustaining selective attention moment by moment on a chosen object" (Lutz et al., "Attention Regulation"); "focuses on a particular item, thought, or object" (Colzato et al., "Meditate to Create"); and "focusing on a specific sensory or mental stimulus to the exclusion of anything else" (Dakwar and Levin, "Emerging Role of Meditation"). The following are descriptions of "insight," "mindfulness," or "open monitoring": "cultivate an objective openness to whatever comes into awareness" (Ospina et al., "Meditation Practices for Health"); "maintaining a specific cognitive perception related to the contents that would spontaneously come to mind" (Goleman, "Meditation and Consciousness"); "maintenance of a particular attentional stance toward all objects of awareness" (Davidson and Goleman, "Role of Attention"); "the non-reactive monitoring of the content of experience from moment to moment, primarily as a means to recognize the nature of emotional and cognitive patterns" (Manna et al., "Neural Correlates"); "enlarge the attentional focus to all incoming sensations, emotions and thoughts from moment to moment without focusing on any of them" (Sperduti et al., "Neurocognitive Model"); "attentive moment by moment to anything that occurs in experience without focusing on any explicit object" (Lutz et al., "Attention Regulation"); "open to perceive and observe any sensation or thought without focusing on a concept in the mind or a fixed item" (Colzato et al., "Meditate to

Create"); and "allowing thoughts, feelings, and sensations to arise while maintaining a non-judgmental, detached, and accepting attitude to them, as well as a heightened perceptual stance attentive to the entire field of perception" (Dakwar and Levin, "Emerging Role of Meditation").

12. Davidson and Goleman, "Role of Attention."

13. Dakwar and Levin, "Emerging Role of Meditation," 257; cf. Cahn and Polich, "Meditation States and Traits"; Raffone and Srinivasan, "Exploration of Meditation."

14. Shapiro, "Overview," 6.

15. Travis and Shear, "Focused Attention."

16. Lutz et al., "Attention Regulation." Ospina et al. also note that "some [mindfulness] practices . . . have phases where concentration is used, and for which certain techniques such as counting or concentrating on a mantra are employed, while at other stages broad spaced mindful attention is encouraged" ("Meditation Practices for Health," 48).

17. Ospina et al., "Meditation Practices for Health," 48.

18. Naranjo, "Meditation," 7ff.; Conze, *Buddhist Meditation*, 13ff.; Koshikawa and Ichii, "Experiment on Classification Methods," 213–224; Holen, "Acem Meditation."

19. Conze (*Buddhist Meditation*, 19ff.) makes a similar distinction but uses the term "concentration" for both types.

20. Cáo and Kǒng, *Hānshān lǎorén mèngyóu jí*. Translations are mine.

21. Hodgson, *Cloud of Unknowing*; translations from Wolters, *Cloud of Unknowing*.

22. Hodgson, *Cloud of Unknowing*, 87; Wolters, *Cloud of Unknowing*, 114.

23. Hodgson, *Cloud of Unknowing*, 62; Wolters, *Cloud of Unknowing*, 95.

24. "Attention Regulation and Monitoring in Meditation," 164.

25. Orig. "Tā qǐ tā de niàn, wǒ niàn wǒ de fó." From Wùkāi, "Jìngyè zhījǐn."

26. Guǎngguì, "Liánbāng shīxuǎn."

27. See Casiday, "Images of Salvation."

28. Palmer et al., *Philokalia*, 165.

29. Müller, *Atthasālinī*, 118; translation from Tin, *Expositor*, 157.

30. Cáo and Kǒng, *Hānshān lǎorén mèngyóu jí*, 2.

31. Palmer et al., *Philokalia*, 164.

32. Eifring, "Spontaneous Thoughts in Meditative Traditions," 210ff.

33. Holen, *Inner Strength*.

34. Kohn, *Meditation Works*, 4.

35. Craven, "Meditation and Psychotherapy"; Cardoso et al., "Meditation in Health"; Ospina et al., "Meditation Practices for Health," 28.

36. Rönnegård, "*Melétē* in Early Christian Ascetic Texts."

37. Cf. Elias, "Sufi *Dhikr*"; Bashir, "Movement and Stillness."

38. A separate list of 1,531 "excluded and nonobtained studies" does include a considerable number of studies of Christian, Jewish, and Islamic practices, but apart from a few "nonobtained" cases, the quality of these studies was deemed insufficient according to the criteria for inclusion in Ospina et al.'s review.

39. Ospina et al., "Meditation Practices for Health," 47–48.

40. West, *Psychology of Meditation*, quoted from Ospina et al., "Meditation Practices for Health," 196.

41. Sarah Shaw's contribution to this volume shows how strongly many apparently technical objects of "insight meditation" are tied to Buddhist doctrine.

42. Cf. Madhu Khanna's and Geoffrey Samuel's contributions to this volume, as well as Baker, "Cinnabar-Field Meditation in Korea"; Rydell-Johnsén, "Early Jesus Prayer"; Elias, "Sufi *Dhikr*"; and Bashir, "Movement and Stillness."

43. Cf. Eifring, "Meditative Pluralism in Hānshān Déqīng." See also Morten Schlütter's contribution to this volume.

44. On meditations on death in Buddhism, see Shaw's contribution to this volume, as well as Dessein, "Contemplation of the Repulsive." On meditations on death in Christianity, see Rönnegård, "*Melétē* in Early Christian Ascetic Texts."

45. Cf. Harold D. Roth's contribution to this volume, as well as Seppälä, "Meditation in the East Syrian Tradition."

46. For the two opposite views of mysticism, see Katz, *Mysticism and Philosophical Analysis*, and Forman, *Problem of Pure Consciousness*.

47. Naranjo, "Meditation."

48. Kohn, *Meditation Works*, 4.

49. Bäumer, "Creative Contemplation."

50. Lindquist, *Methoden des Yoga*.

51. Dasgupta, *Yoga Philosophy*, 352ff.

52. Eliade, *Yoga*, 78f., 99f.

53. Davanger, "Natural Science of Meditation."

54. Brown, "Model for Concentrative Meditation," 243.

55. Lagopoulos, "Increased Theta and Alpha EEG Activity"; Travis and Shear, "Focused Attention."

56. Lutz et al., "Attention Regulation"; Manna et al., "Neural Correlates"; Davanger et al., "Meditation-Specific Prefrontal Cortical Activation."

57. Cahn and Polich, "Meditation States and Traits"; Lutz et al., "Attention Regulation"; Davidson and Goleman, "Role of Attention."

58. Cahn and Polich, "Meditation States and Traits"; Colzato et al., "Meditate to Create."

59. Xu et al., "Nondirective Meditation."

Glossary

bào yī 抱一
dāntián 丹田
fǎ-yǔ 法語
Hānshān Déqīng 憨山德清
huǎnhuǎn 緩緩
jíjí 急急
jílì 極力
Lǎozǐ 老子
niàn 念
qì 氣
sànluàn 散亂
shǒu yī 守一
sǐshǒu huàtóu 死守話頭
"Tā qǐ tā de niàn, wǒ niàn wǒ de fó" 他起他的念，我念我的佛
wàng-niàn 妄念
wàng-xiǎng 妄想
yí niàn 一念
Yùfēng Gǔkūn 玉峯古崑
zá-niàn 雜念
zhí yī 執一

zhuólì 著力
zuò-wàng 坐忘

Bibliography

Baker, Don. "Cinnabar-Field Meditation in Korea." In Eifring, *Meditation and Culture*, 162–171.

Bashir, Shahzad. "Movement and Stillness: The Practice of Sufi Dhikr in Fourteenth-Century Central Asia." In Eifring, *Meditation in Judaism, Christianity and Islam*, 201–211.

Bäumer, Bettina. "'Creative Contemplation' (*Bhāvanā*) in the Vijñāna Bhairava Tantra." In Eifring, *Hindu, Buddhist and Daoist Meditation*, 57–67.

Beary, John F., and Herbert Benson. "A Simple Psychophysiologic Technique Which Elicits the Hypometabolic Changes of the Relaxation Response." *Psychosomatic Medicine* 36, no. 2 (March–April 1974): 115–120.

Benson, Herbert. With Miriam Z. Klipper. *The Relaxation Response*. 1975. Updated and expanded ed. New York: HarperTorch, 2000.

Brown, Daniel P. "A Model for the Levels of Concentrative Meditation." *International Journal of Clinical and Experimental Hypnosis* 25, no. 4 (1977): 236–273.

Cahn, B. Rael, and John Polich. "Meditation States and Traits: EEG, ERP, and Neuroimaging Studies." *Psychological Bulletin* 132, no. 2 (2006): 180–211.

Cáo Yuè 曹越, and Kǒng Hóng 孔宏, eds. *Hānshān lǎorén mèngyóu jí* 憨山老人夢遊集. Originally 17th century. Beijing: Běijīng dàxué chūbǎnshè, 2005.

Cardoso, Roberto, Eduardo de Souza, Luiz Camano, and José Roberto Leite. "Meditation in Health: An Operational Definition." *Brain Research Protocols* 14 (2004): 58–60.

Casiday, Augustine. "Imageless Prayer and Imagistic Meditation in Orthodox Christianity." In Eifring, *Meditation in Judaism, Christianity and Islam*, 173–185.

Colzato, Lorenza S., Ayca Ozturk, and Bernhard Hommel. "Meditate to Create: The Impact of Focused-Attention and Open-Monitoring Training on Convergent and Divergent Thinking." *Frontiers in Psychology* 3 (April 2012): 116.

Conze, Edward. *Buddhist Meditation*. 1956. Reprint, Mineola, NY: Dover, 2003.

Craven, J. L. "Meditation and Psychotherapy." *Canadian Journal of Psychiatry* 34, no. 7 (1989): 648–653.

Dakwar, Elias, and Frances R. Levin. "The Emerging Role of Meditation in Addressing Psychiatric Illness: With a Focus on Substance Use Disorders." *Harvard Review of Psychiatry* 17 (2009): 254–267.

Dasgupta, S. N. *Yoga Philosophy in Relation to Other Systems of Indian Thought*. 1930. Reprint, Delhi: Motilal Banarsidass, 1974.

Davanger, Svend. "The Natural Science of Meditation: A Black Box Perspective." In Eifring, *Meditation in Judaism, Christianity and Islam*, 227–236.

Davanger, Svend, Are Holen, Øyvind Ellingsen, and Kenneth Hugdahl. "Meditation-Specific Prefrontal Cortical Activation during Acem Meditation: An fMRI Study." *Perceptual and Motor Skills* 111, no. 1 (2010): 291–306.

Davidson, Richard J., and Daniel J. Goleman. "The Role of Attention in Meditation and Hypnosis: A Psychobiological Perspective on Transformations of Consciousness." *International Journal of Clinical and Experimental Hypnosis* 25, no. 4 (1977): 291–308.

Dessein, Bart. "Contemplation of the Repulsive: Bones and Skulls as Objects of Meditation." In Eifring, *Hindu, Buddhist and Daoist Meditation*, 117–147.

Eifring, Halvor, ed. *Hindu, Buddhist and Daoist Meditation: Cultural Histories*. Oslo: Hermes, 2014.

———, ed. *Meditation and Culture: The Interplay of Practice and Context*. London: Bloomsbury Academic, 2015.

———, ed. *Meditation in Judaism, Christianity and Islam: Cultural Histories*. London: Bloomsbury Academic, 2013.

———. "Meditative Pluralism in Hānshān Déqīng." In Eifring, *Meditation and Culture*, 102–127.

———. "Spontaneous Thoughts in Meditative Traditions." In Eifring, *Meditation and Culture*, 200–215.

Eliade, Mircea. *Yoga: Immortality and Freedom*. Translated by Willard R. Trask. 2nd ed. Princeton, NJ: Princeton University Press, 1990.

Elias, Jamal. "Sufi *Dhikr* between Meditation and Prayer." In Eifring, *Meditation in Judaism, Christianity and Islam*, 189–200.

Ferrer, Jorge N., and Jacob H. Sherman. "Introduction: The Participatory Turn in Spirituality, Mysticism, and Religious Studies." In *The Participatory Turn: Spirituality, Mysticism, Religious Studies*, edited by Jorge N. Ferrer and Jacob H. Sherman, 1–80. Albany: State University of New York Press, 2008.

Forman, Robert K. C. *The Problem of Pure Consciousness: Mysticism and Philosophy*. New York: Oxford University Press, 1996.

Goleman, Daniel. "Meditation and Consciousness: An Asian Approach to Mental Health." *American Journal of Psychotherapy* 30 (1976): 41–54.

Guǎngguì 廣貴 (fl. ca. 1600). "Liánbāng shīxuǎn" 蓮邦詩選, *Xùzàngjīng* 續藏經 62, no. 1207. Accessed December 20, 2012. http://www.cbeta.org/result/normal/X62/1207_001.htm.

Hodgson, Phyllis, ed. *The Cloud of Unknowing and The Book of Privy Counselling*. Originally 14th century. 1944. Reprint, London: Oxford University Press, 1973.

Holen, Are. "Acem Meditation and Other Meditation Practices." In *Acem Meditation: An Introductory Companion*, edited by Are Holen and Halvor Eifring, 59–66. 2nd ed. Oslo: Dyade Press, 2013.

———. *Inner Strength: The Free Mental Attitude in Acem Meditation*. 2nd ed. Oslo: Acem Publishing, 2007.

Katz, Steven T., ed. *Mysticism and Philosophical Analysis*. New York: Oxford University Press, 1978.

Kohn, Livia. "The Daoist Adaptation of Buddhist Insight Meditation." In Eifring, *Meditation and Culture*, 11–23.

———. *Meditation Works: In the Hindu, Buddhist and Daoist Traditions*. Magdalena, NM: Three Pines Press, 2008.

———. "Taoist Insight Meditation: The Tang Practice of *Neiguan*." In *Taoist Meditation and Longevity Techniques*, edited by Livia Kohn, 191–222. Ann Arbor: University of Michigan Press.

Koshikawa, F., and M. Ichii. "An Experiment on Classification Methods of Meditation Methods: On Procedures, Goals and Effects." In *Comparative and Psychological Study on Meditation*, edited by Y. Haruki, Y. Ishii, and M. Suzuki, 213–224. Delft: Eburon, 1996.

Lagopoulos, Jim, Jian Xu, Inge Rasmussen, Alexandra Vik, Gin S. Malhi, Carl F. Eliassen, Ingrid E. Arntsen, Jardar G. Sæther, Stig Hollup, Are Holen, Svend Davanger, and Øyvind Ellingsen. "Increased Theta and Alpha EEG Activity during Nondirective Meditation." *Journal of Alternative and Complementary Medicine* 15, no. 11 (2009): 1187–1192.

Lindquist, Sigurd. *Die Methoden des Yoga*. Lund: Håkan Ohlssons Buchdruckerei, 1932.

Lutz, A., H. A. Slagter, J. D. Dunne, and R. J. Davidson. "Attention Regulation and Monitoring in Meditation." *Trends in Cognitive Sciences* 12, no. 4 (April 2008): 163–169.

Manna, A., A. Raffone, M. G. Perrucci, D. Nardo, A. Ferretti, A. Tartaro, A. Londei, C. Del Gratta, M. O. Belardinelli, and G. L. Romani. "Neural Correlates of Focused Attention and Cognitive Monitoring in Meditation." *Brain Research Bulletin* 82, nos. 1–2 (March 2010): 46–56.

Müller, Edward, ed. *The Atthasālinī: Buddhaghosa's Commentary on the "Dhammasaṅgaṇi."* London: Oxford University Press, 1897.

Naranjo, Claudio. "Meditation: Its Spirit and Techniques." In *On the Psychology of Meditation*, edited by Claudio Naranjo and Robert E. Ornstein, 1–132. New York: The Viking Press, 1971.

Nesvold, Anders, Morten W. Fagerland, Svend Davanger, Øyvind Ellingsen, Erik E. Solberg, Are Holen, Knut Sevre, and Dan Atar. "Increased Heart Rate Variability during Nondirective Meditation." *European Journal of Preventive Cardiology* 19 (2012): 773–780.

Ospina, Maria B., Kenneth Bond, Mohammad Karkhaneh, Lisa Tjosvold, Ben Vandermeer, Yuanyuan Liang, Liza Bialy, Nicola Hooton, Nina Buscemi, Donna M. Dryden, and Terry P. Klassen. "Meditation Practices for Health: State of the Research." *Evidence Report / Technology Assessment* no. 155. Rockville, MD: Agency for Healthcare Research and Quality.

Palmer, G. E. H., Philip Sherrard, and Kallistos Ware, transl. and eds. *Philokalia: The Complete Text Compiled by St Nikodimos of the Holy Mountain and St Makarios of Corinth.* London: Faber and Faber, 1979–1999.

Perez de Albeniz, A., and J. Holmes. "Meditation: Concepts, Effects and Uses in Therapy." *International Journal of Psychotherapy* 5, no. 1 (2000): 49–58.

Raffone, A., and N. Srinivasan. "The Exploration of Meditation in the Neuroscience of Attention and Consciousness." *Cognitive Processing* 11 (2010): 1–7.

Rönnegård, Per. "*Melétē* in Early Christian Ascetic Texts." In Eifring, *Meditation in Judaism, Christianity and Islam*, 79–92.

Rydell-Johnsén, Henrik. "The Early Jesus Prayer and Meditation in Greco-Roman Philosophy." In Eifring, *Meditation in Judaism, Christianity and Islam*, 93–106.

Seppälä, Serafim. "Meditation in the East Syrian Tradition." In Eifring, *Meditation in the Judaic, Christian, and Islamic Traditions*, 107–121.

Shapiro, Deane H., Jr. "Overview: Clinical and Physiological Comparison of Meditation with Other Self-Control Strategies." In *Meditation: Classic and Contemporary Perspectives*, edited by Deane H. Shapiro, Jr., and Roger N. Walsh, 5–12. New York: Aldine, 1984.

Sperduti, Marco, Pénélope Martinelli, and Pascale Piolino. "A Neurocognitive Model of Meditation Based on Activation Likelihood Estimation (ALE) Meta-Analysis." *Consciousness and Cognition* 21 (2012): 269–276.

Tin, Maung, transl. *The Expositor (Atthasālinī): Buddhaghosa's Commentary on the "Dhammsangaṇi," the First Book of the "Abhidhamma Piṭaka."* Vol. 1. London: Oxford University Press, 1920.

Travis, Fred, and Jonathan Shear. "Focused Attention, Open Monitoring and Automatic Self-Transcending: Categories to Organize Meditations from Vedic, Buddhist and Chinese Traditions." *Consciousness and Cognition* 19 (2010): 1110–1118.

Walsh, R., and S. L. Shapiro. "The Meeting of Meditative Disciplines and Western Psychology." *American Psychologist* 61, no. 3 (2006): 227–239.

West, Michael A., ed. *The Psychology of Meditation.* New York: Oxford University Press, 1987.

Wolters, Clifton, transl. *The Cloud of Unknowing and Other Works*. 1961. Reprint, Harmondsworth, UK: Penguin Books, 1978.

Wùkāi 悟開 (d. 1830). "Jìngyè zhījīn" 淨業知津. *Xùzàngjīng* 續藏經62, no. 1183. Accessed December 20, 2012. http://www.cbeta.org/result/normal/X62/1183_001.htm.

Xu, Jian, Alexandra Vik, Inge R. Groote, Jim Lagopoulos, Are Holen, Øyvind Ellingsen, Asta K. Håberg, and Svend Davanger. "Nondirective Meditation Activates Default Mode Network and Areas Associated with Memory Retrieval and Emotional Processing." *Frontiers in Human Neuroscience* 8 (2014), article 86.

Samādhi *in the* Yoga Sūtras

The Indic traditions have a rich variegated history of meditational and contemplative practices that go back two and a half millennia. The systematization of these techniques as expressed in the *Yoga Sūtras* of Patañjali eventually emerged as the recognized standard and generic model of meditative praxis for orthodox Hinduism that was then accommodated within the theologies and metaphysics of the heterogeneous traditions. This chapter examines the seven ultimate states of consciousness that culminate from progressive stages of meditative focus, with the aim of providing the reader with a historical sense of the metaphysical presuppositions of traditional yoga (i.e., prior to the colonial encounter). Issues pertaining to actual practice (for which there is limited premodern textual material associated with the classical Yoga school) lies beyond the scope of this chapter.

Historical Background

The first clear references to Yoga as a meditational practice emerge in the late Vedic period in a genre of texts called the Upaniṣads, and from then on references to Yoga and *yogīs* pervade the literary landscape of India, both orthodox (upholding allegiance to the old Vedic corpus of texts, such as the Epics, Purāṇas, and emerging theological and philosophical traditions) and heterodox (traditions developing new non-Vedic canons, such as the Buddhists and Jains).[1] The Indian traditions have never had a transsectarian centralizing entity in the form of an ecclesiastical person or body defining praxis (or dogma), and, other than nominal allegiance to the (already very variegated) Vedic corpus, de facto yogic authority lay (and continues to lie) in allegiance to the charismatic ascetic practitioner, the *yogī* virtuoso. Thus, already in the earliest sources we see a wide variety of yogic schema—with eight limbs, six limbs,[2] eight qualities,[3] seven *dhāraṇās* (concentration), twelve yogas, and so on—and find common technical philosophical terms, such as *vitarka* (state of absorption with physical awareness) and *vicāra* (state of absorption with subtle awareness), used in very different ways.[4] A number of interconnected and cross-fertilizing variants of meditational *yoga* were evolving out of a common Upaniṣadic core, spearheaded by renunciants (Buddhist and Jain as well as Hindu) prior to Patañjali, and all drawing from a common but variously understood pool of terminologies, practices, and concepts (and, indeed, many strains continue to the present day).

Since there was never one uniform school of ur-Yoga (or of any Indic school of thought, for that matter), but rather this plurality of variants embedded in different conceptualizations of meditative practices, all going under the name *yoga*, pre-Pātañjalian *yoga* is best understood as a cluster of techniques, some more and some less systematized, that pervaded the landscape of ancient India. There is, however, a common denominator of these variegated references to *yoga*: they all involve some form of effort aimed at *dhyāna*, stilling the mind, often accompanied by preparatory breathing techniques.[5] These techniques overlapped and were incorporated into the various philosophical and devotional traditions of the day, such as the *jñāna* (knowledge) and *bhakti* (devotional) traditions, providing these systems with practical, time-worn, and universally accepted methods and generic techniques for attaining an experienced-based transformation of consciousness in accordance with the particular theologies of each specific tradition.

From this rich and fertile post-Vedic context, then, emerged an individual called Patañjali, dated by scholars to the first and second centuries CE,[6] whose schematization of the heterogeneous practices of *yoga* came to be authoritative for all subsequent practitioners, and whose system eventually became reified as the classical orthodox source of authority in this regard. Patañjali systematized the preexisting traditions, pinpointing their commonality or methodological core of concentrative praxis, and formulated what came to be the seminal text for *yoga* discipline, that is, his particular systematization of these techniques was in time to emerge as the most dominant and authoritative source on generic yogic practice, and was eventually to gain the status of being one of the six schools of Indian philosophy.[7] Patañjali's system was to provide the generic "blueprint," so to speak, for most subsequent traditions, many of which then tinkered with it by adding their sectarian sect-specific qualities (*tantric* physiologies, *bhakti* visualizations, *jñāna* metaphysics, and so on.[8] This chapter will present an overview of the highest stages of this generic meditation, the *samādhis*, as presented in Patañjali's *Yoga Sūtras*.

Metaphysics of Yoga Psychology

Yoga is not to be considered as a school distinct from the oldest metaphysical system in ancient India, Sāṃkhya, until well after Patañjali's time. Sāṃkhya provided the metaphysical or theoretical basis for the realization of *puruṣa* (self, soul), and Yoga the technique or practice itself. Since the Yoga stages of *samādhi* are embedded in this metaphysics, some understanding of the categories of Sāṃkhya is required.[9] In the generic Sāṃkhya (lit. "numeration") system, the universe of animate and inanimate entities is perceived as ultimately the product of two ontologically distinct categories; hence this system is quintessentially dualistic (*dvaita*) in presupposition. These two categories are *prakṛti*, or the primordial material matrix of the physical universe, and *puruṣa*, the innumerable conscious selves embedded within it. The two are inherently, eternally, and fundamentally distinct types of things, the former being unconscious and active, and the latter conscious and passive.

As a result of the interaction between these two entities, the material universe evolves in a series of stages. The actual catalysts in this evolutionary process are the three *guṇas* (lit. "strands" or "qualities") that are inherent in *prakṛti*. These are *sattva* (lucidity), *rajas* (action), and *tamas* (inertia). These *guṇas* are sometimes compared to the threads that make up a rope: just as a rope is a combination of threads, so all manifest reality consists of a combination of the *guṇas*. Another comparison can be made to the wick, fire, and oil of a lamp, which, while opposed to each other in their nature, come together to produce light.

Given the meditative focus of Yoga, the *guṇas* are especially significant in terms of their psychological manifestation; in Yoga, the mind and therefore all psychological dispositions are *prakṛti*, and therefore also composed of the *guṇas*—the only difference between mind and elemental matter being that the former has a larger preponderance of *sattva*, and the latter of *tamas*. Therefore, according to the specific intermixture and proportionality of the *guṇas*, living beings exhibit different types of mindsets and psychological dispositions. Thus, when *sattva* is predominant in an individual, the qualities of lucidity, tranquility, wisdom, discrimination, detachment, happiness, and peacefulness manifest; when *rajas* is predominant, hankering, attachment, energetic endeavor, passion, power, restlessness, and creative activity are present; and when *tamas*, the *guṇa* least favorable for *yoga*, is predominant, there is ignorance, delusion, disinterest, lethargy, sleep, and disinclination toward constructive activity. It is *sattva* that we will focus on in the high meditative states discussed in this chapter.

The *guṇas* are continually interacting and competing with one another, with one *guṇa* becoming prominent for a while and overpowering the others, only to be eventually dominated in turn by the increase of one of the other *guṇas*. Just as there is an unlimited variety of colors stemming from the intermixture of the three primary colors, the different hues being simply expressions of the specific proportionality of red, yellow and blue that are always open to adjustment, so the unlimited psychological dispositions of living creatures and of physical forms stem from the intermixture of the *guṇas*, specific states being the reflections of the particular proportionality of the intermixture of the three *guṇas*.

The *guṇas* not only underpin the metaphysics of mind in Yoga but the activation and interaction of these *guṇa* qualities result in the production of the entirety of gross physical forms that also evolve from the primordial material matrix, *prakṛti*, by the same principle. Thus the physical composition of objects such as air, water, stone, fire, and so on, differs because of the constitutional makeup of specific *guṇas*: air contains more of the buoyancy of *sattva*, stone more of the sluggishness of *tamas*, and fire more of *rajas*. The *guṇas* allow for the infinite plasticity of *prakṛti* and the objects of the world.

The process by which the universe evolves from *prakṛti* is usefully compared to the churning of milk: when milk receives a citric catalyst, yogurt, curds, or butter emerge. These immediate products, in turn, can be further manipulated to produce a further series of products—milk desserts, cheese, and so on. Similarly, according to classical Sāmkhya, the first evolute emerging from *prakṛti* when it is churned by the *guṇas* (*sattva* specifically) is *buddhi*, intelligence (see figure 3.1). Intelligence is characterized by the functions of judgment, discrimination, knowledge, ascertainment, will, virtue, and detachment, and *sattva* is predominant in it. This means that in its purest state, when the potential of *rajas* and *tamas* are minimized, *buddhi* is primarily lucid, peaceful, happy, tranquil, and discriminatory, all qualities of *sattva*. Intelligence is the interface between *puruṣa* and all other *prakṛtic* evolutes. From this vantage point, it can direct awareness out into the objects and embroilments of the world, or, in its highest potential, can become aware of the presence of *puruṣa* and consequently redirect itself toward complete realization of the true source of consciousness that transcends and pervades it.

From *buddhi*, *ahaṃkāra*, or ego is produced (*aham* "I" + *kāra* "doing"; referred to as *asmitā* in the *Yoga Sūtras*). *Ahaṃkāra* is characterized by the function of self-awareness and self-identity. It is the cognitive aspect that processes and appropriates external reality from the perspective of an individualized sense of self or ego—the notion of "I" and "mine" in human awareness. *Ahaṃkāra* also limits the range of awareness to fit within and identify with the contours of the particular psychophysical organism within which it finds itself in any one embodiment, as opposed to another.

When *ahaṃkāra*, or ego, is in turn "churned" by the *guṇa* of *sattva* inherent in it, *manas*, the mind, is produced. The mind is the seat of the emotions, of like and dislike, and is characterized by control of the senses—filtering and

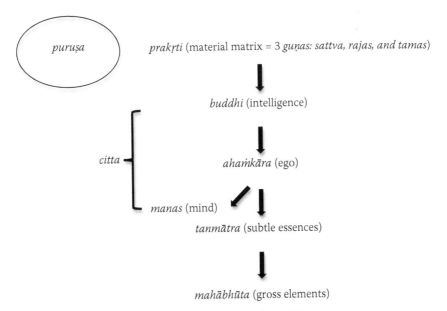

Figure 3.1. *Puruṣa* and *prakṛti. Image courtesy of Edwin F. Bryant.*

processing the potentially enormous amount of incoming sensual data. It primarily receives, sorts, categorizes, and then transmits. It serves as the liaison between the activities of the senses channeling input from the external world, and *buddhi*, intelligence. It therefore partakes both of internal and external cognition: internally, it is characterized by reflective synthesis, while simultaneously being a sense because it is involved in sensual processes. From ego emerge the five *tanmātras*, the subtle essences of sound, touch, sight, taste, and smell, which are the qualities perceived through sense perception. Finally, from these qualities emerge the five *mahābhūta* substances underpinning them, the corresponding gross atoms of ether, air, fire, water, and earth. These evolutes of *buddhi, ahaṁkāra, tanmātra,* and *mahābhūta* are essential to an understanding of the various states of *samādhi.*

The Yoga school, while using the terminology of *buddhi* in particular, but also of *ahaṁkāra* and *manas*, differs somewhat from that of Sāṁkhya in conceiving these three as interacting functions of the one *citta*, mind, rather than as three distinct metaphysical layers. *Citta*, then, as the term used by Patañjali and the commentators to refer to all three of these cognitive functions combined, is one of the most important terms in the *Yoga Sūtras*. Most importantly for the understanding of Yoga, the *puruṣa*, pure consciousness, is cloaked in the psychic layers of this *citta* (as are the gross elements of the material body). The *puruṣa* is not only completely ontologically and metaphysically distinct from the *citta* but potentially separable and autonomous. Indeed, such separation is the very goal of Yoga, a goal that is known by such terms as *mokṣa, mukti, hana,* and *kaivalya*—all synonyms for "freedom."

It is imperative to absorb this essential metaphysical presupposition in order to grasp the basics of Yoga. While the notion of a distinction between the material body and a conscious soul has a well-known history in Western Graeco-Abrahamic religion and thought, Yoga differs from most comparable Western schools of dualism by regarding not just the physical body but also the mind, ego, will, judgment, and all cognitive, conative, and affective functions and intentional thought as belonging to the realm of inert matter. The dualism fundamental to Platonic or Aristotelian thought, or to Paul or Augustine, is not at all the dualism of Yoga. In the Yoga tradition, the dualism is not between the material body and physical reality on one hand, and spiritual and mental reality characterized by thought on the other, but between pure awareness and all objects of awareness—whether these objects are physical and extended, or internal and nonextended. In other words, in Sāṁkhya and Yoga, perception, thought, feeling, emotion, memory (*saṁskāra*), and so on are as material, physical, and objective as the visible ingredients of the empirical world. Pure consciousness, called *puruṣa* in this system, animates and pervades the incessant states and fluctuations of the *citta*, but the two are completely distinct entities.[10]

The Seven Stages of *Samādhi*

In the opening verses of the *Yoga Sūtras*, Patañjali defines *yoga* in general as *citta vṛtti nirodhaḥ*, the stilling of all states of the mind. After a brief discussion of the five states of mind, or *vṛttis*,[11] and of the basic process involved in stilling them, in I.17, we find the following verse, with the Sanskrit text followed by its English translation:

> *vitarka vicārānandāsmitā rūpānugamāt samprajñātaḥ*
>
> *Samprajñāta* [*samādhi*] consists of [the consecutive] mental stages of: absorption with "physical awareness," absorption with "subtle awareness," absorption with "bliss," and absorption with "the sense of I-ness."

Here we encounter the schematized nature of the *Yoga Sūtras* as Patañjali turns his attention to the various stages of *samādhi*, the consecutive levels of mental states ensuing when all thought has, in fact, been stilled, *nirodhaḥ*, the final goal of *yoga*. The technical way that the Sanskrit terms for these stages—*vitarka*, *vicāra*, *ānanda*, and *asmitā*—are being used in this verse here cannot be captured by a suitable English equivalent—in fact, even the Sanskrit terms are something of an artificiality, as the fifteenth-century commentator Vijñānabhikṣu points out, and not to be correlated with their conventional Sanskrit dictionary meanings. They are used variously even within the *sūtras* themselves.[12] And even when terms such as *vitarka* and *vicāra* are used elsewhere to denote meditational states (e.g., in the *Mahābhārata* and Buddhist texts), the definitions given differ considerably from how Patañjali's commentators understand them in this verse.[13] Thus, although the understandings of these terms differ among these traditions,[14] there is clearly a common substratum of practice and terminology. It is important to be aware of the shared context of meditational practices in ancient India: Hindu, Buddhist, or Jain expressions in their formative periods may not have been as distinctly demarcated as they later became in scholastic literature.

In any event, these terms are appropriated by Patañjali as labels to point to supernormal states of consciousness (just as, say, we appropriate existing Latin terms to denote new and previously unknown species of flora that we might discover). Georg Feuerstein likes to think of these terms as "maps," as the symbols of a map denote far greater entities than the simple signs themselves (the circles, squares, triangles, and so on), and inform and alert the traveler in symbolic form as to what to expect on the road ahead, so the technical terms in this *sūtra* represent altered states of consciousness far beyond those of everyday conceptual awareness, and thus beyond the ability of conventional concepts and terminologies to describe.[15] They are guides for the *yogī*, alerting him or her to some of the meditative experiences that will be encountered on the path.[16]

The first and most seminal commentator, Vyāsa (usually dated ca. 3rd–4th century CE), whose commentary was to become to all intents and purposes as canonical as Patañjali's work, is curiously not very effusive in his explanation of this rather complex *sūtra* in his commentary to I.17, but these stages of *samādhi* are discussed in more depth in I.40–45, so we will consider all of these verses as a unit. Vyāsa notes that *vitarka, vicāra, ānanda,* and *asmitā* are four stages of *samprajñāta samādhi,*[17] all of which have an *ālambana,* a support (and the intervening verses between I.17 and I.40 primarily deal with a variety of these *ālambanas*). The *ālambana* is an object of concentrative focus upon which the consciousness of the *puruṣa,* which is still flowing through the *citta* mind, is supported (albeit in progressively more subtle ways), resisting change into any other state. This *ālambana,* whatever it might be, produces an unwavering image on the concentrated mind called a *pratyaya.*[18] So, if, as comes highly recommended in the *Yoga Sūtras,* one concentrates the mind on Īśvara, God, manifest in the sound *om,* then *om* is the *ālambana* and, in these elevated states, produces an undeviating *pratyaya,* or impression, on the mind of this sound, unbroken by any other thought or sense impression.

I.41 is crucial in understanding the differences between these stilled states of *samādhi.* After discussing a variety of *ālambanas,* in I.41, Patañjali resumes the discussion he briefly initiated in I.17:

> **kṣīṇa-vṛtter-abhijātasyeva maṇer-grahītṛ-grahaṇa-grāhyeṣu**
> **tat-stha-tad-añjanatā samāpattiḥ**
>
> *Samāpatti,* complete absorption of the mind when it is free from its *vṛttis,* occurs when the mind becomes just like a transparent jewel, taking the form of whatever object is placed before it, whether the object be the knower, the instrument of knowledge, or the object of knowledge.

We will here correlate the technical term *samāpatti,* introduced in this *sūtra* for the first time, with *samādhi,* even as the terms are not technically synonymous, since the states of mind they represent overlap, and the difference need not detain us here.[19] This verse indicates that, when the mind is freed from all distractions in the form of the *vṛttis,* it becomes like a pure crystal, *maṇi.*[20] Just as a crystal exactly reflects the color of whatever object is placed adjacent to it, such as a red hibiscus flower, so the peaceful mind, when fixed and focused one-pointedly on the object of concentration, is colored by and reflects that object; that is, in advanced meditation, the mind becomes completely absorbed in the presence of that object. Moreover, Patañjali states here that the mind can reflect and assume the form of any object, whether the object be an external object made of gross or subtle elements (*grāhya*), the very instruments of knowledge themselves, such as the sense organs (*grahaṇa*), or the intelligence (*grahītṛ*), the knower, even in its purest and most subtle function, which will be discussed below. As discussed above, the gross elements and subtle qualities evolve out of *citta* (mind stuff—intelligence and ego and so on), in Sāṁkhya, and thus the mind, being more subtle than its evolutes, and, indeed, their very essence, can pervade them (whether these objects are the *grahya,* the *grahaṇa,* or the *grahitṛ*). The mind can not only internally mold its own *guṇic* essence into the *prakṛtic* form of an object or sense organ but can intrusively penetrate, or, better, merge into and percolate the object's very essence.[21] In a sense it becomes the object by merging with it, and thereby gains ultimate insight into its nature. Additionally, when completely pure and steady, the mind can ultimately reflect *puruṣa* back to itself, the penultimate stage of *yoga* practice. This will become clearer as we proceed.

Returning to the states of *samādhi* indicated in I.17, the ninth-century commentator Vācaspati Miśra considers the first state on Patañjali's list, *vitarka samādhi*, to be contemplation on a gross physical object, that is to say, meditating on an object which one experiences as a manifestation or construct of the gross physical or atomic elements. It is the first level of experiencing an object in *samādhi*. In I.42–43, this first stage is further refined by Patañjali and subdivided into two subdivisions: *sa-* (with) *vitarka* and *nir-* (without) *vitarka*. I.42 states,

tatra śabdārtha jñāna vikalpaiḥ saṁkīrṇā savitarkā samāpattiḥ

Savitarka samāpatti, "*samādhi* absorption with physical awareness," is intermixed with the notions of word, meaning, and idea.

Vyāsa takes a cow to exemplify *savitarka*. The actual physical object, the two-syllable word used in speech to refer to that object, and the knowledge, or idea, produced in the mind of a person who hears that word are all different categories of things. They have different characteristics, even though they are conflated in normal cognition: the first is a real-life object made of flesh and blood, the second is a linguistic indicator consisting of a vibrational phoneme, and the third is a mental image or idea predicated on memory recognition and containing meaning—a *pratyaya* or *saṁskāra*.

When the *yogī* uses an object such as a cow as the *ālambana*, but the *yogī's* awareness of this object is conflated with the word for and semantic-laden concept of a cow, this level of *samādhi* absorption is known as *savitarka samāpatti*, "absorption with physical awareness." In other words, the *yogī's* experience of the object is still subtly or perhaps subconsciously tinged with awareness of what the object is called, and with the memory or knowledge corresponding to that object—*śabdārthajñāna-vikalpa*, that is, the experience of the object is mixed up (*saṅkīrṇā*) with a mental construct in the form of language and idea. Consequently, direct experience of the object in its own right and on its own ground of being is tainted by the imposition of recognition or conceptual semantic thought upon it.

Vācaspati Miśra calls this type of *samādhi* lower perception, *apara pratyakṣa* (with an eye to the *para pratyakṣa*, higher perception, that Vyāsa will call the next state of *samādhi* outlined in I.43). This awareness of the object's "word, meaning, and knowledge" is not to be confused with conventional *vṛttis*. The *yogī* is not deliberating or reasoning about the object in any kind of analytical or intellectually sequential fashion at the level of discursive thought, or consciously activating a memory *saṁskāra* to recognize the object, since that would involve the activation and presence of *vṛttis*: we are at the level of *samādhi* here, when all *vṛttis* have been stilled. Nonetheless, the *yogī's* complete absorption on the object still includes an intuitive level of awareness or spontaneous (i.e., nondiscursive) insight as to the object's name and its meaning, and this can only mean that the subconscious memory *saṁskāras* of recognition are still not fully latent or inactive.

Savitarka might be better understood in comparison with *nirvitarka*, the next stage of *samādhi* in I.43, which is when, in contrast, the object stands out in its own right *without* (*nir-*) being conflated with the conventional terminologies of language that might refer to it, and without being conflated with any knowledge, recognition, or meaning it might generate:

smṛti-pariśuddhau svarūpa-śūnyevārtha-mātra-nirbhāsā nirvitarkā
Nirvitarka [*samāpatti*] "absorption without conceptualization" occurs when memory has been purged and the mind is empty, as it were, of its own [reflective] nature. Now only the object [of meditation] shines forth [in its own right].

Nirvitarka means "nonconceptual," or, better, "transconceptual." This occurs when the *yogī*'s *citta* has been purged of any memory awareness of what the object is or what it is called. In other words, no *saṁskāra* imprints pertaining to the *ālambana*, the "cow" in Vyāsa'a example, activate on any subconscious or intuitive level whatsoever. Vācaspati Miśra states that this type of object awareness is real *yogic* perception, because conceptual or artificial notions and names are not superimposed upon the object. The object can "shine forth" in its own autonomous existence. When the mind allows itself to be colored exclusively by the object of focus itself without any cognitive awareness of the object's place in the greater scheme of things and without the normal instinctive impulse to identify it, then the *yogī* has attained the stage of *nirvitarka samāpatti*, or *nirvitarka samādhi*. After all, word and knowledge are different from the ultimate *prakṛtic* metaphysical ingredients that make up a cow in reality. In *nirvitarka samāpatti*, the object itself stands forth in its own right, free of projected designation or mental imaging and clutter.

In this state, the mind has also given up being conscious of itself as an organ of knowledge; in other words, the mind is not even aware of itself as an instrument channeling awareness onto an object. In a sense, all "knowledge" of the object as conventionally understood has been suspended, and the mind has completely transformed itself into the object, free from either any objective cognitive intention or subjective self-awareness. The object can now shine forth in its own right as an object with its own inherent existence, *artha-mātra-nirbhāsa*, free from labels, categorizations, or situatedness in the grand scheme of things. In effect, the object has become the *yogī*'s entire universe; awareness is focused on it exclusively and is thus unaware of anything else, not even the cognitive process itself.

Vyāsa notes that the type of insightful perception into the true nature of an object gained through *savitarka samāpatti* supersedes the other two means of gaining right knowledge of reality recognized by the schools of Yoga: inference (logic) and verbal authority (I.7). Both inference and verbal authority (whether human, *pauruṣeya*, or transhuman, *apauruṣeya*, viz., scripture) are mediate: they depend on sense perception, words, and ideas to impart knowledge. And words and ideas are different from the things they denote; they are secondhand.

Nirvitarka samāpatti is based on firsthand experiential and unmediated direct perception that transcends words and ideas, and penetrates the essential nature of an object itself at a far more profound level than clumsy and artificial words and meanings or ideas. Vyāsa calls it *para pratyakṣa,* "supreme perception," and therefore distinct from *loka [apara] pratyakṣa,* "mundane perception." However, says Vyāsa, *nirvitarka samāpatti* can and does become the "seed" from which logic and scripture may sprout. In other words, says Vācaspati Miśra, *yogīs* who have experienced the lofty levels of *samādhi* discussed in these *sūtras* might use words and logic to share their experiences with ordinary people—as indeed, Patañjali is doing—and their words thus become the basis of scripture, as is the case with the *Yoga Sūtras.* Put differently, scripture can be the product of a *nirvitarka* (higher) level of awareness of reality expressed by God or by the sages through words and concepts.

Once these truths become filtered through and expressed in words, ideas, and logical thought, however, they become subject to the faults and limitations inherent in the adoption of words and ideas (one need only consider, for example, how different commentators sometimes understand cryptic *sūtras* differently—especially in the Vedānta tradition[22]). Therefore, in Yoga, direct perception is the highest form of epistemology; one must practice and experience the truths of Yoga, not merely read about, discuss, or try to understand them theoretically. By definition, then, since *nirvitarka samādhi* is a state beyond the ability of words and concepts to describe, a theoretical analysis on *sūtras* such as I.17 (as we are undertaking here) is a priori oxymoronic. Vijñānabhikṣu adds that since words and ideas are subject to error, and inference and scripture are consequent and derived from them, one must take recourse of a *guru* who has experienced such states. Even then, says Vijñānabhikṣu, despite the fact that the *guru* may have realized the true nature of things, it is not possible to give experiential insight into such things through words, even the words of the *guru,* any more than one can convey through words the actual taste of sugarcane or milk to one who has not experienced them. Therefore, ultimately, one returns to the *yogic* truism that one must experience these states for oneself. Analyses such as this are useful only insofar as they might inspire individuals to take up the actual practice of *yoga.*

In this hierarchization of *nirvitarka* over *savitarka,* Patañjali, and certainly the commentators, are essentially reversing the two stages of conventional perception as understood by a number of Indic philosophical traditions,[23] including (with differences in vocabulary) Sāṁkhya.[24] In conventional non-*yogic* cognition, when one, say, ambles along the road and encounters an unfamiliar object, one first becomes aware of it in a vague sort of way, as raw sense data, without assigning a name or identification to it, like the preconceptual awareness of an infant. After this moment, the mind processes the data, and memory *saṁskāras* identify and recognize the object in terms of its specific name, the category of thing that it is, and its function in the grand scheme of things, for example, "This is a red clay pot for carrying water."[25] The first stage of indeterminate awareness is called *nirvikalpa,* and the second, *savikalpa.* Thus, in

conventional perception, *nirvikalpa pratyakṣa*, preverbal, preconceptual awareness, is followed by *savikalpa pratyakṣa*, the recognition of the name, category,
and function of an object; the latter is considered a more exact form of cognition. In *samādhi* the reverse holds true—*savitarka*, when there is still awareness of an object's name and function, is superseded by *nirvitarka*, where the
object stands out freed from the mental clutter of naming, identification, and
recognition. Thus, in *samādhi*, in contrast to mundane perception, *nirvitarka*
is considered to be a superior level of awareness due to experiencing the object
ontologically, rather than conceptually. Returning to I.17, the next level of
samādhi after *vitarka* is *vicāra*. The overall difference between *vitarka* and
vicāra samādhi (*samāpatti*), Vyāsa informs us, is that the focus of the former
is on the gross physical elements that comprise an object, and the focus of the
latter is on the subtle essences, *sūkṣma-viṣayatvam*, that underpin these gross
elements. As indicated in figure 3.2, in Sāṃkhya metaphysics, gross atomic elements are densifications[26] of the qualities perceived by the senses (made of subtler vibrational energies, as ice, say, is to water), and (with a view to the higher
stages of *samādhi* that are to come), water to vapor. In I.44, Patañjali also divides *vicāra samādhi* into two subdivisions, *sa-* (with) and *nir-* (without), as he
did with *vitarka:*

etayaiva savicārā nirvicārā ca sūkṣma-viṣayā vyākhyātā
The states of *samādhi* with "subtle awareness" and without "subtle awareness,"
whose object of focus is the subtle nature [of things], are explained in the same
manner.

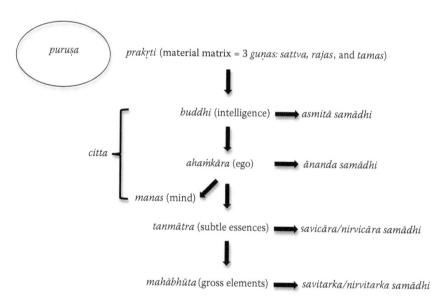

Figure 3.2. *Puruṣa, prakṛti* and the four stages of *samādhi. Image courtesy of Edwin
F. Bryant.*

The subtler essences from which the atomic elements constituting gross physical objects evolve are the *tanmātras,* the five qualities. Vācaspati Miśra states that *vicāra samādhi* involves mental absorption in this more subtle aspect of the object of meditation, the direct experiencing of the object as actually consisting of these more subtle ingredients.

In fact, I.44 informs us that the subtle substructure of physical reality can refer to any of the evolutes from *prakṛti* as conceived of by Sāmkhya, since, as can be seen from the chart, even the *tanmātras* evolve from *ahamkāra,* ego, which in turn evolves from *buddhi,* intelligence. Thus, the latter can also be considered *sūkṣma,* subtle. (Vijñānabhikṣu defines "subtle" as that which is the source or cause of something that evolves from it—that is, since the gross elements are evolutes from the subtle elements, the latter are thereby their causes and thus subtle vis-à-vis the former).

As a new archer first aims at large objects, says Vācaspati Miśra, and then at progressively smaller ones, so the neophyte *yogī* first experiences the gross nature of the object in meditation, and then its progressively more subtle nature. Thus, instead of experiencing the object as comprised of compact quantum masses, the *mahābhūta* gross elements, as in the first state of *vitarka,* the *yogī* experiences them in *vicāra,* as the vibratory, potential, subtle essences underpinning the qualities as perceived by the senses.

As noted, this process of penetrating into the subtle or essential nature of an object might be analogous to seeing a piece of ice as a hard chunk of solid substance, or perceiving its deeper nature as essentially the fluid element of water, or, penetrating deeper still, seeing it as solidified vapor. And one can go further in the analogy and see all of these as combinations of yet finer entities—hydrogen and oxygen molecules—and these can in turn be dissolved into their still finer subatomic physical constituents. As this principle that a gross object is in fact constituted of finer and then still finer elements and essences holds good in modern physics, so it does in Sāmkhyan physics—one difference from normative physics perhaps being that in modern science, the atomic or subatomic structures of matter can be perceived (or inferred as existing) only with advanced mechanical instrumentation, whereas Patañjali and the Yoga tradition claim that the *yogī* can actually and directly perceive, or, more accurately, experience with the mind, the subtle essences of an object without any such instrumental extensions. The subtle essences are directly experiential, since the subtle (and gross) elements are evolutes of a substratum of mind stuff, and the Sāmkhyan principle of perception is that subtler dimensions of *prakṛti* can experience grosser ones. In other words, since one's *buddhi* (intelligence aspect of the *citta*) is composed of the same substance as the *buddhi* substratum of any object, gross or subtle, it can blend with this substratum and thus percolate the object intimately from within, so to speak (a principle fundamental to understanding the metaphysics underpinning the *siddhis,* mystic powers, claimed by the Yoga tradition[27]).

Vicāra, then, is when meditative focus becomes absorbed in the *tanmātras,* the subtle energies underpinning any object of meditation, but it too is divided into *sa-* and *nir-* forms. Thus, when the intensity of focus on the object of meditation has deepened such that the *yogī* has penetrated its gross externalization, transcended language and conceptualization, and is experiencing the object as consisting of *tanmātras*, subtle essences, but subtle essences circumscribed as existing in time and space, then the ensuing concentrative state of awareness is known as *savicāra*. In other words, in *savicāra* meditation, while the object is perceived as consisting of subtle essences, it is still experienced as existing in the present time, rather than in the past or future, and is still bounded by space, that is, it is taking up some distinct physical space in the presence of the meditator rather than being situated anywhere else. Briefly put, at this stage, the *yogī*'s consciousness is spatially and temporally circumscribed—it still has some level of awareness of space and time.

When, however, the *yogī* can focus on the object unconditioned by such dimensionality, in other words when he or she can not just focus on the subtle nature of an object but transcend space and time and perceive that these subtle essences pervade and underpin all things at all times, then the *yogī* has attained the state of *nirvicāra*. In this state, the *yogī* is no longer aware of spatiality and temporality—the here and now. The object is no longer a distinct object taking up extension in a portion of space different from other spatial objects, nor is it any longer experienced as existing in the present, rather than any other time, because the *yogī* experiences the subtle qualities of the object as underpinning all objects at all times. In other words, the form of the object dissolves as it were under the power of the *yogī*'s focus, and the *yogī* is now simply experiencing vibrant subtle energies eternally pervading all reality everywhere and at all times. This is a preliminary experience of a certain level of objectified eternality and infinity.

The nineteenth-century commentator Hariharānanda uses the sun as a rough but useful example for the four types of *samāpatti* (*samādhi*). *Savitarka samādhi* is analogous to focusing without distraction on the sun, cognizing it as an object of a certain shape composed of fire atoms and situated at a certain distance, with some intuitive awareness of its name and function in the natural scheme of things. *Nirvitarka samādhi* can be compared to the deepening of one's focus until one sees the sun only as a luminous object in the heavens, but without awareness of its name, size, distance, function, shape, composition, and so on. *Savicāra* corresponds to perceiving that the fire element of the sun is actually the pure energetic *tanmātra*, subtle element, of light, but one's awareness is still circumscribed by the specific location of the sun in the universe and by the fact that it is perceived in the present, rather than the past or future. When, however, all awareness of space and time dissolves, and one sees pure light, devoid of color, pervading not just the sun but all things at all times, in other words, one is only aware of omnipresent eternal light, then one's meditative state is known as *nirvicāra*.

As a prelude to the still higher stages of *samādhi* that will be discussed next, we note from figure 3.2 that the *tanmātras* are not the only subtle elements underpinning the metaphysics of an object—they themselves are evolutes from still subtler entities such as *ahaṁkāra*, ego, and *buddhi*, intelligence. In order to best understand the third of the four stages of *samādhi*, let us recall that an entity with a "subtle nature," *sūkṣma-viṣayatva*, can be defined as something that can generate a product grosser than itself. We know that the five *mahābhūta* gross elements do not produce any products or evolutes—they are the last link in the chain, so to speak—so they are not considered subtle, while the *tanmātras* are considered subtle essences because they produce grosser by-products. But they are themselves the product of something subtler still, *ahaṁkāra*, ego. As the subtle cause of the *tanmātras*, *ahaṁkāra* is by extension also the indirect subtle cause of the gross elements, but twice removed, so to speak. And *ahaṁkāra* itself, too, has a still subtler cause, *buddhi*, intelligence.[28] *Prakṛti* is the ultimate subtlest cause of everything (because *prakṛti* cannot dissolve into anything subtler). With all this in mind, Patañjali indicates in I.45, "The subtle nature of things extends all the way up to *prakṛti*." In other words, the *samāpatti* or meditative focus of the *yogī* can penetrate the nature of the object and experience it on progressively even more subtle levels than those indicated in *vitarka* and *vicāra* states, namely those of *ahaṁkāra* and *buddhi*. Additionally, as one approaches the more subtle levels of *prakṛti*, the *sattva guṇa* becomes more dominant.

There is no consensus among the commentators as to the exact nature of the last two stages of *samādhi*, *ānanda* and *asmitā*, underscoring the fact that such states are experiential and do not lend themselves to scholastic schematization and analysis. Vācaspati Miśra's version perhaps surfaces most commonly, and is coherently predicated on I.41 quoted above. He correlates the three standard components of knowledge identified in Hindu philosophical discourse referred to in I.41, with the differences between these four stages of *samādhi*. Specifically we can recall that, in any act of knowledge, there is the "knower," or subject of knowledge; the instruments of knowledge (mind and senses, etc.); and the object of knowledge (the *gṛhītṛ*, *grahaṇa*, and *grāhya*; lit. the "grasper," the "instrument of grasping," and "that which is grasped," respectively). In the first two stages of *samādhi* outlined so far, *vitarka* and *vicāra*, the object upon which the mind is fixed, whether perceived as its grosser outer form or as subtler inner constituents, and irrespective of the *sa-* and *nir-* variants of these stages, is an external one and therefore considered *grāhya* (that which is grasped).

Now, in the third stage, *ānanda samādhi*, the *yogī* transfers awareness from the objects of the senses, *grāhya*, to the organs of the senses themselves, *grahaṇa* (the instruments of grasping). Vācaspati Miśra specifies that these are the powers (*śakti*) behind the sensual abilities of seeing, touching, smelling, tasting, and hearing, rather than the gross physical organs of eye, ear, nose, and so on. The *citta* mind now becomes aware of the subtler mechanisms of cognition, the instruments of the senses. In other words, it becomes aware of the knowledge-acquiring aspects of the internal organ through which external objects are "grasped," rather than the external objects themselves, whether experienced in their gross or subtle constitutions.

Since, in Sāṁkhya, the *grahaṇa* includes the internal organ, *manas*, mind; *buddhi*, intelligence; and *ahaṁkāra*, ego, all of which comprise the *citta* in Yoga, the eleventh-century commentator Bhoja Rāja differs somewhat from Vācaspati Miśra by understanding the support of the mind in *ānanda samādhī* to be the *citta* itself (specifically in its aspect as *ahaṁkāra*), rather than with the powers of the senses. (Vācaspati Miśra, in contrast, correlates *ahaṁkāra* with the fourth stage of *samādhi*.) Thus, in Bhoja's perspective, in this third stage, awareness becomes aware of the *citta* itself, which is the higher faculty of acquiring knowledge, as the "instrument" which "grasps" the objects of the senses. In other words, the mind focuses on its own cognizing nature. Since from the three *guṇas* of *prakṛti*, the *guṇa* of *sattva* predominates in *ahaṁkāra* and *buddhi*, and *sattva* is the source of bliss, Patañjali calls this stage *ānanda samādhi*, the "blissful absorption."[29] This is because this state involves experiencing a rarified, pure, and sustainable (and thus supernormal) form of *sāttvic* bliss. Vijñānabhikṣu quotes Kṛṣṇa's description of this state in the *Gītā* here: "When the *yogī* experiences that endless happiness [*sukham*] which is grasped by the discriminative faculty [*buddhi*], but beyond the grasp of the senses, he remains fixed in this state and never strays from the truth . . . this state, free from any trace of suffering, is called *yoga*." VI.21–23). Thus, despite the difference between Vācaspati Miśra and Bhoja Rāja, the prevalent view seems to be that in the third state of *samādhi*, the mind becomes absorbed on some aspect of the instruments of cognition themselves, rather than supported by or concentrated on the gross or subtle constituents of the *ālambana* support as an external object of the senses. All commentators at least agree that at this stage of *ānanda samādhi*, the mind becomes immersed in the *sattva* prevalent at this state of awareness, one of the qualities of which is bliss. Additionally, space, dimensionality, time, and so on having already been surpassed in the previous stage of *nirvicāra*, the *yogī's* focused mind becomes absorbed in the *sattva* essence of not just the mind but the *sāttvic* and blissful quality underpinning all reality, hence the *yogī* experiences all-pervading bliss. But it is important to note that this is not the bliss of *brahman* (=*ātman/puruṣa*)[30] indicated in Upaniṣads such as the *Taittirīya Upaniṣad*; the bliss indicated here is *prakṛtic*, material; it is not the experience inherent in the *puruṣa*, the ultimate goal. The *citta* of the *yogī* is immersed in the *sāttvic* aspect of *prakṛti*, which produces a very refined but nonetheless still *prakṛtic* type of blissfulness in the external covering of mind, not in pure consciousness itself.

Therefore, and as an aside, *Gītā* XIV.6 warns of becoming attached to this *sāttvic* happiness: there is a danger at this stage that the *yogī* may mistake this sense of bliss and unprecedented insight with the ultimate goal of *yoga*, that is, may confound this rapturous state of supernormal attainment with the ultimate experience of *puruṣa* (or for Vedāntins, of *ātmānanada*, the bliss of the self). Indeed, the commentators all take Patañjali's reference in I.19 to the two categories of *yogīs* who attain states of *samprajñāta samādhi*—the *videhas*, those who are "unembodied," and the *prakṛtilayās*, those who are "merged in matter"—as warnings in this regard. The common denominator of these two categories is that such *yogīs* still maintain notions of self-identity that are connected with material (*prakṛtic*) existence.[31] Just as normal people misidentify the self with the gross physical body, there are higher beings and *yogīs* who, through some type of *yogic* practice, have managed to transcend the grosser levels of self-misidentification but who nonetheless remain subject to more subtle levels of misidentification. Absorbed in various subtle dimensions of *prakṛti*, the *yogīs* in this category remain stranded as it were at various heights of supernormal awareness accrued from the *yoga* path; thus Bhoja Rāja considers the states indicated in I.19 to point to "semblances of *yoga*."

Finally, by involuting awareness further still and penetrating the internal organ of meditation to its still more essential nature, one transcends even the instruments of knowledge and arrives at *ahaṁkāra*, ego (if one follows Vācaspati Miśra), or *buddhi*, intelligence (if one follows Bhoja Rāja)—either way, at the closest *prakṛtic* coverings to the *puruṣa* itself, from which all the other evolutes have evolved. Having nothing further external or outside of itself upon which to meditate, at least in the realm of *prakṛti*, since it itself is the source of all *prakṛtic* evolutes, only *puruṣa* now remains as an object of contemplation for the *yogī*'s *buddhi*. Relentless in the pursuit of true and ultimate knowledge, at this point, the *yogī* attains the fourth and final stage of *samprajñāta samādhi* listed by Patañjali in I.17: *asmitā samādhi*. Now, following Bhoja Rāja's schema, having penetrated the constituents of the external object of meditation through its gross and subtle elements consecutively in the first two stages of *samādhi*, and having withdrawn itself from external cognition and into a state of contemplating the essences behind the very organs of cognition in the third stage, awareness penetrates the *citta* further still, absorbing itself in the *citta*'s feature of *buddhi*, the *grahitṛ*, "the grasper," the *prakṛtic* covering adjacent to the *puruṣa* itself.[32] *Buddhi*, in this highly *sāttvic* state, is so pure and luminous it can reflect the consciousness of *puruṣa* back to itself like a mirror. At this point, since it has already transcended all objects outside of itself, including the internal organs of cognition themselves, *buddhi* focuses inward, reflecting *puruṣa* itself as its object of meditation.

Another way of putting this is that the *yogī* now finally becomes aware of *puruṣa* itself as pure consciousness by means of its reflection in *buddhi*. In other words, the *citta* of the *yogī* becomes indirectly aware of *puruṣa* (since this awareness is still mediated by *buddhi*). Obviously, the mind cannot know *puruṣa* in its own true nature, as the commentator Śaṅkara points out, since the mind is inanimate and *puruṣa* is more subtle than the mind. Things can only "grasp" or perceive things grosser than themselves: the senses can perceive the sense objects, but not vice versa; the mind can perceive the senses, but not vice versa; and the *puruṣa* can perceive the mind, but not vice versa (this is a favorite trope of the Upaniṣads[33]). Only *puruṣa* can know "itself in itself, through itself" as the *Gītā* puts it (VI.20, 22).

But mind can, however, redirect awareness back to its own original source and thus indirectly reflect *puruṣa*, just as a mirror can reflect a face. In other words, *puruṣa* can attain a mediated awareness of itself by means of the reflective nature of the pure *sāttvic* mind; the *yogī* becomes aware of "I-am-ness" (the etymological meaning of this fourth state of *asmitā*), rather than any external material *prakṛtic* object or internal organ of cognition.[34] This occurs when the *citta* contemplates the awareness of *puruṣa* by means of its reflection in the pure mirror of the *sāttvic citta*. Consequently, the *citta* gains a genuine knowledge of the real source and identity of the consciousness pervading it, and consciousness becomes indirectly aware of its true self. Whereas in the previous level the mind was aware that "I am blissful," in this fourth level it is now simply experiencing a state of "I am." This is pure I-am-ness with no external object or specific content of self-identification, so it is very close to the goal of direct realization of *puruṣa*. This fourth stage is still within the realm of *prakṛti*, however, hence still at a stage of *samprajñāta samādhi*. In other words, it is "supported" by some connection with *prakṛti*, because the *citta* is still used as an instrument to channel awareness (even though the object of awareness is now *puruṣa* itself rather than any external manifestation of *prakṛti*). The *puruṣa* at this point is still not fully autonomous or extricated from its appropriation by the mind.

Howsoever one takes the various higher levels of *samprajñāta samādhi*, one final step now remains in which this ultimate uncoupling of *puruṣa* from all connection with *prakṛti* and all involvement with the *citta* occurs. This is *asamprajñāta samādhi*, *samādhi* without support (an "*a*" prefixed to any noun in Sanskrit negates that noun[35]), which will be outlined in the next *sūtra*. According to Patañjali in the next verse, I.46, "These above mentioned *samāpatti* states are [known as] *sabīja samādhi*, meditative absorption 'with seed.'" The stages of *samādhi* referred to here as *sabīja samādhi* are referred to as *samprajñāta samādhi* in I.17; thus they, along with their counterparts of *nirbīja samādhi* and *asamprajñāta samādhis*, are essentially used synonymously by our commentators. Vyāsa explains that the four states outlined in the previous *sūtras* are known as *samādhi* "with seed," *sabīja*, because they have something external as their object of focus, whether it be the gross form of an object, as in the case of the *savitarka* and *nirvitarka* states, or the subtle form of an object, as in the case of *savicāra* and *nirvicāra*. *Bīja* here technically refers to a seed in the sense of *saṃskāra*. Any object perceived in the concentrated mind leaves a *saṃskāra* seed imprint, just as any other object does in conventional cognition, even if the mind is fixed on it exclusively in the intense stages of *samprajñāta*, hence the latter's synonym, *sabīja*. Since the object of concentration as well as the concentrating mind itself become redundant in *nirbīja*, which will be discussed below, no seeds of *saṃskāras* are deposited (hence its name in I.51, *nir*=without; *bīja*=seed).

To sum up, then, in *samprajñāta*, or *sabīja samādhi*, there are four levels, listed in I.17, two of which, *vitarka* and *vicāra*, are further subdivided into four *samāpattis* in II.42–44. One can thus speak of six levels of *samprajñāta samādhi*, followed by a final stage of *asamprajñāta samādhi*. This makes seven types of *samādhis* in toto.[36] While there are minor differences between the commentators on their understanding of the metaphysical nature of the two final types of *samprajñāta samādhi*—*ānanda* and *asmitā*—all commentators agree that in principle these stages involve refining one's awareness during consecutive stages of meditation through progressively more subtle states of cognition in quest of the source of awareness itself, *puruṣa*.

What then lies beyond these? In I.18, Patañjali uses the term *anya*, "the other" to refer to another state of awareness beyond all these states, which the commentators take to be *asamprajñāta* (a term that actually never occurs in the *sūtras* themselves): "The other [*asamprajñāta samādhi*] is preceded by cultivating the determination to terminate [all thoughts]. [In this state] only latent impressions remain." As we have seen, the four states of *samprajñāta* all involved the *citta* in various ways. *Asamprajñāta* is beyond the mind. It is therefore beyond all intentional cognition, and thus descriptive categorization. To underscore this, perhaps, Patañjali has used the simple pronoun *anya*, "the other," rather than a descriptive term, thereby pointing to *asamprajñāta* as a state that transcends all conceptual construction and nomenclature (which are all products of *citta*). Here he resonates with the *Māṇḍūkya Upaniṣad*'s usage of the term *turīya*, "the fourth," to refer to this state of pure consciousness (7 and 12).[37]

The commentators present *asamprajñāta samādhi*, or *nirbīja samādhi* (without support), as being the state where the awareness of *puruṣa* is no longer aware of any external entity at all, including the *citta*, since the latter has dissolved itself. In this final and ultimate state, the supreme goal of *yoga*, the mind is not supported by any *ālambana*. The *vṛttis* of the mind exist simply as potential, which means the *saṃskāras*, the subconscious imprints that trigger thoughts, memories, and *karma*, are also latent. Since the mind is now empty of all thoughts, or, as Vyāsa puts it, appears as if nonexistent, the awareness of *puruṣa* now no longer has any object whatsoever external to itself of which to be aware, and thus, for the first time, can become only self-aware (loosely speaking[38]). The final goal of *yoga* has been attained. This is the *yogī*'s final birth.

Another way of considering this is that awareness is eternal; it can not ever cease being aware. The Upaniṣads and the first spiritual teaching of the *Gītā* in chapter II articulates this repeatedly—the soul is indestructible, it can not be slain; it does not die when the body is slain, nor is it ever born; it is birthless, eternal, perpetual, original; it cannot be burnt, pierced by weapons, wetted, or blown by the wind; it is unmanifest, beyond thought, unchanging, and so on (II.17ff). Awareness cannot be switched off like a light. That being the case, the soul's only options are of what it is aware: it can be object aware, or (again, loosely speaking) "subject" aware—that is, aware of entities or objects other than itself, or exclusively aware of itself as awareness with no reference to any other entity. After myriad births being aware of the unlimited varieties of *prakṛtic* objects, *puruṣa* has now come to the point of self-realization—realizing itself as distinct from not only objects of thought but the very faculty and process of thought itself, the *citta* and its *vṛttis*. When there are no objects to detain its awareness, *puruṣa* has no alternative but to be self-aware. While the major (Vaiṣṇava) theist schools continue this progressive trans-*prakṛtic* journey further in quest of an awareness of a yet still higher Truth, the Supreme Puruṣa, Īśvara, God,[39] for the generic Yoga traditions, this stage of self-awareness of the individual *ātman* absorbed in its own nature, *asaṁprajñāta samādhi*, is the final goal of the yogic journey.

Notes

1. Dasgupta, *History of Indian Philosophy*; Whicher, *Integrity of the Yoga Darśana*; Larson, *Classical Sāṁkhya*; Bryant, *Yoga Sūtras of Patañjali*.

2. *Maitrī Upaniṣad* 2nd century BCE, (VI.18); *Viṣṇu Purāṇa*, 4th–6th century (VI.7.91).

3. *Mahābhārata*, XII.304.7.

4. Brockington, "Epic Yoga"; Sarbacker, *Samadhi*.

5. Brockington, "Epic Yoga."

6. Jacobi, "Dates of the Philosophical Sūtras"; Dasgupta, *History of Indian Philosophy*; Larson and Battacharya, *Yoga*.

7. Nicholson, *Unifying Hinduism*.

8. Larson and Battacharya, *Yoga*.

9. For histories of Sāṁkhya, see Colebrooke and Wilson, *Sāṅkhya-Kārikā*; Dasgupta, *History of Indian Philosophy*; Johnston, *Early Sāṁkhya*; Chakravarti, *Origin and Development*; Larson, *Classical Sāṁkhya*; Larson, "Classical Yoga as Neo-Sāṁkhya"; Larson and Bhattacharya, *Samkhya*; Jacobsen, *Prakṛti in Sāṁkhya Yoga*; Gopal, *Retrieving Sāṁkhya History*; and Dutta, *Sāṁkhya*.

10. In Christian mysticism, the dualism between the Creator and the created divides the world in a way similar to Sāṁkhya and Yoga; cf. Eifring, "Spontaneous Thoughts in Meditative Traditions."

11. These are right knowledge, error, imagination, deep sleep, and memory (I.5–11).

12. *Vitarka* in II.33, and *asmitā* in II.6, denote very different things from what they are held to denote in I.17 quoted above: in the former, an unwanted *saṁskāra*, memory imprint, surfacing in the mind, and in the latter, an extension of ignorance involving misidentification with the body and mind.

13. The relationship between the four stages of *samādhi* outlined in this verse and the four *jhānas* (Skt. *dhyānas*) outlined in Buddhist meditation has long been noted. (The term *dhyāna* occurs as the seventh of the eight limbs of Patañjali's system, III.2, but is used in Buddhism and also in older Hindu texts such as the *Gītā* and *Mahābhārata* as a synonym for *samādhi*, Patañjali's final stage). The Buddha speaks of attaining the first *dhyāna*, which consists of *vitarka*, *vicāra*, and *viveka*, and then proceeding to attain the other three stages of *dhyāna* (*Majjhima Nikāya* I.246–247). While a full discussion of these Buddhist stages is beyond the scope of this chapter, there are several different lists of the four *dhyāna* (*samādhi*) states in the Buddhist *abhidhamma* schools, and the most important of these include *vitarka* and *vicāra*, the first two items mentioned in this *sūtra* by Patañjali, under the first *dhyāna*. Moreover, *ānanda*, the third item mentioned by Patañjali (or its correlate, *sukha*), is experienced in the first three of the four stages of *dhyāna*. Only the final item from this *sūtra*, *asmitā*, "I-am-ness," does not have a clear parallel in Buddhism—hardly surprising given the Buddhist rejection of an autonomous *puruṣa*. It also is worth mentioning in this regard Bhīṣma's mention of the four *dhyānas* in the Hindu *Mahābhārata* epic (Bhīṣma too is clearly using the term *dhyāna* as a synonym of *samādhi*). Bhīṣma includes in his first stage of *dhyāna* three features (*vitarka*, *vicāra*, and *viveka*), thereby paralleling the Buddhist system (XII.188.1–22), but, unlike Buddhism, within an *ātma*, or self, framework.

14. The Yoga tradition's understanding tends to situate the psychological basis of the *samādhi* states within the cosmological framework of Sāṁkhyan evolution, where the Buddhists do not do so.

15. Feuerstein, *Yoga-Sūtra of Patañjali.*

16. For analyses of these states, see Koelman, *Patañjala Yoga*; Feuerstein, *Philosophy of Classical Yoga*; Feuerstein, *Yoga Tradition*; Whicher, *Integrity of the Yoga Darśana*; Chapple, *Reconciling Yogas*; Larson and Bhattacharya, *Yoga*; and Bryant, *Yoga Sūtras of Patañjali.*

17. Also known as *sabīja samādhi. Sabīja*, "with seed," points to the fact that the mind is still being used to channel awareness onto an object of concentration, albeit exclusively. Any object upon which the mind focuses, leaves a *saṁskāra*, seed imprint of itself.

18. I understand a *pratyaya* as the momentary content of a *vṛtti*, and a *vṛtti* as a particular sequence of *pratyayas*; a *saṁskāra* is the impression left on the mind of every sense object it encounters or thought it entertains, and partly corresponds to memory.

19. Vijñānabhikṣu points out that the various types of *samāpatti* occur as results of *samprajñāta samādhi. Samādhi* in general might best be understood in terms of the goal of *yoga* as defined in the very beginning of the *Yoga Sūtras* in I.2, namely, the state when all *vṛttis* of the mind have been stilled; *samāpatti* is, a bit more specifically, the complete identification of the mind with the object of meditation. Put simply, the former is the more general or overall state of the stilled mind, the latter the more specific content or object upon which the mind has settled itself in order to become still. Complete mental identification with and absorption in an object, *ālambana*, by definition, can obviously only occur when all other *vṛttis* have been stilled, and the mind is without distraction; hence *samāpatti* occurs only in the context of *samādhi.*

20. This simile is encountered numerous times throughout the commentaries, albeit used variously, and has attained wide usage in Hindu philosophical circles.

21. This trait is pivotal in understanding the metaphysics of the *siddhis*, the mystic powers of chapter III, which feature such an act of *samāpatti.* However, in the context of the mystic powers, the act of *samāpatti* is referred to as *saṁyama*, which points to a more active intentional and manipulative potential of mental absorption, rather than a nonintentional, passive one.

22. See, for example, the completely different interpretation given to *Vedānta Sūtra* I.1.5–9 by Madhva compared to that given by Śaṅkara and Rāmānuja.

23. For example, our Yoga commentator Vācaspati Miśra in his *Nyāyavārttika tātparyaṭīkā.*

24. See Vācaspati Miśra's commentary on *Sāṁkhya Kārikā* XXVII. The language used in the *Kārikās* and the *Yuktidīpikā* for the two types of perception differs from the more standard usage in Nyāya and elsewhere.

25. Technically this process of recognition involves identifying the object's *samānya*, universal, and *viśeṣa*, particularity, metaphysical categories of reality that need not detain us here.

26. This means the *tamas* component (the dense quality that produces stillness and inertia) of the three *guṇas*, which are the metaphysical qualities that comprise *prakṛti*, is increased vis-à-vis the other *guṇas* (*rajas*, the energetic quality, and *sattva*, the translucent quality of lightness and wisdom).

27. Almost an entire chapter of the *Yoga Sūtras* is dedicated to the mystic powers that pervade yogic narratives of Hinduism, Buddhism, and Jainism from its earliest beginnings until modern times (see Bryant, *Yoga Sūtras of Patañjali*, 301ff. for discussion).

28. The term *liṅga* (that which is a sign) is used here for *buddhi*, which is in turn an evolute of *prakṛti*, referred to in I.45 as *aliṅga* (that which has no sign). *Liṅga*, a common term in Nyāya, the School of Logic, literally means "a sign," and indicates that *buddhi*'s existence is inferred by its "signs," that is to say its characteristics. In Hindu logic, an inference is made on the basis of a sign or characteristic, for example, the presence of an unperceived fire is inferred based on the perception of smoke, which is the "sign," *liṅga*, of fire). Primordial, precreation *prakṛti* is *aliṅga*, since, being a state in which the *guṇas* are completely latent, it has no "signs"

or characteristics (any characteristics in the form of its evolutes come later, once the *guṇas* have been activated).

29. Vijñānabhikṣu is uncharacteristically vague about this third stage of *ānanda samādhi*, although he explicitly disagrees with Vācaspati Miśra that it is supported by the sense organs. He states that in *ānanda samādhi*, the mind experiences bliss due to an increase of *sattva*, but he does not specify the location of this bliss. He merely notes that at this point the object of meditation is no longer perceived as consisting of even the subtle elements, as was the case in the previous stage, but is experienced as pure *sāttvic* bliss (about which all of the commentators agree, understandably, given the name Patañjali assigns this third type of *samādhi*).

30. II.8ff. For our purposes in this chapter, we can correlate Patañjali's *puruṣa* not only with the *ātman* of the Upaniṣads but also with the references to *brahman* in these texts without engaging the millennia-old discussion of the Vedānta tradition as to whether and how there are differences between *ātman/puruṣa* and *brahman*.

31. The commentators take the *prakṛtilāyas*, those "merged in *prakṛti*, matter" to refer to entities who consider themselves to be either unmanifest, primordial *prakṛti*, or *buddhi*, the first evolute from *prakṛti*, or the second evolute, *ahaṁkāra*, or even the *tanmātras*, five subtle elements. In other words, more or less anyone who does not identify the self as being the gross material body made of the five gross elements, but still identifies the self as being some other, more subtle aspect of *prakṛti*, could be considered *prakṛtilāya* "merged in matter." In this the commentators follow the *Sāṁkhya Kārikā* XLVI, in which the state of *prakṛtilāyaḥ* in question is held to come from *vairāgya*, "nonattachment" (I.15). In his commentary to this verse in the *Sāṁkhyā Kārikā*, the commentator Gauḍapāda states, "One might have *vairāgya* but without knowing the twenty-four evolutes of *prakṛti*. This state, which is founded on ignorance, is ... *prakṛtilāyanaḥ*. At death, such a person is not liberated, but is merged into the eight evolutes of *prakṛti*—*pradhāna*, intelligence, ego, and the five subtle elements. From there, he returns again to *saṁsāra*." However, "one merged in this state thinks 'I am liberated.' This is a type of ignorance."

32. We can note that in the last two stages of *samādhi*, by the antireflexivity principle, one can not technically speaking *know* the *grahaṇa* or *grahitṛ*, because "acts of knowing" can take place only via these "instruments of knowledge" and by the "knowers" themselves. Rather, awareness becomes "aware" of them. This consideration can help us better appreciate this relentless progression toward the source of awareness: from gross objects of knowledge to their subtle substrates to the instruments of knowledge themselves and, beyond again, to the ultimate *prakṛtic* "knower," until finally one arrives at *puruṣa* itself, the very source of awareness.

33. "That which one cannot grasp with one's mind [i.e., *ātman/brahman*], by which, they say, the mind is grasped" (*Kena* I.5); "By what means can one know the knower?" (*Bṛhadāraṇyaka* II.4.13); "You can't see the seer who does the seeing; you can't hear the hearer who does the hearing; you can't think the thinker who does the thinking; you can't perceive the perceiver who does the perceiving" (*Bṛhadāraṇyaka* III.4.2); "Sight does not go there, nor does thinking or speech. We don't know it, we can't perceive it, so how one would express it?" (*Kena* I.3); "Not by speech, not by the mind, not by sight can he be grasped. How else can that be experienced, other than by saying 'He is'" (*Kaṭha* VI.12); "The self cannot be grasped by multiple teachings or by the intellect" (*Muṇḍaka* III.2.3).

34. However, as Śaṅkara notes, this "I-am-ness," *asmitā*, is not the same as the *asmitā* listed as an obstacle to *yoga* in II.3. *Asmitā* in the context of the *kleśas* (obstacles, afflictions) in II.2 and II.7 involves a misidentification of *puruṣa* with what it is not, and thus corresponds to *ahaṁkāra*. *Asmitā* as *kleśa* involves an *object* of "I am,"—that is, "I am this body and mind," and so on. The *asmitā* in the context of *samādhi* is when the mind experi-

ences an "I-am-ness" in the sense of the true *subject* of awareness, viz., "the source of my awareness is *puruṣa*."

35. The same phenomenon is also preserved in the English theist/atheist, sexual/asexual, and so on.

36. Or nine types, if one subscribes to Vācaspati Miśra's *sānandā/nirānandā, sāsmitā/ nirasmitā* schema, which need not detain us here (but see Koelman, *Patañjala Yoga*, for an approving analysis of these).

37. The other three states of consciousness are waking, dreaming, and deep sleep.

38. I use the term "self-aware" loosely and heuristically, since "self" implies "other," and the ultimate stage of *asamprajñāta samādhi, kaivalya* (lit. "aloneness"; IV.34), by definition, involves the absence of any "other."

39. God, Īśvara, is introduced by Patañjali only in relation to his stated purpose in the *sūtras*, in terms of his relevance to attaining *citta vṛtti nirodhaḥ*; he provides little information as to the relationship of this entity to the liberated *puruṣa*. For a sense of the Vaiṣṇava theistic position that direct self-perception of the *puruṣa* is a secondary and even undesirable goal compared to the perception and relationship with the supreme and distinct *puruṣa*, Īśvara, see Bryant, *Krishna*, xxxv.

Bibliography

Brockington, John. "Epic Yoga." *Journal of Vaishnava Studies* 14, no. 1 (2005): 123–138.

Bryant, Edwin. *Krishna: The Beautiful Legend of God.* London: Penguin, 2003.

———. *The Yoga Sūtras of Patañjali: A New Edition, Translation, and Commentary.* New York: North Point Press, 2009.

Chakravarti, Pulinbihari. *Origin and Development of the Sāṁkhya System of Thought.* Calcutta: Metropolitan, 1951.

Chapple, Christopher. *Reconciling Yogas.* Albany: State University of New York, 2003.

Colebrooke, H. T., and H. H. Wilson. *Sāṅkhya-Kārikā: Translated from the Sanscrit by H. T. Colebrooke, also The Bhashya, or Commentary of Gaudapada; Translated and Illustrated by an Original Comment, by H. H. Wilson.* Bombay: Tookaram Tatya, 1887.

Dasgupta, S. *A History of Indian Philosophy.* Delhi: Motilal Banarsidass, 1922.

Dutta, Deepti. *Sāṁkhya: A Prologue to Yoga.* New Delhi: Khama, 2001.

Eifring, Halvor. "Spontaneous Thoughts in Meditative Traditions." In *Meditation and Culture: The Interplay of Practice and Context,* edited by Halvor Eifring, 200–215.

Feuerstein, Georg. *The Philosophy of Classical Yoga.* Rochester, VT: Inner Traditions, 1996.

———. *The Yoga-Sutra of Patañjali: A New Translation and Commentary.* Rochester, VT: Inner Traditions, 1989.

———. *The Yoga Tradition: Its History, Literature, Philosophy, and Practice.* Prescott, AZ: Hohm Press, 2001.

Gopal, Lallanji. *Retrieving Sāṁkhya History.* New Delhi: D. K. Printworld, 2000.

Jacobi, H. "The Dates of the Philosophical Sūtras of the Brahmans." *Journal of the American Oriental Society* 31 (1911): 1–29.

Jacobsen, Knut. *Prakṛti in Sāṁkhya Yoga.* New York: Peter Lang, 1999.

Johnston, E. H. *Early Sāṁkhya.* London: Royal Asiatic Society, 1937.

Koelman, Gasper. *Patañjala Yoga: From Related Ego to Absolute Self.* Poona: Papal Athenaeum, 1970.

Larson, Gerald James. *Classical Sāṁkhya.* Delhi: Motilal Banarsidass, 1979.

———. "Classical Yoga as Neo-Sāṁkhya: A Chapter in the History of Indian Philosophy." *Asiatische Studien / Études Asiatiques* 52, no. 3 (1999): 723–732.

Larson, Gerald James, and Ram Shankar Bhattacharya. *Samkhya: A Dualist Tradition in Indian Philosophy.* Encyclopedia of Indian Philosophies. Vol. 4. Princeton, NJ: Princeton University Press, 1987.

———. *Yoga: India's Philosophy of Meditation.* Encyclopedia of Indian Philosophies. Vol. 12. Delhi: Motilal Banarsidass, 2008.

Nicholson, Andrew. *Unifying Hinduism.* New Delhi: Permanent Black, 2011.

Sarbacker, Stuart Ray. *Samadhi.* Albany, NY: SUNY Press, 2005.

Whicher, Ian. *The Integrity of the Yoga Darśana.* New York: SUNY Press, 1998.

Yantra *and* Cakra *in Tantric Meditation*

Śāktism is best defined as a "doctrine of power or energy" personified in female form, centered on the worship of the goddess as a supreme, ultimate principal, who is considered as a source of creation that animates and governs existence. Śāktism is traceable to the oldest layers of India's cultural history. With the rise of Tantric Śākta traditions around the sixth century AD came an affirmation of the concept of Śākti as pure consciousness, her transcendence and all pervasive immanence as supreme godhead. Tantric Śāktism introduced a special method of worshipping the goddess by means of *yantra, mantra, mudrā,* and a host of internal meditations involving the arousal of the latent cosmic energy in the subtle body.

This chapter attempts to give a broad view of some of the meditational practices of the Śrīvidyā school of Hindu Śākta Tantra. The presiding deity of the Śrīvidyā school is the goddess Tripurasundarī, who is worshipped in an all-inclusive linear abstract (aniconic) symbol, the Śrīyantra (also referred to as the Śrīcakra). The Śrīyantra is a primary defining characteristic of the Śrīvidyā school and is conceived as being identical with the goddess and her creation. At the same time, the Śrīyantra is a dominant medium of worship. Given the multifaceted nature of Śākta rituals, I will briefly summarize the diversity inherent in meditation practices, emphasizing shifts of meaning and interpretation. These include simple meditational visualizations of the deity that border on external ritual acts, complex *yantra* meditations discussed in the exegetical writings of the erudite sage-scholar Bhāskararāya Makhin (ca. 1690–1785 AD).

Bhāskararāya Makhin, a polymath of rare brilliance and traditional Sanskrit scholarship, is considered an authority on the Śrīvidyā school of Tantric Śāktism. His commentaries give a brilliant analysis of philosophical and yogic aspects of the Śrīvidyā tradition. His distinction lies in his ability to decode coded passages in a lucid style. In his commentaries, he draws on a large number of authoritative sources from the Vedas down to the Kashmirian Agamas and weaves them together with extraordinary skill so as to reconcile their differences. His exegetical writings attempt to synthesize the orthodox Vedic and Kashmirian Agama tradition, thereby creating an inclusive interpretation of the goddess. While Bhāskararāya provides a specialist's insight of inner meditation supported by a sophisticated theological tradition, there are even more elusive homologies between the external *yantra* and the *cakras* of the subtle body that connect and gather together all the elements and planes of the universe in a single meditative experience. It is essential to comment on the diversity of such meditative technologies of the spirit, as these traditions are entirely lineage-based, and are, therefore, open to any number of variations. Moreover, they arise from a religious culture that is not anchored in inflexible dogma.

To understand the nature and significance of Tantric meditative technologies of a more technical variety, it would be wise to gain an insight of the cognitive structures of the world view and theological principles of the Śākta Tantras, and the nature of the symbolic tools for meditation they use.

The Nature of the Object of Meditation

The presiding deity of the meditation is the supreme goddess Tripurasundarī. The cult of the goddess Tripurasundarī occupies a very significant place in Kashmir and in South Indian Tantrism. Widely known also as Lalitā, Kameśvarī, Ṣoḍaśī, Rājarājesvarī, and Śrīvidyā (after her esoteric fifteen-syllabled *mantra*), Tripurasundarī is one of the most sublime personifications of the divine feminine. The philosophical tradition of Tripurasundarī is traced to the Trika school of the Kashmirian Āgamas. The sophisticated ontology of the *Śaivādvaitavāda* of Kashmir is absorbed in the feminine theology of the Tripurā cult. According to the theology of Śākta Tantra, during worship of Tripurasundarī, the deity may manifest in three forms, along with her retinue. Her concrete anthropomorphic icon (*sthūlarūpa*) is described in her contemplative verse (*dhyāna śloka*), which gives a vivid description of her physical characteristics. More subtle than her concrete physical form is her subtle (*sukṣma*) sonic body consisting of her fifteen-syllabled *mantra*. Even subtler than her sound body is her supreme (*parā*) manifestation known through cognition of her illuminating nature,[1] as mirrored in her aniconic symbol, the Śrīcakra/Śrīyantra.

Yantras and *maṇḍalas* are widely used for Tāntric worship and contemplation. They are a prerequisite of worship and meditation. All Hindu Tantric deities have been assigned their specific *yantras*. As stated in the *Kulārṇava Tantra*, "As body to the soul, oil to the lamp, a yantra is to the deity."[2] The *yantras* and the *mantras* are means of steadying the mind. The *yantras* for meditation and ritual worship form a very distinctive group of sacred symbols. The Hindu Tāntric *yantra* is a simple linear diagram of concentric configurations conceived so as to act as a vehicle of concentration. The most important part of the *yantra* is the center (*bindu*), the point of origin of the linear forces that are gathered around it. An important feature of the Śrīcakra symbolism is the manner in which it is to be understood by the devotee, as a fully manifested emblem of creation and dissolution. In technical terminology the dienergic process is called the order of emanation (*sṛṣṭikrama*) and the order of involution (*saṃhārakrama*).[3]

The theology of Śrīvidyā holds that the universe is composed of two opposing but complementary principles.[4] At the apex of creation, these principles are named Parama-Śiva and Vimarśa-Śakti. Śiva is the male principle understood as pure transcendent consciousness, while Śakti, the supreme goddess, is the female principle, Śiva's dynamic creative power. In their descent for manifestation, Śakti unfolds in three phases. In the first phase, the two principles are harnessed in a unitive embrace. This phase is symbolized by the *bindu* in the Śrīyantra. In the phenomenal context, the first evolute is Śiva as the principle of subjective consciousness (*aham*), and Śakti as the principle of objective awareness (*idam*). At this stage the Śakti principle assumes her three intrinsic powers: the energy of will (*icchā śakti*), energy of knowledge (*jñāna śakti*) and the energy of action (*kriyā śakti*). This is a state of pure consciousness, of nondifferentiation and unity represented by the inverted triangle in the center of the *yantra*. In the next phase, owing to the veiling power of *māyā* (illusion), there is separation of the subject and object through negation of their unlimited powers, which get contracted, as it is were, and give rise to the finite world, composed of twenty-six categories of material existence.

The Śrīyantra in figures 4.1 and 4.2 displays the splendor and manifestation of the whole creation expressed in its visual metaphysics. It is read as a chart of cosmic evolution, stage after stage, from the incipient unity of male and female principles to the differentiated categories of creation. The reality of the first unitive phase of creation, which is the seat of the presiding deity, is reflected in the *bindu*, which rests in the center of the Śrīyantra. The subsequent circuits composed through the interlacing of the nine triangles symbolize the manifold world of pure and impure categories. The *yantra* is composed of two sets of triangles: the four upward-pointing triangles are identified with the Śiva principle, whereas the five downward-pointing inverted triangles represent the Śakti principle. The two sets of interlacing triangles create forty-three smaller ones, to show the imperishable unity of Śiva and Śakti. The diagram so formed is enclosed by two rings of lotus petals and a square. United, the shapes comprise all of the thirty-six categories of creation (see figure 4.1). The *yantra* is presided over by the retinue of the goddess Tripurasundarī who are positioned in a graded order on various parts of the *cakra*. Although this is not immediately apparent, the diagram is divided into nine rings or enclosures. In the course of meditation, the diagram is understood in the reverse order of involution, moving inward circuit after circuit. The nine enclosures are referred to as veils (*āvaraṇa*) that hide the luminous deity in the center. The *yantra* functions as a revelatory symbol of cosmic truths and theological principles, and is indeed a yāntric form of the goddess Tripurasundarī.

Each deity or emblem on the *yantra* is related to the devotee's mental traits, which are equated with psycho-cosmic categories of creation. The exoteric rituals pertaining to *yantra* worship consist of invocations with offerings to the retinue deities who are positioned on different circuits of the *yantra*. Sometimes these deities are depicted through their corresponding *mantras* and the seed syllables included in the *mantras*. In contemplative worship, the deities are internalized in deep meditation as forces of one's states of awareness. Beyond its theological aspect, the *yantra* is seen as a diagram that reflects the inner states of human consciousness and as an all-inclusive symbol

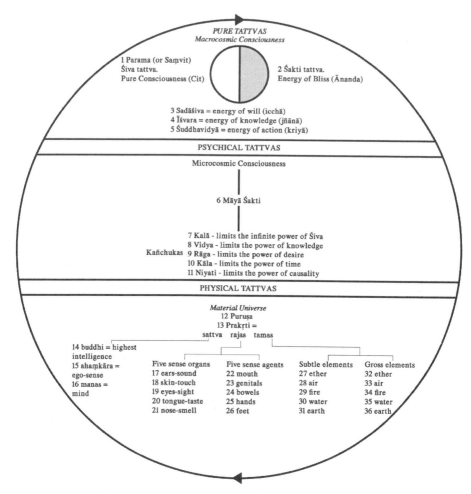

Figure 4.1. The Tattva diagram represents the thirty-six categories of creation. *Image courtesy of Madhu Khanna.*

of the psycho-cosmos. It is, therefore, looked upon as one of the most effective tools for spiritual transformation, projection, concentration, and integration with the envisioned cosmos.

Dhyāna and *Antaryāga*: Contemplative Worship of *Śrīcakra*

The Śākta Tantric ritual has some distinctive features.[5] The ritual is centered on the application of some foundational principles, namely, a well-defined metaphysical ontology (*jñāna*) and a specialized ritual performance (*karman*) that takes place with the aid of *mantra*, *yantra*, *mudrā* (finger poses), and interiorized yogic disciplines, in addition to the correct prescriptive knowledge of phil-

Figure 4.2. The Śrīyantra symbolically mirrors the categories of the Tattva diagram. *Image courtesy of Madhu Khanna.*

osophical principles. For rituals to gain efficacy, the worshipper must inculcate an active experiential awareness of unity and identity with the object of adoration through the process of mentation known as *bhāvanā*. It is *bhāvanā* that forms the basis of yogic meditations.

There are several gradations of practice in which the oneness with the divine is experienced. The highest form of meditation is when the self-luminous light of consciousness is expressed spontaneously. The middle level is one of concentration (*dhāraṇā*) and meditation (*dhyāna*); the lowest form is of laudation and external worship of a sacred image of a deity.[6] The most common form of *dhyāna* is the one that forms a part of the worship of the goddess. It is a combination of concentrated meditation on the physical form of the goddess, as described in her contemplative verse (*dhyāna-śloka*). No external worship can begin without re-creating a mental image of the deity. The descriptions capture minute details of the figure of the goddess, from head to toe, including her color and posture, with meticulous details of her facial features, adornments, jewels, and ornaments. Tripurasundarī's most popular image describes her as one who is "bathing the universe in her rosy effulgence." She holds in her four hands a noose, a goad, a bow, and five flowery arrows. Such simple *dhyāna* practice may be extended into an elaborate internal worship of the goddess with five, eleven, or sixty-four kinds of offerings. In this form of inner visualization, the goddess is mentally invoked in the heart lotus and is gratified by all of the offerings or ingredients such as water for washing her feet, perfumed oils for bathing, garments, unguents, a garland and adornments to deck her from head to toe. The texts often keep reminding the devotee that the true form of *dhyāna* consists in experiencing the identity of essence (*sāmrasyatā*) through immersion in the state of beatitude exuded by the energy of consciousness.[7]

The perfection of meditation is to transcend outer form. Thus the *dhyāna* is unswerving awareness without any object of contemplation for its support. Contemplation of the figure of a deity constitutes the gross form of meditation; the highest level of *dhyāna* is formless and consists in the awareness of the nondifferention of one's self from the absolute principle. This is attained through constant mindfulness of the true nature of the self, which is none other than Śiva in union with Śakti.

The traditions of meditation (*dhyāna* and *antaryāga*) must be viewed within the larger structure of Śrīvidyā rituals. At a generic level, all Hindu forms of ritual begin with a contemplative verse to the guru and the deity. In all forms of Tāntric worship, there is a well-defined structure. It begins with elaborate rites of purification, in which the adept purifies his gross body and re-creates a symbolic divine body (*divyaśarira*) through the rite of the purification of the elements (*bhūtaśuddhi*). Thereafter follow several acts of invocation and consecration. The worshiper performs the rite of infusing the deity's energy into various parts of his body (*nyāsa*) to make himself eligible for worship. Then begins the outer contemplation, before inviting the goddess in the rite of invocation. The next phase is entirely devoted to the contemplative worship of the goddess. *Antaryāga* literary means "internal sacrifice." This is a very special Tantric ritual. It is prescribed that all forms of exoteric ritual should be preceded by internal worship, because the efficacy of external worship lies in the worshiper's capacity to re-create through inner meditative experience and internal visualization all of the acts of worship on the mental screen. The Śākta Tantras say that there cannot be any outer worship (*bahiryāga*) without accomplishing worship within, as it is the inner meditative experience shaped by our *bhāvanā* that is made explicit in the exoteric ritual. Thus *antaryāga* consists in contemplation on all of the outward acts of worship, from the invocation to the dismissal of the deity during worship symbolically performed in contemplative vision. After its performance, the devotee worships the *yantra* with external offerings and finally takes back the flaming radiance of the goddess into his heart in the rite of dismissal (*visarjana*). It can be seen that the boundaries between the external and the internal, though well defined, merge and mingle at various junctures of the ritual. The true worship of the Śrīcakra consists in the unity of the knower (*jñātā*), the act of worship (*jñāna*), and the object of worship (*jñeya*).

The culmination of the ritual is reached with the total identification of the devotee with the goddess, her *cakra/yantra*, and her *mantra*, as they all are sparks of the same fire.

The Dynamics of *Śrīyantra* Meditation according to the *Bhāvanopaniṣad*

A devotee's spiritual journey from the stage of material existence to ultimate enlightenment is mapped on the greatest of *yantras*, the Śrīyantra. We find the sequence of meditation set out in the learned and erudite commentary in one of Bhāskararāya's greatest works, the *Bhāvanopaniṣad Bhāṣyā*,[8] which is divided into two sections. The commentary expounds the view of the Kādi school of Śrīvidyā that holds that the exoteric rituals should be interiorized in symbolic internal meditations. The first part of the commentary describes the meta significance of internal worship. The second part, the *Prayogavidhi*, designated as the *Mahāyaga Krama*, illustrates the injunctions (*vidhi*) for ritual practice through internal meditation of the symbolic representations described in the earlier section. Its distinctive feature is that Bhāskararāya's interpretation expounds the secret meaning (*atirahasya*) of the Śrīcakra by relating it to each part of the microcosm.

The main concern of the *Bhāvanopaniṣad Bhāṣyā* is to establish a unity between the Śrīcakra and the yogic structures of the subtle body. An attempt is made to align and harmonize the macro cosmos reflected in the Śrīcakra symbolism with various aspects of the microcosm, thereby emphasizing a unity between the two.

As is the convention, the text opens with a salutation to the preceptors, who are regarded as a fountainhead of the tradition. Thereafter, it outlines the structures of the physical, mental, vital, and psychological levels of the microcosm, equating these multiple levels to the deities who preside over the nine enclosures of the Śrīcakra. The Bhāṣyā lays great stress on the subtle nature of *bhāvanā*, contemplative meditation (after which the text is named). This form of Śrīvidyā internal worship (*antar-yāga*) takes precedence over the gross form of external worship (*bahir-yāga*). The internal worship is generally performed in two stages: first with the aid of external props such as the Śrīcakra, gestures, and recitations of *mantra*, which are then interiorized as manifestations of the light of consciousness. The internal worship is a form of contemplative immersion whereby the devotee's consciousness transforms through visualization of identity of the devotee's essence with that of the goddess. Such a transformation reflects the acme of the concept of *bhāvanā*. *Bhāvanā*, or an inwardly-directed contemplation, has emerged as a foundational concept in the Śrīvidyā school established by Bhāskararāya. It helped to sublimate the external forms of ritual to a highly subtle level of cognitive conscious worship, thereby refining the paraphernalia of external acts into a profound experience of unity of essence (*sāmarasya*) between the adorer and the adored.

According to Bhaskararaya, abstract philosophical investigation about the visual metaphysics of Śrīcakra is part and parcel of liberative knowledge. This requires both rational reflection (*sat-tarka*), correct understanding of structures and symbolism of the Śrīcakra, the microcosm and the active participation in the ritual known as Śrīcakra-pūjā. The composite form of knowledge (*jñāna*) and ritual action (*kriyā*) leads the devotee to the state of uninterrupted nondual cognition. The mere outward form of ritual acts without this knowledge does not bear any efficacy.

The meditation as described in the text is based on the theory of the affinity between the microcosm and the macrocosm. According to the text, the universe, the macrocosm, and the microcosm are integrally related. There are fundamental affinities between the ontological categories of creation, the subtle (or psychic) body scheme of the adept, and the *yantra*,[9] the object of adoration. In this form of meditation, the external *yantra* is transformed into an internal *yantra*. Energizing psycho-cosmic affinities, the adept can begin to make the ascent, or journey of return. This is demonstrated in the opening lines of the text in which the nine exits of the body (i.e, two ears, two nostrils, two eyes, the two organs of elimination and procreation, and the mouth) are identified with the nine preceptors, and the subtle nerves. Hence it is important to view such *yantras* not merely as symbols of the cosmos but as symbols of the integrated psycho-cosmos, as reflecting a human-universe continuum.

In most, if not all, *yantras* for meditation, the progressive stages from material or gross levels are symbolized by square enclosures with four gates opening out to the four directions, while the highest stage of perfection is identified with the *bindu* in the center. Closed concentric circuits (*maṇḍalas*) of various geometric shapes correspond to the intermediary planes of the consciousness. Each enclosure is circuit or a way station, a plateau (*dhāmani*), leading toward the sanctum sanctorum.

The number of circuits or enclosures in each *yantra* is prescribed by tradition and codified in Tantric texts. It can vary considerably. The Śrīyantra has nine concentric configurations, known as *cakras*, literally "wheels." *Cakra* is a generic term used to describe any circular diagram or symbol. In each of the enclosures, specific deities are invoked, each circuit being considered a cosmological form that supports *devatā* circles, or groups of goddesses. The power and harmony of each circle of deities is relative to the central deity: the deity clusters are like veils concealing the *yantra*'s innermost essence. After the practitioner has invoked all of the deities in the prescribed manner for meditation, he reaches a level of consciousness in which all of the *devatā* circles are fused to become the presiding deity at the center of the *yantra*. Gradually, this central deity itself disappears and merges into the center of spiritual consciousness, the *bindu* of the *yantra* and the highest psychic center between the adept's eyebrows.

The *bindu* is a fusion of all directions and of all levels, a point of termination where *all is*. From the gates that are his own subconscious forces, the yogi has passed through the circuits to be reunited with the permanent element of the universe. The ultimate state of union is achieved when he experiences the out-petaling of the soul flower, the thousand-petaled lotus, rising out of the crown of the head. The awareness that ensues from such meditation constitutes a spiritual climax, a state of yogic enstasis (*samādhi*). This is a state of psychic continuum, free from mental fluctuations, in which there is a perfect merging of symbol and psyche. The journey from the periphery to the center of the *yantra* may be measured physically in a few inches, but psychologically the return to the primordial source represented by the *bindu* is a vast mental distance, demanding the discipline of a lifetime.

The spiritual journey, then, is taken as a pilgrimage in which every step is an ascent of the center, a movement beyond one's limited existence, and every level is nearer to the goal, an affirmation of the unity of existence. Traditionally such a journey is mapped in nine stages, and each of these stages corresponds with one of the nine closed circuits of which the *yantra* is composed. Starting from the outer square and moving inward, the nine rings of the Śrīcakra bear specific names, related to their characteristics; the first circuit (Trailokyamohana *cakra*) "enchants the three worlds"; the second (Sarvāśāparipūraka *cakra*) "fulfills all expectations"; the third (Sarvasaṅkṣobhaṇa *cakra*) "agitates all"; the fourth (Sarvasaubhāgyadāyaka *cakra*) "grants fortune and excellence"; the fifth (Sarvārthasādhaka *cakra*) is the "accomplisher of all"; the sixth (Sarvarakṣākara *cakra*), "protects all"; the seventh (Sarvaroghara *cakra*) "cures all ills"; the eighth (Sarvasiddhiprada *cakra*) "grants all perfection"; and the highest (Sarvānandamaya *cakra*) is "replete with bliss."

In the first circuit of the Śrīcakra (see figure 4.3), there are three square enclosures, and the first line of the square is presided over by the ten forms of yogic accomplishments (*siddhis*): (1) the power to become small as an atom (*aṇimā*); (2) the power to attain weightlessness (*laghimā*); (3) the power to become large (*mahimā*); (4) the power of lordship (*īśitva*); (5) power over others (*vaśitva*); (6) assuming the form deserved (*prākāmya*); (7) the power to enjoy (*bhukti*); (8) attainment (*prāpti*); and (10) the power to fulfill all desires (*sarvakāma*). These ten accomplishments correspond to the ten aesthetic sentiments that propel our karmic actions, namely calmness (*śānta*), a sense of wonder (*adbhuta*), pity (*karuṇā*), valor (*vīra*), humor (*hāsya*), disgust (*bibhatsa*), anger (*raudra*), fear (*bhayānaka*), love (*śṛṅgāra*), and the natural state (*niyati*). In the second line of the square, the adept contemplates his own passions, such as anger, fear, lust, and so on, so as to overcome or conquer them. The eight

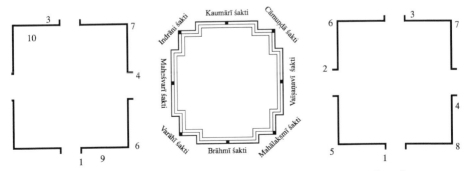

Figure 4.3. First circuit: Trailokyamohana *cakra*. *Image courtesy of Madhu Khanna.*

psychological tendencies that are considered obstacles of the mind are also invoked, through the eight Mātṛkā Śaktis (goddesses) that either flank the four
"doors" of the *yantra* or are invoked in the square band (*bhūpura*). Generally
they are what we experience of the world through sense activity and the crav-
ings of our egotism. Thus the first Mātṛkā Śakti, (1) Brāhmī, is associated with
worldly desire, the passion that impels us to seek ephemeral joys; (2) Māheśvarī
is representative of anger; (3) Kaumārī, of constant avarice and greed; (4)
Vaishnavī fascinates and infatuates; (5) Vārāhī is symbolic of obstinacy and
false pride; (6) Indrānī, of jealousy; (7) Cāmuṇḍā, of earthly rewards; and finally, (8) Mahālakṣmī, symbolizes our deficiencies and blameworthiness in
general.

Around the Mātṛkā Śakti, in the third line innermost of the square, preside
the Mudrā Śaktis: (1) The Agitator of All (Sarvasaṅkṣobhinī); (2) The Chaser of
All (Sarvavidrāvinī); (3) The Attractor of All (Sarvākarṣinī); (4) The Subjugator
of All (Sarvavaśaṅkarī); (5) The Intoxicator of All (Sarvonmādinī); (6) The Re-
strainer of All (Sarvamahāṅkuśa); (7), The Wanderer in Space (Sarvakhecarī) [as
Consciousness] of All; (8) The Seed of All (Sarvabīja); (9) The Womb of All (Sar-
vayoni); and (10) The Triadic [Nature] of All (Trikhaṇḍā). These represent the
ten *cakras* of the subtle body.

Now let us move to the second circuit (see figure 4.4). Our bodies are the
locus of our sense experiences, our likes and dislikes, and our emotions, feelings, and responses. According to the teaching of the Śrīvidyā school, the physical being is composed of sixteen components: the five elements (earth, water,
fire, air, and ether), ten sense organs of perception and action (ears, skin, eyes,
tongue, nose, mouth, feet, hands, arms, and genitals), and the oscillating mind.
These sixteen components are related to the sixteen petals of the Śrīyantra
lotus. Each petal is presided over by a deity of attraction who stimulates our
"sense consciousness" through our bodily faculties, which leaves us spellbound
in infatuation with ourselves. These sixteen "attractions" veil our existence, blind
our spiritual sight, keep us from knowledge, and chain us to the ceaseless cycle

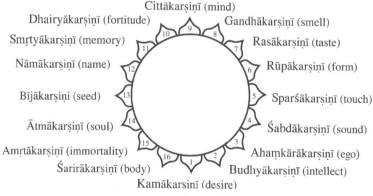

Figure 4.4. Second circuit: Sarvāśāparipūraka *cakra. Image courtesy of Madhu Khanna.*

of life. Since they mirror our consciousness at the stage of false knowing, these Śaktis must be contemplated at the beginning of the spiritual journey.

The eight-petaled lotus, the third circuit (see figure 4.5), governs speech, grasping, locomotion, evacuation, enjoyment, and the three attitudes of rejection, acceptance, and indifference. These petals are also each presided over by a Śakti.

The two principal symbols of the subtle body are the subtle channels (*nāḍīs*) and the *cakras* symbolized as lotuses (see figure 4.6). *Nāḍīs* are subtle channels or nerves that act as conduits of *prāṇic* currents. They are pathways of life currents energized through the practice of Kuṇḍalinī yoga. Of the fourteen channels, there are three principle ones: Iḍā, the lunar channel on the left side of the cerebrospinal axis, the spinal column, Piṅgalā, the solar channel on the right side of the Suṣumnā, the central channel, which extends from the base of the spine to the crown of the head.

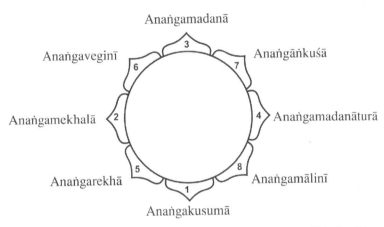

Figure 4.5. Third circuit: Sarvaśaṅkshobaṇa *cakra*. *Image courtesy of Madhu Khanna.*

Figure 4.6. Fourth circuit: Sarvasaubhāgyadāyaka *cakra*. *Image courtesy of Madhu Khanna.*

After transcending the limitations of the physical self, the meditator has to attain an understanding of the *prāṇic* structure of his subtle body, from the physical shell he must enter into his psychic self represented by the subtle nerves, etheric channels, and vital energy of the body-cosmos. Accordingly, the fourth, fifth, and sixth circuits of the Śrīyantra symbolically illustrate the subtle nerves and the modification of the vital energy (*prāṇa*) that regulates the vitality of the subtle body. The first of these, the fourteen-triangled circuit, corresponds with the fourteen energy channels in the subtle body: six run through the right side of the body, starting at the ankle and moving toward and through the right thigh, shoulder, and cheek and ultimately meeting at the center of the forehead; four are on the left, and the rest are along the axis of the subtle body (see figure 4.6).

The fifth circuit of ten triangles shown in figure 4.7 exemplifies the dynamic life force called *prāṇa*, the essential link between mind and body. The triangles represent the tenfold functions of the universal *prāṇic* energy in the individual subtle body, the five vital currents (Prāṇa, which draws life force into the body; Apāna, which expels life force; Vyāna, which distributes and circulates energy; Samāna, which controls digestion; Udāna, which controls circulation), and the five medial currents (Nāga, Kūrma, Kṛkara, Devadatta, and Dhananjaya) that are linked with the functions of the five *prāṇas* that mirror them.

The sixth circuit shown in figure 4.8 embodies the yogic functions of the *prāṇa*, life force that acts in conjunction with the fivefold digestive fire. In Āyurveda, fire is looked upon as the cleansing and transformative element. It is the task of fire (*agni*) in the body to break up solids, transform them, and nourish the body at the cellular level. There are ten recognized functions of fire mentioned in Bhāskararāya's commentary. *Agni* acts as a corroder (*kṣaraka*), ejector (*udgāraka*), agitator (*kṣobhaka*), bloater (*jṛmbhaka*), and dissolver (*mohaka*). It

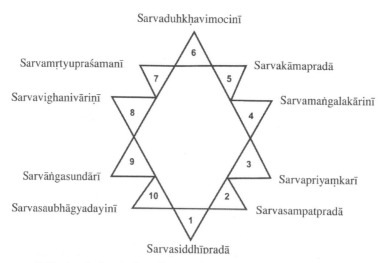

Figure 4.7. Fifth circuit: Sarvārthasādhaka *cakra. Image courtesy of Madhu Khanna.*

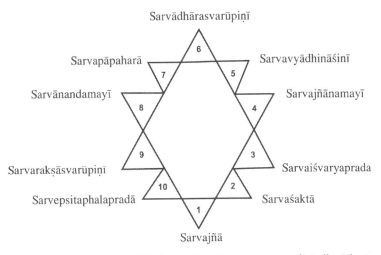

Figure 4.8. Sixth circuit: Sarvarakshakara *cakra*. *Image courtesy of Madhu Khanna.*

facilitates active action in the form of food that is eaten, chewed, sucked, licked, and drunk.

While the digestive fire is responsible for absorption and the elimination of waste at the physical level, on the symbolic plane, the element of fire represents spiritual transformation from the plane of darkness to the light of awareness, a wiping out of negative emotions and memory traits that separate the devotee from his true identity. The contemplation of the sixth circuit, presided over by goddesses, represents the symbolic transformation of consciousness through the conjunction of *prāṇa* and *agni* that brings about a perfect psycho-physical balance to enter the final, albeit unitive, state of consciousness represented by the next circuit.

Conscious experience of the psychic spectrum becomes increasingly subtle as one moves to the Śrīyantra's inner enclosures. The seventh, eight-triangled circuit (Sarvarogahara, see figure 4.9) represents the three constituent principles of material nature: *sattva*, associated with purity or the stuff of intelligence; *rajas*, denoting the force or energy activating and impelling creation; and *tamas*, mass or matter equated with inertia. These three qualities exist in individuals in varying degrees and are variously manifested: *sattva* is expressed psychologically as purity, tranquility, and calmness of mind; *rajas* as passion, egoism, and restlessness; and *tamas* as resistance to all change. The devotee can cultivate any of these qualities by his actions and thoughts; ideally, an aspirant will cultivate the *sattva* element of his nature over *rajas* or *tamas*. Ultimately, however, the devotee will strive to overcome even the *sattva* element, as the ultimate essence is above and beyond all. The other five triangles of this circuit represent two sets of polarities—pleasure/pain, cold/heat—and the individual's will or capacity to decide upon action. Decisiveness guides the psyche to balance the continuous flux of mental activity.

Before reaching the finale of *yantra* meditation represented by the *bindu*, the adept is made to once again come face to face with mental fluctuations caused by the existential reality of the world at large. At this stage, the adept is once again confronted by the four symbols of the weapons of goddess Tripurasundarī, which she holds in her four hands. Although the weapons are not depicted in the diagram, they are visualized around the primal triangle (figure 4.10). The noose that the goddess holds in her lower right hand embodies the gross form of desire. The elephant hook that she holds in her lower left hand is a symbol of the negative traits, such as anger and hatred, that lie at the subliminal levels of

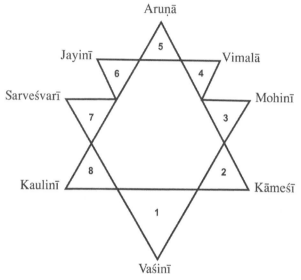

Figure 4.9. Seventh circuit: Sarvarogahara *cakra. Image courtesy of Madhu Khanna.*

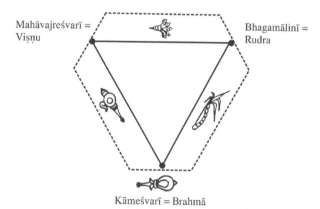

Figure 4.10. Eighth circuit: Sarvasiddhiprada *cakra. Image courtesy of Madhu Khanna.*

the psyche. In her upper two arms, the goddess holds a bow and five arrows. The bow symbolizes the higher faculties of cognition that controls the five flowery arrows, symbols of the five gross and five subtle elements that attract our senses but leave us unfulfilled.

As meditation nears the innermost triangle, a dramatic change takes place with the fading of the goddesses presiding over the previous circuits into the emptiness of the center. The innumerable Śaktis of the earlier phases are reduced to three principles of existence of impure creation: the unmanifest principle of creation (Avyakta), the cosmic principle of force (Mahat), and the principle of ego-formation (Ahamkāra) give rise to the experiences of subject and object through which the adept perceives the distinctions and diversity of external nature.

The ninth *cakra*, the *bindu* (figure 4.11), is the symbol of final release. It is the summit of reality and represents the innermost center of the consciousness, the abode of the supreme goddess Tripurasundarī, whose mysterious presence is experienced in the depths of one's being. The *bindu* marks the end of the spiritual pilgrimage. Where outer life ends, the inner life begins: there is no shape, no form; all is immersed in the void. According to the *Prayogavidhi* of Bhāskararāya, the internalization of the Śrīyantra is accomplished by chanting the appropriate *mantras* that invokes the aforesaid symbolism through the ritual of *nyāsa*. The contemplative ritual consists in touching specific spots on the body to infuse it with the energies of the deities who represent all of the symbolic categories described above. A more extreme but knowledge-centered meditative practice was propounded by Lakṣmīdhara (ca. 1200 AD) and is followed by the Samayācārins, who outright reject the use of any form of external aid or sacred symbol but retain the inner and mentally directed contemplations.

The Śrīyantra's nine circuits are thus nine levels separating the devotee from his primordial wholeness, or, conversely, nine steps that can lead him through the principles of spiritual evolution. When the highest stage of exaltation is reached, the *yantra* is internalized; it becomes a psychic complex. The truth of the cosmos, illuminated in the *yantra*, is the devotee himself illumined, and his body itself becomes the *yantra*.

In another type of subtle and abstract meditation, the adept experiences the dynamic flow of evolution and involution through the Śrīyantra. In deep concentration, the adept mentally constructs the entire image of the Śrīyantra from the center, in the same fashion in which the cosmos is held to unfurl itself in the process of evolution. After the whole image has been visualized, the adept begins his meditation from the outermost periphery of the figure. Moving inward, enclosure after enclosure, he is symbolically involved in the "dissolution" of all of the cosmic principles projected by the nine Śiva-Śakti triangles. In such meditation, the adept lives through the whole drama of descent and ascent, as

Figure 4.11. Ninth circuit: Sarvānandamaya cakra, as one's innermost self. *Image courtesy of Madhu Khanna.*

an act of purging his consciousness. He is summoned by and surrenders to initiatory death, through which he is reborn. When he has attained the sought-after identity, the extended universe (of the *yantra*) symbolically collapses into the *bindu*, which itself vanishes into the void.

Kuṇḍalinī *Dhyāna* and *Cakra* Homologies

In the Śākta Tantras, the human body acquires a unique role and is considered the most perfect and powerful of all vehicles of worship. The adept looks upon himself as an extension of divine consciousness expressing the fundamental unity of creation. His life, like the cosmos, is bound by a purpose; his biological rhythms are tuned by planetary phenomena. Human existence is ordained and regulated by the governing principles of nature. The external macrocosmic world and the microcosmic inner world are formed of the same "stuff" and are related by an indivisible web of mutually conditioned affinities.

To illustrate the mutual correspondences between the microcosmic body and the cosmos, Śākta Tantra has created a complex map of psychic "crosspoints" in which the infinite world of time and space are seen reflected in the psychophysical structure of the subtle body. The cosmos, according to the Tantras, consists of seven ascending planes of existence, starting from earthly, gross existence, and this hierarchy is mirrored in the psychic vortices functioning as invisible *yantras* in the human body. In the Hindu tradition, the seven major points of power in the subtle body function as *yantras* for inner meditative experience in Kuṇḍalinī yoga. They are visualized as geometrical figures, as wheels (*cakras*) or lotuses, spaced on the vertical axis of the subtle body, the Suṣumnā, which corresponds roughly to the spinal column and the brain. Since these *cakras* embrace the entire psycho-cosmos, each is associated with a sound vibration, element, color, deity, or animal symbol. The first *cakra*, known as the Mūlādhāra (Root) Cakra, is situated at the base of the spine and is the gathering point of the energy of the psychic body. Its symbol is a square with an inverted triangle. In the center of this *yantra* is the snake symbol of the latent microcosmic form of energy, Devī Kuṇḍalinī, coiled around a *liṅga* emblem. It is governed by the element earth, and its seed *mantra* is Laṃ.

The second *cakra*, the Svādhiṣṭhāna Cakra, lies behind the genitals. It is vermilion, and its form is a circle with six petals, containing a white crescent moon. In the center is inscribed the *mantra* of the water element, Vaṃ.

The third *cakra*, the Maṇipura Cakra, is the navel center, governed by the element fire. Its symbol is a lotus of ten petals. Within the lotus is a red triangle with three T-shaped swastika marks. Its seed *mantra* is Raṃ.

The fourth *cakra*, the Anāhata Cakra, is located at the level of the heart, and is conceived as a lotus of twelve petals with a hexagon at the center. This *cakra* is the seat of the air element, and is a prime revealer of cosmic sound during meditation. Its seed *mantra* is Yaṃ.

The fifth *cakra* is known as the Viśuddha Cakra and is situated at the level of the throat. It is of smoky purple hue, and its symbol is a sixteen-petaled lotus with a downward-pointing triangle. At its center is the symbol of the ether element, represented by a circle, with the seed *mantra* Ham.

The sixth *cakra*, the Ājñā Cakra, is located between the eyebrows and commands the various levels of meditation. Its symbol is a circle with two petals and an inverted triangle bearing a *liṅga* emblem. Its seed *mantra* is the primordial vibration Om.

The seventh *cakra*, the Sahasrāra Cakra, represents the apex of yogic meditation, the seat of the Absolute (Śiva-Śakti). It is visualized as measuring four fingers' breadth above the crown of the head, and is represented by an inverted lotus of a thousand petals, symbolically showering the subtle body with spiritual radiance. The Sahasrāra neutralizes all colors and sounds, and is represented as colorless.

These internal symbols in the subtle body mark the phases of the spiritual journey of the Kuṇḍalinī Śakti, the energy that is aroused in meditation for the ascent of the path of the Suṣumnā to unite with the Sahasrāra Cakra. They indicate the seven stages of meditation through which the adept works out his identity with the cosmos. Each of the inner *cakras* may be meditated upon either independently or with the aid of an external *yantra*. A common practice is to equate the various circuits of the external *yantras* with each of the seven or nine *cakras* in the subtle body (see figure 4.12). In pyramidal-shaped *yantras*, each level of the hierarchy may be identified with each level of the *cakras*.

The technique of Kuṇḍalinī yoga consists in using the vital energy (*prāṇa*) to awaken the consciousness-as-power (Śakti) in the root *cakra* (Mūlādhāra), located in the region of the perineum, and causing it to rise up the Suṣumnā, the central channel of the subtle body, energizing the *cakras* through which the Tantric universe can be absorbed into the body. Once the Kuṇḍalinī Śakti has ascended to Sahasrāra, the highest psychic center at the crown of the head, it is made to reverse its course and return to rest in the base center again.

Figure 4.12. The *cakra* of the subtle body corresponding to the circuits of the *yantra*. *Image courtesy of Madhu Khanna.*

In a special method of meditation practiced by advanced adepts, under the guidance of a guru, the adept learns to achieve union between the Kuṇḍalinī of the microcosm (*piṇḍa*) and the macrocosm (*brāhmaṇḍa*). These affinities are struck in the subtle body by meditation on its *cakras* and by finding correlations and similarities between the subtle body and the totality of the cosmos. The inner *cakras* may be meditated upon in turn with the aid of an external *yantra*. A common practice, however, is to equate the circuits of the *yantra* with the body *cakras*.

In an authoritative text devoted to Śakti worship, the *cakras* of the subtle body are related to the nine enclosures of the Śrīyantra as follows:[10]

Śrīyantra	*Cakra*
1. Outer square (Trailokyamohana)	Mūlādhāra (root *cakra*)
2. Sixteen-petaled lotus (Sarvāśāparipūraka)	Svādhiṣṭhāna (*cakra* below the navel)
3. Eight-petaled lotus (Sarvasaṅkshobana)	Maṇipūra (navel *cakra*)
4. Fourteen-angled figure (Sarvasāubhāgyadāyaka)	Anāhata (heart *cakra*)
5. Ten-angled figure (Sarvārthasādhaka)	Viśuddha (throat *cakra*)
6. Ten-angled figure (Sarvarakṣākara)	Ājñā (*cakra* between the eyebrows)
7. Eight-angled figure (Sarvaroghara)	Brahmarandhra (*cakra* of palate)
8. Triangle (Sarvasiddhiprada)	Brahman (*cakra* of the Supreme)
9. *Bindu* (Sarvānandamaya)	Sahasrāra (*cakra* of space)

In such meditations, the Śrīyantra can be viewed as a composite image of the psycho-cosmos.

Other homologies are drawn between the subtle body and the Śrīyantra. In the Śrīyantra's three-dimensional form, for instance, when it is known as Meru (after Mount Meru, the mythical axis of the earth), its nine circuits are divided into three elevations that match the scheme of the subtle body, whose *cakras* can also be divided into triads (see figure 4.13). Alternatively, three *cakras*, each containing the *liṅga* emblem of the male principle, are seen as marking the three levels corresponding to the three elevations of the Meru form of the Śrīyantra:

Meru Form of the Śrīyantra	*Cakra*	*Deity*	*Liṅga Emblem*
1. A square and two lotus rings	Mūlādhāra (root)	Brahmā = creation	Svayambhū *liṅga*
2. A fourteen- and two ten-angled figures	Anāhata (heart)	Viṣṇu = preservation	Bāṇa *liṅga*
3. An eight-angled figure, a triangle, and a *bindu*	Ājñā (eyebrows)	Śiva = destruction	Itara *liṅga*

These *cakras* are called "knots" (*granthi*) and are nodes where the transformation of the adept is said to take place. They are associated with the

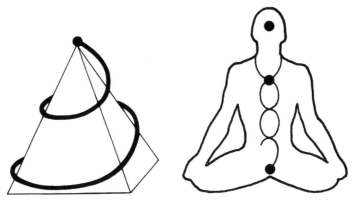

Figure 4.13. The three elevations of the Śrīyantra (*left*) and the three corresponding planes of the body-cosmos (*right*). *Image courtesy of Madhu Khanna.*

earthly desires and passions to be overcome during the process of Kuṇḍalinī yoga.

Meditation without Visual Aids

Meditation on the *yantra* takes the more subtle and advanced form when it consists of inner illumination, a method of meditation without any yogic, ritual, or visual aids.

In the early phases of the practice, the devotee is instructed in the iconic images of deities. Later, even yāntric symbols are discarded, and worship becomes highly abstract, subtle, and esoteric. It is at this stage that meditation on internal *yantras* composed of simple graphic symbols is performed. This technique is divulged only to those practitioners who have been through all of the primary stages of practice (*sādhanā*), and is attained after a long and arduous training under the strict instruction of highly advanced gurus. The authorities of the discipline state that all of the ritual offerings made in the external form of worship are spontaneously present in the interior form, and it is for this reason that in many texts the contemplative experience is called "mental oblation" (*antaryajña*).

The whole process of mental oblation is described in the *Kaulāvalīnirṇaya*,[11] an authoritative work of the Kaula sect of Tantrism. After preliminary purifying rites, the devotee builds up, in deep concentration, a square *yantra* enclosed by three concentric circles. In the center of the square, he visualizes the emblem of the yoni (a half moon and a *bindu*). The square symbolizes the vessel of consciousness (*cit-kuṇḍa*) in which burns the fire of consciousness, and into this symbolic fire the adept "surrenders" all of his mental offerings. The devotee first makes an offering of his impulses, then his senses, his selfhood, his acts, both good and evil, and finally his entire inner and outer self, which is simply a variant of the thirty-six cosmic principles of which the universe is composed (see figure 4.1). Through this unconditional surrender, the adept dissolves every bond with outer life. This mental offering of his entire being is the prelude to new birth. The devotee apprehends the true nature of the absolute principle as void, the undifferentiated ultimate ground of reality. He is then said to become indistinguishable from the vessel into which the symbolic oblations were offered: in this final stage, his entire being is perfectly assimilated with the cosmos. The act of offering is Brahman, the reality of the offering is Brahman, the person offering is Brahman.

The essential difference between the outer form of *yantra* worship (*pūjā*) and inward meditation through yāntric symbols is that the former produces mental states that are like "seeds" for the future workings of consciousness, while the latter is "without seed" (*nirbīja*), in the sense that the adept no longer needs to work upon himself, as he has reached the highest stage of perfection, where no kārmic seeds will fructify or impel him to perform any form of worship. This is the highest grade of spiritual attainment, called Sahaja-avasthā, a state of consciousness in which oneness with the Absolute is experienced spontaneously and naturally, the ontological plenitude in which being, knowledge, and bliss are inseparable and indistinguishable.

The culmination of *yantra* meditation is reached when the devotee begins to internalize the centered *bindu* in the *yantra* as an inner, still center. The spiritual experience of the *bindu* marks the end of spiritual involution. The "*bindu* state" experience is unique. Psychically, it implies the practitioner's awareness of his wholeness, which is spontaneously discovered through inward illumination. All of the outward-directed energies of the phenomenal ego are brought together to an inward state of rest and unity by the ultimate realization of the oneness of Śiva and Śakti. Neutrality of the senses has superseded the creative play of Māyā Śakti, and she is now the silent seer, no longer attached to the world of phenomena. In this state, the adept neither laughs nor weeps, neither loves nor hates, for he has transcended all dualities. The adept attains precisely the state, mentally and spiritually, that the symbol of the *bindu* of the *yantra* denotes, an ideal mind point, the balancing of all polarities. But this is not the end; the aspirant is still to soar beyond the *bindu* state to merge with the Void—the primordial plenitude of Śiva-Śakti in oneness.

This highest stage of spiritual absorption (*samādhi*) achieved through *yantra* ritual worship and meditation is not susceptible to any verbal analysis. It is contemplated in absolute silence: "Higher than the original syllable is the point, the echo higher than this; the syllable vanishes with the sound, the highest state is silent."[12] This is the state of identity attained through holding on firmly to the awareness that "I am" the universe, which is nondifferent from Śiva and Śakti in union.

At this stage, all external aids, such as *yantras* and *mantras*, have become like shadows. In the most advanced form of internal meditation, when ecstasy bordering on trance has been reached, even the inner *yantra* is regarded as obsolete, serving no spiritual purpose. The yogi engaged in *samādhi* cannot be controlled by *yantra* or *mantra*; he is beyond the power of all corporeal beings. At this stage, the *yantra* is abandoned and may be passed to another devotee or immersed in holy water. For the adept has internalized the truth of the cosmos mirrored in the *yantra* in his own being.

Notes

1. Sastri, "Tripurā Upaniṣad," 1–10; for discussion on the theme, see Brooks, *Secret of the Three Cities*, 80–81.

2. Avalon, *Kulārṇava Tantra*, chap. V, 86; ch. XVII, 154.

3. For a detailed discussion on the two *kramas* of the Śrīyantra, see Khanna, "Sṛṣṭi and Saṃhāra," 255–266.

4. For the ontology supporting the Śrīyantra, see Avalon, *Kāmakalāvilāsa*; Dvivedi, *Nityaṣoḍaśikārṇava*, chap. 1, 28–45; and Kavirāja, *Yoginīhṛdaya*, part 1, verses 2–15.

5. For a detailed exposition of the ritual worship of Śrīyantra, see Khanna, "Concept and Liturgy," parts II and III.

6. Singh, *Vijñānabhairava*, verse 146.

7. Sastry, "Śrīlalitācatuṣṣaṣṭyupacāra saṃgrahaḥ," verses 1–26.

8. Rao, *Bhāvanopaniṣat*. The text in its first recension (edited by A. Mahadeva Shastri and K. Rangacharya) was published in 1896 by Government Oriental Library, Mysore; in 1925 by Adyar Library Bulletin, Adyar Madras; in 1917 by Nirnaya Sugar Press, Bombay (edited by W. L. Pansikar). A newer version, along with the *Prayogavidhi*, has been published in Sarasvatī, *Śrīvidyā-ratnākaraḥ*, 497–509, which we have followed. To my knowledge, this exclusive form of meditative practice has not been commented upon by John Woodroffe.

9. For a detailed exposition on Kuṇḍalinī Śakti, see Bhattacharya, *Śrītattvacintāmaṇi*, chap. VI, 183–210; Avalon, *Serpent Power*; and Tripathi, *Śāktānandatāraṅgiṇī*, chaps. I and IV.

10. Sastri, "Saubhāgyalakṣmī Upaniṣad," chap. III, 1–9.

11. Avalon, *Kaulavalīnirṇaya*, chap. III, verse 103.

12. *Dhyānabindu Upaniṣad*, cited in Deussen, *Philosophy of the Upanishads*, 392.

Bibliography

Avalon, Arthur, ed. *Kāmakalāvilāsa by Puṇyānanda with Comm. Cidvalli by Naṭnānandanātha*. Madras: Ganesh and Company, 1953.

———. *Kaulavalīnirṇaya of Jñānānanda Paramhaṃsa*. Calcutta: University Press, 1928.

———. *Kulārṇava Tantra*. Madras: Ganesh and Company, 1965.

———. *The Serpent Power, Being the Sat-Cakra-Nirupana and Pāduka-Pañcaka, Two Works on Laya-Yoga, Translated from the Sanskrit, with Introduction and Commentary*. New York: Dover Publications, 1974.

Bhattacharya, Chintamani, ed. *Śrītattvacintāmaṇi of Pūrnānanda. Critically Edited from Original Manuscripts (Chapters I–XVIII) with an Original Commentary by Bhuvanamohan Sankhyatirtha and (Chapters XIX–XXVI) with Notes by Chintamani Bhattacharya*. Delhi: Motilal Banarasidass, 1994.

Brooks, Douglas Renfrew. *The Secret of the Three Cities: An Introduction to Hindu Śākta Tantrism*. Chicago: University of Chicago Press, 1990.

Deussen, Paul. *The Philosophy of the Upanishads*. New York: Dover Publications, 1966.

Dvivedi, V. V., ed. *Nityaṣoḍaśikārṇava with Comms. Ṛjuvimarśinī by Śivānanda and Artharatnāvalī by Vidyānanda*. Varanasi: Varanaseya Sanskrit Viśvavidyālaya, 1968.

Kavirāja, Gopinātha, ed. *Yoginīhṛdaya with Two Sansk. Comms. Dīpikā by Amṛtānanda-nātha and Setubandha by Bhāskararāya.* Sanskrit Bhavana Granthamālā 7. Varanasi, India: Varanaseya Sanskrit Viśvavidyālaya, 1963.

Khanna, Madhu. "The Concept and Liturgy of the Śrīcakra Based on Śivānanda's Trilogy." PhD thesis, Oxford University, 1986.

———. "Sṛṣṭi and Saṃhāra: Dinergic Order in the Symbolism of the Śrīcakra." In *Ṛta: The Cosmic Order,* edited by Madhu Khanna, 255–266. New Delhi: Indira Gandhi National Centre for the Arts / D. K. Printworld, 2004.

Rao, S. K. Ramachandran, ed. *Bhāvanopaniṣat with Commentary by Bhāskararāya.* Bangalore: Kalpatharu Research Academy, 2002.

Sarasvatī, Harihārananda, *Śrīvidyā-ratnākaraḥ.* Edited by Dattatreyānandanātha, 5th ed. Varanasi: Sādhanā Pītha, 2000.

Sastri, A. Mahadev, ed. *The Śākta Upanisads.* Adyar, Madras: Adyar Library, 1950.

———. "Saubhāgyalakṣmī Upaniṣad." In Sastri, *Śākta Upanisads,* 54–66.

———. "Tripurā Upaniṣad." In Sastri, *Śākta Upanisads,* 35–40.

Sastry, K. P. Narayana, ed. *Sri Lalitāmahātripurasundarī Yāgakramaḥ by Bhāskararāya.* Bangalore: Sri Chamarajendra Sanskrit College, 1956.

———. "Śrīlalitācatuṣṣaṣṭyupacāra samgrahaḥ." In Sastry, *Srilalitāmahātripurasundarī,* 1–3 (after p. 18).

Singh, Jaideva, ed. *Vijñānabhairava or Divine Consciousness—A Treasury of 112 Types of Yoga.* Delhi: Motilal Banarsidass, 1979.

Tripathi, Rajanatha, ed. *Śāktānandatāraṅginī of Brahmanandagiri.* Yogatantra Granthamālā. Vol. 2. Varanasi, India: Sampūrṇānanda Sanskrit University.

The History of Jaina Meditation

The history of Jaina meditation reveals a number of discontinuities and innovations that show that there was much uncertainty with regard to the way in which Jaina monastics (and perhaps lay followers) were supposed to meditate, or whether they were supposed to meditate at all.[1] Authors were confronted with canonical guidelines that were difficult to make sense of, and more than once felt free to deviate from these guidelines; they even went to the extent of borrowing elements from non-Jaina schools of meditation. This chapter will consider some examples.

Canonical Meditation

The difficulties had started early. The canonical texts of the largest sect of Jainism, Śvetāmbara, contain very little information about meditation. The information they do contain can be summarized as follows.[2]

The earliest road to liberation that is still discernible in the texts, especially in the *Āyāraṅga*, is a direct response to the idea that suffering is the result of activity. The evil effects of activity are avoided by renouncing activity. In this way no new karma is bound by the soul, and karma that has already been bound is destroyed, as the *Uttarajjhayaṇa* (29.37/1139) explains. Renouncing activity is done in a most radical way, culminating in motionlessness until death. Motionlessness of the mind is but one aspect of this, which does not receive much attention in the old texts. One early passage (*Uttarajjhayaṇa* 29.72/1174) speaks of a "pure meditation" (*sukkajjhāṇa*; Skt. *śukla dhyāna*) that is entered when less than the time of a *muhūrta* is left of life.[3] In this "pure meditation" only subtle activity remains initially; then—after the activities of mind, speech, and body, including breathing, have been stopped—the monk is in "pure meditation" in which all activity has been cut off, and in which the last remains of karma are being destroyed. The ninth (sometimes considered the eighth) chapter of *Āyāraṅga* 1 indicates that meditation (*jhāṇa*; Skt. *dhyāna*) was not confined to the last moments before death. Mahāvīra is here said to meditate "day and night." He is also said to meditate on objects in the external world.

Beside these few early passages, there are more extensive descriptions in later classificatory (but still canonical) texts. These texts enumerate how many kinds of this or that chosen item there are. In conformity with this goal, they enumerate everything that can be covered by the term *jhāṇa* (Skt. *dhyāna*). This is much more than "meditation" alone; "thinking" or mental activity in general is also covered.[4] The resulting enumeration contains four types of *dhyāna*: (i) afflicted (*aṭṭa*; Skt. *ārta*); (ii) wrathful (*rodda*; Skt. *raudra*); (iii) pious (*dhamma*; Skt. *dharmya*); and (iv) pure (*sukka*; Skt. *śukla*). They are described as follows in the *Ṭhāṇaṅga* (4.1.61–72/247), and described almost identically in the *Viyāhapaṇṇatti* and *Uvavāiya*:

> Afflicted *dhyāna* is of four kinds: (1) [one] is joined with what is not liked and also accompanied by the thought of separation therefrom; (2) [one] is joined with what is liked and also accompanied by the thought of non-separation therefrom; (3) [one] is joined with disease and also accompanied by the thought of separation therefrom; (4) [one] is joined with the experience of agreeable pleasures and also accompanied by the thought of non-separation therefrom. These are the four characteristics of afflicted *dhyāna*: crying, grief, weeping, lamentation.

> Wrathful *dhyāna* is of four kinds: connected with injury, connected with robbery, connected with theft, connected with the protection [of worldly goods]. These are the four characteristics of wrathful *dhyāna*: [one] has abundant hatred, much hatred, hatred due to ignorance, hatred until the end[,] which is death.

> Pious *dhyāna* is of four kinds and has four manifestations: examination of the commandments [of the Jinas, the enlightened Jaina masters], examination of sins, examination of the results [of actions], examination of the forms [of the constituents of the world]. These are the four characteristics of pious *dhyāna*: liking for the commandments [of the Jinas], liking for the natural state, liking for the scriptures, liking for pervasive study [of the sacred texts]. These are the four supports of pious *dhyāna*: recitation, questioning, repetition, reflection. These are the four reflections of pious *dhyāna*: reflection on being alone, reflection on transitoriness, reflection on there being no refuge, reflection on birth and rebirth of living beings.

> Pure *dhyāna* is of four kinds and has four manifestations: (i) in which there is consideration of multiplicity and change of object; (ii) in which there is consideration of oneness and no change of object; (iii) in which activity has become subtle and from which there is no return; (iv) in which [all] activity has been cut off and from which one does not fall back. These are the four characteristics of pure meditation: absence of agitation, absence of delusion, discriminating insight, renunciation. These are the four supports of pure meditation: forbearance, freedom, softness, straightness. These are the four reflections of pure meditation: reflection on infinity, reflection on change, reflection on what is inauspicious, reflection on sin.

These four kinds of *dhyāna* came to be looked upon as four types of meditation, enumerated among the different kinds of inner asceticism.[5] The later tradition, when it looked for canonical guidance regarding meditation, was henceforth confronted with a list of four kinds of "meditation," only the last one of which, namely "pure meditation," should properly be regarded as such.

The strange confusion described above was followed by an even more dramatic development. "Pure meditation" came to be considered inaccessible in the present age (in this world). Sometimes this is stated explicitly, as for example in Hemacandra's *Yogaśāstra*.[6] More often it is expressed by saying that one has to know the *Pūrva*s in order to reach the first two stages of "pure meditation." The fourteen *Pūrva*s once constituted the twelfth major subdivision (*aṅga*) of the Jaina canon. But they were lost at an early date. Already the *Tattvārtha Sūtra* (9.40)[7] states that knowledge of the *Pūrva*s is a precondition for entering "pure meditation." This means that already in the time between 150 and 350 CE "pure meditation" was considered no longer attainable in this world.

Such an early date finds support elsewhere. We have seen that the canonical description of the four *dhyāna*s assigns four reflections (*anuprekṣā*) each to "pious meditation" (*dharmya dhyāna*) and "pure meditation" (*śukla dhyāna*), in the following manner (in the case of "pious meditation," the Sanskrit equivalents are here given, for comparison with what follows):[8]

In "pious meditation":

  (i) reflection on being alone (*ekatvānuprekṣā*)
  (ii) reflection on transitoriness (*anityānuprekṣā*)
  (iii) reflection on there being no refuge (*aśaraṇānuprekṣā*)
  (iv) reflection on birth and rebirth of living beings (*saṃsārānuprekṣā*)

In "pure meditation":

  (i) reflection on infinity (*aṇaṃtavattiyāṇuppehā*)
  (ii) reflection on change (*vippariṇāmāṇuppehā*)
  (iii) reflection on what is inauspicious (*asubhāṇuppehā*)
  (iv) reflection on sin (*avāyāṇuppehā*)

The *Tattvārtha Sūtra* (9.7) enumerates twelve reflections. They are:

  (i) reflection on transitoriness (*anityānuprekṣā*)
  (ii) reflection on there being no refuge (*aśaraṇānuprekṣā*)
  (iii) reflection on birth and rebirth of living beings (*saṃsārānuprekṣā*)
  (iv) reflection on being alone (*ekatvānuprekṣā*)
  (v) reflection on the otherness (of body and soul; *anyatvānuprekṣā*)
  (vi) reflection on impurity (*aśucitvānuprekṣā*)
  (vii) reflection on influx (of karma; *āsravānuprekṣā*)
  (viii) reflection on restraint (*saṃvarānuprekṣā*)
  (ix) reflection on the destruction of karma (*nirjarānuprekṣā*)
  (x) reflection on the world (*lokānuprekṣā*)
  (xi) reflection on the difficulty of attaining enlightenment (*bodhidurlabhānuprekṣā*)
  (xii) reflection on the truth well explained by the doctrine (*dharmasvākhyātatattvānuprekṣā*)

We see that the *Tattvārtha Sūtra* includes the four reflections connected with "pious meditation," but not the four connected with "pure meditation."[9] This list, in the same or a slightly different order, and sometimes substituting *bhāvanā* for *anuprekṣā*, occurs in numerous other works, some of them late canonical (*Mahānisīha, Maraṇasamāhī*) or early non canonical (Kundakunda, Vaṭṭakera, Śivārya).[10] But the four reflections of "pure meditation" are absent from all of these lists. This supports the view that "pure meditation" was no longer attainable when these lists were made. Interestingly, Śivārya's *Bhagavatī-Ārādhanā* (1705, 1710) describes all twelve of the reflections as supports (*ālambana*) of "pious meditation" (*dharmya dhyāna*).

The reasons why "pure meditation" came to be looked upon as no longer attainable in this world seem clear. It appears to be the almost unavoidable consequence of the gradual exaltation of the Jina, the enlightened Jaina master, and of the state of liberation preached by him. A comparable development took place in Buddhism, where already superhuman qualities came to be ascribed to Arhats[11] and release was postponed to a next life.[12]

Whatever the reason that "pure meditation" came to be excluded from actual practice, it is clear that all existing practice had henceforth to be assimilated into the descriptions of "pious meditation." ("Afflicted *dhyāna*" and "wrathful *dhyāna*" were, very understandably, considered bad forms of meditation.) This means that two historical developments—first, the addition of "pious meditation" under the heading "meditation" (*dhyāna*), and second, the exclusion of "pure meditation" from it—left later meditators with a canonical "description of meditation" that was never meant for such a purpose.[13]

Postcanonical Meditation

It can cause no surprise that the practice of meditation has often been neglected in the subsequent history of Jainism. Yet Jainism never totally abandoned it. Adelheid Mette, in "Gotama und die Asketen," has drawn attention to a legend from the early postcanonical *Āvaśyakacūrṇi*, in which Mahāvīra's main disciple, Gotama, emphasizes the importance of thought control (*dhyānanigraha*) above outward signs of penance.[14] This tendency persisted. A number of later Jaina works deal with meditation. But how did these later authors treat the subject? One option was to simply repeat the canonical classification, thus ignoring the problem. Several authors, however, chose other solutions, such as the following:

> 1. An obvious step to take was to drop afflicted (*ārta*) and wrathful (*raudra*) *dhyāna* from the canonical classification, and retain only pious (*dharmya*) and pure (*śukla*) *dhyāna*. This is done in Vīrasena's *Dhavalā* on the *Ṣaṭkhaṃḍāgama Sūtra* 5.4.26 (13, 70–88). Another interesting feature of the description in the *Dhavalā* is that the only difference between "pious meditation" and "pure meditation" is stated to lie in the duration: short in the former, long in the latter (74–75). Nothing in the canonical description of these two forms of meditation warrants such an idea.

2. An extension of the canonical description are the four types of *dhyāna* called *piṇḍastha, padastha, rūpastha,* and *rūpātīta*. These are looked upon as belonging to the fourth manifestation of "pious meditation": "examination of forms" (*saṃsthānavicaya*). They are mentioned in a number of works, among them Yogīndudeva's *Yogasāra* (verse 98) and Śubhacandra's *Jñānārṇava* (chapters 37–40). The lengthy description of these forms of meditation in the *Jñānārṇava* shows that they consist in visualizing objects and *mantras* inside and outside the body; the *rūpātīta* meditation, in particular, has as its object "the highest self" (*paramātman*), which consists of consciousness and bliss (*cidānandamaya*) and is without form (*amūrta*). Since these are not notions we find in early Jainism but which *are* common in many forms of Hinduism, a suspicion of influence by similar forms of Hindu meditation seems justified. We do indeed find the same four kinds of meditation mentioned and comparably described in a number of Hindu texts, among them the *Kubjikāmata Tantra* (chapters 17–19), the *Mālinīvijayottara Tantra* (chapters 2 and 19), Abhinavagupta's *Tantrāloka* (10.241 f.), the *Navacakreśvara Tantra* (Mahāprajña, *Jaina Yoga*, 9), and the *Gurugītā* (verses 119 f.).[15] Note that by adopting these forms of meditation the Jainas could interpret *dharmya dhyāna* as a form of real "meditation," not of "thinking."

3. A far more drastic departure from the scriptures is made by Haribhadra in his *Yogadṛṣṭisamuccaya* (verses 5–6). Haribhadra does not deny that what he writes goes beyond the scriptures:[16] "This [kind of Yoga] called '[Yoga of] competence' is best; its means have been indicated in the scriptures [but] its range goes beyond them in matters of detail because of the abundance of energy. / The precise causes leading to the state called *siddhi* are not in their totality correctly understood by the Yogins from the scriptures alone." Haribhadra then proceeds to collect information on "this best form of Yoga" from "various works on Yoga," as he admits towards the end of his book (verse 207). The course of Yoga that he describes consists of eight stages. These stages are said to correspond with the eight stages mentioned in works by other authors, among them Patañjali.[17] All of these stages cover far more than meditation alone, but even in the last stages nothing resembling the canonical descriptions of meditation shows up. Haribhadra's break with tradition is complete in this respect.

4. Hemacandra's *Yogaśāstra* constitutes a special case. Hemacandra describes traditional forms of meditation in chapters (*prakāśa*) 7 through 11. Here he follows to a large extent earlier texts—in particular the *Jñānārṇava*; this means that he includes forms of meditation such as *piṇḍastha, padastha, rūpastha,* and *rūpātīta*. What makes Hemacandra special is his twelfth chapter. It begins with a verse that deserves to be quoted: "What is learnt from the ocean of scriptures [and] from the mouth of the teacher has here been completely shown; now [however] the pure truth as it has been obtained through experience will be explained."[18] From what

follows in chapter 12 it is clear that something quite different from what precedes it has been introduced. Most noteworthy is Hemacandra's insistence on not using constraint. If one exerts no restraint on the mind it will reach peace, not otherwise: "Wherever the mind goes, don't restrain it from [going] there; for what is restrained becomes stronger, what is not restrained becomes peaceful. / The mind is like an elephant in rut, which becomes stronger when restrained with effort, but comes to peace after satisfying its needs without restraint."[19] Nothing could better illustrate the remarkability of Hemacandra's views in the context of Jainism than the example of an elephant that must satisfy its sexual needs. Equally remarkable is verse 51, in which Hemacandra expresses indifference concerning the question of whether the result of these practices is liberation or not: "It may be liberation or not, but it certainly is the highest bliss, in which all forms of happiness appear as if nothing."[20] The editor of the *Yogaśāstra*, Muni Jambuvijaya, has found very similar ideas, often expressed in virtually identical words, in a work titled *Amanaska Yoga*, which is attributed to Gorakṣa Nātha. It seems therefore that Hemacandra again introduced new practices into the Jaina tradition, beside or perhaps rather instead of the traditional practices. In this case, the "traditional" practices included the additions made by such authors as Śubhacandra.

5. One further innovation that has taken place in recent years must be mentioned. Ācārya Mahāprajña (1920–2010) of the Terāpantha tradition of the Śvetāmbara sect of Jainism introduced, in 1975, what he called *prekṣā-dhyāna*, "*prekṣā* meditation." Samani Pratibha Pragya, who is preparing a doctoral dissertation on this innovation, points out in a recent article that this innovation was the result of an encounter with modern Buddhist systems of meditation.[21] Moreover, she clarifies that "*prekṣā* meditation becomes a means of purification rather than liberation." For details about the precise influences that Ācārya Mahāprajña underwent (the Buddhist *vipassanā* meditation taught by the Burmese teacher S. N. Goenka played an important role) and the way he used these influences to create this form of meditation, we will have to wait until the completion of Samani Pratibha Pragya's doctoral dissertation.[22]

Discontinuity and Innovation

These few examples must suffice to show that the history of Jaina meditation is not continuous. The canonical description that came to be held authoritative was itself the result of scholastic activity that had little understanding of the practice of meditation. Those later authors who had a practical interest in meditation felt free to work rather independently from the canonical description, often borrowing elements from non-Jaina schools of meditation.

One of the reasons for this peculiar development was, as we have seen, the hand that people of greater scholastic than meditational capability had in the development and interpretation of the canonical texts. Another factor must have been the relatively minor role played by meditation in Jaina circles. It is true that every now and then there were individuals who had a strong interest in its practice, and this might sometimes lead to a "revival" in a certain period and region, such as we seem to be witnessing today among the Terapanthis of northern India. But these individuals had to start almost from scratch, so to speak. They had to look for a teacher among the Jainas, but perhaps more often elsewhere. They also had to decide how far the canonical guidelines could be considered adequate. This led to the peculiar developments to which the preceding pages draw attention.

Notes

1. "Certainly it is difficult to avoid the conclusion that later Jain writers discussed [meditation] only because participation in the pan-Indian socio-religious world made it necessary to do so" (Dundas, *Jains*, 167).

2. For details, see Bronkhorst, *Two Traditions*, chap. 3; and Schubring, *Doctrine of the Jainas*, 313 ff. For a brief characterization of the difference between Buddhism and Jainism as presented in the early Buddhist texts, see Bronkhorst, *Buddhist Teaching in India*, 44 ff.

3. A *muhūrta* often corresponds to forty-eight minutes, but the term can also be used loosely to refer to any short period of time.

4. See Dundas, *Jains*, 167: "The fact that an early source . . . uses the term *dhyāna* with reference to carnivorous birds contemplating fish and heretics considering sensual pleasures suggests that the term in origin implied for the Jains not so much calm meditation as unhealthy and obsessive brooding."

5. See *Viyāhapannatti Sutta* 25.7.217, 237 f./580, 600 f.; and *Uvavāiya*, section 30. The confusion is complete in *Āvassaya Sutta* 4.23.4, where the monk is made to *repent* these four types of *dhyāna*; obviously only the first two are such as should be repented of, and these are not forms of meditation.

6. Hemacandra, *Yogaśāstra* 11.4: "Duṣkaraṃ apy ādhunikaiḥ śukladhyānaṃ yathāśāstram." The editor of the *Yogaśāstra*, Muni Jambuvijaya, quotes in this connection *Tattvānuśāsana* 36: "Dhyātuṃ śuklam ihākṣamān aidaṃyugīnān uddiśya" (1149).

7. See Bronkhorst, "Chronology of the Tattvārtha Sūtra," 176, 179f.

8. The order is slightly different in *Uvavāiya*, section 30.

9. Perhaps *aśucitva-* must be identified with *asubha-* or *asubhaya-*, as it is substituted by the latter in at least one text; see Upadhye, *Swāmi-Kumāra's Kārttikeyānuprekṣā*, 14 (*Maraṇasamāhī*).

10. See Upadhye, *Swāmi-Kumāra's Kārttikeyānuprekṣā*, Intr.

11. See Bareau, "Les controverses relatives."

12. In later times, the reason adduced for this was often that liberation would become possible after rebirth in the time of a future Buddha, especially Maitreya; see Kloppenborg, "Place of Maitreya," 47.

13. This is not to say that the canonical description of "pure meditation" is very satisfactory. Hemacandra (*Yogaśāstra* 11.11), for example, rightly points out that the last two stages of "pure meditation" concern the body rather than the mind.

14. See Mette, "Gotama und die Asketen."

15. See Goudriaan, "Introduction, History and Philosophy," 61; 1981: 54; and Gupta, "Modes of Worship and Meditation," 178.

16. Haribhadra, *Yogadṛṣṭisamuccaya* verses 5–6: "Śāstrasandarśitopāyas tadatikrāntagocaraḥ / śaktyudrekād viśeṣeṇa sāmarthyākhyo'yam uttamaḥ // siddhyākhyapadasamprāptihetubh edā na tattvataḥ / śāstrād evāvagamyante sarvathaiveha yogibhiḥ."

17. The authors and their lists of stages are enumerated in Haribhadra's own commentary on verse 16, and are tabulated in K. K. Dixit's edition, also under verse 16.

18. Hemacandra, *Yogaśāstra* 12.1: "Śrutasindhor gurumukhato yad adhigataṃ tad iha darśitaṃ samyak / anubhavasiddham idānīṃ prakāśyate tattvam idam amalam."

19. Hemacandra, *Yogaśāstra* 12.27–28: "Ceto'pi yatra yatra pravartate no tatas tato vāryam / adhikībhavati hi vāritam avāritaṃ śāntim upayāti // matto hastī yatnān nivāryamāṇo'dhikībhavati yadvat / anivāritas tu kāmān labdhvā śāmyati manas tadvat."

20. Hemacandra, *Yogaśāstra* 12.51: "Mokṣo'stu mā'stu yadi vā paramānandas tu vidyate sa khalu / yasmin nikhilasukhāni pratibhāsante na kiñcid iva."

21. Pragya, "Prekṣā Meditation."

22. See the various publications of Yuvācārya Mahāprajña in the bibliography. The "revival" initiated by Mahāprajña may not be unconnected with the interest in meditation among non-Indians; see, for example, Mahāprajña, *Prekṣādhyāna*, 3.

Bibliography

Note: For further bibliographical information, the following works may be consulted: *Jainendra Siddhānta Kośa*; Dige, *Jaina Yoga kā Ālocanātmaka Adhyayana*; Mahāprajña, *Jaina Yoga*, 7–12 (Prastuti); Mehatā and Kāpaḍiyā, *Jaina Sāhitya kā Bṛhad Itihāsa*, 227–266; Tatia, "Jaina Yoga."

Abhinavagupta. *Tantrāloka*. Edited, with commentary by Rājānaka Jayaratha, by Madhusūdan Kaul. Kashmir Series of Texts and Studies, no. 41. Vol. 7 (Āhnikas X, XI and XII). Bombay, 1924.

Āvassaya Sutta. Edited by Muni Shri Puṇyavijayaji and Pt. Amritlāl Mohanlāl Bhojak. Jaina-Āgama-Series no. 15. Bombay: Shri Mahāvīra Jaina Vidyālaya. 1977.

Bareau, André. "Les controverses relatives à la nature de l'Arhant dans le Bouddhisme ancien." *Indo-Iranian Journal* 1 (1957): 241–250.

Bronkhorst, Johannes. *Buddhist Teaching in India*. Boston: Wisdom Publications, 2009.

———. "On the Chronology of the Tattvārtha Sūtra and Some Early Commentaries." *Wiener Zeitschrift für die Kunde Südasiens* 29 (1985): 155–184.

———. *The Two Traditions of Meditation in Ancient India*. Stuttgart: Franz Steiner Verlag Wiesbaden, 1986. (Alt- und Neu-Indische Studien, 28.)

Dige, Arhat Dāsa Baṇḍobā. *Jaina Yoga kā Ālocanātmaka Adhyayana*. Varanasi, India: Pārśvanātha Vidyāśrama Śodha Saṃsthāna, 1981. (Pārśvanātha Vidyāśrama Granthamālā, 23.)

Dundas, Paul. *The Jains*. 2nd ed. London: Routledge, 2002.

Goudriaan, Teun. "Hindu Tantric literature in Sanskrit." In Goudriaan and Gupta, *Hindu Tantric and Śākta Literature*, 1–172.

———. "Introduction, History and Philosophy." In Gupta, Hoens, and Goudriaan, *Hindu Tantrism*, 1–67.

Goudriaan, Teun, and Sanjukta Gupta. *Hindu Tantric and Śākta Literature*. Wiesbaden, Germany: Otto Harrassowitz, 1981. (A History of Indian Literature II, 2.)

Gupta, Sanjukta. "Modes of Worship and Meditation." In Gupta, Hoens, and Goudriaan, *Hindu Tantrism*, 119–185.

Gupta, Sanjukta, Dirk Jan Hoens, and Teun Goudriaan. *Hindu Tantrism*. Leiden: E. J. Brill, 1979. (Handbuch der Orientalistik 2/4/2.)

Gurugītā. Ganeshpuri, India: Shree Gurudev Ashram, 1972.

Haribhadra. *Yogadṛṣṭisamuccaya*. (1) Edited, with Haribhadra's own commentary, by Muni Jayasuṃdara Vijaya, in Hāribhadrayogabhāratī. Bombay: Divyadarśana Trust, n.d. Vi. Saṃ. 2036. 67–129. (2) Edited, with English translation, notes, and introduction, by K. K. Dixit, in Yogadṛṣṭisamuccaya and Yogaviṃśikā of Ācārya Haribhadrasūri. Ahmedabad, India: Lalbhai Dalpatbhai Bharatiya Sanskriti Vidyamandira. (Lalbhai Dalpatbhai Series, No. 27.)

Hemacandra. *Yogaśāstra*. Edited by Muni Jambuvijaya. Bombay: Jaina Sāhitya Vikāsa Maṇḍala. 1977, 1981, 1986.

Jacobi, Hermann. "Eine Jaina-Dogmatik: Umāsvāti's Tattvārthādhigama Sūtra." *Zeitschrift der Deutschen Morgenländischen Gesellschaft* 60 (1906): 287–325 and 512–551.

Jainendra Siddhānta Kośa. By Jinendra Vaṇī. Parts 1–4. New Delhi: Bhāratīya Jñānapīṭha, 1970–1973. (Jñānapīṭha Mūrtidevī Granthamālā: Sanskrit Granthas 38, 40, 42, 44.)

Kloppenborg, Ria. "The Place of Maitreya in Early and Theravāda Buddhism and the Conditions for Rebirth in His Time." *30th International Congress of Human Sciences in Asia and North Africa, 1976*. South Asia 3 (1982): 37–48.

Kubjikāmata Tantra. Kulālikāmnāya version. Critical edition by T. Goudriaan and J. A. Schoterman. Leiden: E. J. Brill. 1988. (Orientalia Rheno-Traiectina, 30.)

Mahāprajña, Yuvācārya. *Cetanā kā Urdhvāropaṇa*. 3rd ed. Cūrū (Rajasthan). India: Ādarśa Sāhitya Saṃgha, 1980.

———. *Jaina Yoga* (in Hindi). Cūrū (Rajasthan), India: Ādarśa Sāhitya Saṃgha, 1978. (2nd ed. 1980).

———. *Kisa ne kahā Mana Caṃcala hai*. Cūrū (Rajasthan) , India: Ādarśa Sāhitya Saṃgha, 1979. (2nd ed. 1981).

———. *Mana ke Jīte Jīta*. 4th ed. Cūrū (Rajasthan), India: Ādarśa Sāhitya Saṃgha, 1981.

———. *Mind: Beyond Mind*. Translated by S. K. L. Goswami. Churu, India: Adarsh Sahitya Sangh, 1980.

———. *Prekṣādhyāna: Ādhāra aura Svarūpa*. Ladnun (Rajasthan), India: Jaina Viśva Bhāratī, 1980.

———. *Prekṣādhyāna: Śvāsa-Prekṣā*. Ladnun, India: Jaina Viśva Bhāratī, 1981.

Mālinīvijayottara Tantra. Edited by Madhusūdan Kaul. Bombay, 1922. (Kashmir Series of Texts and Studies, no. XXXVII.)

Mehatā, Mohanalāla, and Hīrālāla R. Kāpaḍiyā. *Jaina Sāhitya kā Bṛhad Itihāsa*. Part 4. Varanasi, India: Pārśvanātha Vidyāśrama Śodha Saṃsthāna, Hindu University, 1968. (Pārśvanātha Vidyāśrama Granthamālā, 12.)

Mette, Adelheid. "Gotama und die Asketen—Eine jinistische Legende." *Studien zur Indologie und Iranistik* 13/14 (Festschrift Wilhelm Rau, 1987), 139–148.

Pragya, Samani Pratibha. "Prekṣā Meditation: History and Methods." *Jaina Studies: Newsletter of the Centre of Jaina Studies, SOAS* 8 (March 2013): 36–37.

Schubring, Walther. *The Doctrine of the Jainas, Described after the Old Sources*. Translated from the revised German edition by Wolfgang Beurlen. 2nd rev. ed. Delhi: Motilal Banarsidass, 2000.

Śīvārya. *Bhagavatī-Ārādhanā*. Edited, with Hindi translation, by Pandit Kailaschandra Shastri. Sholapur, India: Jain Samskriti Samrakshaka Sangha, 1978.

Śubhacandra. *Jñānārṇava*. Edited, with Hindi translation, by Pannālāla Bākalīvāla. Agas, India: Śrīmad Rājacandra Āśrama, 1975.

Tatia, Nathmal. "Jaina Yoga." In *Studies in Jaina Philosophy*, by Nathmal Tatia, 261–304. Banaras, India: Jain Cultural Research Society, 1951.

Tattvārtha Sūtra. See Jacobi, "Eine Jaina-Dogmatik."

Ṭhāṇaṃga Sutta. (1) Edited by Muni Jambuvijaya. Bombay: Shrī Mahāvīra Jaina Vidyālaya. 1985. (Jaina-Āgama-Series No. 3, 1–322.) (2) Edited by Muni Nathamal. Ladnun, India: Jain Vishwa Bhārati, n.d. V. S. 2031. (Anga Suttāni I, 489–823.)

Upadhye, A. N., ed. *Swāmi-Kumāra's Kārttikeyānuprekṣā.* Agas, India: Srimad Rajchandra Ashram, 1960.

Uttarajjhayaṇa. (1) The Uttarādhyayanasūtra, edited by Jarl Charpentier. New Delhi: Ajay Book Service. 1980. 2) Edited by Muni Shri Puṇyavijayaji and Pt. Amritlāl Mohanlāl Bhojak. Bombay: Shri Mahāvīra Jaina Vidyālaya. 1977. (Jaina-Āgama-Series No. 15, 85–329.)

Uvavāiya. Das Aupapātika Sūtra, erstes Upānga der Jaina. I. Theil. Einleitung, Text und Glossar. Von Ernst Leumann. Leipzig, 1883. Genehmigter Nachdruck, Kraus Reprint Ltd., Nendeln, Liechtenstein, 1966. (Abhandlungen für die Kunde des Morgenlandes, VIII. Band, No. 2.)

Vīrasena: *Dhavalā.* In: The Ṣaṭkhaṃḍāgama of Puṣpadanta and Bhūtabali, with the Commentary Dhavalā of Vīrasena, Vol. XIII, edited with (Hindi) translation, notes and indexes, by Hiralal Jain. Bhilsa (M. B.): Jaina Sāhitya Uddhāraka Fund Kāryālaya, 1955.

Viyāhapaṇṇatti Sutta / Bhagavaī. (1) Edited by Pt. Bechardas J. Doshi, assisted by Pt. Amritlal Mohanlal Bhojak. Bombay: Shrī Mahāvīra Jaina Vidyālaya, 1974–1978. (Jaina-Āgama-Series No. 4.) (2) Edited by Muni Nathamal. Ladnun, India: Jain Viswa Bhārati. V. S. 2031. (Anga Suttāni II.)

Yogīndudeva. *Yogasāra.* In: Sri Yogīndudeva's Paramātmaprakāśa and Yogasāra, edited, with Hindi translation, by A. N. Upadhye. Agas, India: Shrimad Rajachandra Ashram, 1978. (Srimad Rajachandra Jaina Sastramala, 3.)

Nām Simran *in the Sikh Religion*

When a Sikh friend in India on one occasion wished to communicate what in his view was a sensitive matter regarding his family and himself, he started by reciting *vāhigurū*—the sacred Sikh formula representing God—and then began to explain the circumstances. A few sentences into the talk, however, he paused and closed his eyes to repeat the sacred formula a few more times, and then again continued with the explanation. In a similar fashion, our conversation evolved, with several shorter intermissions for his low-voiced recitative meditation on the divine. The friend was a *khālsā* Sikh who routinely dedicated himself to readings from the Sikh scripture, Gurū Granth Sāhib, and practiced *nām simran*, remembrance and recitation of the divine name. In a moment when he felt distressed for having private matters revealed to someone else, he sought divine support by resorting to repetitions of *vāhigurū*, believing that this would transform his inner fear into courage and provide peace and calm when feelings ran high.

The Sikh religion does not specify a single meditation technique to be practiced for spiritual gains, but emphasizes the importance of inner loving devotion (*bhakti*) to a supreme and nonincarnated god. The Punjabi language and Sikh terminology include several words derived from the broader Indian religious culture that can be translated as "meditation" in the English language and often carry wider connotations to devotion and worship.[1] What is presented as a meditative practice of the Sikhs in contemporary interpretations, however, is *nām simran*, which literally means "to remember" or "to hold in mind" (*simran*) the divine name (*nām*). Commentators on the Sikh teaching have frequently engaged in discussions on the interior aspects of *nām simran* from a textual, historical, and philosophical viewpoint, while downplaying external and ritual dimensions of the practice. The practice of *nām simran* has been presented as a "meditation" during which Sikh disciples internally contemplate on the nature and qualities of God and constantly hold the divine name in remembrance. This meditative practice is believed to internally transform humans, who gradually become less self-centered and realize the divine power in all—an experience that eventually leads to liberation.

Based on fieldwork among Sikhs in India, this chapter explores some understandings and practices of *nām simran* in lived practices among contemporary Sikhs.[2] After a brief introduction to the Sikh religion, the chapter exemplifies how the concept and practice of *nām simran* unfolds in interpretations of the gurus' teaching and is mentioned in manuals for the Sikh code of conduct. These normative texts are important sources for legitimizing beliefs and practices among the Sikhs today, even if they do not provide detailed instructions on specific meditation techniques. The practice of *nām simran* is rather presented as a broader spiritual discipline, which includes various mental and physical activities to appropriate and internalize the divine name, such as remembrance, contemplation, chanting, singing, and recitation. An ethnographic description of individual and collective practices among contemporary Sikhs in India further illustrates how *nām simran* is understood to be both spontaneous and highly formalized methods of reciting the sacred formula *vāhigurū*, sometimes within restricted time and space and with distinct breathing techniques. From this perspective, *nām simran* is a discipline that incorporates both mental and recitative meditation practices and that ideally should have a firm base in a sincere devotional stance of the devotee. While interpretations of normative texts present realization of the divine and liberation from the cycle of birth and death as the ultimate goal of the Sikh discipline, local people often find these soteriological discussions remote and consider liberation granted to only a spiritually gifted few. Instead they may ascribe a wide range of spiritual, material, and bodily effects and meanings to contemplations and recitations of *vāhigurū* that are derived from and adjusted to their own situational contexts.

The Sikh Religion

Sikhism is one of the youngest world religions today, with about twenty-three million adherents. The large majority resides in India (more than nineteen million) and is concentrated in the northwestern state of Punjab, even if Sikhs can be found on almost every continent due to an extensive migration.[3] Sikh historiography traces the origin and uniqueness of Sikhism to the first guru, Nānak (1469–1539), who in his late twenties had a mystical experience and set out on extensive travels for two decades to refine and spread his message before he settled in Kartarpur (Punjab) and established a community of Sikhs, meaning "disciples." Scholarship has frequently approached the beginning of Sikhism from a more contextual perspective to demonstrate that Gurū Nānak was firmly rooted in the Sant tradition of Northern India, which he reinterpreted in light of his own experiences. The Sant tradition flourished in Hindi-speaking areas from the fifteenth century onward and drew its elements primarily from Vaiṣṇava bhakti, the Nāth *yogī* tradition and Sufism. The tradition was more loosely organized around different Sants or saint-poets of various backgrounds, such as Kabīr, Nāmdev, and Ravidās, who eschewed formalized religious worship, asceticism, and caste distinctions in Indian society and emphasized inner and true devotion (*bhakti*) to a supreme formless god beyond qualifications (*nirguṇa*), remembrance of God through the divine name (*nām*), devotion to the guru, and the importance of a holy congregation (*satsang*) for spiritual progress.[4]

In line with these ideas, Gurū Nānak's teaching was centered on the monotheistic concept of a timeless god who creates and rules the whole universe by a divine order (*hukam*) and is known to humans through its name (*nām*) and word (*śabad*). Like other Indian religions, the Sikh teaching presumes that humans are subjected to the cycle of birth and rebirth and the laws of karma that uphold bonds to life and determine conditions in the present and coming births. A human life provides a unique opportunity to be freed from transmigration and attain liberation by developing a relationship with God that is based on devotion and eventually will obliterate human self-centeredness (*haumai*) and attachments to the world (*māyā*). For Gurū Nānak humans do not pursue liberation by renunciation from the social world, but they should cultivate devotion and divine qualities while living a domestic life and actively working for the betterment of society. It is commonly held that Gurū Nānak ensured the preservation of his teaching by committing his devotional compositions to writing in the *gurmukhī* script (lit. "the mouth of the guru") and establishing a succession line of human gurus who operated as spiritual leaders for almost two hundred years.

A central event in Sikh history occurred when the tenth guru, Gobind Singh (1666–1708), in 1699 declared the Sikhs as *khālsā*, "the pure," and formed a new religious and military community and identity for the Sikhs. Disciples were requested to undergo an initiation ceremony and drink sanctified water over which the hymns of the gurus had been recited while stirring with a double-edged sword. The first five Sikhs who took the nectar were called "the five beloved" (*panj pyare*) and changed their original names to Singh, "lion." The initiated were expected to do daily readings of the gurus' hymns, abstain from intoxicants, and keep unshorn hair, a comb, a steel bracelet, a dagger, and a pair of breeches. The creation of *khālsā* has been interpreted as a transformation of Sikhism from a pacifist to a militarized community caused by political tensions between the Sikhs and the Mogul administration in the seventeenth century. By declaring *khālsā*, Gobind Singh initiated the process of dissolving his office of personal guru and shifted the authority to the Sikh community and the scripture.

In 1604 the fifth guru, Arjan (1563–1606), compiled the religious poetry of the first five Sikh gurus as well as compositions by like-minded Hindu and Muslim poet-saints of different traditions. A century later, the writings of the ninth guru, Tegh Bahādur (1621–1675), were added to what became the *Ādi Granth*, literally "the original book." By the time of Gobind Singh, the scripture had gained considerable status in the community, and this development reached its peak when in 1708 the guru on his deathbed declared the scripture as the eternal guru of the Sikhs. This decision marked the end to a succession line of human gurus, as the scripture, hereafter called the Gurū Granth, with an added suffix of reverence, Sāhib, succeeded to the office of guru and was endowed with the spiritual authority to guide the Sikhs.

Wherever the Sikhs have settled in the world today, the Gurū Granth Sāhib is the focal point of their religious life. A Sikh place of worship—the *gurdwārā*, or literally the "guru's door/house"—is by definition a place in which the scripture is ceremonially installed on a throne to receive worshippers. Almost every Sikh ceremony is conducted in the presence of the physical book, and hymns from the text are rendered in recitation (*pāth*) and devotional singing (*kīrtan*) and are explicated in oral expositions (*kathā*). The majority of Sikhs perceive the

Gurū Granth Sāhib as a collection of the historical Sikh gurus' divinely inspired utterances and teachings, simultaneously as the scripture is believed to be their living guru. Given this authority and status of scripture in Sikhism, the Gurū Granth Sāhib is the primary source for Sikh understandings on *nām simran*.

The Sikh scripture is not a manual providing metacommentaries and detailed instructions on how to perform meditative practices, but rather falls into the category of religious poetry, which over and over again eulogizes the significance and magnitude of devotion (*bhakti*). The confluence of verbal and musical components in Gurū Granth Sāhib anticipates that it is a "performative" text to be read and performed to music.[5] Consequently the text does not offer systematic analyses of Sikh beliefs and practices but presents a rich tapestry of devotional expressions that bear witness of the human gurus' religious experiences and messages dressed in poetic form. Rather than prescribing particular meditation techniques, the early Sikh sources unveil a much broader spiritual enterprise comprised of meditative and recitative practices, prayers, praises, and devotion of God that can be summarized in the doctrine and practice of *nām*.

Nām in the Sikh Tradition

The doctrine of *nām* is frequently presented as a key aspect of the Sikh teaching enshrined in Gurū Granth Sāhib. Innumerable verses in the scripture eulogize *nām* and leave little doubt that the gurus considered it a fundamental truth and a way toward liberation.[6] Already in *Japjī Sāhib*, the opening composition of the scripture, Gurū Nānak writes, "Early in the morning [*amritvela*] utter the True Name and reflect upon God's greatness."[7] Because of the centrality of *nām*, Sikh scholars have sometimes termed their religion *nām marga*, or "the way of *nām*,"[8] and suggested that Sikhism advocates a "science of *nām*."[9] The oft-quoted credo that states that Sikhs should recite and remember *nām* (*nām japō*), work hard and live truthful (*kirat karō*), and share their earnings with others (*vaṇḍ chhakō*), attributed to Gurū Nānak, is presented as a main principle in the guru's teaching and a moral imperative for all Sikhs. Given this importance, scholars and religious expounders of Gurū Granth Sāhib have been preoccupied with explaining how the concept and practice of *nām* can be interpreted from theological, historical, and psychological perspectives with a firm base in the scriptural verses.[10] Although Sikh interpretations of *nām* differ in details, one can distinguish two general approaches that explain *nām* as the goal and the method of spiritual progress.

First, *nām* signifies the divine name, which can be explained as "a summary expression for the whole nature of Akal Purakh [the Timeless One] and all that constitutes the divine being."[11] The Sikh scripture is teeming with more than a hundred individual names of gods in various religious traditions, such as Hari, Rām, Niraṇkār, Gopāl, Gobind, Prabhu, Nārāyan, and Allāh.[12] From a Sikh perspective, these attributive names are used for personal gods or for describing aspects of God, while *nām* signifies the universal divine power that sustains and directs the cosmos and is manifested in the world. In numerous verses of the

Gurū Granth Sāhib, *nām* is presented synonymously with "God," as an imma-
nent quality of the transcendent divine that existed before the creation and is
infused in the creation. Human beings can attain knowledge of the divine name
and secure the rewards it confers if they are able to perceive the divine order
and harmony that exist within and around all humans.

Many Sikhs believe that Gurū Nānak had a direct and mystical experience
of God, which laid the foundation of his spiritual teaching. Historical *janam-
sākhīs* (life stories) of Nānak, recorded from the seventeenth century onward,
dressed this central idea in prose stories that embroidered how the guru gathered into the divine presence to hear the voice of God and be given a celestial
bowl with the immortal nectar (*amrit*) of *nām*. By ingesting *nām*, Nānak was
invested with the office of guru and received a robe of honor that sanctified his
spiritual authority and mission.[13] As many Sikhs would assert, Nānak's teaching emanates from this revelatory experience, when he was imbued with the
divine name and returned to the world to mediate a divine message. By obeying
the commands of God and immersing himself in relentless meditation on the
divine name, Nānak became an enlightened guru for the world and opened up
a path toward liberation. Sikh disciples who have been graced with the power
and capacity to submit to this spiritual teaching are similarly able to realize
the divine.

Second, *nām* also refers to a spiritual discipline that includes a wide range of
devotional practices. In Sikh textual sources, as well as in the broader Sant tradition, remembrance of the divine name (*nām simran*) and repetition of the divine name (*nām japna*) stand out as two key methods by which commentators
have given various interpretations.[14] Considering that the Sikh gurus did not
hesitate to criticize their Hindu and Muslim contemporaries for reliance on formal rituals without inner commitment, scholars have often given preference to
interpretations that privilege interior and soteriological meanings of *nām simran*. According to the historian W. H. McLeod, for example, the literal understanding of *nām simran* is "nearer to a description of Guru Nanak's practice than
'repeating the Name,'" and the prescribed method for engrafting the divine into
the human mind and heart is "meditation on the nature of God, on His qualities and His attributes as revealed in the Word (*Śabad*)."[15] Another example is
given by the linguist Christopher Shackle and the historian Arvind-Pal Singh
Mandair, who emphasize the inner transformation of the human ego and describe *nām simran* as "the constant holding in remembrance of the Name, which
goes beyond ritualistic repetition to become a spontaneous form of loving meditation in which the ego is disappropriated."[16] Interpretations such as these impart a picture of *nām simran* as a discipline primarily involving contemplative
and meditative practices, while exterior acts, such as the recitation and repetition of sacred words and formulas, are given a secondary and instrumental
importance. As God is beyond birth and death and cannot incarnate in Sikh
theology, the object of focus for these exercises is the divine word (*śabad*) and
name (*nām*). The primary target for transformation is the human mind/heart
(*man*), which is considered to be a powerful mental and emotional faculty that

attempts to divert humans from their divine inner self and make their actions be driven by attachment to the world.

The discipline of *nām simran* is frequently presented as a progressive spiritual path on which a person gains different types of understanding and experiences, and ultimately consciousness and knowledge of God (*giān*). A model for this spiritual progression is found in *Japjī Sāhib*, which describes five *khaṇḍs*, or "realms"—duty, knowledge, effort, grace and truth—as representing different ascending or overlapping stages of spiritual development.[17] The five realms are supposed to correspond to a process of expanding the human consciousness and knowledge: In the first stages, perceptual and rational knowledge is attained through mental perception and intellectual reason, while the final stage—*sach khaṇḍ* or "the realm of truth"—implies a realization and union with the divine. This realization is not approached as an intellectual understanding of God but rather as a mystical experience, in which a person is graced with intuitive knowledge and unites with a higher truth.[18]

Different methods of implementing the guru's messages presumably evolved in the early Sikh community and came to include performances of silent meditation as well as verbal repetitions of sacred words and the singing of religious compositions.[19] Sikh narrative traditions, for example, provide a wealth of stories about the Sikh gurus' intensive and disciplined meditation (*tapasiā*) and about how they advised others to engage in various devotional and meditative practices.[20] Written manuals of the Sikh code of conduct, so-called *rahit-nāmās*, from the beginning of the eighteenth century present *nām simran* as an essential form of worship, in which Sikhs should engage. These documents reflect an attempt to define and standardize normative practices in writing, especially when the succession line of human gurus ended with the death of Gobind Singh in 1708, and the Sikh scripture ascended to the office of the guru. In the *Tanakhāh-nāmā*, attributed to Bhai Nand Lal, who many believe was a contemporary of Gobind Singh, a *khālsā* Sikh is defined as a person who "remains absorbed in the divine Name."[21] This *rahit-nāmā* tells how Bhai Nand Lal asked the guru about the fundamental deeds of the Sikhs, whereupon he got the ideals summarized by the words *nām* (divine name), *dān* (charity), and *ishnān* (bathing).[22] Later manuals similarly describe the meditation on and repetition, hearing, and reading of the divine name as defining practices for Sikhs who follow the gurus' teaching.[23] The present code of conduct from 1950 (*Sikh Rahit Maryādā*) states that meditation on *nām* should be an incorporated part of the Sikh personal life: The Sikhs are to wake up early in the morning, take a bath, contemplate on God (*akāl purakh*), and repeat *vāhigurū*.[24]

Textual sources indicate that at some point in history the Sikhs came to understand and use *vāhigurū*, literally meaning "wonderful guru," as the specific name for the divine and a sanctioned formula for meditative practices. The term *vāhigurū* is one of the many epithets for God mentioned in Gurū Granth Sāhib, and in later sources described as a *gurmantra* that was given by the historical gurus to their disciples for remembrance and meditation.[25] For example, the eighteenth-century *rahit-nāmā* of Daya Singh provides an instructive line about how continuous repetition of *vāhigurū* will imbue the human inner with the divine name: "The Singh's duty is to repeat the Word (*shabad*), to learn to wield weapons, and to enshrine the *mantra Vāh gurū* in his heart, repeating it with every breath in and every breath out, and thereby fixing it within his inner being (*man*)."[26] Sikh commentators frequently evoke references to the exegete Bhai Gurdas (1551–1636), who at the turn of the sixteenth century explained the term as being composed of four holy syllables—Vava, Haha, Gaga, and Rara—representing four divine names—Vāsudev, Hari, Gobind, and Rām—in the four ages of creation (*sat, dvāpar, tretā,* and *kali*).[27] From this understanding *vāhigurū* is considered to be the amalgam of different labels of a single and formless power, not to be associated with incarnated deities in the Hindu tradition. The four separate syllables joined into a compound represent different designations of the divine, which become powerful when brought together.[28]

A perusal of contemporary descriptions of the Sikh teaching suggests that *nām simran* is a unifying term for a spiritual discipline that may cover a wide range of individual and collective practices. It includes methods of silent contemplation during which the devotee inwardly reflects upon the nature and qualities of God, but also verbal repetition of words and sacred formulas that represent the divine name, such as *vāhigurū*. Singing devotional hymns (*kīrtan*) from the scripture is considered another form of *nām simran* through which devotees can attune with a higher power. In the widest definition it implies a larger devotional lifestyle in which a person actively seeks divine knowledge by reading and understanding the guru's teaching in Gurū Granth Sāhib, participates in various religious activities, upholds moral standards, and works for others in their social life while remembering God in every thought, speech, and deed. Various modern movements and groups (*jathās*) within Sikhism have further nuanced this picture by stipulating their own distinctive codes of conduct and techniques for performing *nām simran*.[29]

The following sections provide a few ethnographic glimpses of how contemporary Sikhs in the local setting of Varanasi may interpret, perform, and provide a wide range of meanings to *nām simran*. As the description illustrates, *nām simran* has become a highly formalized practice of reciting the *gurmantra* with specific breathing techniques and concerns about time and space. The practice is not merely a mental activity but also a recitative meditation that combines sound, word, meaning, and devotion.

Individual Practices of *Nām Simran*

The ways in which local Sikhs have come to practice *nām simran* in their religious and social lives are countless. In everyday life, people may repeat the name of God, *vāhigurū*, internally when they are riding a scooter, walking, traveling by bus, performing domestic duties, or when going to bed. In moments of emotional distress or physical discomfort, many Sikhs recite the name of God in a voiced or soundless manner to gain inner strength and courage. This is particularly noticeable in speech acts that seek divine assistance to shield from human or supernatural ill-wishers. An elderly Sikh man in Varanasi said he used to repeat the *gurmantra* to ward off all possible dangers caused by humans and spirits when he sometimes had to walk alone through the city in the middle of the night. When facing evildoers in reality or in dreams, uttering *vāhigurū* is believed to invoke the power behind the name for protection.

Among Sikhs who have undergone the initiation ceremony and follow the normative *khālsā* discipline more strictly, a *nām simran* technique is occasionally used for greetings. When two friends meet, they first embrace each other and adjust their breathing to one another and then repeat *vāhigurū* in unison for a couple of minutes. The chanting will frame their conversation and only after having formally ended the session with an exclamation of the standardized *khālsā* ovation (*vāhigurū jī kā khālsā, vāhigurū jī kī fateh*), they will start everyday talk. According to a popular opinion, the gurus instituted recitative repetition of the divine name (*nām japna*) as a devotional practice for Sikhs in general, and for illiterates in particular, since repeating *vāhigurū* numerous times with inner devotion and pure intentions can grant them the same fruits as readings from the Sikh scripture.

Although *nām simran* can be performed spontaneously in numerous improvised ways and is not regulated by strict techniques as are meditation practices in other Indian traditions, there are a few general directives that aim to create a suitable context for the exercise. Preferably a devotee should create a daily routine of performing *nām simran* at least once a day. The "nectar hours" (*amritvela*) from 2 to 6 a.m. are considered to be an auspicious time of the day and the most favorable for contemplation, when the mind is fresh and the surroundings peaceful. As the devotee is expected to contemplate the divine attentively without distractions, the ideal environment is a secluded and quiet spot, whether this can be found at home, in the *gurdwārā*, or elsewhere. To aid the concentration, many of my interlocutors emphasized the importance of sitting on the ground in a straight and alert position, preferably in a posture with the legs folded and drawn up, without leaning against a wall.

The repetition of *vāhigurū* can be uttered loudly or soundlessly in unison with the heartbeat or the breath. According to a distinct breathing technique that is sometimes used, the devotee should utter the first syllables of the *gurmantra*—*vāhi*—while inhaling, followed by an exhalation of the last syllables—*gurū*—with long intonation on the ending vowel. During a practical demonstration of the method in Varanasi, a younger man said that *vāhi* should emanate from the inside, as if being pulled out from the belly button, whereas the sound of *gurū* flows from the mouth. When the *gurmantra* is repeated at a hurried pace, the first syllable is replaced by the sound of an exaggerated inhalation and a sharper pronunciation of the consonants—*gru*—when breathing out. To assist the repetition, the devotee can use a rosary with 27 or 108 beads, each of which is rolled off with the forefinger and thumb to the utterance of the *gurmantra*. There is no instruction on how many times *vāhigurū* should be recited, but rather the guiding rule seems to be as much as possible according to individual ability.

Although many of these individual practices stand out as ritualized techniques that hardly correspond to definitions of meditation as a mental technique for self-cultivation or inner transformation, many Sikhs will emphasize over and over again that merely a mechanical repetition of *vāhigurū* from one's lips is not sufficient. Different formalized ways of repeating sacred words, either soundlessly or audibly, can be considered as effective means to attentively focus the mind and deepen the contemplation and will prove favorable only when propelled by sincere devotion and concentration. While these are basic ideals to strive toward, many would quickly admit to the difficulty of following such a discipline in everyday life, for varying reasons. While conversing on this subject, a middle-aged woman in Varanasi stigmatized herself as a "sinner" because she used to keep later hours and could not wake up in the early nectar-hours for *nām simran*. A younger man, who indeed rose before dawn to devote himself to recitative meditation, admitted that his concentration was frequently tottering. Whenever this happened he just broke off his repetition and performed a prayer in which he pleaded to God for more strength the following day. The attentiveness, dedication, and power of mind necessary to keep up a regular and disciplined individual practice is ultimately considered to be a gift graced by God.

Collective Practices of *Nām Simran*

Participation in *sādh sangat*—the assembly of like-minded who have gathered for devotional singing and chanting—is important in the Sikh religion and is considered extremely favorable to concentration and encouragement. During daily ceremonies in the *gurdwārā*, Sikh musicians (*rāgis*) frequently insert shorter sessions of *nām simran*, accompanied with harmonium and tabla, as a prelude to or conclusion of the ordinary program. The musicians may lead the tuneful chanting for several minutes to create a religious atmosphere and engage the congregation in meditation. Similarly, when preparing and distributing food from the communal kitchen of the *gurdwārā*, devotees usually repeat *satnām vāhigurū* (true name, wonderful guru) to allow every portion of vegetables, rice, and bread be accompanied by the name of God and to call attention to the divine giver. Whenever the Sikh scripture is to be moved from one location to another, the assembled people likewise chant the *gurmantra* in a melodious chorus.[30]

A far more formalized type of collective *nām simran* are "gatherings" (*samāgams*) or "spiritual practices" (*sādhnās*) that are organized in *gurdwārās* or at private houses by groups of devotees who undertake a discipline to sing and repeat the *gurmantra* jointly for one or sometimes several hours. During my fieldwork in Varanasi, around thirty Sikhs used to assemble in the house of a family every Sunday morning at 4 am. Refraining from unnecessary talk, they removed their sandals before entering a selected room and took seats on the floor, men and women in separate rows. To cut themselves off from social reality and create a meditative space, they closed the doors, drew the curtains and put out all lights in the room. In darkness the host would put on a cassette tape titled "simran practice" (*simran sādhnā*), which was a recorded version of a devotional performance by a pious Sikh musician who combined the singing of hymns from the scripture with repetitions of *vāhigurū*. While keeping their eyes shut, people would listen and soon start to join in, imitating the recorded performance that was reverberating in the confined space. After some thirty minutes the devotional music would fade into a unison chanting of the name of God—*vāhigurū*—led by the recorded performer. Gradually the sound of instruments disappeared and the pace of the repetition intensified. All participants regulated their breathing to the pronunciation—inhaling with the utterance of *vāhi* and aspirating *gurū*—at a faster speed until every respiring second in the room was imbued with loud polyphonic sounds of female and male voices. Depending on which tape was selected, the intensive repetition under control of the breath could continue for several minutes, relapse into a slower melodious singing, and then be repeated again. This oscillation between slow and fast rhythms was seen as a method to prevent the participants from sinking into drowsiness or moving into trance-like states. Instead they were expected to individually experience the divine from within while retaining consciousness and concentration. At the very end of these gatherings, about one and a half hours later, the lights were switched on and everyone rose to a standing position for a joint reading of the Sikh prayer (*ardās*) before they continued home to their daily duties at daybreak.

The reason why local Sikhs prefer to use audio recordings in collective *nām simran* programs can be found, firstly, in the positive reception of modern technology within the broader Sikh community.[31] Recordings of devotional music (*kīrtan*), exegetical discourses (*kathā*), and recitations of hymns from the Gurū Granth Sāhib (*pāth*) are today mass-produced for a growing market in India and abroad. In major *gurdwārās* in Punjab the daily services are broadcast on TV channels and the Internet for a global Sikh community. Secondly, it is typical that the tapes and DVDs used specifically for *nām simran* programs are often recordings of live performances, fully embedded in a traditional context of *sādh sangat* led by a religious person. This seems to be rooted in a belief that only individuals who are deemed saintly and fully engaged in devotion can be appropriate guides for common people in the disciplined practice. The recordings provide an easy accessible means of receiving the instructions of a saintly person and a devotional congregation irrespective of geographical location. People may gather at a place and form a group that listens to and joins in the playback as if they were participating in a larger congregation in the presence of a devout instructor. That *nām simran* recordings are usually live performances, rather than studio productions, seems to emphasize this participatory aspect.

Another example of more organized *nām simran* programs in Punjab are the *samāgams* arranged by the Brahm Bunga Trust in the village Dodra of the Mansa district. The organization was established by the retired army man Jaswant Singh, often called Bauji, who in the 1970s began to hold *nām simran* meetings in private houses in Dodra and other villages every month. Because of a growing interest, the congregation around Bauji constructed a *gurdwārā* (Gurdwara

Brahm Bunga Sahib) in the 1970s and a decade later handed over the administration to a trust.[32] Today the organization is responsible for large gatherings that attract devotees from all over the world. Except for two-day gatherings every fortnight in different villages and cities, the trust arranges continuous eight-day *nām simran* programs in the *gurdwārā* every March and September, and an eleven-day program at the end of December. During these intensive spiritual retreats, the devotees will adopt a simple lifestyle and be fully dedicated to meditation, which is believed to gradually generate spiritual powers (*siddī*) in the doers. People who have participated in these events sometimes testify that the *gurmantra* vibrating between the walls of the *gurdwārā* at Dodra helps people forget about worldly worries and fully engage in devotion. As popular stories add, the early practitioners of the congregation were imbued with the divine name to such an extent that their bodies emitted sweet electrical shocks; through their intensive practices they pursued internal powers that created perceptible bodily effects.[33] Inspired by these and other devotional endeavors, Sikhs in India and in the diaspora regularly engage in different types of collective *nām simran* practices exercised with or without religious instructors.

A demanding method is the so-called *akhaṇḍ jāp*, or "unbroken repetition," of *vāhigurū* uninterruptedly from a few hours up to twenty-four hours or more. These events are typically staged for special occasions, such as festivals in the Sikh calendar, anniversary days, or whenever human conditions require urgent divine intervention, such as at times of natural disasters or war.[34] The unbroken *nām simran* can begin after the obligatory reading of the Sikh evening prayers at dusk and may continue throughout the night until the ambrosial hours (*amritvela*) and the break of dawn, or may be scheduled as a day program, occurring between the rising and setting of the sun. Devotees may then take turns in keeping the repetition unbroken, and may sometimes divide the chanting assembly so that women and children are doing *akhaṇḍ jāp* during the day, and men throughout the night.

Results and Meanings of *Nām Simran*

From a textual and normative perspective, it is obvious that *nām simran*, as a broader spiritual discipline, is believed to bestow multifold merits and is considered the Sikh path toward liberation. In Gurū Granth Sāhib, the beloved composition *Sukhmani Sāhib* (The Jewel of Peace) by the fifth Gurū Arjan develops a long exposition of all of the virtues gained from the contemplation and remembrance of *nām*. Given the centrality of *simran* in this text, contemporary Sikhs sometimes approach it as a guide as to what can be achieved from the practice.[35] A few lines of this lengthy poem may help to illustrate:

> I am ever a sacrifice unto those, who contemplate [*simran*] over the Master.
> Beauteous are the faces of those, who contemplate [*simran*] over the Master.
> They, who contemplate [*simran*] over the Master, pass their life in peace.
> They, who contemplate [*simran*] over the Master, conquer their mind.

They, who contemplate [*simran*] over the Master, have the pious way of life.
They, who contemplate [*simran*] over the Master, have manifold joys.
They, who contemplate [*simran*] over the Master, abide near God.
By the favour of Saints they remain watchful night and day.
Nānak, Lord's meditation [*simran*] is obtained by perfect luck.[36]

People graced with the ability to be dedicated and concentrated in the various practices covered within the concept of *nām* are able to gradually transform their inner self-centeredness (*haumai*), cultivate devotion, and eventually realize the divine power within themselves and in the whole of creation. The Sikh gurus describe this transition by contrasting two different types of existence: The self-oriented human (*manmukh*), who is entangled with the self and the material world, and the god-oriented person (*gurmukh*), who follows the guru's teaching and shuns the five principal vices (i.e., lust, anger, greed, attachment to the world, and pride) to live a life in humility, fearless of death. The *gurmukhs* are believed to purge the ego and master worldly desires to become immersed in a ceaseless and effortless remembrance and meditation on the divine—a chant without chanting (*ajpā jāp*)—for which their body and mind become merely instruments.[37] The ultimate goal of this spiritual journey is *mukti*—liberation, release, and emancipation—when the infinite dimensions of the spiritual self realizes its belonging to a divine power. This realization is presented in terms of enlightenment or a mystical experience in which the formless divine speaks "the unspoken word" (*anahad śabad*)—the internalized word that cannot be reduced to discursive forms—and the person becomes a *jivan mukt*, one who has attained liberation while remaining alive in a corporeal state, and will end the cycle of rebirths after death, when the soul merges with the divine light (*joti joti samāuṇā*).

Looking at how local Sikhs explain and view the meaning of conducting religious practices that can be included in a broader definition of *nām simran*, however, surmounting life and death for a final liberation is not necessarily visualized as an attainable goal, nor is it considered the ultimate aim of their practices. On the contrary, many Sikhs will find *mukti* remote in the present dark and degenerating age (*kaliyug*), when only those who are exceptionally spiritually gifted have the chance to merge with God. Rather than ending the transmigratory process, many of my interlocutors have explained that their various devotional practices are a means of accumulating good karma for rewards in this and coming lives, which makes it possible to develop devotion. In Sikh discourses, devotion is often presented as both the means and the end in itself; to fully engage in various religious practices, with no other purpose but to praise the divine, is considered a sign of humbleness in compliance with the gurus' teaching.

This emphasis on devotion is also significant for understanding how local Sikhs recognize recitative practices as a form of meditation and meritorious worship acts. As the above description illustrates, individual and collective *nām simran* include different methods of repeatedly reciting the sacred formula *vāhigurū*, and as such appear as exterior and highly formalized activities. It would be possible to assert that contemporary Sikhs are engaging in the kind of ritualism and worship of sacred sound that the gurus so harshly criticized in their time. However, these external practices should ideally be anchored in two important conditions with transformative capacity: concentration of the mind (*dhyān*) and devotion to the divine from a true heart. The spiritual gains of any religious activity in the life of a Sikh are believed to depend upon the actor's emotional and cognitive state in the moment of acting. A term often used in this context is *bhāvnā*, which designates both the devotional quality of a person's intention and a feeling of "meaning to mean" something in the enactment of an action. It signifies a kind of sincerity that can be felt internally and acknowledged only by the individual devotee but has the power to saturate religious acts with certain qualities and thereby regulate the results. Recitation can be understood as a mechanical repetition of sound without meaning or merits if the performing person is devoid of this kind of sincerity. But if the same acts are carried out with full *bhāvnā*, they can leave a strong imprint on the human mind and affect the person's karmic conditions.

Related to this discussion is also the idea that enactments of *nām simran* should not be goal-oriented or driven by ulterior motives to procure spiritual or material ends, but "selfless" (*nishkām*) acts carried out without thought of reward. The disciple should take up a condition or an attitude according to which s/he virtually drains the human mind/heart from selfish purposes, even if there may very well be prior intentions that motivated the practice in the first place. The underlying idea presupposes that desires are inherent in humans' minds and hearts and hold them ensnared to the world. This is also explained as a reason why Gurū Nānak and his successors criticized yogis, ascetics, and others of their time, claiming that their desire for spiritual rewards would only amplify their egoism and worldly attachment. The person who cultivates devotion to the divine name, however, is believed to gradually transform and cleanse the mind/heart from all desires and to engage in devotion only for its own sake.

This does not mean that Sikhs are not ascribing various effects to their practices. Quite the contrary, many lay Sikhs are pragmatically more inclined to speak about the inward and outward gains they expect from mental and recitative meditation on the divine name in particular contexts than to occupy themselves with exegetical and soteriological elaborations. For example, a Sikh man in his thirties recalled how he was continuously reciting *vāhigurū* when his pregnant wife was taken to the hospital in labor. For him a spontaneous *nām simran* was evoked and uttered for the protection of his wife and to relieve her from bodily pain. In a similar fashion, an elderly woman explained that people who are not performing *nām simran* with regularity are more liable to spirit possession and other types of afflictions, as they have not filled their interior with the divine name. Both of these interlocutors presumed that the recitative meditation of *vāhigurū* had causal power to affect the human body and mind in positive and tangible ways.

The practice is also believed to have moral effects. Over and over again my informants coupled *nām simran* with the term *sēvā*, the selfless service to the guru, codevotees, and society at large, and described these two concepts as interdependent aspects of the Sikh life. *Nām simran* is believed to induce people to do righteous deeds, and should ideally underlie all acts in the Sikh life. Contemplating only for one's own spiritual progress could lead to self-centeredness, which *sēvā* is capable of eliminating. Selfless acts to others performed in continuous remembrance of God, however, will be more beneficial to a doer. Spontaneous as well as more disciplined *nām simran* is believed to charge ordinary acts with spiritual properties and transform them into virtuous deeds. In fact, all ordinary acts, such as preparing food or cleaning, can become meritorious acts if coupled with remembrance and repetition of the divine name.

From an analytical perspective it would be possible to argue that local interpretations of *nām simran*, like those described above, reveal the existence of a "performativist language" ideology, which values sacred words not only for their semantic properties but also for what they are capable of doing. A performativist language ideology views language as an effective means to present, constitute, and act upon the world, compared to a referentialist language ideology, which privileges semantic meanings.[38] As the anthropologist Verne Dusenbery has suggested, the language ideology prevalent among the Sikhs is nondualistic, as it "recognizes the material as well as cognitive properties of language (especially articulated speech) and refuses to privilege semantico-referential meaning at the expense of other properties that language is thought to possess."[39] For Sikhs who are brought up with this ideology, sacred words are valued not only for their propositional meanings but also for their transformative power to affect the human mind and body in a positive way. When a sacred formula such as *vāhigurū* moves into performance and is uttered during a religious session it becomes a performative act that is believed to evoke powerful forces and a presence of the divine that have spiritual and material effects in the world. To verbally repeat and internally contemplate the name of God becomes a device to invoke and activate an agentive divine power believed to have the capacity to alter the inner mind and heart of humans, transform outer actions into virtuous deeds, and provide divine protection and support in real-life situations.[40]

To summarize these ethnographic glimpses, one could say that, on a general level, *nām simran* has been given importance and status as a Sikh spiritual discipline that is comprised of various devotional practices, including mental and recitative meditation. The gurus' teaching, enshrined in Gurū Granth Sāhib, as well as the normative code of conduct sanctioned by the Sikh community, remain the primary sources on which the Sikhs base and legitimize their devotional practices. But these normative texts are always open to interpretation, and the gaps that sometimes emerge between what is recorded and what is left out can become dynamic sites of negotiation and interpretation in a local community. The examples mentioned above illustrate that there is neither a single method by which local Sikhs perform *nām simran* nor a single meaning that they attached to the practice, even if authoritative voices within the community may claim something else. People ascribe to their practices a variety of motives, purposes, and functions that are evoked in situational and shifting contexts or are drawn from more conventional and socially shared ideas within the tradition. In the interplay between religious tradition and social context, the practice of *nām simran* is always being reconstructed and new meanings created.

Notes

1. The noun *dhiān* is commonly used for a mental process of reflection, remembrance, and concentration within the mind, and is translated as "meditation" or "contemplation," while *simrat* similarly signifies recollection, remembrance, and meditation. Other words commonly used are *tap* or *tapasiā*, which connotes meditation, severe austerity practice, and devotion; *jap*, which is translated as meditation, devotion, or prayer; and *bhagatī*, which stands for meditation, devotion, worship, and religious observation. For literal translations, see Gill and Joshi, *Punjabi English Dictionary*, 115, 342, 417, 478, 634.

2. The fieldwork in Varanasi was conducted between 1999 and 2001, with revisits in 2003 and 2005. The fieldwork experience on which this chapter is based also includes interviews and interactions with Sikhs at different locations in Punjab during fieldtrips in 2000, 2004, and from 2008 to 2011.

3. The academic study of Sikhs in the English-speaking diaspora has been continously expanding, while research on Sikhs in Europe is an emerging field. For references, see, for example, Jacobsen and Myrvold, *Sikhs in Europe*; Jacobsen and Myrvold, *Sikhs across Borders*.

4. See W. H. McLeod, *Gurū Nānak*; Schomer and McLeod, *Sants*.

5. Apart from three initial compositions (*Japjī Sāhib*, *Rehrās Sāhib*, and *Kirtan Sohilā*) and a collection of poems at the end, the major portion of the scripture is arranged in thirty-one *rāga*s, different musical modes of both classical and regional kinds, by which the text is indexed. Individual poems are further subdivided into poetic meters and singing styles, such as *Asthapadi*, *Vār*, and *Ghoṛiān*, which assimilate both classical and folk styles of music. The scripture will even provide detailed musical digits and signs to instruct on the way in which each hymn should be performed.

6. According to Sikh scholars, the word *nām* is mentioned 5,999 times in Gurū Granth Sāhib. See Joshi, *Sikhism*, 73–74.

7. M. Singh, *Sri Guru Granth Sahib*, 2.

8. Daljeet Singh, "Doctrine of Naam in Sikhism," 27.

9. See, for example, G. J. Singh, *Understanding Naamsimran*. The monthly magazine *Sikh Review* (www.sikhreview.org) frequently publishes articles by scholars and believers under a special section called "Naamology."

10. See, for example, Daljeet Singh, "Doctrine of Naam in Sikhism"; Dewan Singh, "Guru Nanak"; G. Singh, *NaamSimran Bhakti in Sikhism*; W. H. McLeod, *Gurū Nānak*; W. H. McLeod, *Sikhs and Sikhism*; Sethi, "Mystical Consciousness in Sikhism"; Sethi, "Ethical and Spiritual Aspects"; N. Singh, *Philosophy of Sikhism*.

11. H, McLeod, *Sikhism*, 98.

12. See, for example, the list of Hindu and Muslim names of God in Rahi, *Sri Guru Granth Sahib Discovered*, 5–7.

13. For example, the tenth chapter of *Purātan Janam-sākhī* tells about Nānak's mystical experience. See B. V. Singh, *Purātan Janam Sākhī*, 40–43; and the analysis in N. G. K. Singh, "Myth of the Founder."

14. For practices in the Sant tradition, see Vaudeville, "Sant Mat," 32.

15. W. H. McLeod, *Guru Nānak*, 216. In modern English translations of Gurū Granth Sāhib, such as those available on the Internet (e.g., www.srigranth.org), *jap* is frequently translated as "meditation."

16. Shackle and Mandair, *Teachings of the Sikh Gurus*, xxxiii.

17. These "realms" are Dharam khaṇḍ, Giān khaṇḍ, Saram khaṇḍ, Karam khaṇḍ, and Sach khaṇḍ. For one interpretation of the realms, see, for example, W. H. McLeod, *Gurū Nānak*, 221–226.

18. See, for example, N. Singh, *Philosophy of Sikhism*, 175–193. It has been alleged that *nām simran* finds parallels in a combination of Sufi meditation (*muraqaba*) and its practice of re-membering and invoking God (*dhikr*), and that Gurū Nānak's model of spiritual development through five "realms" corresponds to the Sufi thought of different stages (*maqāms*) on the journey of ascension. Because of these and other conceptual overlaps, scholars have suggested that Nānak was to a lesser or greater extent influenced by Sufi traditions. This influence, how-ever, has been characterized as a "thematic correspondence" that was indirect and was com-municated to Nānak through the broader North Indian Sant tradition, partly because Sufi references and terms are absent from the guru's writings, in contrast to the rich imaginary and language derived from various Hindu sources and traditions. For conflicting views, see Lawrence, "Sant Movement and North Indian Sufis"; and W. H. McLeod, *Gurū Nānak*.

19. H. McLeod, *Sikhism*, 13.

20. The landscape of Punjab is today dotted with sacred places that are believed to mark the sites where the Sikh gurus undertook secluded meditation for periods. See, for example, Myr-vold, *Inside the Guru's Gate*; Myrvold, "I guruns fotspår." The *janam-sākhīs* include several references to more ritualized recitals of divine names and *mantras* and meditative practices in other religious traditions. See, for example, W. H. McLeod, *Early Sikh Tradition*. The B40 *janam-sākhī*, for instance, includes an apocryphal hymn in which Gurū Nānak recommends that a Muslim disciple meditate on God while keeping Lady Fatimah Zahra, Hussain, and Hassan in the heart. According to Francisco Jose Luis, this is "a reference to meditation tech-niques in the Shi'a mystical tradition," involving "the visualisation of either the Infallibles or their names, often in a mandala-like structure" (Luis, "Khanda and the Dhulfiqar," 156).

21. W. H. McLeod, *Sikhs of the Khalsa*, 83. See also Bawa, *Biography and Writings*.

22. T. Singh, *Turban and the Sword of the Sikhs*, 170. See also the translation in W. H. McLeod, *Sikhs of the Khalsa*, 280. The threefold rule of *nām*, *dān*, and *ishnān* is mentioned a century earlier by Bhai Gurdas in *Vār* 26:4; see J. Singh, *Vārān Bhāī Gurdās*, 2:11.

23. W. H. McLeod, *Sikhs of the Khalsa*.

24. *Sikh Rahit Maryādā*, 9.

25. See, for example, references in W. H. McLeod, *Chaupa Singh Rahit-Nama*, 33; W. H. McLeod, *Sikhs of the Khalsa*, 88, 115; and W. H. McLeod, *Prem Sumārag*.

26. W. H. McLeod, *Sikhs of the Khalsa*, 124. See also the translation in T. Singh, *Turban and the Sword of the Sikhs* 169.

27. J. Singh, *Vārān Bhāī Gurdās*, 1:79.

28. That the formula designates a singular divine power is further emphasized by the way contemporary Sikhs let the word *satnām*, or "the true name," precede the compound in recita-tions.

29. To mention one among many of these groups, the Nānaksar movement has developed more disciplined routines of hour-long recitations of *vāhigurū*. For a description of *nām sim-ran* according to Sant Nand Singh, the founder of the Nānaksar movement, see B. Singh, *Anand Sarovar*, 165–169.

30. For detailed descriptions of the daily ceremonies and practices in the *gurdwārā*, see Myrvold, *Inside the Guru's Gate*.

31. See Mansukhani, *Indian Classical Music*; Manuel, *Cassette Culture*.

32. See the website of Brahm Bunga Trust at www.brahmbungadodra.org (accessed January 20, 2010).

33. See the discussion at www.sikhnet.com/discussion/viewtopic.php?f=2&t=2332 (accessed February 21, 2010).

34. Individual and collective continuous repetitions of the *gurmantra* and verses of the Gurū Granth Sāhib were, for instance, organized for the victims of the tsunami in 2004. Some Sikh organizations let people register their individual recitations on the Internet to have them mentioned in a collective prayer for the victims. For examples of *akhaṇḍ jāp* programs organized in the Sikh diaspora, see Myrvold, "Osjälvisk tjänst av sikherna," and the websites http://akhandjaap.com (accessed February 21, 2010) and http://akhandjaapforworldpeace.com (accessed February 21, 2010).

35. See, for example, G. J. Singh, *Understanding Naamsimran*, 40.

36. M. Singh, *Sri Guru Granth Sahib*, 263.

37. See, for example, M. Singh, *Sri Guru Granth Sahib*, 840, 1291.

38. Kang, "'Staged' Rituals and 'Veiled' Spells"; Rumsey, "Wording, Meaning, and Linguistic Ideology."

39. Dusenbery, "Word as Guru," 389.

40. Similar to what Tambiah purports, words are cosubstantiated with the things they denote, and thus to name a thing is to make it manifest. See Tambiah, "Magical Power of Words."

Bibliography

Bawa, Ujagar Singh. *Biography and Writings of Bhai Nand Lal Ji*. English translation. New Delhi: Hemkunt Publishers, 2006.

Dusenbery, Verne A. "The Word as Guru: Sikh Scripture and the Translation Controversy." *History of Religion* 31, no. 4 (1992): 385–402.

Gill, Mukhtiar Singh, and Joshi S. S. *Punjabi English Dictionary*. Patiala, India: Punjabi University, 1999.

Jacobsen, Knut A., and Kristina Myrvold, eds. *Sikhs across Borders: Transnational Practices of European Sikhs*. New York: Continuum, 2012.

———. *Sikhs in Europe: Migration, Identities and Representations*. Farnham, UK: Ashgate, 2011.

Joshi, L. M., ed. *Sikhism*. Patiala, India: Publication Bureau Punjabi University, 2000.

Kang, Yoonhee. "'Staged' Rituals and 'Veiled' Spells: Multiple Language Ideologies and Transformations in Petalangan Verbal Magic." *Journal of Linguistic Anthropology* 16, no. 1 (2006): 1–22.

Lawrence, Bruce B. "The Sant Movement and North Indian Sufis." In *The Sants: Studies in a Devotional Tradition of India*, edited by Karin Schomer and W. H. McLeod, 259–373. New Delhi: Motilal Banarsidass, 1987.

Luis, Francisco Jose. "The Khanda and the Dhulfiqar: Sikh-Shi'a Parallelisms and Crossings in History and Text, Concept of the Divine Guide and Sacred Chivalry." *Sikh Formations* 2, no. 2 (2006): 153–179.

Mansukhani, Gobind Singh. *Indian Classical Music and Sikh Kirtan*. New Delhi: Oxford and IBH Publishing, 1982.

Manuel, Peter. *Cassette Culture: Popular Music and Technology in North India*. Chicago: University of Chicago Press, 1993.

McLeod, Hew. *Sikhism*. London: Penguin Books, 1997.

McLeod, W. H. *The Chaupa Singh Rahit-Nama*. Dunedin, New Zealand: University of Otago Press, 1987.

———. *Early Sikh Tradition: A Study of the Janam-sakhis*. Oxford: Clarendon Press, 1980.

———. *Gurū Nānak and the Sikh Religion*. New Delhi: Oxford University Press, 1996 (1968).

———. *Prem Sumārag: The Testimony of a Sanatan Sikh*. New Delhi: Oxford University Press, 2006.

———. *Sikhs and Sikhism*. New Delhi: Oxford University Press, 1999.

———. *Sikhs of the Khalsa: A History of the Khalsa Rahit*. New Delhi: Oxford University Press, 2003.

Myrvold, Kristina. "I guruns fotspår: Pilgrimsresor och platser i samtida sikhism." In *Heliga platser, pilgrimsfärder och andliga resor i vår samtid*, edited by Bodil Liljefors Persson and Emma Hall, 31–41. Malmö, Sweden: Föreningen lärare i religionskunskap, 2009.

———. *Inside the Guru's Gate: Ritual Uses of Texts among the Sikhs in Varanasi*. Lund, Sweden: Media-Tryck, 2007.

———. "Osjälvisk tjänst av sikherna." *Chakra—tidskrift för indiska religioner*, no. 3 (2005): 42–48.

Rahi, Hakim S. *Sri Guru Granth Sahib Discovered: A Reference Book of Quotations*. New Delhi: Motilal Banarsidass, 1998.

Rumsey, Alan. "Wording, Meaning, and Linguistic Ideology." *American Anthropologist* 92 (1990): 346–361.

Schomer, Karin, and W. H. McLeod, eds. *The Sants: Studies in a Devotional Tradition of India*. New Delhi: Motilal Banarsidass, 1987.

Sethi, Amarjit Singh. "Ethical and Spiritual Aspects of Nam-Simaran." In *Sikh History and Religion in the Twentieth Century*, edited by Joseph T. O'Connell et al., 44–51. New Delhi: Manohar Publications, 1990.

———. "Mystical Consciousness in Sikhism." *Journal of Sikh Studies* 10, no.1 (1983): 13–19.

Shackle, Christopher, and Arvind-Pal Singh Mandair, eds. *Teachings of the Sikh Gurus: Selections from the Sikh Scripture*. London: Routledge, 2005.

Sikh Rahit Maryādā. Amritsar, India: Golden Offset Press, 1997.

Singh, Bhagat. *Anand Sarovar / The Holy Pond of Blissful Joy: Biography of Sant Baba Nand Singh Ji*. Vol 3. Hardwar, India: Nanak Dar, Sant Baba Nand Singh-Sant Baba Ishar Singh, Spiritual Mission, 2000.

Singh, Bhai Vir. *Purātan Janam Sākhī Srī Gurū Nānak Dev Jī*. 1926; repr., New Delhi: Bhai Vir Singh Sahitya Sadan, 1999.

Singh, Daljeet. "The Doctrine of *Naam* in Sikhism." *Journal of Sikh Studies* 2, no. 2 (1975): 27–65.

Singh, Dewan. "Guru Nanak and the Mystic Concept of *Nām*." *Journal of Sikh Studies* 7, nos. 1–2 (1980): 43–48.

Singh, Gulshan Jeet. *Understanding Naamsimran (The Practicing of the Divine Word: Being an Anthology of Sikh Naamology)*. New Delhi: Young Brothers, 2004.

Singh, Gurbax. *NaamSimran Bhakti in Sikhism*. New Delhi: Hemkunt Press, 1998.

Singh, Jodh, ed. and trans. *Vārān Bhāī Gurdās: Text, Transliteration and Translation*. Patiala, India: Vision and Venture, 1998.

Singh, Manmohan, trans. *Sri Guru Granth Sahib*. Amritsar, India: Shiromani Gurdwara Parbandhak Committee, 1996.

Singh, Nikky Guninder Kaur. "The Myth of the Founder: The Janamsakhis and the Sikh Tradition." *History of Religions* 31, no. 4 (1992): 329–343.

Singh, Nirbhai. *Philosophy of Sikhism*. New Delhi: Atlantic Publishers and Distributors, 1990.

Singh, Sher. *Philosophy of Sikhism.* Amritsar, India: Golden Offset Press, 1998.

Singh, Trilochan. *The Turban and the Sword of the Sikhs: Essence of Sikhism (History and Exposition of Sikh Baptism, Sikh Symbols and Moral Code of the Sikhs: Rehitnāmās).* Amritsar, India: B. Chattar Singh Jiwan Singh, 2001.

Tambiah, Stanley J. "The Magical Power of Words." *Man* 3, no. 2 (1968): 175–208.

Vaudeville, Charlotte. "Sant Mat: Santism as the Universal Path to Sanctity." In *The Sants: Studies in a Devotional Tradition of India*, edited by Karin Schomer and W. H. McLeod, 21–40. New Delhi: Motilal Banarsidass, 1987.

Meditation Objects in Pāli Buddhist Texts

The *Dhammapada* commentary, whose series of pleasingly intricate stories are associated with the verses of that famous collection, describes a young man struggling unsuccessfully with meditation. He has been asked to recollect "the foul" by visually considering the sight of a decomposing corpse, a practice that from the earliest times seems to have been peculiar to Buddhism.[1] He cannot progress. The Buddha, seeing him with his divine eye, a faculty associated with many awakened beings in these stories, realizes the boy will not succeed, and that his object is unsuitable. He divines that he is now, and was in many past lives, a hereditary goldsmith, and needs a different meditation. So he visits him and conjures a magical vision of a golden-red flower. The young man takes this object, and murmuring the words "red, red" soon enters *jhāna*, a meditation described in Buddhist texts as characterized by initial thinking, discursive examination, joy, happiness, and one-pointedness: a peaceful bodily, emotional, and mental unification. He attains three further *jhānas*: the second, where thinking is dropped and "internal silence" is present; the third, where joy is discarded, and happiness, mindfulness, or alertness and equanimity become strong; and finally the fourth, a state where feeling has been purified. The mind, untroubled by painful feelings or even excessively pleasant feelings, becomes fluid and flexible: the meditator is free to turn to insight, other meditations, or psychic powers. The Buddha sees that the man is now ready for insight. He causes the flower, the basis of his meditative attainments, to wither and blacken. The boy, established in calm (*samatha*), gains insight (*vipassanā*) too: he sees what are known in Buddhism as the three signs—impermanence (*anicca*), unsatisfactoriness (*dukkha*), and the lack of a solid and enduring self (*anattā*)—understood through the decomposition of this visual object. The Buddha leaves the boy, but now the young man's mind is attuned. He passes a bank of flowers, some lustrous and fresh, others putrefying. He reaches further insight into these three "signs." Finally the teacher returns: he sees the young man is ready for the last stage of insight. Making a magical image of himself, he brushes the boy's cheek. Through the combination of surprise and the aptness of this external event, the boy is filled with devotion, the last necessary step in his own path, and attains *arahatship*—in Buddhist terms, the last vestiges of greed, hatred, and delusion drop away, and the boy is free.

Individual Paths

Through such tales most Southern Buddhists, monks, and laity have historically been taught about meditation, its objects, and its practice: children hear *Dhammapada* stories as their first contact with Buddhist teaching.[2] So it is a good starting point for this chapter, as it epitomizes a creative and adaptable attitude to meditation objects that is found in the canon and commentarial stories as well as in the varieties of technique in modern Southern Buddhism.[3] As so often in early Buddhist discourse, the detail of sustained narrative communicates much that theory cannot. Specificity of object to individual, appropriateness of different objects at various stages of development, and variety of method in a graduated path are all characteristic of the texts and of much Southern Buddhist meditation teaching today. The meditator has been given an object that does not suit; he is given another, dovetailing with his predisposition and past experience. When he has achieved results in calm, he is asked to observe it differently: he sees the defects of his object, in a way that produces insight, rather than frustration, and, through a mixture of his own creative observation, of the bank of dead and live flowers, and the surprise of an odd and apposite step by his teacher inspiring a moment of faith (*saddhā*), achieves awakening. Modern interpretations might vary on features such as "magical" flowers, visits from a teacher who projects himself to the meditator to give guidance, or the occurrence of "past lives" that have active influence on present disposition. But whether these features are taken as metaphors, imaginative ways of describing idiosyncracies of temperament, or literal "truths" (and the story is rich on all of these levels), the incidents stress, as many texts do, that the individual is in part the product of past experience, that this affects what will work, that there is a right time to offer advice and intervene, that some objects are suitable at different times, and that the practice of meditation, as it is described in Buddhism, requires some spontaneous creativity on the part of the practitioner. In *Dhammapada* stories meditation objects are sometimes carefully chosen and prescribed, and sometimes, where there is also a graduated path that might be different for different people, they arise fortuitously. The underlying assumption is that it is up to the meditator to use advice skillfully and to exercise intuition in observing events in the world that can help his or her practice.

The interplay of character, environments, and distinct, precisely delineated individual paths, in this and other Pāli collections, indicate that in Buddhist practice and theory, no technique stands alone. The young monk would also be living his daily life, with recommendations for bodily mindfulness and attentiveness to others, and often discussing and hearing talks to loosen views that, according to the Buddhist *Abhidhamma*, are associated with rigidity and lack of healthiness in body and mind.[4] These would all be considered important to support the body and mind for meditation, ensuring the practitioner's well-being for the return to "normal" life. The practice of awareness during daily life and the various kinds of chanting, often the recollections (*anussatis*) listed below, are comparable supports for the laity too.

The golden flower, "real" or "not real," conjured, or perhaps visualized, is classified among the category of the first ten objects, the visually "beautiful" (which will be discussed later), the *kasiṇa*, but it should also be noted that as an external visual object, it does not quite match the contained carefully arranged *kasiṇa* disc Buddhaghosa prefers.[5] And when it has been mastered, the object itself changes, "magically," as a flower would in "real" life, so the boy can observe decay and putrefaction, features he could not grasp at the outset of the tale. Commentarial lists and advice in working with different techniques need to be read alongside such stories. They show the interchange of teacher, person, and object. In the texts and in much modern practice, "objects" are devised, crafted, and changed for particular situations and people. As so often in early Buddhist texts, the flower, perhaps imaginary, is a spontaneous creation for the moment, for the person concerned, "created" by both teacher and meditator.

This chapter considers briefly a large number of objects—the basic forty described by the commentaries—with the intention of identifying key features that contribute to what is called a "place of work," a meditation object (*kammaṭṭhāna*). The objects will be discussed in the seven groups described under "enumeration" in the *Visuddhimagga* (*Visuddhimagga* III 104), and some broad indication given of modern variations. While each category is frequent in early texts, no such extended list exists in the canon.[6] The groupings are the ten *kasiṇas*; the ten "unlovely" (*asubha*); the ten recollections; the four divine abidings; the four formless spheres; and, finally, two objects that, like the recollections, are intended to change views and understanding about the relationship between the practitioner and his or her bodily environment. The very range of categories and variations in teaching them are indicative of the diverse ways "objects" are regarded in canon, commentary, and modern practice.

These objects, like medicines or nutriments, are described in texts as assigned in combinations to encourage particular features and to eliminate those that are unhelpful or destructive. Within the space available, only a thumbnail sketch can be offered, but it is hoped that the adaptive nature of early Buddhist meditative practice manifest in such stories, and the modern adjustments and variations within some Southern Buddhist schools, will be demonstrated. Wherever possible, specific narrative instances will be given, as more true to the sense of individual applicability that animates meditation teaching as it is described within early Buddhist texts. The purpose of considering a wide range is to ascertain whether more general conclusions can be made about the nature of meditation objects and how they are used in Southern Buddhism. Texts cited will include the often overlooked *Dhammapada-aṭṭhakathā* (translated as *Buddhist Legends*), the manuals of Buddhaghosa (*Visuddhimagga*) and Upatissa (*Vimuttimagga*), and the Pāli canon.

The Beautiful Object: *Kasiṇa* 1–10

So how would the boy consider the golden flower and address it as a meditation object? The object, a *kasiṇa*, is here "created" outside, found internally, and, later in the story, found again by the pupil externally and in "real" multiple form in the world around him. In early and modern Southern Buddhist practice there is a greater emphasis on the external, "real-life" starting object. Internally derived visualization practices do exist, however, and skill in such fields as a preparation for meditation are suggested by the *Mahāsudassana-Sutta*, the *Piṅgiya-Sutta* and the *Mahāsamaya-Sutta*, in which the listener is encouraged to create in the mind's eye the contents of what in later Buddhist texts becomes the more frequent, formally constructed mandalas and visualized figures organized on predetermined lines.[7]

The commentaries and some modern monasteries advise the practitioner to construct a *kasiṇa* as part of the preparation. Buddhaghosa gives careful instructions: for a *kasiṇa*, a disc or a larger area of the color is made, or a means of containing the elements of earth, water, air, fire, or space. In Southern Buddhist countries, where many follow commentarial guidelines, discs for the colors are already constructed, and hang in monasteries. Buddhaghosa also discusses naturally occurring fields of objects, though cautiously. That they were used at the time of the Buddha, however, is suggested in very early texts: the canonical list of the spheres of transcendence (*abhibhāyatana*) compares the "external object" to the flowers of blue flax, the yellow *kaṇṇikāra* flower, the red *bandhujīvaka* flower, and the white morning star, as well as fine muslin of these colors (*Majjhimanikāya* II 12–15).[8] The taking of a field of earth is described in the *Culasuññata-Sutta* as "just as a bull's hide becomes free from folds when fully stretched with a hundred pegs" (*Majjhimanikāya* III 105).[9] In the *Dhammapada* story told at the beginning, as well as in others, a meditator spontaneously finds a natural occurrence of an external object.

In the commentaries, the practitioner is asked to allow the eyes to rest on the external visual object, placed at a set distance away, so that it occupies his whole attention: the word *kasiṇa* is derived from the Sanskrit word meaning "entire" or "whole."[10] The eyes should not be so open as to cause strain, or half-closed, inducing drowsiness: it should be like seeing one's face in a mirror (*Visuddhimagga* IV 28). The meditator then shuts the eyes, with the same rested attention as if they were open (*Visuddhimagga* IV 30), until a counter-part image (*uggaha-nimitta*) of the object appears spontaneously in the mind's eye. He repeats this a "hundred, a thousand times." This is a delicate process and may take time and require guidance: too much strain and the mind becomes tense or tired. The boy in the story is described as following such guidelines, as given by Buddhaghosa and Upatissa (Ehara, *Path of Freedom*, 76). From the outset, as the boy settles his attention and examines the flower, he would bring to mind the descriptive denoter "red, red," an aid to sustaining alertness. Although Buddhaghosa does not specify this, it involves an "internal," perhaps auditory factor.[11] For each object a comparable descriptive formula is taught, though no significance or mantric power is associated with this. As indicated earlier, meditation objects are chosen to suit specific temperamental needs: the canonical *Mahāniddesa* says that the "beautiful" object, the *kasiṇas* of earth, water, fire, air, blue-black, yellow, red, white, space, consciousness, and, in some lists, light, are regarded as an antidote to dispositions inclined to ill will.[12]

In time, when *jhāna* factors start to develop, an image arises spontaneously in the practitioner's own mind (*patibhaga-nimitta*), when the eyes are shut. Now it is not necessary to return to the external object; the image is made stable, and the factors of *jhāna* begin to strengthen and support one another. Advice from the meditation teacher and care in behavior are recommended at this sensitive stage of practice (Ehara, *Path of Freedom*, 76–79). Two qualities come to balance: the application of the mind to the object (*vitakka*) and examination (*vicāra*), usually associated with speech and internal dialogue, become cooperative in wholehearted engagement and examination of the object. When this occurs, joy, happiness and one-pointedness (*ekaggatā*, literally "gone-to-oneness") are said to arise, as the interest the mind takes in outside distractions and internal hindrances, such as hatred, resentment, or restlessness, falls away. In time *vitakka* and *vicāra* drop away, then joy and happiness, while other qualities, such as mindfulness and equanimity, intensify and grow. This is what the boy in the story would have been practicing, in a process preparing him for insight, after establishing calm first.[13]

Throughout early stories, such objects are used as means of producing unification of mind. The size of the object is carefully considered: both Upatissa and Buddhaghosa recommend a specific size.[14] The great variety of the methods described in the *Dhammapada* commentary, however, supports the possibility that more fluid forms were employed in early times. The *Dhammasaṅgani* associates skill in the limited (*paritta*) and the immeasurable (*appamāṇa*) with the *kasiṇa*, and describes making forms large and small, perhaps an indication that techniques, in extending an object to make it wide or diminishing it to make it tiny, contribute to mastery in these meditations (*Dhammasaṅgani* 160–247).[15] These features of early and later texts suggest the use of varied naturally occurring objects. Certainly some meditation teachers in Thailand today also teach *samatha* meditation using simple objects, principally naturally found features, such as a candle flame, the space between trees, and running water. The object is used to arouse a *nimitta*, an image, that can then be applied, changed, extended, and moved around in the mind's eye.[16] Alongside this, five masteries—adverting, entering, sustaining, emerging, and recollecting—are also enjoined for flexibility and nonattachment. These ensure that the object for calm is easily entered into but also left behind at the end of meditation practice. Meditators in texts always "emerge" (*vuṭṭhati*) from meditation. This practice is usually conducted as a sitting, or occasionally a standing, practice, in seclusion. It is not usually undertaken in what we call "daily life," though Buddhaghosa notes the mastery of *arahats* who could enter and emerge from such states for a moment. Variations involving skill and mastery over the object and its appearance are taught at Wat Dhammakaya, Bangkok, with the internally visualized "crystal ball" techniques, as well as by some other meditation teachers in Thailand.

Beautiful visual objects are the classic means of arousing calm in secluded *jhāna* practice in early Buddhism, but they are also considered restorative outside sitting meditation and likely to elicit a response in the human mind that resonates with their auspiciousness. They are thought to produce a corresponding health and well-being in the mind for daily life as well as for meditation, provided there is mindfulness. It is usual for meditation centers, if they are particularly associated with *samatha* practice, to be set in natural surroundings. The risk of attachment is recognized in canon and commentary: Buddhaghosa, for instance, suggests one given to desire should not be placed in surroundings that are too well regulated, decorated, or beautiful (*Visuddhimagga* III 97). The underlying assumption, however, is that where mindfulness is practiced, *kusala-citta*, wholesome mind, is thought likely to be aroused by continued observation of the movement of sensory experience in response to the natural world, and the consequent alertness to the "beautiful" resultant (*vipāka*) objects received at the physical sense-doors. The practitioner is considered able to find the mind's innate health or balance through such mindfulness of external objects, where attention is appropriately and alertly applied (*yonisomanasikāra*).[17]

In addition, "beautiful" features—both internal, in the *nimitta*, and in the external world—can also be viewed for insight, too, the other side of meditative practice. The meditator is encouraged in the canon to see defects after the meditation in the external form of the object, to discourage attachment. In *Dhammapada* stories and other stories of the monks and nuns who attain *arahatship*, all kinds of natural objects elicit the attainment of *arahatship*. In one such story, an unsuccessful meditator, given a meditation object that does not work, goes in search of his teacher to receive a better one, but he sees a great forest fire on his way, so he climbs up a mountain and says to himself, "Even as this fire advances, consuming all obstacles both great and small, so also ought I to advance, consuming all obstacles both great and small by the fire of knowledge of the noble path" (*Buddhist Legends* 1 ii 8). The Buddha, seeing this man's insight, sends a luminous image of himself, and reassures him: "The monk who delights in heedfulness and views heedlessness with fear / Advances like a fire, consuming attachments both small and great" (*Dhammapada* 31). The monk, now suddenly awakened, soars through the air to thank the Buddha in person. In yet another story, a whole group of monks see a mirage and realize the truth of impermanence of events; then, seeing the bubbles forming in the cascades of a tumbling waterfall, they all become awakened. In another story a nun, Kisā Gotamī, who has lost her child and joined the order, lights a lamp and sees the flickering of its flame, and notices that that some lamps flare, while others flicker out. She takes this for her subject of meditation and meditates as follows: "Even as it is with these flames, so also is it with living beings here in the world: some flare up, while others flicker out; they only that have reached *nibbāna* are no more seen" (*Buddhist Legends* 2 viii 13). The Buddha appears magically to her and confirms her own formulation of her spiritual path, at which she becomes an *arahat*.

So, do we say that such incidents are the product of *samatha* or *vipassanā*? What sort of object is a bubble dissolving in water, a flickering flame, a mirage, or an uncontained fire? These are "beautiful objects"—but also triggers to awakening that defy conventional classification. Perhaps they are intended to. These meditators seem to find insight through a fusion of *samatha* and *vipassanā*, which they see and articulate for themselves, and that is then supported and confirmed by the teacher. The *Dhammapada-aṭṭakaṭṭhā* has many stories of people, after meditative work, intuitively formulating for themselves the very insight, made on the basis of the externally observed object, that brings their meditations to fruition. In some cases the meditators have been pursuing unspecified meditations; their apprehension is so sharpened, however, that they attain enlightenment through some external natural object, undergoing natural processes of change. So the bereaved nun sees water trickling, and compares it to life ebbing away, or a group of monks see jasmine flowers bloom and die in one day (e.g., *Buddhist Legends* 2 viii 12 and 3 xxv 7).

One important additional property of "beautiful" objects is that they are often invoked after awakening, in delighted observation of the natural environment, a feature of Southern Buddhism that is sometimes less appreciated. In such verses, the speaker finds in the landscape the objects that can describe or mirror his enlightened state: the world is described as observed, without desire or craving, and auditory, visual, and tactile elements in the natural surroundings are evoked. The monk Ramāṇeyyaka speaks this verse on attaining enlightenment: "Amidst the sound of chirping and the cries of birds, this mind of mine does not waver, for devotion to solitude is mine" (*Theragāthā* 49). The monk Vimala speaks this verse: "The earth is sprinkled, the wind blows, lightning flashes in the sky. My thoughts are quietened, my mind is well-concentrated" (*Theragāthā* 50).

In conclusion, the "beautiful" visual object, the *kasiṇa*, is regarded as the paradigm of the meditation object for secluded *jhāna* practice. On a general level, as an object of mindfulness rather than of concentration, in manifold forms, it is also, along with other objects of the physical senses, implicitly considered to offer a restorative influence in daily life. Joy and happiness arising from observing beauty seem key: beauty in the natural world provides a counterpart to an auspiciousness considered latent within the skillful human mind (*kusala-citta*). As these stories indicate, the meditation object can, when linked to a sense of impermanence and to unsatisfactoriness, awaken insight. In its varied and complex manifestations, the natural world then contributes to a rich field of observation for awakened beings.

The Formless Spheres

After the attainment of the fourth *jhāna*, the mind is described as purified, malleable, and ready for work. The boy in the story that the Buddha taught proceeded to further investigation of the object, insight, and *arahatship*. Four other meditations can be pursued, however, exercising the flexibility and mastery of the mind in different ways. They are described here, as they are classically considered dependent on *kasiṇa* practice, though in the list of forty they are numbers 35 through 38, and can follow a number of *jhānic* meditations described in this chapter, such as the *brahmavihāras*.[18]

That these meditations are a natural progression from the simplicity of the beautiful object is implied by a canonical list, the "deliverances" (*vimokkha*; see, for instance, *Majjhimanikāya*, II 12–15). Found frequently in the canon, this series of eight means by which the mind is "delivered" describes the meditator first seeing forms within his own body, then seeing them externally, and then, in the third "deliverance," of "releasing the mind onto the beautiful," which is said by the commentaries to be the beauty of the *kasiṇa* object, after which he enters into formless meditation.[19]

All formless meditations are described in the *Abhidhamma* as involving the same mental factors as the fourth *jhāna*, which appears to act as a crossroad for meditators described in the canon and the commentaries, before the final stages of insight, the development of psychic powers, or the attainment of formlessness (*Dhammasaṅgani* 265–268). In the first formless meditation, the sphere of infinite space (*ākāsānañcāyatana*), objectness itself is examined through an infinite and undifferentiated ground within which objects usually occur. In the second, the sphere of infinite consciousness (*viññāṇañcāyatana*), subjectness, or *nāma*, is explored to an infinite extent, through examining the infinite ground of the very means by which objectness is usually apprehended. A modern teacher, Ajahn Lee Dhammadharo, describes this as "being absorbed in boundless consciousness as one's preoccupation, with no form or figure acting as the sign or focal point of one's concentration."[20] In the third formless meditation, the sphere of nothingness (*ākiñcaññāyatana*), denoters or categories of "subject," "object," or "thingness" cease to apply. Dhammadharo describes this as "focusing exclusively on a fainter or more subtle sense of cognizance that has no limit and in which nothing appears or disappears, to the point where one almost understands it to be *nibbāna*" (*Basic Themes*). The fourth formless meditation examines the nature of consciousness itself, before the application of differentiation or categories of "space," "consciousness," "thingness," and "nothingness." Dhammadharo says, "There is awareness, but with no thinking, no focusing of awareness on what it knows" (*Basic Themes*).

In these spheres, the nature of mind and its relationship to object are successively refined and explored, until, it appears, their emergence and differentiation are themselves observed. Descriptions of their attainment are sparse in the canon, though extensively delineated by Buddhaghosa (*Visuddhimagga* X). Dhammadharo says they are merely resting places for the mind, because they are states that the mind enters, stays in, and leaves.

A wide range of objects lead to the first four *jhānas*, indeed, the first may be accessed by twenty-five of the forty objects.[21] Each formless sphere, however, defines through a single term its object, in the ground of awareness in which it is derived, the state with which it is associated, and the sphere in which the mind of the practitioner enters and "surmounts" the *jhāna* that it supersedes. Each sphere can be found only through the very characteristics that allow it to be experienced by the meditator: these are the only "objects" in which object, state, and meditational technique are not differentiated.

So in the formless spheres, the mind and its field are examined, with a loosening of fixed views or attachments to *any* objects—images (*nimittas*) that arise in the "form" sphere, externally derived meditation objects, or any other objects of the senses in daily experience. The spheres (*āyatanas*), although subsequently termed *jhānas* by the *Abhidhamma* traditions, seem, however, to act as fields outside the parameters of "constructings" or "forms" defining any given meditation, state, meditative procedure, or object. They do not lead to awakening but seem to be "resting places," and perhaps these are essential features of their identity. Awakening requires some "grit" or interplay of object and subject in the world of flux: the apprehension of differentiation, and a clear distinction between name (*nāma*) and form (*rūpa*). These realms, however, which are described in the texts as a kind of specialism, enact a freedom from the very nature of "subject" and "object," "name" and "form," as skills taught for their own sake. The last deliverance, from cessation, is reserved for those who have attained this path.

These meditations are not discussed much in modern contexts, though they are taught to advanced practitioners. In the canon and the commentaries, a number of people in the texts practice them, particularly those cultivating masteries in *samatha* practice; they are treated in the canon perhaps as a kind of spiritual aerobics for the experienced meditator, loosening attachments to forms and appearances. Moggallāna, the Buddha's great disciple who stands to his left (while his partner, Sāriputta, stands to the right), is considered the great exponent of calm meditation, and practices each one of these formless realms in turn on his route to awakening (*Saṃyuttanikāya* IV 263 / *Connected Discourses of the Buddha* II 1302–1308). His experiences act as an encouragement to anyone awed by such rarefied objects: he has a tendency to sleepiness, at each stage, but after some dozy detours, attains *arahatship* and becomes a master of the psychic powers.[22]

The importance of these meditations is much debated, and they are not considered "necessary" to the path; that they are there, though, refreshes the sense of what it is that constitutes an object, a meditation state, and the means of attaining it. These factors are themselves perhaps indicative of some function they serve within Southern Buddhist practice.

The Foul: *Asubha* 11–20

For the beautiful object, various practices involving mastery over the appearance of the external or internal manifestation, and the counterpart image that arises on the basis of that, are designed to improve skill in entering and leaving meditation. They also prevent attachment, or views that, for instance, any experience associated with that object constitutes a noetic or ontological insight.[23] Beautiful objects, though understandably treated with caution for their capacity to entice and arouse desire, are considered particularly suitable, through their simplicity, for arousing all four *jhānas* and thence the formless spheres. But an apparently diametrically opposed object, the visually foul (*asubha*), as in the various stages of decomposition of a corpse, also characterizes Buddhist meditation. Perhaps for its disturbing and unsettling attributes, or, as the commentators indicate, more particularly for its inherent complicatedness and scattered nature, the "foul" object is described in the commentaries as being unable to provide sufficient simplicity to act as a support for all *jhānas*.[24] It just seems too complicated. The "foul" is recommended for those with excessive attachment. Because of the obvious risk arising from its scary, disgusting nature, careful warnings from Buddhaghosa, Upatissa, and modern teachers stress its practice only under close supervision, alongside other balancing meditations (*Visuddhimagga* VI). It is taught in Bangkok now by visits to morgues for monks, as a collective exercise, unlike the practice conducted alone in the open charnel grounds of ancient times. For a meditator one feature, such as color, within the corpse, or one element, is required to attain to higher *jhānas*. From the point of view of this chapter, it seems that the simplicity of the *kasiṇa* is more suited to allowing calm meditation, through the abstract possibilities of a "beautiful" form, to develop and grow; the "foul," necessarily involving complication, is less suited, except inasmuch as it arouses disenchantment (*nibbidā*), or turning away from the senses. But just as decay and ugliness are manifest potentially in the beautiful object, as the boy's experience with the flower demonstrates, "beauty" too may be found by attention to one detail, such as color, in "foul" meditation.[25] The category "foul" usually denotes a corpse in the manuals, but the canon and the commentary often describe it applying to living beings, and as an object producing insight as well as calm.

The "foul" is regarded as an antidote to attachment, but does not, according to the commentaries, produce calm beyond that of the first meditation. For its associations, and perhaps in addition for its complexity and differentiation, the "foul" also provides a frequent means of eliciting insight into the three signs of impermanence, suffering, and non-self. In the *Dhammapada-atthakathā*, the decay and decomposition of the body is frequently taught, either through a "real" experience of a corpse, or through the magical conjurings or perhaps visualization of a beautiful woman exhibiting accelerated decay, old age, and death (*Buddhist Legends* 2 xi 5 and 3 xxv 10). Such "conjurations" perhaps suggest also that internally visualized techniques, from the meditator's own imagination, were employed in early times. In early texts and modern practice, the beautiful object is described as requiring care; the foul, however, requires a knife-edge of attention, and is only recommended for those receiving extended guidance on meditation retreats or for monastics, who would be paying careful attention to supporting practices.

The Ten Recollections

Most of the *samatha* practices considered so far are conducted in seclusion, sitting down, in the *samādhi* posture, with eyes open at the outset, then closed to pursue the meditation object, or, if the object is visualized, with eyes closed throughout, though no reference explicitly enjoins this. Apart from the *kasiṇa* practices, there seems to be no reference to visual awareness in other meditations, apart from the hairs of the head in the first part of the practice on bodily parts.[26] Little is said about posture in early Buddhist texts, other than that the back should be straight, the legs crossed, and that the meditator be, or perhaps thereby becomes, "nobly born"—a simple lack of specificity in which one scholar, A. P. Pradhan, has discerned an implicit critique of more arduous and precisely delineated bodily practices associated with Indian yogic systems.[27] Some features of sitting meditation seem to have been constant from early times. For instance, the hand position seen in the *samādhi* posture of early Buddha figures is usually used now.[28] There are important meditative, practical, and doctrinal implications in the adoption of a stable, fixed posture for a certain period of time, usually in seclusion. The *samādhi* posture can be assumed for all of the objects described in this chapter, but requires time and space away from bustle. Other postures should also be noted; Buddhaghosa recommends specific postures for different temperaments. The sculptural depictions of Southern Buddhists show varied postures for Buddha figures, and there is a rich iconography linking gesture, life event, and associated narrative in the Southeast Asian typology of poses of the Buddha.[29] It is worth noting that in this volume the adoption of posture as a meditative preparation is also emphasized generally by Eifring, and for specific schools by Mabuchi (neo-Confucianism), Roth (Daoism), Samuel (Tibetan longevity practices), and Myrvold (Sikhism).

The following group of *samatha* exercises are the "recollections" (*anussati*): (1) the Buddha, (2) the teaching, (3) the *sangha*, the community of those who have attained stages of path, whose representatives are the community of monks and nuns, (4) good conduct or morality (*sīla*), (5) generosity (*cāga*), (6) sense-sphere deities (*devas*), (7) mindfulness of death, (8) mindfulness of body, (9) breathing mindfulness, and (10) mindfulness of peace.

These exercises are sometimes conducted sitting—as is usually the case for breathing mindfulness—but are distinguished in part by the fact that they can often be practiced in other postures, such as standing or walking, as accompaniments to sitting practice, or even in some cases as exercises to be pursued in daily life. Some, in particular the body and the breath, practiced in particular ways, may be undertaken as secluded sitting exercises leading to the first four *jhānas*. Others, however, are often undertaken as walking practices and even as daily life practices. Change of posture seems always to have featured as an important part of meditation practice.

The first three recollections, recollections of the attributes of the Triple Gem, are recommended before meditation. They are also sometimes walking practices, undertaken in groups in collective, chanted meditations at shrines. The first six, including the Triple Gem recollection as well as remembering one's own good conduct or virtue, generosity, and the presence of *devas* (the sense-sphere gods who live in happiness and whom one may in time join) are often given by the Buddha to busy people with children around, to businessmen, and to housewives as ways practicing in daily life when there is not time or space for extended sitting practice (*Saṃyuttanikāya* V 394; *Aṅguttaranikāya* I 206–11;

Aṅguttaranikāya V 332–4). The inclusion of this range of varied supportive meditations, sometimes conducted in different postures, must be stressed, as the recollections are such frequent features in canonical advice. Many are presented within the tradition as essential accompaniments to sitting practice, aimed at addressing one's orientation to the world and ensuring that the mind and the body are in balance to support meditation. They do not all lead to *jhāna*, and hence are sometimes overlooked, but by arousing in varied ways qualities such as cheerfulness, confidence, and freedom from fear, as well as allowing meditation involving physical movement, they render other practices sustainable, ensure that the mind is not overstimulated or bored, and allow it to find its own balance under less static or controlled conditions.[30] Clearly such difficulties have always been a problem, even in apparently more leisurely times.

In the first six recollections, qualities are brought to mind discursively. For generosity, for instance, one remembers acts of generosity that one has performed, a practice particularly favored for the dying. For morality, one recollects times one has kept the five precepts. These meditations, often overlooked in modern discussions of the subject, are held to be important for their capacity to bring about confidence and happiness in daily life. One *Dhammapada* story tells of a suicidal monk, who, just as he is about to use the razor, recollects his own good conduct; filled with joy, he then enters one of the stages of the path (*Buddhist Legends* 2 viii 11). All six of these recollections, while distinct, are felt to contribute to one another, are often taught together, and while not "simple" enough to lead to *jhāna*, are thought to bring about an underlying health of mind in daily life and, crucially, in meditation. Their practice, and to some extent their content, is often a little social.

The other four recollections are termed "mindfulnesses." The recollection of death is said to produce urgency (*saṃvega*).[31] Then follows mindfulness of body—as Buddhaghosa describes it, this is mindfulness directed toward viewing the parts of the body internally in the mind's eye. The meditator reviews bodily features, such as bones, blood, phlegm, and so on, with regard to element and color, and learns mastery and equanimity through them. This is presumably always conducted in seclusion. This and the next recollection, breathing mindfulness, are said to take the mind to deeper concentration and *jhāna*. Indeed, the third recollection in this group, breathing mindfulness, is the most widely used object in the list of forty. As a daily background practice, even during interchanges with others, it can also be used to develop all four *jhānas*, as well as providing a basis for formless meditation. Indeed, it is noteworthy that the breath also features prominently in systems described by Geoffrey Samuel (Tibetan), Harold D. Roth (Daoist), and Edwin F. Bryant (Yoga Sutras) in this volume. Breathing mindfulness is perhaps the most popular practice in Southeast Asia and, as Buddhism spreads, in the North Atlantic and in Europe. Dhammadharo writes,

With one exception, all of the meditation themes mentioned here are simply *gocara dhamma*—foraging places for the mind. They're not places for the

mind to stay. If we try to go live in the things we see when we're out foraging, we'll end up in trouble. Thus, there is one theme that's termed *"vihara
dhamma"* or *"anagocara"*: Once you've developed it, you can use it as a place to
stay. When you practice meditation, you don't have to go foraging in other
themes; you can stay in the single theme that's the apex of all meditation
themes: *anapanasati*, keeping the breath in mind. This theme, unlike the
others, has none of the features or various deceptions that can upset or dis-
turb the heart.[32]

The *Ānāpānasati-sutta* gives a range of recommendations, which are outside the
scope of this study. Breathing mindfulness is, however, taught today as a practice for daily life, with background awareness of breath, or as a practice leading
to either *samatha* or *vipassanā*, or with elements of both: the breath is moving,
unsatisfactory, and impermanent in its manifestation and not "owned," so it is a
natural object for arousing insight into the three "signs." It also, however, has
the capacity to gladden the mind and bring about tranquility, as described in
the sixteen stages of breathing mindfulness. In this regard, it is also a natural
samatha practice, said to lead to all four *jhānas*, as well as offer a basis for
formless meditation.[33] In some schools, the breath is counted, followed, "touched,"
and settled, the four stages recommended by Buddhaghosa, and when the visual
nimitta has arisen in the mind's eye, the *jhāna* factors are developed on the
basis of it (*Visuddhimagga* VIII 145–244).

The last of these recollections is that of peace. Any moments of tranquility
are brought to mind and remembered, an exercise particularly recommended
for the practitioner who has attained any stage of the path (*Visuddhimagga* VIII
245–251).

The recollections represent an essential, often overlooked element of Buddhist
"meditation." Many are not always sitting practices, though all can be. But the
term *bhāvanā*, meaning "mental development" or "cultivation," is most commonly used in early texts and modern practice to describe a range of activities,
including meditation, discussion, guided thinking about a number of attributes
intended to arouse specific qualities (as in the first six recollections), listening
to chanting and texts, and participation in investigative *dhamma* discussion.[34]
Discussion and investigation are also seen as particularly important *bhāvanā*,
correcting strong views, overpowering hindrances, or even, perhaps most
commonly, particularly in monastic settings, overcoming boredom and lassi-
tude. The word *bhāvanā* means "bringing into being" and is associated with the
verb used for the fourth noble truth, the path to awakening, and requires not
only "meditation" but other path factors too. Indeed, it would be difficult to find
some activity, where the precepts are kept, which is *not bhāvanā*. So the importance of these recollections cannot be underestimated, and a mix of activities
along with "sitting practice" is the usual way of teaching and describing meditation in the texts. Changes of posture, types of activities, and kinds of meditation are often enjoined.[35] Very few texts in the canon deal only with "sitting
meditation." The prevalence of such a variety of features involving adaptive

change suggests the balance derived from mixing one's activities, bodily, emo-
tionally, and socially, during the day. This is central and perhaps peculiar to
early Buddhist meditative procedure, in a context in which extremes that test
body and mind seem to have been more usual.[36] In modern practice also, chant,
ritual, listening, change of posture, and a good mix of collective and solitary
practice are frequent variations and accompaniments to the pursuit of sitting
meditation. In many *suttas* to individual meditators the Buddha gives a number
of practices, pursued collectively or singly, and in others suggests a number of
postures, including walking.[37]

The *Brahmavihāras*

The next grouping comprises the meditations on loving-kindness, compassion, sympathetic joy, and equanimity, the divine abidings (*brahmavihāras*),
also leading to *jhāna*. These are also considered "beautiful," but in an emotional sense. In their nonmeditative application, they are considered essential on
the Buddhist path; the *Dhammasaṅgani* list of the factors of a skillful mind
(*kusala-citta*) stresses that one of these is always present in any skillful state, in
daily life, as well as those path factors particular to that activity. So these meditations too can and should be cultivated at any time, as part of daily life, without
being used as means to obtain *jhāna*. The *Mettā-sutta*, a short text wishing
happiness to all beings, is constantly employed in Southern Buddhism, for all
kinds of purificatory, ceremonial, and restorative purposes, in both public and
private contexts (*Suttanipāta* 143–152). As sitting meditations, both collective
and solitary, they are frequently given to lay people, particularly by Sri Lankan
teachers, with adaptations so that specific locations are given for the various
beings that are mentioned, a practice suggested by the early texts' instructions
to pervade the directions with loving-kindness. So in Halvorsbøle, Norway (at
the conference where this essay was first presented), a monk might encourage
lay meditators to wish happiness to all beings around Halvorsbøle and the local
fjord before allowing the feeling to pervade Norway, and then move out in all
directions.[38] In the *Jātakas* and the canonical *Mahāsudassana-sutta*, these
meditations are practiced by lay Universal Monarchs, Gotama in his past lives.
They are considered peaceful and restorative, allowing the mind not to be trou-
bled by suffering or excitement.[39] The Buddha and his followers frequently
practiced these meditations after becoming enlightened.

The formless spheres we have already considered, so all that remains of the
forty meditation objects are the two last: considering the loathsomeness of food,
and awareness of the presence of the four elements in one human body, that of
the practitioner. The loathsomeness of food is only ever recommended in the
canon alongside other practices; a variation is suggested in some modern monastic contexts, though it does not seem to be a lay practice. The last, the defining of the elements, is interesting in that it seems to have become linked with a
rich variety of practices popular in recent times. In Laos and Northern Thailand some *samatha* practices on the elements are conducted in the traditions

described by François Bizot, and use meditative diagrams (*yantras*), often depicted on amulets, as ways of communicating balance and the interplay of the elements within the body. As perhaps suggested by the canonical *Mahārahulavāda-sutta*, the elements and the balance between them acquire a metaphoric meaning to denote attributes necessary for the *jhāna* itself, with "earth" related to the "father" and the first *jhāna* factor, *vitakka* (the syllable *mo*); the syllable *na* (water) to the "mother" and the *jhāna* factor of *vicāra*; the syllable *ddha* (fire) to the "monarch" and the factor of joy (*pīti*); the syllable *bu* (air) to the "family" and the factor of happiness (*sukha*), and the syllable *ya* (space), the unifying factor, to *ekaggattā*.[40] Extensive meditation teaching is encoded in these *yantra*, amulet, and ritual procedures, whose source is unknown, though their affinity with Śaivite practices suggests a common heritage.[41] Indeed, while hasty generalizations are rash given the highly differentiated nature of the contexts discussed in this volume, practices of various kinds discussed by Madhu Khanna, Geoffrey Samuel, and Kristina Myrvold in this volume suggest that the interweaving of chanting, invocation, visualization, and using a *yantra* as a guide to a complex investigation of manifestations of the four elements in the body was common in varying degrees to many traditions in India beginning sometime in the first millennium. There seems to have existed a pool of meditative features involving various interplays between them from which various traditions drew. The presence of such features, even perhaps those dating from recent centuries, indicates the continued interchange between folk knowledge, lay practice, ritual, and meditative procedure that seems to animate the Buddhist meditation. "The body" depicted in the *yantra* is in part a physical one, as the diagrams in figures 7.1 and 7.2 show; with the association of the five *jhāna* factors, or "limbs" of *jhāna*, the integration of the physical with the emotional and the mental is suggested with this meditative body.

These practices indicate that the interplay between meditative practice, modern accretions, and traditional canonical and commentarial recommendations is rich and complex in modern Southern Buddhism.

Forty Meditation Objects

In some ways this attempt to ascertain what features within early Buddhism could be said to characterize a meditation object, a "place of work," has been inconclusive, but the variety of objects, and the way they are matched together, in life and meditation, seem key. Simplicity and the attribute described as "beauty" are primary in practices intended to calm the mind, apparently performing essential roles in effecting unification and an ecstatic calm that nonetheless retains alertness and wisdom. Purification through joy and happiness are central to this process. At the higher stages of meditation, joy and happiness are transcended, though not rejected, as the mind is said to develop skill; they return however, in the sense-sphere, in lower *jhānas*, and in the process of attaining awakening. Joy (*pīti*) is a factor of awakening; happiness (*sukha*) is

Figure 7.1. *Yantra. Courtesy of Dr. Paul Dennison, Samatha Trust ("Na Yan: Continued," in* Samatha, *21).*

Figure 7.2. *Yantra. Courtesy of Dr. Paul Dennison, Samatha Trust ("Na Yan: Continued," in* Samatha, *21).*

always described as an important concomitant at each stage of practice, including the path and the attainment of *nibbāna.* So these factors are also central features in the complexity and complicatedness of other meditations associated with contact with the world and the activities of daily life, and the commentaries constantly cite them as benefits as well. These meditations seem to fulfill a number of functions in calming the mind, but also in allowing appropriate responses to develop to objects that shock the mind—such as death or loathsomeness—by ensuring that peacefulness and cheerfulness become habitual in the underlying tenor of one's mental state. There is also throughout the texts a sense of a graduated, taught path. Perhaps as is the case with the Jain objects

(Johannes Bronkhorst) and yoga techniques (Edwin F. Bryant) discussed in this volume, meditations are graduated and have different levels and stages. In Buddhism, the route can be very different for different meditators, however, and attainments may vary considerably.

There does not seem to be any description of what constitutes a meditation object in early texts. An overall category does not seem to have been thought necessary: "meditation" is perhaps a modern construct, where *bhāvanā* is more generally used in Buddhism. Buddhaghosa gives ten ways of describing a *kammaṭṭhāna*, or meditation object, that refer specifically only to the meditations on his list.[42] The list, however, does not seem to be definitive or prescriptive; some meditations are mentioned in the canon only once and are not included in the list of forty.[43]

Meditation Objects and Events in the World

In many *Dhammapada* stories, as we have seen, meditation objects, chosen and engaged with intent, overlap with surprise objects, or external events, occurring at crucial and timely moments. This phenomenon is famous in Eastern Buddhism, but is a striking feature of Southern Buddhism as well. Like the Kashmir practices described by Bettina Bäumer,[44] they require something more than "technique," a willing openness to the fortuitous and the fortunate in helping to bring about realization. In early Buddhist understanding, the key term was strong support (*upanissaya*), the causal condition, such as food or a teacher or a season, that acts as the trigger for meditative change and awakening.[45] This will in part be the product of the meditator's karma, perhaps from past lives.

Many *Dhammapada* stories describe enlightenment prompted by such external events. Meditators are described as needing a practice, methods to follow it, and a teacher. But there also seems to be a need to be open to the surprising and the unplanned. The prompt, or trigger that finally arouses inner transformation and liberation, is often some aspect of the deficiency of an object—say, its witheredness or its potential for decay. Sometimes, however, it is puzzling and koanlike. In one story, a young man is struggling with his meditation—a frequent narrative motif, as we have seen, presumably designed to encourage those lacking in confidence. He is given a cloth to rub, with the words "purity, purity" as an internal accompaniment. The cloth, however, gets dirtier and dirtier, and through this contradiction the meditator comes to awakening, seeing that it is internal, not external, purity that constitutes his own route to freedom. He formulates this insight himself, at the attainment of the path (*Buddhist Legends* I ii 3). In this regard Chán/Zen/Sŏn koans—as described by Morten Schlütter in this volume—are oddly anticipated, an understanding that grappling with a fortuitous paradox may offer the final means of release.

This chapter has considered a large range of objects, including the visual, the discursive, the emotional, and the inner, as well as those involving perceptions of the breath and the body. There is an emphasis on the visual, perhaps more than other Indic practices. The use of an auditory element to sustain alertness is, however, central to many. Some modern practices link the breath to the internal repetition of words such as "Buddho," whose sound is supposed to be linked to meaning as well.[46] Southeast Asian meditative practice is inventive and various in ways that can only be suggested here. Some modern meditation teaching aligns itself with commentarial procedures, but some is innovative too.

It might seem that this exploration of objects is focused on method. The intention, however, is to demonstrate that method is governed by the practitioner, steered by the teacher who assigns the object, and supporting conditions, met with openness. In exploration of the operating principles, some unifying strands have emerged: a wide diversity of objects, a graduated path, an emphasis on applicability, the importance of the relationship with the teacher or the good friend, and, in stories, the initiative of the meditator in finding and articulating the practice that brings final awakening. This awakening is often on the basis of an unexpected, fortuitous event in the world that completes that individual's path. Many stories describe meditators spontaneously alighting upon the object that brings awakening. This often forms the basis of the delighted utterances on attainment, a frequent feature of early Buddhist texts. Any object, it seems, could do this.

Notes

1. *Buddhist Legends*, 3 xx 9. For accessibility and ease of reference, the translation of the *Dhammapada-aṭṭhakathā*, the commentary to the *Dhammapada*, by E. W. Burlingame (*Buddhist Legends*), is cited throughout this article. All Pali Texts cited in this article may be found in the original, with Roman transliteration, in publications by the Pali Text Society.

2. I am grateful to Dr. Valerie Roebuck and the late L. S. Cousins for pointing this out to me. Dr. Mahinda Degalle told me (March 25, 2010) that since at least the nineteenth century the usual store of stories for "Sunday school" teaching within Sri Lanka was the *Dhammapada-Attakathā*, along with associated Sinhala versions and tales, and *Jātakas*. For shortened summaries of stories and the verses, see Roebuck, *Dhammapada*.

3. *The Path of Purification* (*Visuddhimagga*), by the fifth-century commentator Buddhaghosa, has been the most influential manual in South and Southeast Asia, closely followed by *The Path of Freedom* (*Vimuttimagga)* of Upatissa, probably written earlier. The classification of objects for this chapter have been taken from these. Again, for ease of reference, citations of *The Path of Purification* (*Visuddhimagga*) in this article are given with the chapter number (uppercase Roman numerals) and paragraph number of the Bhikkhu Ñāṇamoli translation. At the time of writing, the only translation of Upatissa's work from the Chinese is the Sri Lankan, undertaken by N. R. M. Ehara, Soma Thera, and Kheminda Thera, and citations are from that. The manuals present the methods probably associated with their own monasteries: Buddhaghosa's, written at the Mahāvihāra, in Sri Lanka, the home of the Sthāvira/Theravāda, reflects the monastic methods of the time. Upatissa is a mysterious figure, but seems to have been associated with the Abhayagiri Monastery, Sri Lanka, whose methods were probably influenced by Indian Buddhism. See introduction to *Path to Freedom* (*Vimuttimagga*), xxxiv–xxxv; and Shaw, *Buddhist Meditation*, 4–6.

4. "Wrong views" (*micchādiṭṭhi*) are said to produce rigidity of mind and body (*Atthasālini*, 134).

5. The word "object" is used here to describe a *kammaṭṭhāna*. Some teachers use the word "theme" or a "grazing place," *gocara*. See Dhammadharo, "Basic Themes."

6. Many short lists are delineated, and "permed" variously, but, significantly, the Buddha himself never gave a definitive compendium. A possible exception would be the *Aṅguttaranikāya*'s group of ones (I 34–40), which includes many other features of the path.

7. See *Aṭṭhasalini* 189; and, for the *suttas*, *Dīghanikāya* (*Sutta* 17) II 169–199 / *Long Discourses of the Buddha*, 279–290; *Suttanipāta* 1133–1149; *Dīghanikāya* II 253–262 (*Sutta* 20) / *Long Discourses of the Buddha*, 315–320. See also Shaw, *Buddhist Meditation*, 113–118.

8. For Buddhaghosa's caution, see, for instance, *Visuddhimagga* V 26. On this subject, see Shaw, *Buddhist Meditation*, 92–96.

9. Bhikkhu Ñāṇamoli and Bhikkhu Bodhi's translation of this passage is excellent (*Middle Length Discourses of the Buddha*, 966).

10. See *Dictionary of Pali* I 661; for "pervasiveness" as a meaning, see *Path to Freedom*, 72.

11. Unlike the mantric meditations of ancient and modern India and some modern Southeast Asian contexts, at this time no significance is attached to the syllables themselves other than as denoters. Meditations involving words whose meaning is felt to be communicated within the syllable soon enter many forms of Buddhism as *dhāraṇis*, spells, *mantras*, and *yantras*.

12. See Shaw, *Buddhist Meditation*, 28, 49, and 90; *Udāna* 34–37 / Shaw, *Buddhist Meditation*, 26–28; *Aṅguttaranikāya* I 3; and *Paṭisambhidāmagga* II 39.

13. Establishing calm before insight does seem the most common method described in the canon, as in, for instance, in the *Meghiya-Sutta*, *Udāna* 34–37 / Shaw, *Buddhist Meditation*, 26–28. Other routes are also described in Cousins, "*Samatha-Yāna* and *Vipassanā-Yāna*."

14. The size and the quality of the object are also adjusted to temperament: the desiring temperament is recommended to use a color *kasiṇa*, starting with "blue," that is not quite "pure"; the hating temperament is also recommended to do this, though with a pure color, while the deluded temperament should have a small object, so that the mind does not wander (*Visuddhimagga* III 97–102).

15. For the way objects may be made small or large, see *Dhammasaṅgani* 160–247. And for discussion of the *kasiṇa*, see Shaw, *Buddhist Meditation*, 86–100.

16. The *Mahāsakulayādi-sutta* says for all ten *kasiṇas*, "One is aware of the earth *kasiṇa* above, below, across, undivided, immeasurable" (*Majjhimanikāya* II 15), a formula repeated for all ten.

17. For closer examination of the Abhidhammic explanation for the affinity between the human *bhavaṅga* consciousness and the experience of beautiful objects as *vipāka*, see *Aṭṭhasalini* 270 / Shaw, *Buddhist Meditation*, 89–92 and 212n25. These are more likely to arouse skillful consciousness in the active stage of the thought process.

18. See *Samyuttanikāya* V 119–121; *Visuddhimagga* IX 121–122; and Shaw, *Buddhist Meditation*, 166.

19. For full canonical account of the "deliverances" see *Middle Length Discourses of the Buddha*, 1284–1285n2, quoted in Shaw, *Buddhist Meditation*, 212n38.

20. See Dhammadharo, "Basic Themes."

21. These are ten *kasiṇa*, ten *asubha*, four divine abidings, and the breath.

22. For some of the varied advice given to Moggallāna by the Buddha, see *Aṅguttaranikāya* IV 85–88 / Shaw, *Buddhist Meditation* 56–58.

23. For an explicit association between the *kasiṇa* practice and worldview, see *Majjhimanikāya* II 229–223 / *Middle Length Discourses of the Buddha*, 840; and *Paṭisambhidāmagga* I 143–144. See also Shaw, *Buddhist Meditation*, 91,212n30. See also Dessein, "Contemplation of the Repulsive."

24. For discussion of the limits of this meditation, which cannot go to higher *jhānas* as it is said to require the "rudder" of the repeated application of the mind to the object (*vitakka*), a feature present only in the first of the *jhānas*, see *Visuddhimagga* VI 86.

25. See Deleanu, "Śrāvakayāna," 3–11, for a description of this practice in early Yogācāra meditation.

26. The *Visuddhimagga* and the *Vimuttimagga* do not seem to give any specific instructions regarding the eyes for other meditations. The body mindfulness practice described by Buddhaghosa is not the practice for daily activities also recommended in the *Satipaṭṭhāna Sutta* (*Majjhimanikāya* I 47), but takes the thirty-two parts of the body in turn as properties defined through the *kasiṇa* method; e.g., teeth, skin, and hair of the head are taken as earth; bodily fluids as water; and so on (*Majjhimanikāya* I 158). The color of the respective part can also be used for this method. Where the object is external, such as hair of the head, the commentary describes it as a visual *kasiṇa* object, blue-black or white, depending on color. The eyes are presumably shut for other, internal parts of the body (*Visuddhimagga* VIII 81–141). Breathing mindfulness practice is conducted with closed eyes, as the breath *nimitta* is seen in the mind's eye (*Visuddhimagga* VIII 214–221).

27. See Pradhan, *Buddha's System of Meditation*, 3:1381–1385.

28. Early depictions of the Buddha in India at Ajanta, Amaravati, Nagarjunakonda, and so on, suggest that the arrangement of the right hand resting gently cupped on the left was usual, as it is now. In modern practice, a number of posture variations are pursued, including folding the legs to the side. Thai custom permits the meditator to make a graceful and finely planned sweep of the legs within a sitting meditation when very uncomfortable, though some honor is associated with sticking it out.

29. Buddhaghosa, for instance, mentions standing and walking postures as suitable for "greed" types, and lying or sitting postures for "hate" types (*Visuddhimagga* III 97–103). For the iconography of gestures and posture, see Matics, *Gestures of the Buddha*.

30. As an example of the benefits of this sort of recollection, see *Visuddhimagga* VII 114, where, it is said, the meditator starts to become intent on generosity (*cāga*), acts in conformity to loving-kindness (*mettā*), is fearless, experiences happiness and gladness, and is headed for a heavenly or happy rebirth. For these six recollections, see *Visuddhimagga* VII; and *Path to Freedom*, 140–155.

31. Death is also a frequent object of meditation in Western practices; cf. Rönnegård, "Melétē in Early Christian Ascetic Texts."

32. See note 5.

33. See Buddhadāsa Bhikkhu, *Mindfulness with Breathing*. See also Nyanaponika Thera, *The Heart of Buddhist Meditation*, which describes the practice with a stronger emphasis on *vipassanā*. See also Shaw, *Buddhist Meditation*, 146–158.

34. This contrasts with the much narrower meaning of the word in Tantric traditions. See Bäumer, "Creative Contemplation"; and Madhu Khanna's contribution to this volume.

35. See, for example, *Aṅguttaranikāya* IV 84–88 / *Buddhist Meditation*, 56–58.

36. See Bronkhorst, *Two Traditions*, 1–30.

37. For the most part, walking practices seem to balance sitting meditation. There are many varieties in the present day, emphasizing either calm (associating the rhythm of the walk with a feeling of well-being and of following the movement of the feet and body as the weight changes) or insight, through analysis of the stages of the process of lifting and moving the feet (see Dhammasami, *Mindfulness Meditation*). Although walking practices are not described in detail in any canonical or commentarial material, stories describe meditators walking, often within the set limits of a *caṅkamana*, specifically designed walking grounds, as a regular practice, are frequent (*Majjhimanikāya* I 56–57; *Aṅguttaranikāya* V 333–334; *Aṅguttaranikāya* III 29).

38. There does not seem to be any textual recommendation for this, though monks frequently "localize" the directional aspect of the loving-kindness practice, as described in say, the *Cūla-Assapura-Sutta* (*Majjhimanikāya* I 283–284), with wishes for the happiness of beings locally, and then over a larger geographical extent, and then in all directions. So, in Letchworth, in the United Kingdom, Venerable Rāhula wishes happiness to all beings in the surrounding environs; Venerable Piyatissa, now abbot of the *vihāra* in New York, when he was visiting Manchester led a practice wishing all beings in the area well before encouraging sending good wishes to areas further afield.

39. "As for the four sublime abodes, if you don't have *jhāna* as a dwelling for the mind, feelings of good will, compassion, and appreciation can all cause you to suffer. Only if you have *jhāna* can these qualities truly become sublime abodes, that is, restful places for the heart to stay." Dhammadharo, "Basic Themes."

40. Buddhaghosa does not describe space as the fifth element in this practice, but the *Mahārahulovāda-Sutta* (*Majjhimanikāya* 1 420–426 / Shaw 2006, 190–193) does. For some sense of the diversity of modern Southeast Asian practice, see D. K. Swearer, "Thailand." Bizot has drawn attention to the rich variety of amulet, chant and *yantra* practice in the region in *Le Bouddhisme des Thais*. See also Crosby, "Tantric Theravāda."

41. At the Cultural History of Meditation conference held in Oslo in May 2010, the fivefold interplay of Na Mo Śi Va Ya was discussed by M. D. Muthukumaraswamy. This has obvious affinities with the Na Mo Bu Ddha Ya formula of recent Southeast Asian practice. Cf. Muthukumaraswamy, "Vedic Chanting."

42. See *Visuddhimagga* III 103–121. These ten descriptions are (1) enumeration, as in the seven groups described in this paper; (2) as to whether they bring access meditation (*upacāra-samādhi*), a joyful state not yet stable enough to arouse *jhāna*, produced by some of the recollections, or *jhāna*; (3) as to the *jhāna* they produce; (4) as to surmounting; *kasiṇas*, and form meditations, "surmount" by means of mental factors, such as joy, but the formless surmount by means of an object; (5) as to extension and nonextension; *kasiṇas* can be extended, and will arouse psychic powers, but the breath and the foul do not; (6) as to object; some involve a "counterpart sign," and some do not; (7) as to "plane"; some, such as the foul and breathing mindfulness, can be practiced only by those in the sense-sphere, not by those in a Brahma heaven, where the body is too refined; (8) as to apprehending; nine *kasiṇas* (omitting air) and the foul are practiced initially by sight alone, body mindfulness (as taught by Buddhaghosa) by sight and hearsay (*suta*), breathing mindfulness by touch, air *kasiṇa* by sight and touch, and the remaining eighteen by "hearsay," in that they have attributes whose qualities have been "heard" described; (9) as to conditions, as to the states for which they can be conditions; for instance, according to Buddhaghosa, nine *kasiṇas* (excluding space) are conditions for formless meditation; (10) as to suitability for particular temperaments.

43. Many meditations taught by the Buddha fit no list; the recommendation to remember good friends to Nandiya (*Aṅguttaranikāya* V 336 / Shaw, *Buddhist Meditation*, 132), for instance, or the teaching on space as an internal object in the *Rāhulovāda-Sutta* (*Majjhimanikāya* I 423 / Shaw, *Buddhist Meditation*, 192). It is not a closed, exclusive, or definitive list noting all possible meditations, but rather only those that are most suitable (see Shaw, *Buddhist Meditation*, 6–8; and Vajirañāṇa, *Buddhist Meditation*, 75).

44. Bäumer, "Creative Contemplation."

45. This is the ninth of the twenty-four causal relationships, and its arising is considered dependent on the person's past karma (*Visuddhimagga* XVII 18–24).

46. See Dhammadharo, *Keeping the Breath in Mind*, 26–63.

Bibliography

All original Pali texts cited are published by the Pali Text Society.

Bäumer, Bettina. "'Creative Contemplation' (*Bhāvanā*) in the Vijñāna Bhairava." In *Hindu, Buddhist and Daoist Meditation: Cultural Histories*, edited by Halvor Eifring, 57–67. Oslo: Hermes, 2014.

Bizot, F. *Le Bouddhisme des Thais*. Bangkok: Editions des Cahiers de France, 1993.

Bronkhorst, J. *The Two Traditions of Meditation in Ancient India*. Delhi: Motilal Banarsidass, 1993.

Buddhadāsa Bhikkhu. *Mindfulness with Breathing: Unveiling the Secrets of Life (A Manual for Serious Beginners)*. Bangkok: The Dhamma Study and Practice Group, 1989.

Burlingame, E. W. *Buddhist Legends*. 3 vols. First published in the Harvard Oriental Series, 1921. Oxford: Pali Text Society, 1990.

Chalmers, Robert, ed. *Majjhimanikāya*. Oxford: Pali Text Society. First published in London in 1899. Oxford: Pali Text Society, 2003.

Cone, Margaret. *Dictionary of Pali*. Volume 1. Oxford: Pali Text Society, 2001.

Crosby, K. "Tantric Theravāda: A Bibliographic Essay on the Writings of François Bizot and Others on the Yogāvacāra Tradition." *Contemporary Buddhism: An Interdisciplinary Journal* 1, no. 2 (November 2000): 141–198.

Cousins, L. S. "*Samatha-Yāna* and *Vipassanā-Yāna*." In *Buddhist Studies in Honour of Hammalava Saddhatissa*, edited by Gatare Dhammapala, R. F. Gombrich, and K. R. Norman, 46–68. Nugegoda, Sri Lanka: Hammalava Saddhatissa Felicitation Volume Committee, 1984.

Deleanu, F. "Śrāvakayāna Yoga Practices and Mahāyāna Buddhism." Special issue. *Waseda Daigaku Daigaku-in bungaku kenkyū-ka kiyō (Bulletin of the Graduate Division of Literature of Waseda University)* 20 (1993): 3–11.

Dennison, P. "Na Yan: An Introduction." *Samatha: Insight from a Meditation Tradition* 2 (1996): 16–18.

———. "Na Yan: Continued." *Samatha: Insight from a Meditation Tradition* 3 (1997): 19–23.

Dessein, Bart. "Contemplation of the Repulsive: Bones and Skulls as Objects of Meditation." In *Hindu, Buddhist and Daoist Meditation: Cultural Histories*, edited by Halvor Eifring, 117–147. Oslo: Hermes, 2014.

Dhammadharo Ajahn Lee. "Basic Themes." Translated from the Thai by Thanissaro Bhikkhu. *Access to Insight*, August 23, 2010 (unpaginated), http://www.accesstoinsight.org/lib/thai/lee/themes.html (accessed April 12, 2012).

———. *Keeping the Breath in Mind: Lessons in Samādhi*. Translated by Geoffrey DeGraff. Rayong, Thailand: N.p, talks cover the period of 1956–1960.

Dhammasami, Bhikkhu. *Mindfulness Meditation Made Easy*. Penang, Malaysia: Inward Path, 1999.

Ehara, N. R. M., Soma Thera, and Kheminda Thera, trans. *The Path of Freedom (Vimuttimagga) by Arahant Upatissa*. Kandy, Sri Lanka: Buddhist Publication Society, 1977.

Matics, K. I. *Gestures of the Buddha*. 4th ed. Bangkok: Chulalongkorn University Press, 2008.

Muthukumaraswamy, M. D. "Vedic Chanting as a Householder's Meditation Practice in the Tamil Śaiva Siddhānta Tradition." In *Meditation and Culture: The Interplay of Practice and Context*, edited by Halvor Eifring, 186–199. London: Bloomsbury Academic, 2015.

Ñāṇamoli, Bhikkhu, trans. *The Path of Purification (Visuddhimagga) of Buddhaghosa: The Classic Manual of Buddhist Doctrine and Meditation*. 5th ed. Kandy, Sri Lanka: Buddhist Publication Society, 1991.

Ñāṇamoli, Bhikkhu, and Bhikkhu Bodhi, trans. *The Middle Length Discourses of the Buddha*. Revised edition. Oxford, Pali Text Society, 2001.

Norman, K. R. *Theragāthā (Poems of Early Buddhist Monks)*. London, Pali Text Society, 1969.

Nyanaponika Thera. *The Heart of Buddhist Meditation: A Handbook of Mental Training Based on the Buddha's Way of Mindfulness with an Anthology of Relevant Texts translated from the Pāli and Sanskrit*. London: Rider and Company, 1962.

Pradhan, A. P. *The Buddha's System of Meditation*. 4 vols., New Delhi: Oriental University Press, 1986.

Roebuck, V. *The Dhammapada*. Penguin Classics Series. London: Penguin, 2010.

Rönnegård, Per. "*Melétē* in Early Christian Ascetic Texts." In *Meditation in Judaism, Christianity and Islam*, edited by Halvor Eifring, 79–92. London: Bloomsbury Academic, 2013.

Shaw S., *Buddhist Meditation: An Anthology of Texts*. London: Routledge, 2006.

———. *Introduction to Buddhist Meditation*. London: Routledge, 2009.

Swearer, D. K. "Thailand." In *Encyclopedia of Buddhism*, edited by Robert Buswell, 2:830–836. New York: Macmillan, 2003.

Vajirañāṇa, Mahāthera. 1975. *Buddhist Meditation in Theory and Practice*. Kuala Lumpur: Buddhist Missionary Society, 1975.

Walshe, Maurice. *The Long Discourses of the Buddha*. Boston, MA: Wisdom Publications, 1987/1995.

Tibetan Longevity Meditation

Tibetan meditation techniques can at first seem complex, even bewildering, to those familiar with Buddhist meditation primarily through the simpler forms of Theravāda and Zen Buddhist practice commonly taught in the West. Much Tibetan imagery is complex, and meditation is intertwined with elaborate, even theatrical, ritual techniques. In addition, Tibetan meditation is intrinsically Tantric, and for Westerners the term "Tantra" tends to be associated primarily with ritualized sex, an association that is certainly evoked by much Tibetan imagery, though it has little to do with most Tibetan practice.

In fact, much of this elaborate ritual can be performed through visualization and creative imagination, without the use of elaborate props, and the most advanced levels of Tibetan practice can be very direct and simple. Simplicity in the Tibetan tradition, however, tends to come at the later stages, not at the beginning. One might say that this is because the Tibetan traditions see a need to deconstruct the conditioning of everyday life, and to dissolve or weaken the ways in which our experience of the world is entrained by deeply engrained emotions and habitual tendencies, before moving to the levels of direct experience.

As for Tantric sex, sexual practices in the literal sense do not form part of most Tibetan meditation. Today, they are confined to a small minority of committed yogic practitioners within certain specific traditions. At the same time, sexuality as a dimension of human existence is certainly not excluded from Tantric practice, and appears both in the imagery of Tantric ritual and meditational procedures, and as part of the general understanding of human psychophysiological processes that underlies the practices.

Thus the striking and dramatic imagery and symbolism of Tibetan Buddhist practice today is deployed in the service of essentially the same goals as Buddhist practice elsewhere. Whether this was so in the earlier days of Indian Tantra is open to question. Earlier versions of Tantra in India, at any rate in non-Buddhist circles, seem to have centered around techniques of magic and sorcery, often employed for destructive purposes on behalf of local kings and chieftains.[1] For the Tibetans, while some of the imagery may seem to hark back to such contexts, Buddhist Tantra, or Vajrayāna Buddhism, as it is often termed, derives by definition from a revelation of the wisdom and compassion of an enlightened Buddha. It should only be practiced with the highest of motivations, which is *bodhicitta*, the altruistic desire to attain Buddhahood in order to relieve the suffering of all sentient beings, a category that includes gods, animals, hell beings, and other spirits as well as humans. The relationship between Mahāyāna Buddhism and Vajrayāna Buddhism in Tibet is essentially one between theory and practice. The Mahāyāna teachings define the structure of the path and the goal toward which it is oriented, and the Vajrayāna provides the techniques by which it is to be attained.[2]

Here it is worth outlining some basic assumptions of Mahāyāna and Tantric Buddhism in Tibet. Western understandings of Buddhism see the historical Buddha, Śākyamuni, as a human teacher living at a particular point in time whose activities formed the starting point of a tradition developed by a succession of later historical personages. By contrast, the Tibetan perspective has a different and much expanded sense of the nature of the Buddha and of Buddhahood. Within this perspective, the historical Buddha was an example, an emanation, or a projection (I am deliberately keeping this a little vague since a detailed explanation would go well beyond the scope of this chapter) of a universal principle or capability that is variously called Buddhahood, Buddha nature, Enlightenment, or the Dharmakāya. Buddha nature is present in all life, and particularly in all beings that have consciousness (the "sentient beings" referred to above). Thus Buddhahood can be seen as a potential mode of being that any living consciousness can potentially adopt. Put somewhat differently, Buddha nature is within all phenomena, and constitutes the underlying nature of the universe seen "as it really is." There is a basic opposition here between things as ordinary beings see and experience them, with dualistic vision, and things as they are seen in their enlightened form, through "pure vision" (Tib. *dag snang*).[3]

The various Tantric deities, in the Tibetan perspective, are aspects of this pure vision. They are devices through which ritual practitioners can access both the knowledge and, very importantly, the power of the Buddha. Lamas perform their work through the power of creative imagination, visualizing the deities and then summoning the real presence of the deities to enter the visualized forms. The deities may be evoked externally or internally, a distinction that is in any case illusory from the point of view of ultimate reality.

While the explicit central goal of these practices is for the ritual performer to attain Buddhahood in order to relieve the sufferings of living beings, the deities can also be invoked for more immediate and this-worldly purposes, such as the attainment of health and long life, of good fortune and prosperity, or for defense against malevolent spirits and other obstacles and forces of evil. The ability to do this is grounded in the activity of lamas of the past, who established the ongoing lineages of Tantric practice by which today's Tantric practitioners continue to control the forces of the apparent world. These ongoing traditions of Tantric practice became the property of major monasteries, passed on through the centuries by hereditary or reincarnate lamas much of whose status, charisma, and political power was associated with their connection to one or another of the lineages of Tantric practice.

Thus Tantric lamas are above all ritual performers and teachers of the skills of ritual performance, skills that historically have been seen as of central value to Tibetan society. These skills involve the creative manipulation of the forces represented by the Tantric deities, and this is routinely done through the practitioner's imaginative identification with Tantric deities, supported by visualization, gesture, liturgy, and a variety of ritual implements and offerings.

Tshe-sgrub, or longevity practices, are among the most significant of the meditative processes carried out through this Tantric methodology. Their purpose is to attain a long and healthy life. At the same time, as we will see, the orientation toward the achievement of Buddhahood remains very much part of the wider context within which the practice is performed. *Tshe-sgrub* practices form part of a much wider repertoire of Tibetan longevity-related practices, which include medical preparations, dietary practices involving the ritual empowerment of pills made from herbal and mineral substances and their ingestion under controlled circumstances, and physical exercises, as well as practices such as the liberation of animals to generate positive *karma* or the performance of Tantric ritual to avert and eliminate obstacles to health and well-being or to avert the time of death. While *tshe-sgrub* practices are characteristically Vajrayāna Buddhist in their form and procedures, and refer explicitly to the Indian Tantric ideas of the *siddhi*, or attainment of power over the duration of life, these practices also incorporate both elements from the Indian alchemical tradition, and also other elements that suggest procedures of Himalayan shamanism, such as the recalling of soul-substance or spirit that has been stolen by demonic forces or otherwise lost to the surrounding environment.

Elsewhere I have discussed the history of Indo-Tibetan alchemy[4] and the evolution of longevity practice in Tibet,[5] and I have also considered how one might understand these practices in anthropological terms.[6] Here I will present a description of one specific cycle of longevity practices, the *'Chi-med Srog Thig*, a set of practices that originated with the late nineteenth-century lama Zil-gnon Nam-mkha'i rdo-rje and is particularly associated with the late Dudjom Rinpoche (bDud-'joms Rin-po-che 'Jigs-bral Ye-shes rdo-rje).[7]

The Origins of the *'Chi-med Srog Thig* Cycle

What is the *'Chi-med Srog Thig* (the name means something like *Creative Seed of Immortal Life*)? To start with, like all Tibetan Tantric practices, the *'Chi-med Srog Thig* is an ongoing continuity of practice, passed down from teacher to student. Thus, while there is a body of texts that relate to it, the *'Chi-med Srog Thig* is essentially the ongoing practice tradition rather than the text. As such, it is one of the many practice traditions within Tibetan Buddhism mentioned earlier. Some of these have been handed down over many centuries, in some cases going back to Indian Buddhism; others, such as the *'Chi-med Srog Thig*, go back to a specific vision or revelation at a more recent point in time. The *'Chi-med Srog Thig* was revealed at the beginning of the twentieth century, in this case to a *gter-ston*, a term often translated somewhat literally as "treasure finder" but which we can tentatively render as "visionary lama."[8] It should be noted that none of these practices is regarded as being of simply human origin; there is always some kind of contact with the levels of ultimate reality represented by the

Buddha and his various Tantric manifestations. The *gter-ston* is one way in which this contact can take place.

A *gter-ston* is a person who is thought of as having a link back to Padma-sambhava (generally known in Tibetan as Padma 'Byung-gnas or Guru Rin-po-che), the principal originating lama of the Rnying-ma-pa (Old Ones) tradition, regarded as the earliest of the major Tibetan Buddhist traditions. The Rnying-ma-pa is also the tradition that is closest to what one could call, with reservations, the "shamanic" side of Tibetan religion.[9] Padmasambhava is probably a historical figure who came to Tibet from India in the late eighth century. During his visit to Tibet he is held to have bound the local gods of Tibet in obedience to the Buddhist teachings, and to have helped establish the first Tibetan monastery. He is also said to have gathered together a group of twenty-five close disciples, including the then King, Khri-srong Lde'u-btsan, and a princess, Ye-shes Mtsho-rgyal, who acted as one of his Tantric consorts and wrote down his teachings, which were concealed in cryptic forms. Buddhist *gter-ston*[10] are regarded as rebirths of one or more of these twenty-five disciples, who carry within their mind-streams the imprint of the original teachings given by Padmasambhava. The idiom of visionary revelation is complex, but the general idea is that some precipitating event awakens these memories, and the *gter-ston* has access to them and can transcribe or dictate them in a form that can be practiced by his followers. The *gter-ston* may find physical texts and other objects that catalyze the rediscovery, or may simply uncover the teachings within the depths of his own consciousness.[11]

A *gter-ston* may or may not be able to produce a formal textual presentation of the teachings he or she reveals. His talents may be more for visionary work than for scholarship, and it is not unusual for a *gter-ston* to work with one or more lamas with more gifts for the compilation of the teachings in liturgical form. These lamas may also be responsible for the further propagation of the teachings. If they are heads of major monasteries, the teachings may become part of the ongoing "property" of that monastery and its lamas, and be passed on through successive generations of lamas and students in that tradition alongside the other teachings associated with the monastery. In other cases, a lama may establish a major new teaching tradition on the basis of a particular set of revelations (*gter-ma*, a term that can refer both to physical objects and to texts discovered, and also, as here, to a body of discovered teachings and practices). This was the case, for example, with the lama Karma 'Chags-med, who worked with the *gter-ston* Mi-'gyur Rdo-rje in the early seventeenth century, in the codification of his Gnam Chos (Sky Dharma) revelations. These became the basis of liturgical practice at the newly founded monastery of Dpal-yul, and in time the Dpal-yul tradition became one of the six major teaching monasteries of the Rnying-ma-pa tradition, with numerous dependent monasteries all practicing the Gnam Chos teachings.

A complete *gter-ma* cycle generally includes a whole range of liturgical and practice texts relating to a specific deity and his or her *maṇḍala*, along with associated historical texts, empowerment texts, explanatory and commentarial material, and so on. Thus one can carry out a wide range of activities, from solo meditational practices to large-scale public rituals, on the basis of a single *gter-ma*. We will see some of how this works later when I run through the material in the *'Chi-med Srog Thig* cycle.

This whole process of *gter-ma* revelation has close relationships to a variety of other visionary practices in Tibetan religion, and there is much more that could be said about it, and indeed much that has been said by others and by myself in other contexts,[12] but here it is perhaps enough to note that it introduces an important dynamic element into Tibetan Buddhism. A *gter-ma*-revelation is not necessarily automatically accepted. Much depends on the status of the original lama and of the people who take up the teachings. Many *gter-ma* teachings doubtless disappeared with little or no trace. Others became major traditions of practice within contemporary religion, as with the main *gter-ma* cycles associated with Dudjom Rinpoche, of which the *'Chi-med Srog Thig* is one.

Dudjom Rinpoche was himself a *gter-ston*, but he was not in fact the discoverer of the *'Chi-med Srog Thig* cycle. The original revelation of the *'Chi-med Srog Thig* took place at the start of the twentieth century, through a lama called Zil-gnon Nam-mkha'i Rdo-rje.[13] The initial revelation took place in Southern Tibet in 1902, and was followed by a more public revelation at a sacred site in Bhutan in 1904.[14] The *'Chi-med Srog Thig* formed part of a series of revelations that were received by Zil-gnon Nam-mkha'i Rdo-rje, and was associated as a set of accessory practices to a group of Vajrakīlaya teachings.

We do not as yet know a great deal about Zil-gnon, but he lived in Eastern Tibet, and was apparently associated with the Zur-mangs group of monasteries, part of the Karma Bka'-brgyud-pa tradition of Tibetan Buddhism. While *gter-ma* discovery is more associated with the Rnying-ma-pa than with the various branches of the Bka'-brgyud-pa, there were close links between Rnying-ma-pa and Bka'-brgyud-pa in Eastern Tibet in the nineteenth century. The Karma Bka'-brgyud-pa were closely involved in the great Buddhist revival centered at the court of Sde-dge (Derge) in the mid- to late nineteenth century and generally referred to as the Ris-med (eclectic or nonsectarian) movement, in which *gter-ma* revelations were of particular importance. Zil-gnon appears to have made a deep impression on the principal lama of the Karma Bka'-brgyud-pa, the fifteenth Karmapa (Rgyal-ba Karma-pa Mkha-khyab Rdo-rje, 1871–1922), who wrote the basic empowerment ritual and several other texts for the *'Chi-med Srog Thig* cycle between 1911 and 1916, and was recognized as the *chos-bdag*, or owner and propagator, of Zil-gnon's revelation.

The fifteenth Karmapa died, however, in 1922, and although the texts for the *'Chi-med Srog Thig* are included in his Gsung-'bum (Collected Works), there is as far as we know no continuing practice tradition of the *'Chi-med Srog Thig* among the Karma Bka'-brgyud-pa today. The large-scale propagation of Zil-gnon's teachings was the work of another, much younger East Tibetan lama, Dudjom Rinpoche (Bdud-'joms Rin-po-che, 1904–1987), whose personal name was 'Jigs-bral Ye-shes Rdo-rje. Dudjom Rinpoche, as mentioned earlier, was himself a *gter-ston*, as well as being the recognized rebirth of another well-known visionary lama, Bdud-'joms Gling-pa, and he is said to have found his own first *gter-ma* at the age of five.[15] Dudjom Rinpoche took over as *chos-bdag* or chief propagator of the *'Chi-med Srog Thig* practices. He wrote most of the other ritual and liturgical texts for the cycle, and seems to have taken it up with some enthusiasm, perhaps because his own health was poor for much of his life (he suffered badly from emphysema). The *'Chi-med Srog Thig* became one of his principal practices and was taught widely to his many students and followers.

Crucially for the later history of this cycle of teachings, Dudjom Rinpoche left Tibet in 1958, initially settling at Kalimpong in West Bengal, India. He was a major figure among the Tibetan refugees, and along with the sixteenth Karmapa (1924–1981), who went to Sikkim, and Dilgo Khyentse Rinpoche (1910–1991), who had settled in Bhutan, formed the principal counterweight to the refugee administration at Dharamsala, which was dominated by the Dalai Lama's Dge-lugs-pa tradition. Dudjom later also lived in Nepal and in France, where he died in 1987. Today there are many lamas, particularly in Nepal and the Kalimpong area, who are followers of his teachings. He was also one of the first senior lamas to have Western students and patrons.

The Factors of Long Life

What is long-life practice supposed to do? The English term "long-life practice," or "longevity practice," is a translation of the Tibetan *tshe-sgrub*, literally "realization or accomplishment of *tshe*" where *tshe* means life in the sense of life duration. *Tshe ring-po*, a long life span, is certainly an explicit goal of the practices. More technically, the practices are described as being aimed at the attainment or accomplishment of the *siddhi* (Tib. *dngos-grub*) of long life, the Tantric power of control over life span. This was held to be one of a number of "powers" or "abilities" of the Enlightened Buddha and so of the Tantric adept. Indian Tantric adepts (*siddha*) such as the great Nāgārjuna were thought of as having attained the *siddhi* of long life, and so as being able to live as long as they desired.[16] As we will see, Padmasambhava was also believed to have attained this *siddhi*. However, the situation becomes complicated in two ways.

Firstly, it may be asked whether the practice is really concerned with long life in the sense of an increased duration of time in this ordinary and by definition very unsatisfactory and largely illusory existence in *saṃsāra*, the world of cyclic existence, of life, death and rebirth, which the Buddhist teachings are explicitly aimed at transcending. It is not uncommon to encounter direct denials that this is the case. The *real* long-life *siddhi*, one may be told, is Enlightenment itself, and the state of Enlightenment or Buddhahood is beyond ordinary notions of space and time.[17] The mere mundane question of adding a few months or years onto one's current rebirth is not a matter to be taken seriously.[18] Within this perspective, extension of the duration of life is at best a question of *upāyakauśalya*, or skill in means, by which the student is lured toward a goal that actually far transcends such meaningless concerns.

A position of this kind is in radical contrast to the general Tibetan lay perception that long-life practice is precisely about living longer in this life, admittedly a problematic goal for a tradition such as Buddhism that regards ordinary *saṃsāric* life as radically unsatisfactory and ultimately largely illusory, and sees attachment to *saṃsāra* as a basic problem to be countered through practice. What is more common in the learned discourse about long-life practice is a kind of compromise position, by which the extension in life duration is real (at least as far as anything in this life has reality), but its purpose is explicitly Dharmic.

Thus one strives to achieve a longer and healthier life so as to have more time and more ability to practice the Dharma, with the ultimate aim of altogether transcending such relative concepts and then of aiding others to follow one along the same path. This is very much in line with the familiar Tibetan emphasis, deriving from Indian Mahāyāna sources, on human life as a unique opportunity for the achievement of Buddhahood. Since we have this opportunity, we should seek to make as good a use of it as possible.

It goes along with this that the deities of long life, such as the form of Amitāyus who is at the center of the *'Chi-med Srog Thig* cycle, are thought of, like almost all of the deities at the center of specific Tantric practices, as themselves aspects of the Enlightened Buddha. The ultimate attainment of Amitāyus is therefore equivalent to Buddhahood itself, or at least takes you a fair way along the path to it. This helps remove the conflict between the apparently *saṃsāric* goal to which the practice is oriented, and the explicitly trans-*saṃsāric* intention of any proper Mahāyāna practice. Most *tshe-sgrub* practice texts ensure that you are regularly reminded of this trans-*saṃsāric* motivation, as in fact do most other kinds of Buddhist practice aimed at superficially worldly ends. Thus the *'Chi-med Srog Thig* practice begins with verses in which the practitioner takes refuge in the deity of long life, who is in effect treated as a form of the Buddha, and in which the altruistic motivation for the practice is generated. It ends with a dedication of merit and auspicious wishes, which again return us very explicitly to the central aims of Buddhist practice.

Secondly, long-life practice is thought of as operating on a number of factors or components, among which *tshe* (life duration) itself is listed as one. This raises the question of the relationship between *tshe* in the sense of the overall goal of the practice, and *tshe* as one of the factors that is being manipulated through the practice. One can think of this in at least two ways. Firstly, part of the process of achievement of long life consists in mastery over these other aspects of health and longevity; secondly, the aim of the practice is in fact rather more than long life itself, since (for example) long life as a permanent invalid in continual pain is not necessarily helpful for the achievement of Enlightenment. This is particularly true on the Tantric path, where Buddhahood is closely linked with mastery over the inner flows of the subtle body, for which good physical health is a major asset.

What then are the various factors or components on which long-life practice might be seen as operating? Here there are generally three or four principal factors mentioned in the practice texts, though the precise lists vary. The *'Chi-med Srog Thig* uses four factors: *tshe*, life span or life duration; *srog*, which can be translated approximately as "life force" or "vital strength"; *bla*, a term for separable life essence or protective energy; and *dbugs*, literally meaning "breath." Other factors that may be involved include *rlung-rta* (good fortune) and *dbang-thang* (personal power, ability to enforce one's will).

As Barbara Gerke has demonstrated in her own research on the contemporary ethnography of long-life concepts and practices,[19] these form part of a body of Tibetan terms that occur both in popular discourse and in a variety of learned contexts, including medicine, astrology, and other forms of divination. Thus in astrology the variations over time of *srog*, *bla*, *lus* (body), *rlung-rta*, and *dbang-thang* are tracked and correlated with the cycles of the five elements (metal, wood, water, air, and fire) fundamental to the Chinese-derived system of Tibetan astrology (*nag-rtsis*). The *rlung-rta*, or "prayer flag" rituals, that are an ubiquitous feature of Tibetan communities are not just concerned with increasing the *rlung-rta* (good fortune) after which they are named. They also explicitly ask in most cases for the increase of *srog*, *lus*, *tshe*, and *dbang-thang*. The movement of *bla* around the body is traced in the medical context and is significant in terms of the use of various medical procedures, such as moxibustion.

Whether these factors have the same meaning in each of these different contexts is another question. *Bla* is a particularly significant factor in this regard since it appears to have a direct derivation from pre-Buddhist Tibetan ideas of a separable soul or life essence similar to that found in many Asian and American contexts.[20] Such souls can generally be lost, and the work of shamanic practitioners is, as is well known, often conceived of in terms of its recovery. This is true in the Tibetan case as well, and as we will see that this becomes extended to the other factors; *tshe* or *srog* may also be seen as potentially able to be lost to the surrounding environment and also able to be recovered from that environment through the practice. Thus the body in longevity practice is seen as open to the surrounding environment and intimately connected with it, and the practice itself, like a range of other Tibetan Tantric practices, can be seen as a reworking within a sophisticated literate culture of ideas of lost or stolen souls.

In relation to the environment, it is worth saying a few more things about the concept of *bla*. Firstly, *bla* may pertain to social groups or regions as well as to individuals. Secondly, specific places, plants, or animals in the environment may be thought of as external homes of the *bla* and their vitality linked to the vitality of the corresponding person or group. Such ideas are common in the Tibetan epic of Gling Ge-sar, where defeating a particularly powerful human or demonic opponent can involve tracking his or her *bla*-object, and in various folk and popular ritual contexts. They have also remained quite alive in popular understandings, and easily shade over into ideas of relationships to local deities: thus the *bla ri* (*bla* mountain) or *bla mtsho* (*bla* lake) of a region is also the home of its guardian deity, so that the health of the *bla* may also be figured in terms of maintaining good relations with the local deity.

These relationships to the environment are not referenced directly in longevity practice but can probably be thought of as part of a network of associations that support longevity practice's environmental dimension and give it plausibility and naturalness in the Tibetan setting. To put this differently, the idea of an ecological or environmental dimension to health may be found in a variety of premodern Tibetan contexts, and these can be thought of as reinforcing one another. The extent to which these concepts may be reworked or rethought in terms of modern ideas of environmental health is a complex and interesting question, but one into which I shall not go here.

The key transaction in longevity practice does however retain a strong environmental dimension. Put simply, in longevity practice, deterioration in *bla srog tshe* and other related factors is remedied by recovering the "lost" *bla srog tshe* and so on from the surrounding environment and returning it to the individual, and also by strengthening the individual with the aid of positive forces or essences in the environment. This can be done by the individual practitioner on his or her own behalf, or by a lama, with or without a supporting ritual team, on behalf of others.

The Structure of the Teachings

I have referred to the *'Chi-med Srog Thig* as a cycle of teachings but so far have avoided being explicit about what this means. The central feature of a *gter-ma* cycle is a specific revelation or series of revelations that normally focus around a specific form of a deity and the associated *maṇḍala.* In the case of the *'Chi-med Srog Thig*, the central deities are as already mentioned forms of Amitāyus, more specifically a male-female couple (Padma Thod-'phreng-rtsal and consort) who are held to represent the specific forms of Amitāyus and of his consort Caṇḍalī that were realized by Padmasambhava and his consort, the Indian princess Mandāravā, when they themselves achieved the long-life *siddhi*, an episode that was held to have happened at a location known as Māratika and today mostly identified with the Hindu-Buddhist cave shrine of Halase in Nepal.[21]

These two figures are surrounded by a *maṇḍala* of subsidiary figures: four further Buddha figures, each with female consort, in the four directions, six goddesses of sensory enjoyment, eight offering goddesses, and four door-keeper goddesses. These are portrayed as images in figure 8.1, and are represented by dots in figure 8.2. The door-keeper goddesses again have male consorts, so this comes to a total of thirty-two deities, including the central figures. There are also four symbolic supports for the four life forces. Figure 8.1 also portrays the two *sambhogakāya* deities (Padma Gar-dbang and consort), of which Padma Thod-'phreng rtsal and consort are *nirmāṇakāya* projections or emanations, and the *dharmakāya* deities (Samantabhadra and consort) from which they in turn derive, as well as the deified lamas of the lineage through which the teachings have been passed down, at the top of the painting, and the worldly protector gods associated with the teachings at the foot.

It is the imaginative recreation by the practitioner of this *maṇḍala* of deities that effectively defines the practice of the *'Chi-med Srog Thig.* None of the

Figure 8.1. The *'Chi med srog thig* deities, Kalimpong, 2009. *Photo by Geoffrey Samuel.*

Figure 8.2. Sand *maṇḍala* for the *'Chi med Srog Thig* major practice session, Jangsa Dechen Choling Monastery, Kalimpong, 2009. *Photo by Cathy Cantwell.*

individual deities is unique to the *'Chi-med Srog Thig*, but the specific configuration, and specific details of the iconography (such as the implements held by the various figures) are not repeated exactly in any other cycle, and a primary function of the initiation or empowerment ritual (*dbang gi cho-ga*, or *dbang chog* for short) in the cycle is to introduce future practitioners to this specific constellation of deities, which they will invoke and bring into being through visualization and active imagination in the practice.

Major *gter-ma* cycles such as the *'Chi-med Srog Thig* contain a large number of individual texts carried out in relation to the *maṇḍala* of deities of that particular *gter-ma*. These form the basis for a variety of meditational practices and ritual activities. To get a sense of what the *'Chi-med Srog Thig* contains in textual terms, I now turn to a brief survey of the texts in volume 14 (volume Pha[22]) of Dudjom Rinpoche's Gsung-'bum (Collected Works). These texts center around the longevity deity Guru Amitāyus (Bla-ma Tshe-dpag-med), a Tibetan development of the important Indian Buddhist deity Amitāyus, whose name (meaning "limitless life") already indicates his close association with long-life practices.

The overall title of these practices is worth a brief glance: it is *Rdo rje'i phur pa yang gsang phrin las bcud dril gyi las tshe sgrub 'chi med srog thig* (The Creative Seed of Immortal Life Longevity Practice, an Activity of the Extra-secret Essential Vajrakīlaya Practice). As this implies, these practices are technically an appendix to a set of practices associated with the fierce Tantric deity Phurba or Vajrakīlaya, also originally revealed by the same lama, Zil-gnon Nam-mkha'i Rdo-rje. The first few texts in volume 14 are in fact about these Vajrakīlaya practices, but the bulk of the volume is about the long-life practices of Guru Amitāyus, and in fact includes little or no reference to their supposed context as part of a Vajrakīlaya cycle. The balance is quite telling; the Vajrakīlaya texts take up 70 pages, the 'Chi med srog thig practices some 480 pages, so the latter hardly appear as an appendix to the former.

This imbalance makes more sense when one appreciates that, as one of our lama-consultants, Lopön Ogyan Tandzin, pointed out, Dudjom Rinpoche also had two major Vajrakīlaya cycles of his own, one of them (Gnam-lcags Spu-gri) said to be based on a discovery by his previous rebirth, bDud-'joms gLing-pa, and the other (Spu-gri Reg-phung) from his own personal *gter ma*. These two Vajrakīlaya cycles were central components of Dudjom's overall body of practices and are extensively performed by his students, so it is understandable that the Zil-gnon Vajrakīlaya practice became somewhat superfluous. Dudjom went to some trouble, however, to compose the basic texts for this practice, perhaps out of respect for the lama who had entrusted it to him.[23]

There is, however, a possible association between the Vajrakīlaya practice and the longevity practice that is worth noting. As Lopön Ogyan Tandzin noted, Vajrakīlaya practice involves the ritual killing or liberation of dangerous and malevolent spirit beings, and killing someone creates extreme negative karma that is specifically regarded as having a potential effect on the killer's life span. Provided that the performer of these practices maintains an awareness of *śūnyatā*, the emptiness or voidness of phenomena, which of course includes the demonic beings who are being destroyed, he or she does not suffer any negative karmic consequences. However, it is possible that the practitioners may not always succeed in maintaining such an awareness, and it is therefore important to complement such potentially risky practices as Vajrakīlaya with the life-strengthening practices of *tshe-sgrub*.[24]

We now turn to look at the *'Chi-med Srog Thig* texts in this volume:

Page numbers	Short Tibetan title	Description
75–143/144	*las-byang*	main ritual manual
145–148	*rgyun-khyer*	short text for regular practice
149–154	*sbas-sgom rgyun-khyer*	short text for more advanced regular practice
155–156	*brgyud 'debs*	lineage invocation
157–184	*skong ba* texts	reconciliation-offering texts

185–186	*sman mchod*	offering of medicinal herbs
187–192	*zur 'debs*	additional prayer
193–208	*khrigs zin*	explanation of texts
209–212	*gter srung*	invocation of protective deities
213–231/232	*bdag 'jug*	self-empowerment to renew link to deity
233–296	*sgrub khog*	instructions for practice
297–315/316	*sbyin-sreg*	fire offering
317–343/344	*brten-bzhugs*	request for long life of lama
345–358	*'chi bslu*	ritual to avert death
359–406	*dbang chog*	empowerment
407–429/430	*tshe-dbang*	life-empowerment
431–509	*bsnyen-yig*	text providing explanation and commentary on longevity practice
511–512	*'phrul-'khor*	physical yogic practices
513–517/518	*bcud-len*	dietary practice
519–543/544	*yang-zab*	concise practice
545–549/550	*tshogs glu*	song for *tshogs* offering
551–554	*tshogs glu*	song for *tshogs* offering

As can be seen, this is quite a substantial body of material. Two of these texts also occur in the fifteenth Karmapa's *Collected Works*, along with a longer version of the *dbang chog*, or empowerment text, and an additional longer supplementary prayer (*zur 'debs*).

Almost all of these texts refer to the central practice in which the practitioners construct a relationship with the deity Guru Amitāyus, and provide various ways of operating within this relationship. Here the principal text is the *las-byang*, which we will look at in a few moments, and the others are mainly adaptations of the basic ritual given in the *las-byang* for other specific purposes (conferring the empowerment to those being initiated into the practice, conveying long life to others, carrying out a fire offering, and so on), or else supplementary texts, such as the lineage invocation or offering songs that would be used as subsidiary parts of a full ritual sequence (one would, for example, normally include the lineage invocation at or near the start of a practice session). There are also shorter, more concise forms of the practice suitable for daily use, and an extended treatise (the *bsnyen-yig*) discussing techniques for achieving longevity in general and providing a commentary on the *'Chi-med Srog Thig* practice itself.

Two texts that present a rather different kind of material are the *bcud len* and *'phrul 'khor* texts. *Bcud len* translates as the Sanskrit *rasāyana*, and *bcud* is equivalent to that significant and polyvalent Sanskrit term *rasa*. In the present context, one might translate *rasa* as "essence" or "juice" (in the literal sense but also in the sense that something that has *rasa* is "juicy," has vitality and life). *Bcud* is also part of a familiar Tibetan compound, *snod-bcud*, meaning the universe, seen as container, and the essence or life that is contained within it. Another closely related term is *bdud-rtsi*, the Tibetan equivalent of the Sanskrit *amṛta*, the immortality-bestowing essence churned from the oceans by the gods and *asuras* in Brahmanical mythology. *Bdud-rtsi/amṛta*, the positive life essence of the universe, is closely linked to *bcud/rasa*, and both terms occur extensively in these and other longevity texts.

The Sanskrit term *rasāyana* is generally translated into English as "alchemy," and refers to techniques (spiritual, medical, and protochemical) for longevity or spiritual realization.[25] The Tibetan term *bcud-len*, although used to translate *rasāyana* and corresponding etymologically to it, is somewhat more specific in meaning. It generally refers to the preparation of ritually empowered herbal and mineral substances that are taken as part of Tantric practice, particularly practices aimed at health and long life.[26] In *bcud-len* practice, one takes one or more *bcud-len* pills each day and progressively refrains from ordinary food.

The *'phrul-'khor* text, as noted, is a text on physical yogic exercises, though it is brief and does not give much detail of the exercises.[27] In fact, the *las-byang* also includes a number of references to one of the basic *'phrul-'khor* exercises, though without any detailed explanation; these practices are regarded as somewhat secret and the details are taught orally. It may be helpful to explain for readers unfamiliar with Tibetan Tantric practices that the basic ritual itself includes body movements, both the *mudrā*, or hand gestures, that form part of many ritual sequences, and a number of sequences in which the practitioner walks or dances around the practice area. The *mudrā* are always performed, but the dance sequences might simply be visualized or performed symbolically in an everyday practice context. They would generally be included in a large-scale collective ritual, or *sgrub chen*.

To return to the *las-byang* and the basic ritual sequence, it is worth quickly summarizing the main components:

Page no.	
75	Title
75	Opening statement by Padmasambhava in which he describes his powers and his activities in India and Tibet, including his attainment of long life at Māratika, the occasion that forms the basis for the present practice
77	(A) Preparations: preparing the site, refuge and bodhicitta verses, confession and restoration of samaya, consecration of place and substances
86	(B) Main practice: generation of deity and *maṇḍala*
91	Invitation of deities into the *maṇḍala*
94	Establishment, salutation, offerings
99	Praises of the deities

101	Four stages of *mantra* recitation, followed by supplementary visualizations
106	Requesting the bestowal of *siddhi*
108	**Requesting the various deities in turn to recover the lost or deteriorated life forces (*tshe-'gugs*)**
121	Sealing of the accumulated life forces
121	(C) *Tshogs* offering including liberative killing and offering of excess; enjoining heart vow, proclaiming Tantric command, offering to the *brtan-ma* goddesses (protectors of Tibet); Heruka Horse Dance, confession, dissolution of *maṇḍala*, dedication and aspiration, auspicious verses
140	Final verses of Padmasambhava and account of the concealment of the *gter-ma*
143	Colophon describing the discovery of the *gter-ma* and its public revelation in the Wood Dragon year (1904–1905)

A key element here is the *tshe-'gugs* (marked in bold above), and it is really to this that the whole ritual sequence leads. This is the section in which the deities of the *maṇḍala* are asked in turn to recover and restore the lost life forces and to bring in positive life forces to strengthen the practitioner. Here the practitioner chants the main *mantra* of the practice while imagining its letters rotating around a *mantra* seed syllable at his or her heart center, which is of course also the visualized heart center of the deity. From it, light radiates out, gathers, and reabsorbs the pure essence of both samsara and nirvana (*srid zhi'i tshe bcud dwangs ma*), another term for the *rasa/bcud* referred to above. This pure essence repairs any deterioration of one's life elements (*bla tshe srog dbugs*), so leading to the attainment of power over life and health.

A noticeable feature of the *las-byang* is the outer frame of Padmasambhava's speech. In the opening and closing sequences, and at a number of key points, he explains that this is his text and his practice. The deity with which the practitioner is identified is, as explained earlier, a form of Padmasambhava himself as identifying with Amitāyus. At the end of the text, Padmasambhava gives directions to his Tibetan consort Ye-shes mTsho-rgyal, who generally acts in *gter-ma* texts as his scribe, to write the text down and conceal it. This is then followed by the colophon, in which the *gter-ston* states that he found it in a cave in Bhutan that is associated with Ye-shes mTsho-rgyal and deciphered it (since these texts are thought of as a series of indications in a script only readable by *gter-ston*, and act more as a stimulus to recovery than as an actual text).

The two extended statements by Padmasambhava form a frame that encloses the three phases of preparation, actual practice, and concluding rituals, and that is in itself included in the text by an outer frame formed by the title and colophon.

We might also note the strong female and sexualized aspects of this practice; the deities are either male-female couples in sexual embrace, or goddesses who are described as sexually attractive and alluring, and the *rasa*, or juice, itself has clear sexual associations at several points in the text. This links up with a frequent theme of long-life practice that goes back to Indian Tantric lineages such as those associated with the *Kālacakra Tantra*. In the root text of the *Kālacakra Tantra* and its commentary, the *Vimalaprabhā*, long-life practice is recommended for performance by older men with young women in order to restore their health and vitality.[28] In the *'Chi-med Srog Thig* practices we have been discussing here, the women are visualized goddesses, and the practice can be and is performed by women as well as men, but there are undoubted traces of Indian and Tibetan gender attitudes in which young women are seen as key signifiers of purity, good fortune, and life energy.

What is more critical from the contemporary Tibetan perspective is the deep grounding of the practice both in the key Tibetan Buddhist narrative of Padmasambhava's presence in Tibet, a narrative that is also present materially through the countless sites, images, and shrines associated with Padmasambhava, and in the central Buddhist orientation toward the attainment of Buddhahood. This may be, in a sense, a reworking of a common shamanic theme found in many cultural contexts outside Tibet, but it has been very thoroughly transformed into a Tibetan Buddhist conceptual and symbolic vocabulary.

Finally, though, we can ask what this practice does, and how it might work, assuming that processes of this kind may indeed have some real effect on the health of the human organism.[29] At the core of *tshe-sgrub*, particularly as performed by an individual meditator in retreat context or as part of a regular personal practice, is, as we have seen, the constructed relationship between the meditator's own bodymind complex and the wider environment, mediated by the image of the Tantric deity. The bodymind in *tshe-sgrub* is understood as a site open to outward and inward flows of various kinds of life essence that may be both lost to external forces and recovered and brought back into the body.

The revitalizing flows of life essence are associated both with the imaginative recreation of the universe typical of Tibetan Tantric practice, with associated *mantra* recitation, *mudrā* (ritual gestures), and so on, and also with specific breathing and visualization techniques that link the individual with the wider environment. Thus *tshe-sgrub* implies that the vitality of the bodymind is critically affected by ongoing transactions with the wider environment. However, the transformation of the environment through "pure vision" into the *maṇḍala* of the Tantric deities, who then act to retrieve lost life energy and to replenish the meditator with the pure, health-giving essence of the transfigured universe, moves the person undertaking the practice from a situation in which the environment is a source of threat and danger to one in which it is a source of health and positive support.

Thus the "message" of *tshe-sgrub* to the bodymind of the person undertaking the practice, if we can speak in such terms, is that health is intimately related to the wider environment, but that the wider environment, as transformed by the practice, is fundamentally positive and benevolent.

The Buddhist relativizing of the self-concept provides both a theoretical basis for this view and an underlying vision that is constantly referred to in the practices. So is the soteriological orientation of the entire tradition; long life and vitality in the Tibetan vision are achieved not for their own sake but to provide the material basis for further progress toward the attainment of Buddhahood. A more detailed study of the textual material and the way in which it is practiced would demonstrate this point in a great deal more detail. However, I hope that the description presented here is sufficient both to explain something of the structure and content of Tibetan longevity meditation, and of the way in which it is understood to operate.

Notes

1. Samuel, *Origins of Yoga and Tantra*.

2. This is a simplified account, both because there are forms of practice that derive from the Mahāyāna teachings, and also because the Vajrayāna does have its own theoretical assumptions, such as those underlying the internal structure of *cakras* and *nāḍīs* that make up the "subtle body" (cf. Madhu Khanna's contribution to this volume).

3. Tibetan names and terms are transcribed according to the Wylie system, except for some places and people well known under other forms (Lhasa, Dudjom Rinpoche).

4. For example, Millard and Samuel, "Precious Pills"; Samuel, "Short History."

5. Samuel, "Amitāyus."

6. Samuel, "Healing, Efficacy and the Spirits"; Samuel, "Inner work."

7. The description and analysis here derives from a three-year research project, "Longevity Practices and Concepts in Tibet: A Study of Long-Life Practices in the Dudjom Tradition" (2006–2009), funded by the UK Arts and Humanities Research Council. I was the director on this project, and worked with two other researchers, Cathy Cantwell and Robert Mayer, and two lama consultants, Lama Ogyan P. Tandzin and Lama Kunzang Dorjee. I would like to acknowledge the generous help of my collaborators, and also of Barbara Gerke, Thomas Shor, and Santi Rozario. This was the first full-scale study of Tibetan longevity practices, though *tshe-sgrub* and *tshe-dbang* rituals are discussed at some length in Beyer, *Cult of Tārā*; and in Kohn, *Lord of the Dance*.

8. On *gter ston* and *gter ma*, see Thondup, *Hidden Teachings*; Gyatso, *Literary Transmission of the Traditions of Thang-stong rGyal-po*; Gyatso, *Apparitions of the Self*; and Samuel, *Civilized Shamans*, 229–230, 294–302.

9. Samuel, *Civilized Shamans*; Samuel, *Tantric Revisionings*, 8–17 and 72–93.

10. There are also Bon *gter ston*, on which, see, for example, Samuel, *Civilized Shamans*, 462–463; Martin, *Unearthing Bon Treasures*.

11. It is unusual for a *gter ston* to be female, although there are one or two examples (e g., Hanna, "Vast as the Sky"; Jacoby, *Consorts and Revelation*).

12. See, for example, Samuel, *Civilized Shamans*, 229–230, 294–302, 462–463.

13. Zil-gnon is a title; *zil gnon*=Skt. *abhibhāva*, a state of meditative control (over external forces).

14. Cantwell and Mayer, "Textual Corpus."

15. See http://www.dudjomba.org/issue1/ENGLISH/e12.html (accessed February 20, 2013).

16. Cf. Ray, "Nāgārjuna's Longevity"; Mabbett, "Historical Nāgārjuna Revisited."

17. See, for example, the argument in the *Suvarṇaprabhāsa Sūtra*, chapter 2 (=Emmerick, *Sūtra of Golden Light*, 3–8).

18. For example, the contemporary lama Changling Rinpoche presented this argument to Robert Mayer and myself (personal communication, London, September 2006).

19. Gerke, *Time and Longevity*.

20. Samuel, *Civilized Shamans*, 186–187, 263–264.

21. Cf. Buffetrille, *Halase-Maratika Caves*; Buffetrille, *Pèlerins, Lamas et Visionnaires*, 293–341.

22. The volumes of a large multivolume work such as this are numbered using the letters of the Tibetan alphabet (*ka*=volume 1, *kha*=volume 2, etc.).

23. See Cantwell and Mayer, "Textual Corpus."

24. Lama Kunsang Dorjee of Jangsa Gompa, however, explicitly denied that this was why the *tshe-sgrub* practice was included in the context of a Vajrakīlaya cycle (interview, London, 2007). As he noted, Vajrakīlaya includes its own longevity practice.

25. Cf. Samuel, "Short History."

26. There is a probable historical relationship here to similar Chinese practices (Schipper, *Taoist Body*; Shawn, "Life without Grains"), though whether this is entirely mediated via India or whether there might be some more direct influences is hard to say (cf. Samuel, *Origins of Yoga and Tantra*, 278–282).

27. Cathy Cantwell notes that this text is "drawn from the long longevity practice of the Padma gling-pa tradition. [It] fills the necessary niche for such a section within a self-sufficient cycle, although in practice, it may be considered too short to be of more than symbolic value, and when needed, more substantial yogic practices for controlling the channels and air currents (*rtsa rlung*) from other Dudjom cycles may be done instead, such as from the *mKha' 'gro thugs thig* (in Volume *ma*) or the *gNam lcags spu gri* (Volume *da*)." (Personal communication, 2007.)

28. Wallace, *Kālacakratantra*.

29. Cf. Moerman, *Meaning*; Wilce and Price, "Metaphors"; Samuel "Healing, Efficacy and the Spirits"; Samuel, "Inner Work"; and Samuel, "Healing in Tibetan Buddhism."

Bibliography

Beyer, Stephan. *The Cult of Tārā: Magic and Ritual in Tibet.* Berkeley: University of California Press, 1973.

Buffetrille, Katia. *The Halase-Maratika Caves (Eastern Nepal): A Sacred Place Claimed by Both Hindus and Buddhists.* Pondy Papers in Social Science, 16. Pondicherry: Institut français de Pondichery, 1994.

———. *Pèlerins, Lamas et Visionnaires: Sources orales et écrits sur les pèlerinages tibétains.* Vienna: Arbeitskreis für tibetische und buddhistische Studien Universität Wien, 2000.

Cantwell, Cathy, and Robert Mayer. "The Creation and Transmission of a Textual Corpus in the Twentieth Century: The *'Chi med srog thig.*" In *Edition, éditions: L'écrit au Tibet, evolution et devenir* [The evolution and future of writing in Tibet], edited by Anne Chayet, Cristina Scherrer-Schaub, Françoise Robin, and Jean-Luc Achard, 65–83. Munich: Indus-Verlag, 2010.

Emmerick, R. E. *The Sūtra of Golden Light.* London: Luzac, 1970.

Gerke, Barbara. *Time and Longevity in a Tibetan Context.* PhD diss., Institute of Social and Cultural Anthropology, University of Oxford, 2008.

Gyatso, Janet. *Apparitions of the Self: The Secret Autobiographies of a Tibetan Visionary: A Translation and Study of Jigme Lingpa's Dancing Moon in the Water and Dākki's Grand Secret-Talk.* Princeton, NJ: Princeton University Press, 1998.

———. *The Literary Transmission of the Traditions of Thang-stong rGyal-po: A Study of Visionary Buddhism in Tibet.* PhD diss., University of California, Berkeley, 1981.

Hanna, Span. "Vast as the Sky: The Terma Tradition in Modern Tibet." In *Tantra and Popular Religion in Tibet,* edited by Geoffrey Samuel, Hamish Gregor, and Elizabeth Stutchbury, 1–14. Śata-Piṭaka Series, 376. New Delhi: International Academy of Indian Culture and Aditya Prakashan, 1994.

Jacoby, Sarah Hieatt. *Consorts and Revelation in Eastern Tibet: The Auto/Biographical Writings of the Treasure Revealer Sera Khandro (1892–1940).* PhD diss., University of Virginia, 2007.

Kohn, Richard J. *Lord of the Dance: The Mani Rimdu Festival in Tibet and Nepal.* Albany: State University of New York Press, 2001.

Mabbett, Ian W. "The Problem of the Historical Nāgārjuna Revisited." *Journal of the American Oriental Society* 118 (1998): 332–346.

Martin, Dan. *Unearthing Bon Treasures: Life and Contested Legacy of a Tibetan Scripture Revealer, with a General Bibliography of Bon.* Boston: Brill, 2001.

Millard, Colin, and Geoffrey Samuel. "Precious Pills in the Bon Medical Tradition." Paper for Seventh International Congress on Traditional Asian Medicine (ICTAM 7), Thimphu, Bhutan, September 7–11, 2008.

Moerman, Daniel E. *Meaning, Medicine and the "Placebo Effect."* New York: Cambridge University Press, 2002.

Ray, Reginald A. "Nāgārjuna's Longevity." In *Sacred Biography in the Buddhist Traditions of South and South Asia,* edited by Juliane Schober and Mark Woodward, 129–159. Honolulu: University of Hawai'i Press, 1997.

Samuel, Geoffrey. "Amitāyus and the Development of Tantric Practices for Longevity and Health in Tibet." In *Transformations and Transfer of Tantra in Asia and Beyond,* edited by István Keul, 263–286. Berlin: Walter de Gruyter, 2012.

———. *Civilized Shamans: Buddhism in Tibetan Societies.* Washington, DC: Smithsonian Institution Press, 1993.

———. "Healing, Efficacy and the Spirits." *Journal of Ritual Studies* 24, no. 2 (2010): 7–20. (*The Efficacy of Rituals, Part 2.* Second volume of two-volume special issue edited by William S. Sax and Johannes Quack.)

———. "Healing in Tibetan Buddhism." In *The Wiley Blackwell Companion to East and Inner Asian Buddhism,* edited by Mario Poceski, 278–296. Chichester, UK: John Wiley, 2014.

———. "Inner Work and the Connection between Anthropological and Psychological Analysis." In "The Varieties of Ritual Experience," edited by Jan Weinhold and Geoffrey Samuel, a section of *Ritual Dynamics and the Science of Ritual,* vol. 2, *Body, Performance, Agency and Experience,* edited by Axel Michaels et al., 301–316. Wiesbaden, Germany: Harrassowitz, 2010.

———. *The Origins of Yoga and Tantra: Indic Religions to the Thirteenth Century.* Cambridge: Cambridge University Press, 2008.

———. "A Short History of Indo-Tibetan Alchemy." In *Studies of Medical Pluralism in Tibetan History and Society,* edited by Sienna Craig, Mingji Cuomu, Frances Garrett, and Mona Schrempf, 221–233. Proceedings of the Eleventh Seminar of the International Association for Tibetan Studies (PIATS), Königswinter, 2006. Andiast, Switzerland: International Institute for Tibetan and Buddhist Studies GmbH, 2011.

———. *Tantric Revisionings: New Understandings of Tibetan Buddhism and Indian Religion.* Delhi: Motilal Banarsidass / London: Ashgate, 2005.

———. "Tibetan Longevity Practice and the Ecology of Mind." Paper for the Society for the Anthropology of Religion/Society for Psychological Anthropology Joint Spring Meeting, "Moments of Crisis: Decision, Transformation, Catharsis, Critique," March 27–29, 2009, Asilomar, California.

Schipper, Kristofer. *The Taoist Body.* Translated by Karen C. Duval. Taipei: SMC Publishing, 1994. First published in 1982 as *Le corps taoïste* by Librairie Arthème Fayard, Paris.

Shawn, Arthur. "Life without Grains: *Bigu* and the Daoist Body." In *Daoist Body Cultivation: Traditional Models and Contemporary Practices*, edited by Livia Kohn, 91–122. St Petersburg, FL: Three Pines Press, 2006.

Thondup, Tulku. *Hidden Teachings of Tibet: An Explanation of the Terma Tradition of the Nyingma School of Buddhism.* London: Wisdom Publications, 1986.

Wallace, Vesna A., transl. *The Kālacakratantra: The Chapter on the Individual Together with the Vimalaprabhā.* New York: American Institute of Buddhist Studies at Columbia University / Columbia University Center for Buddhist Studies and Tibet House US, 2004. Wilce, James M. and Price, Laurie J. "Metaphors Our Bodyminds Live By." In *Social and Cultural Lives of Immune Systems*, edited by James M. Wilce, 50–81. London: Routledge, 2003.

Kànhuà *Meditation in Chinese Zen*

Over the many centuries that Buddhism developed in East Asia, several distinctive styles of meditation appeared. None, however, is more unique and apparently idiosyncratic than the meditative focus on seemingly impossible questions or bizarre dialogues that originated in the Chinese Chán school (in Korea called Sŏn, but best known under its Japanese name Zen). Nevertheless, this became a standard meditation practice, and for centuries Zen practitioners all over East Asia have meditated on questions such as "What was your original face before your parents gave birth to you?"[1] or on exchanges such as the one where a monk asks Yúnmén Wényǎn (864–949) about whether there can be any fault when one is not giving rise to any thought and Yúnmén answers, "Mount Sumeru."[2]

This form of meditation took shape during the middle of the Sòng dynasty (960–1279) and has come to be known as *kànhuà* Chán (lit. "Chán of observing the keyword"), sometimes referred to as "*kōan* introspection." The development of *Kànhuà* Chán began with the puzzling, sometimes shocking, or even violent "encounter dialogues;" brief stories about great ancient Chán masters that seem to have first started to circulate in the ninth and tenth centuries, and that involve a Chán master and interlocutor, typically a monastic student, a Buddhist master from another tradition, or a lay visitor.[3] Encounter dialogues quickly came to be the hallmark of Chán literature; they were seen as direct expressions of the enlightened mind of a Chán master, that could inspire enlightenment in others by their retelling. Chán masters from the tenth century onward would often quote and comment on encounter dialogues, which then became known as *gōng'àn* (public cases; Jap. *kōan*; Kor. *kongan*).[4] Eventually some masters began to assign *gōng'àn* to their students to mull over during meditation, but it was the famous Dàhuì Zōnggǎo (1089–1163), a master in the Línjì (Jap. Rinzai) tradition, who fully developed *kànhuà* Chán and established it as a distinct form of meditation.[5]

Dàhuì was highly successful in his own lifetime, and his teachings had an enormous impact on the development of Chinese Buddhism, and of Buddhism in Korea and Japan as well. Due to Dàhuì's success, *kànhuà* Chán became widely used in the centuries after his death, even within the competing Cáodòng (Jap. Sōtō) tradition that Dàhuì had strongly criticized. However, although Dàhuì's teachings on *kànhuà* Chán have been studied quite extensively, very little scholarship has focused on the development of this type of meditation in the subsequent centuries. This chapter will therefore first outline Dàhuì's approach to *kànhuà* meditation and then discuss the development of this meditation technique through the Yuán (1279–1368) and Míng (1368–1644) dynasties.[6]

Dàhuì and his *Kànhuà* Chán

Dàhuì Zōnggǎo is, after the semimythical Sixth Patriarch Huìnéng (638–713), perhaps the most famous Chinese Chán master of all times, and his influence on his contemporaries and on the subsequent development of Chinese Chán was immense. Dàhuì is especially known as the tireless advocate of *kànhuà* Chán, an innovative meditation technique. But Dàhuì also became famous for his attacks on approaches to Chán that he felt were mistaken, especially that of "silent illumination" (*mòzhào*), which he associated with the Cáodòng tradition of Chán (which had become a rival to his own Línjì tradition), and which he repeatedly attacked in the years after 1134, when he seems to first have become aware of it. In fact, Dàhuì's creation of *kànhuà* Chán also dates to after 1134 and must, at least in part, be understood as an answer or antidote to the silent illumination meditation that was advocated in the Cáodòng tradition at the time, most prominently by the famous master Hóngzhì Zhèngjué (1091–1157). This again must be placed in the context of competition among Chán lineages for patronage from the educated lay elite, the literati (*shìdàfū*).[7]

Dàhuì was an active teacher and writer throughout his life, and a large corpus of his recorded sayings, sermons, and writings is still extant.[8] Especially interesting in the context of this chapter are the many sermons and letters in which Dàhuì directly addresses members of the literati class, because it is here that he most often discusses *kànhuà* Chán.[9]

Dahui's approach to Chán meditation involves focusing intensely on the *huàtóu*, that is, the "keyword" or "punch line" of a *gōng'àn* story.[10] The story that Dàhuì most often told his students for this purpose was the very simple one of the response Zhàozhōu Cóngshěn (778–897) is said to have given to someone asking whether a dog had the Buddha nature. Thus, in a written sermon addressed to a scholar-official, Dàhuì writes,

> A monk asked Zhàozhōu: "Does even a dog have the Buddha nature?" Zhàozhōu answered: "No!" [*wú*]. Whether you are walking or standing, sitting or lying down, you must not for a moment cease [to hold this "no/*wú*" in your mind]. When deluded thoughts arise, you must also not suppress them with your mind. Only just hold up this *huàtóu* [=the keyword "no/*wú*"]. When you want to meditate ("do quiet sitting," *jìngzuò*) and you begin to feel dull and muddled, you must muster all your energies and hold up this word. Then suddenly you will be like the old blind woman who blows [so diligently] at the fire that her eyebrows and lashes are burned right off.[11]

The *gōng'àn* here is the short exchange between Zhàozhōu and the monk, while the *huàtóu* is the single word "no/*wú*." *Kànhuà* is simply an abbreviation of *kàn huàtóu*, "observing the keyword"; however, Dàhuì himself never uses the terms *kànhuà* or "*kànhuà* Chán," and instead usually simply talks about the method of using the term *huàtóu* (keyword).

Zhàozhōu's dog was Dàhuì's favorite story for use in *kànhuà* meditation, and he returns to it again and again. In another sermon written for a member of the literati, Dàhuì first presents a scathing criticism of the silent illumination that sadly has ensnared some members of the literati and then goes on to advocate *kànhuà* Chán and explain a bit about the mental technique:

> A monk asked Zhàozhōu: "Does even a dog have the Buddha nature?" Zhàozhōu answered: "No!" When you observe it do not ponder it widely, do not try to understand every word, do not try to analyze it, do not consider it to be at the place where you open your mouth [about to say it out loud], do not reason that it is at the place [in your mind] where you hold it up, do not fall into a vacuous state, do not hold on to "mind" and await enlightenment, do not try to experience it through the words of your teacher, and do not get stuck in a shell of unconcern. Just at all times, whether walking or standing, sitting or lying down, hold on to this [no/*wú*]. "Does even a dog have Buddha nature or not [*wú*]?" If you hold on to this "no/*wú*" to a point where it becomes ripe, when no discussion or consideration can reach it, and you are as if caught in a place of one square inch, and when it has no flavor as if you were chewing on a raw iron cudgel, and you get so close to it you cannot pull back,—when you are able to be like this, then that really is good news![12]

Of course, in Chán understanding, like all other sentient beings, dogs *do* have the Buddha nature,[13] and by employing this and other bewildering *gōng'àn* it appears that Dàhuì aimed for *kànhuà* Chán practice to bring the practitioner to a point where no thinking or conceptualizing of any kind is possible. As is clear from Dàhuì's discussion, the objective was not to understand the story in any intellectual way, and the focus of contemplation was not the story itself but the *huàtóu* (keyword), here consisting of the single word "no," or rather *wú*, which seems at this level to become devoid of linguistic content.

Dàhuì appears to have developed this kind of meditation because he believed it was the most effective method for achieving enlightenment, and because other meditation techniques had come to be misused by "heretical" Chán masters. Dàhuì strongly insisted on the need for a decisive moment of enlightenment, without which a person would forever remain in the shadows of delusion, and his main reason for attacking other approaches to meditation such as silent illumination was that he felt that they did not lead to enlightenment.[14]

It is important to be aware of the distinction between *kànhuà* Chán and the practice of using *gōng'àn* stories as a means of instruction, which is sometimes missed in the secondary literature. Dàhuì was far from the first or only Sòng dynasty Chán master to use *gōng'àn* stories in teaching his students. Much of the material in the recorded sayings of individual Sòng Chán masters, no matter what Chán tradition they belong to, consists of the master quoting ("raising," *jǔ*) a piece of encounter dialogue centered on a famous past Chán figure and then offering his own comments on the story. The source was often the famous Chán transmission lineage history *Jǐngdé chuándēng lù* (Record of the transmission of the lamp from the Jǐngdé era; 1004–1008) published in 1009. It was these dialogues that came to be referred to as *gōng'àn* (Jap. *kōan*), which means something like "public case," an expression that seems to have been borrowed from the language of law. The stories are often bizarre, shocking, or just plain puzzling, and Chán masters used them in sermons, letters, and commentaries to instruct their disciples and startle them out of habitual modes of thinking (as well, perhaps, as to demonstrate their own erudition and mastery of the Chán parlance). Some Chán masters, such as Dàhuì's teacher Yuánwù Kèqín (1063–1135), also began assigning specific *gōng'àn* stories to their students to mull over in their daily activities and in meditation.

But although *gōng'àn* were employed as teaching devices in all of Sòng Chán, Dàhuì's use of *gōng'àn* goes far beyond anything that is attested in Chán literature before him. He was the first to insist on the necessity of an intense introspection directed toward the crucial punch line part of the *gōng'àn*, the keyword or *huàtóu*, and this makes his *kànhuà* Chán a unique as well as momentous development in Sòng Chán Buddhism.

In the quotations above, Dàhuì emphasizes that *kànhuà* practice should be a constant endeavor as one goes about one's daily activities and that one must hold the no/*wú* of the dog *gōng'àn* in mind "at all times, whether walking or standing, sitting or lying down." This advice seems especially directed to literati, who usually held administrative jobs and could not engage in prolonged formal meditation practice the way a monastic might. But the question may be raised: If it is something to be practiced at all times in the midst of regular activities, is Dàhuì's *kànhuà* Chán really "meditation"? I will not attempt a cross-cultural definition of the term "meditation" here, but clearly we usually think of meditation as something that is undertaken at specific times, associated with certain ritual (however minimal), and most commonly done in a seated position. But when Dàhuì mentions seated meditation in the first quote above, it almost seems as if he treats it as an additional, perhaps optional, practice. At the very least, *kànhuà* Chán is depicted as going much beyond seated meditation, perhaps even rendering seated meditation unnecessary.

In fact, searching through Dàhuì's extant writings it becomes clear that he almost never uses terms that we customarily translate as "meditation" in a positive sense. In almost all cases, Dàhuì seems to associate these terms with the dreaded silent illumination meditation technique, which he understands to consist of simply passively sitting and awaiting illumination of one's inherent Buddha nature. We might get the impression that, to Dàhuì, seated meditation was something to be avoided, at best an unnecessary practice and potentially a harmful one. In this he follows the rhetoric attributed to earlier legendary Chán masters, who often denigrated meditation or reformulated the term as meaning something very different from just sitting in meditation, as the Sixth Patriarch Huìnéng is supposed to have done.[15]

However, the impression that Dàhuì and other famous Chán masters outright rejected seated meditation is misleading, and there are in fact several instances where Dàhuì does talk about seated meditation in an approving manner. One example is in a sermon that is directed to his monastic students, in which Dàhuì says, "Although we do not approve of silent illumination, it is necessary that each of you face the wall [to meditate in seated position]."[16] This passage says nothing about *kànhuà* practice, and it seems possible that Dàhuì also instructed his monks to sit in traditional Buddhist meditation without focusing on the *huàtóu*. But it is interesting that Dàhuì here mentions silent illumination, clearly marking his disdain for it and noting his fear that any approval of sitting meditation might be understood as an endorsement of the silent illumination approach. However, Dàhuì almost certainly must have routinely instructed his monastic disciples to sit in meditation, which, after all, was standard practice in Chán monasteries in the Sòng.

In addressing his audience of educated lay people, Dàhuì never seems to directly advocate sitting meditation, but may at times be understood to be implying that meditation should be practiced if possible (if it could be done the right way). Below is a passage from a letter Dàhuì wrote to an official who had asked if would not be a good idea for beginners to do some meditation, or quiet sitting:

> In my teaching, no matter whether you are a beginner or an experienced student, without regard to whether you have studied for a long time or are just entering [the Way], if you want true quietness, you must break your mind of birth and death. Without holding on to an effort to practice [quietness], if you break your mind of birth and death, then you will be naturally quiet. The skillful means of stillness and quiet that the former sages talked about is exactly this. It is simply that the heretical teachers of this late age do not understand the former sages' talk about skillful means. . . . When you want to meditate, just light a stick of incense and sit quietly. When you sit, you must not let yourself become dull, and you must also not become agitated. Dullness and agitation are what the former sages criticized. When you meditate and begin to feel these two kinds of diseases appear, then just hold up the words about a dog not having the Buddha nature.[17] Then you do not have to spend energy on dispelling those two diseases, and you will be peaceful right there. As the days and months pass, you begin to feel [that the practice] becomes effortless, and that is when you are obtaining power. There really is no need to work on attaining quietude, just this should be your work.[18]

So, although Dàhuì does not directly state that one must meditate, it seems clear that it is not seated meditation as such that he is against, but the silent illumination approach of just sitting and trying to attain quietness. The way not to fall into that trap is to do *kànhuà* practice, which makes sitting meditation a powerful practice.

In another, very interesting, passage, Dàhuì seems even more positive about practicing sitting meditation. This is in a sermon Dàhuì gave at the request of the mother of the famous statesman and Dàhuì supporter Zhāng Jùn (1096–1154).[19] As Dàhuì explains in the passage, Zhāng's mother, here called Madame Qínguó (Qínguó Tàifūrén, d. 1156) had long been studying Buddhism, but Zhāng Jùn and his brother were concerned that she had had no awakening. They therefore asked Dàhuì's disciple Dàoqiān (d.u.) to tutor her. Dàoqiān taught her to focus on the dog *gōng'àn*—which she did, but she also often read *sūtras* and worshipped the Buddha (this may refer to Buddha invocation [*niànfó*]; see below). Dàoqiān then told her that Dàhuì advised against such practices, which would be distractions when working on a *gōng'àn*. Dàhuì continues, "Having heard Dàoqiān's words, she all at once let go and single-mindedly only did seated meditation [*zuòchán*], contemplating [*kàn*] the saying about the dog not having Buddha nature. I heard that last winter one night when she was sleeping, she all of a sudden woke up. She got up and sat in meditation raising the saying [in her mind]. Suddenly, there was a joyous event."[20] Dàhuì here seems somewhat short of sanctioning Madame Qínguó's experience as a full-fledged enlightenment, although in his annualized biography she is listed among his literati disciples who had attained enlightenment.[21] In any case, this is the only place I am aware of in Dàhuì's extant works where he directly links seated meditation with *kànhuà* practice in an event that leads to an enlightenment experience. From his description, it is clear that the main practice of Madame Qínguó was sitting in meditation and contemplating the dog *gōng'àn*, presumably focusing on the no/*wú*, and it seems to be exactly what Dàhuì would expect her to do.

I think we can conclude that Dàhuì indeed did see *kànhuà* Chán as a technique that ought to be practiced in sitting meditation, if at all possible, although it should also be extended to be practiced during the regular activities of daily life.

It appears that Dàhuì aimed for *kànhuà* practice to bring the practitioner to a point at which no thinking or conceptualizing of any kind is possible, as should be clear from the quotations above. But to Dàhuì, a parallel function of concentrating on the *huàtóu* is that it focuses a person's doubts.[22] Doubts are detrimental to enlightenment, but the unenlightened mind will always have doubts. However, when one is immersed in *kànhuà* practice, all doubts about other things will be forgotten for the one immense doubt generated by the *huàtóu*. According to Dàhuì, once doubt is centered on the *huàtóu*, it will become like a huge growing ball. Eventually this ball of doubt will shatter and all other doubts will disappear with it. This would be the moment of enlightenment. Thus, Dàhuì says, "Great doubt will necessarily be followed by great enlightenment."[23] In this letter to a follower, Dàhuì explains in some detail his views on doubt and *kànhuà* practice:

All the myriad one thousand or ten thousand doubts are just one doubt. If you can shatter the doubt you have on the *huàtóu*, then all the myriad doubts will at once be shattered [too]. If you cannot shatter the *huàtóu*, then you must still face it as if you were opposite a cliff. If you discard the *huàtóu* and then go and let doubts arise about other writings, or about the teachings in the *sūtras*, or about *gōng'àn* by the old masters, or about your day-to-day worldly worries, then you will be in the company of the devil.[24]

Here Dàhuì makes it very clear that doubt is both powerful and dangerous. If doubt can be harnessed and focused on the *huàtóu*, it will lead to enlightenment; if not, it is a destructive force that binds a person to delusion. Thus, it is apparent that Dàhuì was concerned with doubt and with how to use the *huàtóu* to harness it and to further enlightenment. However, in most of the places where Dàhuì discusses *kànhuà* Chán there is no mention of doubt. It seems possible that, to Dàhuì, doubt was just one facet of *kànhuà* practice and might not apply to all practitioners.

Dàhuì would maintain that he did not allow for a gradual approach to enlightenment; either one has it or one does not have it. However, it may take many years of effort to get there; in this way, attaining enlightenment is like archery: after practicing for a long time the archer naturally hits the target.[25] So although enlightenment is instantaneous, the process of getting there would seem to be a gradual one, although Dàhuì never really addresses this issue.

Furthermore, Dàhuì insisted that *kànhuà* practice was, in fact, the only way to enlightenment for Chán practitioners of his day, to the virtual exclusion of other Buddhist meditation practices. In this, Dàhuì is unusual among the Sòng Chán masters, who generally tended to take a rather inclusive view of Buddhist practice. It is, therefore, fair to say that Dàhuì invented an entirely new kind of Chán that in its focus on a single new contemplative technique was a radical departure from anything that had come before.

Dàhuì was very successful in forging close ties with literati (often very prominent ones) and convincing them that his *kànhuà* Chán was the orthodox one. This, I believe, greatly helped the fortunes of the Línjì tradition in the generations after Dàhuì, and it is not surprising if later Chán masters very carefully tried to emulate Dàhuì's example and often invoked his authority. Dàhuì also succeeded in making the term "silent illumination" associated with such negative connotations that it was never used again in a positive sense in Chinese Buddhism.[26] Most importantly, the *kànhuà* Chán that Dàhuì invented became a standard meditation technique in Chinese Chán, even in the Cáodòng tradition that had been the target for his criticism of silent illumination.

During the Yuán and Míng dynasties that followed the Sòng, Chán underwent many institutional, social, and ideological changes while its influence in elite Chinese society waxed and waned; however, *kànhuà* Chán continued as its signature meditation style. But although Dàhuì was still seen as the great sage of *kànhuà* practice, and Chán masters continued to appeal to his authority in their discussions of it, *kànhuà* Chán did undergo a number of developments and changes over the centuries. The following outlines some of these changes, which have been grouped under four headings: the use of the *kànhuà* technique as a way of calming the mind; an even greater emphasis on doubt; the integration of Pure Land practice into *kànhuà* Chán; and the notion that the *huàtóu* could be called out aloud.

Kànhuà Chán as a Device to Calm the Mind

As we have seen, Dàhuì was battling silent illumination, which he felt was imposing a deadening stillness and quietude on the mind of the practitioner. Instead, practitioners were encouraged to put all of their efforts into *kànhuà* Chán and attain a breakthrough enlightenment; once that had been achieved, their minds would be naturally quiet. So to Dàhuì, the *kànhuà* technique was not about calming or quieting the mind.

However, there are indications that *kànhuà* Chán in some forms may have been understood as a device to calm the mind, at least within the Cáodòng tradition. This would no doubt have irked Dàhuì, who had made it very clear that he associated his contemporary Cáodòng masters with the dead-end silent illumination that he attacked.

Although the vast majority of Cáodòng masters of the Yuán and Míng dynasties in general taught a quite orthodox *kànhuà* Chán meditation, in the late Sòng some Cáodòng masters may have invested *kànhuà* Chán with a silent illumination approach. Thus, in an autobiographical narrative (rather unusual for its time), the monk Xuěyán Zǔqīn (1216–1287) talks about his early Chán training with a Cáodòng master in this way:

> I then joined the assembly of venerable Tiějué Yuǎn of Shuānglín[27] to wholeheartedly practice [*dǎ shífāng*]. From morning to night I stayed only in the monk's hall without leaving the building. Even when I was entering the common quarters or going to the washroom, I held my hands in my sleeves, moving about very slowly, and never glancing left or right but only looking no more than three feet in front of me. The worthies of the Cáodòng tradition were wont to teach people to contemplate [*kàn*] the saying about the dog not having Buddha nature. Just when random conceptions and thoughts arose, one was supposed to ever so lightly balance the word *wú*/no on the tip of the nose. When the thought disappeared, you should right away put down [the *wú*/no]. This way you would sit silently waiting for purity to become ripe. After a long time, understanding would naturally occur. Practice in the Cáodòng tradition was very dense and obscure; and therefore people after doing this for ten or twenty years still did not succeed. Thus it was difficult for them to find heirs [to their tradition].[28]

Of course, Zǔqīn went on to get a transmission in the Línjì tradition, and he was no doubt very aware of Dàhuì's attacks on the silent illumination of the Cáodòng tradition. But although he is not a disinterested reporter, his description may well still reflect a use of the *huàtóu* that was designed to calm the mind, rather than to facilitate investigating it and generate doubt. This would be quite in keeping with what we know about Cáodòng practice of a century earlier and its emphasis on the original Buddha nature with which all sentient beings are endowed.

This kind of use of the dog *gōng'àn* can perhaps be traced back to the Cáodòng master Tiāntóng Rújìng (1163–1228), who became famous as the teacher of the founder of the Japanese Sōtō Zen school, Dōgen (1200–1253). Rújìng told his students to use the *huàtóu* "*wú*/no" to sweep out their minds: "Rújìng ascended the hall [and said]: 'When your mind is flying off in different directions, how do you control it? Take the story about Zhàozhōu's dog not having the Buddha nature and just use the word "*wú*/no" to vigorously sweep it out. . . . Suddenly you will sweep through to the Great Void, and lucidly penetrate all the myriad distinctions in the universe.'"[29] Rújìng here seems to suggest an emptying out of the mind, using the *huàtóu* to stop random thoughts.

Although in later times Cáodòng masters seemed eager to demonstrate their orthodox understanding of *kànhuà* Chán, there are some indications that a notion of *kànhuà* Chán as a device for calming the mind may have persisted. Thus, the late-Míng and early Qīng Cáodòng master Wéilín Dàopèi (1615–1702) says in a sermon,

> It is like Chán master Dàhuì always instructing people to contemplate the saying about the dog not having the Buddha nature, stating that the one character "no/*wú*" encompasses the entire universe. Just when delusions and vexations manifest before you, you must maintain your composure and raise the "no/*wú*." It is like pouring a ladle of cold water into a huge boiling cauldron: it will immediately become clear and cool. Bringing up the *huàtóu* [in your mind] is very much like this. Afterwards, the worthy [Dàhuì] also made people give rise to intense feelings of doubt, using these feelings of doubt to generate conditions for enlightenment. Therefore it is said: "Not to doubt the word [the *huàtóu*] is a great calamity: great doubt, great enlightenment; small doubt, small enlightenment; no doubt, no enlightenment." The number of those who have practiced according to this and have obtained the Way is beyond count."[30]

Here we see a typical appeal to Dàhuì as the orthodox arbiter of *kànhuà* Chán, but also an emphasis on the power of the *huàtóu* to calm the turbulent mind that here seems presented as a fundamental function of *kànhuà* Chán.

Doubt in Later *Kànhuà* Chán

In the quotation above, Wéilín Dàopèi emphasizes, as did Dàhuì, that *kànhuà* Chán is a crucial and necessary tool in obtaining enlightenment. But Dàopèi also puts great emphasis on the engendering of doubt. This is, in fact, typical of *kànhuà* Chán in the Yuán and Míng, which tends to emphasize doubt to a much greater degree than Dàhuì does in his surviving writings. Beginning by the late Sòng, the saying "great doubt, great enlightenment; small doubt, small enlightenment; no doubt, no enlightenment" came to be used frequently in discussions of *kànhuà* Chán, although it was not an expression used by Dàhuì.

It seems the earliest instance of the expression is found in Xuěyán Zǔqín's autobiographical account referred to above. Here Zǔqín tells of how he was set on the correct path after his time practicing in the Cáodòng tradition by an old monk who told him, "When practicing Chán, one must give rise to a feeling of doubt. Great doubt, great enlightenment; small doubt, small enlightenment; no doubt, no enlightenment. One must doubt the gōng'àn to get anywhere."[31] The context clearly suggests that this was an expression circulating at the time and not the original invention of the unnamed monk. The passage underscores the great emphasis on doubt in kànhuà practice, and it is in fact virtually impossible to find a discussion of kànhuà Chán from the Yuán or the Míng that does not mention doubt.

Although the dog gōng'àn continued to be used, a number of other gōng'àn also became popular in the centuries after Dàhuì, and were thought to generate the same kind of doubt. For example, the Yuán dynasty (1279–1368) Chán master Zhìchè Duànyún (b. 1309) writes, "Whether you investigate the word "wú/no" [of the dog gōng'àn], or you investigate your original face, or you investigate invoking the name of the Buddha, although the gōng'àn are different, in the end the doubt [they generate] is the same."[32] Duànyún also has an interesting discussion in which he describes doubt in kànhuà Chán exemplified by yet another gōng'àn:

> To begin with, you should raise [the gōng'àn] "The ten-thousand things return to one, where does the one return to?" perhaps three or four times, gathering it up [mentally] as seems right. Then you begin to put less emphasis on the "ten-thousand things return to one," and only let doubt arise on the word "one"; the doubter should doubt this "where does the one return to?" The three words "return to where" should lead you to thoroughly investigate "the one"; where else can you find peace and establish yourself? The three words are not where the doubt should be placed, the doubt is on "the one." If, unfortunately, feelings of doubt on "the one" do not arise, then again raise the "where, after all, does the one return to?" When you raise the huàtóu, saying it out loud or not saying it out loud are both fine, just don't be too fast and also don't be too slow.[33]

This is one of the rare places in Chán literature where we are given a few pointers about how kànhuà meditation is to be carried out. In this scheme, the practitioner starts with the whole gōng'àn and moves toward the most important part of it; then shifts to the huàtóu or keyword, the crucial element of the gōng'àn, which is where doubt should be concentrated. If not successful in focusing doubt on the huàtóu, the practitioner must go back to the second step.

Interestingly, we are also told that the practitioner may say the huàtóu out loud, an issue that is never addressed by Dàhuì. It is clearly implied that if not said out loud the huàtóu should be repeated mentally, in a measured pace. We will return to this in the last section of this chapter.

Doubt seems to have become the sine qua non of kànhuà Chán in the Yuán and Míng dynasties. Even as gōng'àn that Dàhuì had never used became popular, Chán masters kept appealing to his authority, pointing out how *kànhuà* practice with such *gōng'àn* generated the same doubt as the dog *gōng'àn*. This emphasis on doubt in the Yuán and Míng seems to go significantly beyond Dàhuì's own presentation of doubt.

Pure Land Practice and *Kànhuà* Chán

In the quote from Zhìchè Duànyún above, where he lists several different *gōng'àn* that can be used in *kànhuà* Chán meditation, one stands out: the practitioner may investigate the invocation of the name of the Buddha (*niànfó*).[34] This is a reference to a very old and popular practice in China: chanting homage to the Buddha Amitābha (Ch. Ēmítuófó) in the hope of being reborn in his paradisiacal Pure Land (with the phrase "*namo Ēmítuófó*"). In fact, the practice of Buddha invocation has been ubiquitous in Chinese Buddhism for most of its history, and has blended easily with a range of practices and doctrinal positions. It thus cannot be associated with any particular Buddhist school, nor can it be identified as an independent school, although together with other related practices it is often referred to as "Pure Land Buddhism."[35] Although scholars sometimes have been slow to recognize this, the practice of *niànfó* was incorporated into much of the Chinese Chán tradition right from its inception.[36]

It is perhaps not surprising that, as *kànhuà* Chán become increasingly widespread with the Chán school, the name of Amitābha and the practice of *niànfó* came to be integrated into *kànhuà* meditation. This may be the greatest innovation in *kànhuà* Chán after Dàhuì.

Interestingly, the use of the name of Amitābha in *kànhuà*-style meditation was in the Míng and later thought to have begun with Zhēnxiē Qīngliǎo (1088–1151) of the Cáodòng tradition, who was the Dharma brother of the famous Hóngzhì Zhèngjué. Qīngliǎo was one of the main targets of Dàhuì's attacks on heretical masters who taught silent illumination (*mòzhào*),[37] and it seems somewhat surprising that he should be credited with being the first Chán master who applied something like Dàhuì's *kànhuà* technique to Buddha invocation.

None of the extant sermons and writings by Qīngliǎo suggests that he was particularly interested in Pure Land practice, and he certainly nowhere advocates *kànhuà* meditation. But in a work on Pure Land practice from 1381, the *Jìngtǔ jiǎnyào lù*, we find Qīngliǎo quoted as saying:

> If you understand the one mind, then there is no other Dharma. Just take the four characters "Ē mí tuó fó" and make them a *huàtóu*. Twenty-four hours a day, from the time of the first ten recitations in the morning, just like that hold these words up. Do not recite with the mind, do not recite with no-mind, do not recite with both mind and no-mind, and do not recite with neither not-mind nor not-no-mind. Then you will cut off the realms of before and after and not a single thought will arise, and without going through any of the Bodhisattva stages you will suddenly reach Buddhahood.[38]

This passage seems to depict an intense and prolonged focus on Amitābha's name as a *huàtóu*, with the use of a tetralemma in the style of the iconic Mahāyāna philosopher Nāgārjuna (ca. 150–250 CE) to cut off any conceptualizing. It is quite similar to descriptions of the effort needed in regular *kànhuà* Chán meditation, although there is no indication of doubt.

But it seems unlikely that these are the actual words of Qīngliǎo. The *Jìngtǔ huòwèn*, a work by Tiānrú Wéizé (1286–1354), in its standard edition includes a quote by Qīngliǎo that is almost identical to the one above.[39] However, what is probably an earlier version of the *Jìngtǔ huòwèn* is included in the *Jìngtǔ shíyào*, and here Qīngliǎo is quoted rather differently:

> If you understand the one mind, then there is no other Dharma. Just take the four characters "Ē-mí-tuó-fó" and just like that go recite them 24 hours a day. If you can comprehend that the mind that does the reciting fundamentally has no recitation, no non-recitation, no both-have-and-do-not-have recitation, and no neither-have-nor-not-have recitation, then that which recites is thus and that which is recited is also like that.[40]

Here there seems to be a much greater emphasis on the actual recitation, and there is no mention of Amitābha's name as a *huàtóu*, nor any Chán-style claim to a direct realization of Buddhahood. Still, the sentiment is similar to the later version of the quote, and it cannot be ruled out that Qīngliǎo did teach an approach to Pure Land practice as described here. The *Jìngtǔ huòwèn* was first compiled several hundred years after the time of Qīngliǎo, and we cannot know when this passage first began to be attributed to him. But it is not impossible that Qīngliǎo could have advocated a contemplation of the act of invoking the name of Amitābha, which perhaps began the development of using Amitābha recitation in *kànhuà* practice. In any case, the passage attributed to Qīngliǎo in the *Jìngtǔ jiǎnyào lù* and in the standard edition of the *Jìngtǔ huòwèn* became a popular one, and it is quoted and further elaborated upon in a number of works from the Míng and Qing dynasties, although none of the authors actually seem themselves to have advocated using Amitābha's name as a *huàtóu*.

However, there were other Chán masters who advocated an intense focus on Buddha invocation that may be seen as a direct precursor to the use of *niànfó* in *kànhuà* Chán. The Venerable Yìnqiān has recently suggested that Yōután Pǔdù (1255–1330), a well-known leader in the White Lotus movement,[41] was especially influential in this regard. Pǔdù writes,

> If you wish to practice Chán and see your own true nature, then just rely on this Dharma. In a quiet room you must sit firmly in meditation, with the correct body posture. Sweep away all karmic entanglements, and cut off mental defilements. Look straight ahead with open eyes, externally do not attach to objects and internally do not become fixed in concentration. Tracing back the radiance,[42] the internal and external both become still. Then, delicately, you raise the sounds of the recitation "namo Ēmítuófó" several times [in your mind], tracing back the radiance and spontaneously contemplating "seeing

your own nature." What is it, ultimately, that becomes a Buddha? It is the Amitābha of my own original nature. Again, you must contemplate and focus on investigating that which now being raised. This one recitation arises from where? If you can completely penetrate this one recitation, then you can also completely penetrate [the question of] who is doing the analyzing.[43]

It is possible that a practice of contemplating the recitation of the name of Amitābha as described above was at some point fairly common, although it never seems to have become very popular. However, it may have inspired a different *gōng'àn* referring to Pure Land practice that did become widely used in *kànhuà* Chán. This is the question "Who is the one reciting the name of the Buddha [*Niànfó [zhě] shì shuí*]?" that is often referred to as the *niànfó gōng'àn*.

One of the earliest Chán masters associated with the mature *niànfó gōng'àn* is the fourteenth-century Zhìchè Duànyún referred to above. In his *Chánguān cèjìn*, the famous Míng dynasty Buddhist master Yúnqī Zhūhóng (1535–1615) cites Duànyún in this way:

> When you recite the Buddha's name out loud, whether it is three, five, or seven times, silently ask yourself "Where does this one sound of the Buddha['s name] come from?" Also ask "Who is the one reciting the name of the Buddha?" When there is doubt, just go take charge of that doubt. If you cannot get close to the place from where the question comes, don't cut off the feeling of doubt. Once again raise [the question] "Ultimately, who is the one reciting the name of the Buddha?"[44]

In Duànyún's extant work we find no reference to *kànhuà* practice using the *niànfó gōng'àn* as Zhūhóng reported it. But, as we have seen earlier, Duànyún's work does in fact contain a passage in which he equates investigating the invocation of the name of the Buddha with the investigation of the "no/*wú*" of the dog *gōng'àn*. This clearly indicates that Duànyún considered reflection on *niànfó* in *kànhuà* Chán meditation a common and uncontroversial practice. Many examples show that in the centuries after Duànyún this was indeed the case.

For example, the Míng dynasty Chán master Dúfēng Běnshàn (ca. 1400–1480) has this to say in a sermon:

> When you contemplate the "who is the one reciting the name of the Buddha," you must push down on the word "who" and enter deeply into a feeling of doubt. Doubt this "who is the one reciting the name of the Buddha." Therefore it is said: "Great doubt, great enlightenment; small doubt, small enlightenment; no doubt, no enlightenment." Fine words indeed! If you begin to gain a mind of urgency, then the feeling of doubt will be strong, and the *huàtóu* will naturally manifest before you.[45]

It would seem that in its mature form, the Buddha recitation *gōng'àn* as used in *kànhuà* practice functioned very much like the dog *gōng'àn* or the ten-thousand-things-return-to-one *gōng'àn* discussed above. We see the same focus on a single word that functions as the *huàtóu* or keyword, and the now familiar focus on doubt. In fact, several Míng dynasty Chán masters emphasize exactly this similarity and declare the different *gōng'àn* used in *kànhuà* Chán as functionally equivalent. Zhūhóng sums up this position very succinctly in his comments on an (apocryphal) story about Huángbó Xīyùn (d. between 847 and 859) advocating the use of the dog *gōng'àn* in *kànhuà* Chán:[46]

> When these later generations talk about *gōng'àn*, this [dog *gōng'àn*] is the one that is understood to be the beginning of the practice of contemplating the *huàtóu*. However, there is no need to be so attached to the word "no/*wú.*" Whether it is the word "*wú*," or "the ten-thousand things," or "Mt. Sumeru," or "completely dead and cremated," and so on, or investigating the invocation of the name of the Buddha, they all follow the standard of "guarding the one"[47] and have enlightenment as the goal. The focus of the doubt is not the same, but as for enlightenment it is no different.[48]

Calling the *Huàtóu* Out Aloud

As we have seen, Zhūhóng cites Zhìchè Duànyún as instructing practitioners to recite the Buddha's name out loud and then investigate where the sound is coming from and who is doing the reciting. This seems to have been a common practice when using the *niànfó gōng'àn* in *kànhuà* Chán. Dúfēng Běnshàn, in a section different from the one cited above, also instructs practitioners to invoke the Buddha several times and then turn to the *niànfó gōng'àn*: "Invoke the Buddha's name three, five, or seven times and then retreat and turn back [on yourself] the question 'Who is the one reciting the name of the Buddha?'—'Who is the one reciting the name of the Buddha?'—'Ultimately, who is the one reciting the name of the Buddha?' Hūm!"[49] In fact, the notion that employing the *niànfó gōng'àn* in *kànhuà* Chán requires, at least initially, the recitation of it, seems to have been a standard one. Later in the Míng, the famous Buddhist master Hānshān Déqīng (1546–1623) wrote, "Slowly bring up the one sound of the Buddha [recitation] and focus on observing from where this one sound of the Buddha ultimately arises. When you have recited it five or seven times, deluded thoughts will not appear [anymore]. Again you must go into a feeling of doubt, and examine who, ultimately, is the one reciting the name of the Buddha?"[50] I think we have to conclude from this evidence that *kànhuà* Chán with the *niànfó gōng'àn* has an element of orality that is crucial to it.

However, perhaps more surprising, it seems that this use of recitation in *kànhuà* Chán may have been extended to the *huàtóu* itself. As we have seen, in Zhìchè Duànyún's sermon about the *gōng'àn*, "The ten-thousand things return to one, where does the one return to?," Duànyún made it clear that the *huàtóu* should either be recited internally or said out loud. The notion that the *huàtóu* could be said out loud may have been a common one in the Míng. Interestingly, Yúnqī Zhūhóng cites one of his own teachers in a passage that seems to affirm that this was an option in *kànhuà* practice. In his *Chánguān cèjìn*, Zhūhóng has the following quote from Xiàoyán (Yuèxīn) Débǎo (1509–1578):

"When you raise the *huàtóu* . . . the feeling of doubt must be perpetual and constant, and you must be deeply immersed in complete sincerity, whether you keep your mouth shut and practice in silence, or you pursue the investigation out loud."[51]

The notion that the *huàtóu* could be called out loud seems to run counter to the technique as Dàhuì described it, and reminds us of tantric *mantra* recitation practice. It may be counted as another major development within *kànhuà* Chán in the Míng. It seems more than likely that this came into *kànhuà* Chán with the *niànfó gōng'àn*, since *niànfó* is very much an oral practice—if not exclusively so. In this way, the techniques of *niànfó* and *kànhuà* Chán may have come to be brought closer together, an interesting possibility that warrants further investigation.

Conclusion

Kànhuà Chán during the Yuán and Míng dynasties was in many ways remarkably faithful to Dàhuì's vision, and Dàhuì continued to be understood as the ultimate authority of *kànhuà* practice. Nevertheless, several significant developments took place within the practice. The most important of these, no doubt, was the integration of *niànfó* practice into *kànhuà* Chán with the *niànfó gōng'àn*, a development that has been little studied, and which deserves much more attention than I have been able to give it in this chapter.[52]

But several other developments in *kànhuà* Chán are also noteworthy. The notion that *kànhuà* meditation could be a device to calm the mind went directly against Dàhuì's vision. To Dàhuì, *kànhuà* Chán was a tool to gain enlightenment, that is, if it did not lead to enlightenment, a person's efforts were wasted. Meditation therefore had no value in itself, and it did not lead to greater peace, or a calmer mind—or, if it did, this was not really relevant to Dàhuì. Also, it seems unlikely that Dàhuì would have approved of the practice of calling the *huàtóu* out aloud, which makes *kànhuà* Chán seem uncomfortably close to Buddha invocation. And even though Dàhuì did talk about the importance of doubt in *kànhuà* practice, the Chán masters of the Yuán and Míng emphasized doubt to a much greater degree than Dàhuì had done. Thus, *kànhuà* Chán by no means remained static, but continued to evolve as Chinese society and its ideas about Buddhism changed.

Notes

1. See, for example, *Yuánwù Fóguǒ Chánshī yǔlù*, 790, c23–24.

2. *Yúnmén Kuāngzhēn Chánshī guǎnglù*, 547, c1–2.

3. "Encounter dialogue" is John McRae's translation of *kien mondō*, a neologism he attributes to Yanagida Seizan; see McRae, "Ox-head School," 244n48.

4. For further discussion, see Foulk, "Form and Function of Koan Literature."

5. The discussion of Dàhuì that follows is partly based on Schlütter, *How Zen Became Zen*, especially chapter 5.

6. Some of the issues discussed here are also addressed in Wu, *Enlightenment in Dispute*.

7. For an elaboration of these points, see Schlütter, *How Zen Became Zen*.

8. For a discussion of the various works attributed to Dàhuì, see Ishii, "Daie goroku."

9. For an excellent study of Dàhuì and many of the aspects of his relationship with literati figures, see Levering, "Ch'an Enlightenment for Laymen"; see also Levering, "Ta-hui and Lay Buddhists."

10. Both before and after Dàhuì, the word *huàtóu* seems often to have been used synonymously with *gōng'àn*, although Dàhuì himself clearly distinguished the two.

11. *Dàhuì pǔjué Chánshī pǔshuō*, 962, a10–13. This and most of the subsequent passages by Dàhuì are translated in Schlütter, *How Zen Became Zen*.

12. *Dàhuì Pǔjué Chánshī yǔlù*, 901, c27–902, a6.

13. For an interesting analysis of the dog *gōng'àn* in its Chinese context, see Sharf, "How to Think with Chan Gong'an." See also Heine, *Like Cats and Dogs*, for a comprehensive discussion of the use and history of this *gōng'àn* in East Asian Zen.

14. For more discussion of Dàhuì's *kànhuà* Chán, see, for example, Buswell, "'Short-cut' Approach"; Levering, "Ch'an Enlightenment for Laymen"; and Yü, "Ta-hui Tsung-kao."

15. See Yampolsky, *Platform Sutra*, 136–141, Chinese text, 6–8.

16. *Dàhuì pǔjué Chánshī yǔlù*, 828, b16–19.

17. In Schlütter, *How Zen Became Zen*, 118, I translate this as "But it is only when you do quiet-sitting that you will feel these two kinds of diseases appear. If you [instead] just hold up . . ." I now believe this translation is misleading, and depicts Dàhuì as being more negative about seated meditation than he actually was.

18. *Dàhuì pǔjué Chánshī yǔlù*, 922, a24–b8; Araki, *Daie sho*, 57.

19. I am grateful to Miriam Levering for alerting me to this sermon in her presentation at the conference "Buddhism and Society in Song-Dynasty China" at UCLA on May 18, 2002.

20. *Dàhuì pǔjué Chánshī yǔlù*, 869, c11–870, a7.

21. *Dàhuì pǔjué Chánshī niánpǔ*, 807, a1–2.

22. Doubt in Dàhuì's *kànhuà* Chán is discussed by Yanagida, "Chūgoku Zenshūshi," 98–104; Levering, "Ch'an Enlightenment for Laymen," 297–303; and Buswell, "'Short-cut' Approach," 351–356.

23. *Dàhuì Pǔjué Chánshī yǔlù*, 886, a28; cited in Yanagida, "Chūgoku Zenshūshi," 100; and Levering, "Ch'an Enlightenment for Laymen," 302.

24. *Dàhuì Pǔjué Chánshī yǔlù*, 930, a14–18; Araki, *Daie sho*, 127. Cited in Yanagida, "Chūgoku Zenshūshi," 99; and in Levering, "Ch'an Enlightenment for Laymen," 302.

25. See *Dàhuì Pǔjué Chánshī yǔlù*, 927, b5–6; Araki, *Daie sho*, 102. Cited in Buswell, "'Short-cut' Approach," 367n78.

26. Silent illumination is now used by some modern-day Chinese Buddhist masters in a positive sense; see, for example, Sheng Yen, *Method of No-Method*.

27. This seems to be a reference to Duānpéng Yuán (d.u.), who was a third-generation descendant of Hóngzhì Zhèngjué. See the *Kūyá mànlù*, 35, c24.

28. *Xuěyán Zǔqīn Chánshī yǔlù*, 606, b06–13. My translation is based on Wu, *Confucian's Progress*, 77, with numerous changes.

29. See the recorded sayings of Tiāntóng Rújìng in Kagamishima, *Tendō Nyojō*, 282.

30. *Wéilín Dàopèi Chánshī huánshān lù*, 653, a17–23 // Z 2:30, 469, c17–d5 // R125, 938, a17–b5.

31. *Xuěyán Zǔqīn Chánshī yǔlù*, 606, b22–23 // Z 2:27, 257, a7–8 // R122, 513, a7–8. See also Wu, *Confucian's Progress*, 78.

32. *Chánzōng juéyí jí*, 1015, c22–24.

33. *Chánzōng juéyí jí*, 1011, c7–13, cited in Shì Yìnqiān, "Chánzōng."

34. *Niànfó* is a translation of the Sanskrit term *buddhānusmṛti* that can mean "Buddha recollection," "Buddha contemplation," "recitation of the name(s) of the Buddha(s)," or "Buddha invocation." The term *niànfó* holds all of these meanings, but in China the most important aspect of *niànfó* was Buddha invocation, that is, chanting homage to a Buddha. The following section is based on Schlütter, "Reciting the Name."

35. There are considerable issues associated with the notion of distinct "schools" in Chinese Buddhism. See Stanley Weinstein, "Buddhism, Schools of." See also the newer entry by John R. McRae, "Buddhism, Schools of."

36. See Sharf, "On Pure Land Buddhism."

37. See Schlütter, *How Zen Became Zen*, 123–129.

38. *Jìngtǔ jiǎnyào lù*, 419, b11–15 // Z 2:13, 107, c15–d1 // R108, 214, a15–b1.

39. *Jìngtǔ huòwèn*, 296, b10–14.

40. *Jìngtǔ shíyào*, 695, a14–17 // Z 2:13, 379, a4–7 // R108, 757, a4–7, cited in Shì Yìnqiān, "Chánzōng."

41. On Pǔdù and the White Lotus movement, see ter Haar, *White Lotus Teachings*, especially 72–76.

42. Redirecting attention to the mind's activity back to its source. Robert Buswell has discussed this concept in several places; see, for example, "Chinul's Systematization."

43. *Lúshān liánzōng bǎojiàn*, 311, c26–312, a3; cited in Shì Yìnqiān, "Chánzōng."

44. *Chánguān cèjìn*, 1102, b18–22.

45. *Tiānzhēn Dúfēng Shàn Chánshī yàoyǔ*, 138, a13–16.

46. The story is sometimes used to argue that the *kànhuà* technique has a long history, but it doesn't appear until after the Sòng dynasty. See Schlütter, *How Zen Became Zen*, 114.

47. For "guarding the one," see Sharf, *Coming to Terms*, 182–184. Cited in Muller, *Digital Dictionary of Buddhism*.

48. *Chánguān cèjìn*, 1098, b6–9.

49. *Tiānzhēn Dúfēng Shàn Chánshī yàoyǔ*, 138, b4–5.

50. *Hānshān lǎorén mèngyóu jí*, 495, a1–3 // Z 2:32, 138, b16–18 // R127, 275, b16–18. Cf. Eifring, "Meditative Pluralism," 122.

51. *Chánguān cèjìn*, 1105, a11–15.

52. For more discussion of the *niànfó gōng'àn*, see Schlütter, "Reciting the Name."

Glossary

Amitābha (Ēmítuófó 阿彌陀佛)
Cáodòng 曹洞
Chán 禪
Dàhuì Zōnggǎo 大慧宗杲
Dàoqiān 道謙
dǎ shífāng 打十方
Dōgen 道元
Duǎnpéng Yuǎn 短篷遠
Dúfēng Běnshàn 毒峰本善
gōng'àn 公案 (Jap. *kōan*)
Hānshān Déqīng 憨山德清
Hóngzhì Zhèngjué 宏智正覺
Huángbó Xīyùn 黃檗希運
huàtóu 話頭
Huìnéng 惠能

jǔ 舉
kàn 看
kànhuà (Jap. *kanna*) 看話
kànhuà Chán 看話禪
kien mondō 機緣問答
Línjì 臨濟
Míng 明 (dynasty)
mòzhào 默照
namo Ēmítuófó 南無阿彌陀佛
niànfó 念佛
niànfó [zhě] shì shuí 念佛[者]是誰
pǔshuō 普說
Qīng 清 (dynasty)
Qínguó Tàifūrén 秦國太夫人
shìdàfū 士大夫
Sòng 宋 (dynasty)
Sōtō Zen 曹洞禪
Tiāntóng Rújìng 天童如淨
Tiějué Yuǎn of Shuānglín 雙林鐵橛遠
Tiānrú Wéizé 天如惟則
Wéilín Dàopèi 為霖道霈
wú 無
Xiàoyán (Yuèxīn) Débǎo 笑巖 (月心) 德寶
Xuěyán Zǔqīn 雪巖祖欽
Yōután Pǔdù 優曇普度
Yuán 元 (dynasty)
Yuánwù Kèqín 圜悟克勤
Yúnmén Wényǎn 雲門文偃
Yúnqī Zhūhóng 雲棲株宏
Zhāng Jùn 張浚
Zhàozhōu Cóngshěn 趙州從諗
Zhēnxiē Qīngliǎo 真歇清了
Zhìchè Duànyún 智徹斷雲
zuòchán 坐禪

Bibliography

Araki, Kengo 荒木見悟. *Daie sho* 大慧書. Tokyo: Chikuma Shobō, 1969.
Buswell, Robert E., Jr. "Chinul's Systematization of Chinese Meditative Techniques in Korean Sŏn Buddhism." In *Chinese Buddhist Traditions of Meditation*, edited by Peter N. Gregory, 199–242. Honolulu: University of Hawai'i Press, 1986.
———. "The 'Short-cut' Approach of *K'an-hua* Meditation: The Evolution of a Practical Subitism in Chinese Ch'an Buddhism." In *Sudden and Gradual Approaches to Enlightenment in Chinese Thought*, edited by Peter N. Gregory, 321–377. Honolulu: University of Hawai'i Press, 1987.
Chánguān cèjìn 禪關策進. Chinese Buddhist Electronic Text Association (hereafter given as CBETA), T48, no. 2024. Available online at cbeta.org.
Chánzōng juéyí jí 禪宗決疑集. CBETA, T48, no. 2021.
Dàhuì Pǔjué Chánshī niánpǔ 大慧普覺禪師年譜. CBETA, J01, no. A042.

Dàhuì Pǔjué Chánshī pǔshuō 大慧普覺禪師普說. CBETA, M059, no. 1540.

Dàhuì Pǔjué Chánshī yǔlù 大慧普覺禪師語錄. CBETA, T47, no. 1998A.

Eifring, Halvor. "Meditative Pluralism in Hānshān Déqīng." In *Meditation and Culture: The Interplay of Practice and Context*, edited by Halvor Eifring, 102–127. London: Bloomsbury Academic, 2015.

Foulk, T. Griffith. "The Form and Function of Koan Literature: A Historical Overview." In *The Kôan: Texts and Contexts in Zen Buddhism*, edited by Steven Heine and Dale S. Wright, 15–45. New York: Oxford University Press, 2000.

Haar, Barend ter. *White Lotus Teachings in Chinese Religious History.* Honolulu: University of Hawai'i Press, 1999.

Hānshān lǎorén mèngyóu jí 憨山老人夢遊集. CBETA, X73, no. 1456.

Heine, Steven. *Like Cats and Dogs: Contesting the Mu Koan in Zen Buddhism.* New York: Oxford University Press, 2013.

Ishii, Shūdō 石井修道. "Daie goroku no kisoteki kenkyū (jō) 大慧語録の基礎的研 (上)." *Komazawa daigaku bukkyō gakubu kenkyū kiyō* 31 (1973): 283–292.

———. "Yakuchū *Daie Fukaku Zenji hōgo* (zoku) (jō) 訳注『大慧普覚禪師法語』< 続 > (上)." *Komazawa daigaku Zenkenkyūjo nenpō* 4 (1993): 20–62.

Jǐngdé chuándēng lù 景德傳燈錄. CBETA, T49, no. 2037.

Jìngtǔ huòwèn 淨土或問. CBETA, T47, no. 1972.

Jìngtǔ jiǎnyào lù 淨土簡要錄. CBETA, X61, no. 1155.

Jìngtǔ shíyào 淨土十要. CBETA, X61, no. 1164.

Kagamishima, Genryū 鏡島元隆. *Tendō Nyojō zenji no kenkyū* 天童如浄禅師の研究. Tokyo: Shunjūsha, 1983.

Kūyá mànlù 枯崖漫錄. CBETA, X87, no. 1613.

Levering, Miriam. "Ch'an Enlightenment for Laymen: Ta-hui and the New Religious Culture of the Sung." PhD diss., Harvard University, 1978.

———. "Ta-hui and Lay Buddhists: Ch'an Sermons on Death." In *Buddhist and Taoist Practice in Medieval Chinese Society*, edited by David W. Chappell, 181–206. Buddhist and Taoist Studies 2. Honolulu: University of Hawai'i Press, 1987.

Lúshān liánzōng bǎojiàn 廬山蓮宗寶鑑. CBETA, T47, no. 1973.

McRae, John R. "Buddhism, Schools of: Chinese Buddhism." In *Encyclopedia of Religion*, edited by Lindsay Jones, 2:1235–1241. 2nd ed. Macmillan: New York, 2005.

———. "The Ox-head School of Chinese Chán Buddhism: From Early Chán to the Golden Age." In *Studies in Chán and Hua-yen*, edited by Robert M. Gimello and Peter N. Gregory, 169–252. Honolulu: University of Hawai'i Press, 1983.

Muller, A. Charles, ed. *Digital Dictionary of Buddhism.* http://buddhism-dict.net/ddb, February 28, 2012.

Schlütter, Morten. *How Zen Became Zen: The Dispute over Enlightenment and the Formation of Chan Buddhism in Song-Dynasty China.* Honolulu: University of Hawai'i Press, 2008.

———. "'Who Is Reciting the Name of the Buddha?' as Gongan in Chinese Chan Buddhism." *Frontiers of History in China* 8, no. 3 (2013): 366–388.

Sharf, Robert H. "How to Think with Chan Gong'an." In *Thinking with Cases: Specialist Knowledge in Chinese Cultural History*, edited by Charlotte Furth, Judith T. Zeitlin, and Ping-chen Hsiung, 205–243. Honolulu: University of Hawai'i Press, 2007.

———. *Coming to Terms with Chinese Buddhism.* Honolulu: University of Hawai'i Press, 2005.

———. "On Pure Land Buddhism and Ch'an/Pure Land Syncretism in Medieval China." *T'oung Pao* 88 (2002): 282–331.

Sheng Yen. *The Method of No-Method: The Chan Practice of Silent Illumination.* Boston: Shambhala, 2008.

Shì Yìnqiān 釋印謙. "Chánzōng 'niànfózhě shì shuí' gōng'àn qǐyuán kǎo 禪宗「念佛者是誰」公案起源考."Yuánguāng fóxué xuébào 圓光佛學學報 4 (1999): 107–139.

Tiānzhēn Dúfēng Shàn Chánshī yàoyǔ 天真毒峰善禪師要語. CBETA, J25, no. B159.

Wéilín Dàopèi Chánshī huánshān lù. CBETA, X72, no. 1440.

Weinstein, Stanley. "Buddhism, Schools of: Chinese Buddhism." In Encyclopedia of Religion, edited by Mircea Eliade, 2:482–487. Macmillan: New York, 1987.

Wu, Jiang. Enlightenment in Dispute: The Reinvention of Chan Buddhism in Seventeenth-Century China. New York: Oxford University Press, 2008.

Wu, Pei-yi. The Confucian's Progress: Autobiographical Writings in Traditional China. Princeton, NJ: Princeton University Press, 1989.

Xuěyán Zǔqīn Chánshī yǔlù 雪巖祖欽禪師語錄, CBETA, X70, no. 1397.

Yampolsky, Philip B. The Platform Sutra of the Sixth Patriarch. New York: Columbia University Press, 1967. 2nd ed., 2011.

Yanagida, Seizan 柳田聖山. "Chūgoku zenshūshi 中国禪宗史." In Zen no rekishi: Chūgoku 禅の歷史— 中国, Kōza Zen 講座禅 3, edited by Nishitani Keiji 西谷啓治, 7–108. Tokyo: Chikuma Shobō, 1967.

Yü, Chün-fang. "Ta-hui Tsung-kao and Kung-an Ch'an." Journal of Chinese Philosophy 6 (1979): 211–235.

Yuánwù Fóguǒ Chánshī yǔlù 圓悟佛果禪師語錄. CBETA, T47, no. 1997.

Yúnmén Kuāngzhēn Chánshī guǎnglù 雲門匡真禪師廣錄. CBETA, T47, no. 1988.

Meditation in the Classical Daoist Tradition

Meditation in classical China is most often and most readily found in an early tradition of practice, thought, and literature that was later associated with the label "Daoism." Whether or not this label was present before the Hàn dynasty (202 BCE–220 CE), the evidence for the distinct tradition of practice and thought to which it came to refer is contained in a body of extant texts that include works often regarded as the classics of the entire Daoist tradition, such as the *Lǎozǐ* and the *Zhuāngzǐ*, as well as a set of others that have been often overlooked, such as the four "Techniques of the Mind" (Xīnshù) works within the *Guǎnzǐ*, the *Lǚshì chūnqiū*, and some recently excavated works, such as the *Silk Manuscripts of Huáng-Lǎo* (Huáng Lǎo bóshū). These works contain a distinctive series of intellectual categories, philosophical concerns, and literary genres that are simply not found in the same interrelationships or internal structures in other early philosophical works.[1] Hence whether or not the authors of these texts considered themselves "Daoist," they did recognize that they were part of a distinct intellectual lineage that was neither Confucian nor Mohist nor any other lineage. Because their practices and ideas were identified as "Daoist" by Hàn dynasty historian Sīmǎ Tán (ca. 120 BCE), we will be using this label when discussing their unique meditation practices.

While there is only meager information of a precise nature about the social organization of this lineage, it can be said that until the middle of the third century BCE, when the figure of Lǎozǐ and the *Lǎozǐ* text were promoted as lineage founder and canon, it was constituted of very loosely organized collections of teachers and students, all of whom shared a common set of meditation practices and ideas that were set down in writing in a series of texts. Indeed, the very existence and survival of these texts implies that there must have been some sort of social organization to create, copy, and transmit them. Indeed, Mark Lewis posits the existence of groups like these that were outside the "ambit of the state" that "were formed by master-disciple traditions that relied on writing both to transmit doctrine or information and to establish group loyalties."[2] The early Daoist tradition is one such intellectual tradition, and this chapter will present an overview of its distinctive meditative practices. Because the methodologies of the comparative study of religious and mystical experience have only recently been applied to the study of classical Chinese Daoism, and because of the now outdated division of the Daoist tradition into an earlier pure "philosophical" foundation and a later corrupted "religious" institution, some have doubted that there is any evidence of a meditative practice in the early materials we present in this chapter.³ However, not only does the textual evidence provide a solid basis for the existence of meditation in classical Daoism, but the archaeological record does as well, as we shall see.

In these early Daoist texts there are three interlocking categories of ideas linked to meditation: cosmology, self-cultivation, and political thought. Setting aside the last of these categories for the time being as being a somewhat later development in the tradition, within the others there is a distinctive set of ideas that was found in particular relationships in these works and *only* in these works—not in the *Analects*, *Mencius*, or the *Mòzǐ*, for example.⁴ These ideas in many ways begin and end with a common understanding of the Way (Dào) as the ultimate source of the cosmos, with potency (*dé*) as its manifestation in terms of concrete phenomena and experience, nonaction (*wúwéi*) as its definitive movement, and formlessness (*wúxíng*) as its characteristic mode. There is also a common meditation or "self-cultivation" vocabulary that includes stillness and silence (*jìmò*), tranquility (*jìng*), emptiness (*xū*), and a variety of apophatic self-negating techniques and qualities of mind that lead to a direct apprehension of the Way.

The Classical Daoist Inner Cultivation Tradition

In previous publications I have hypothesized the existence of an "inner cultivation" tradition of practice and theory that produced a series of texts, some of which the Chinese have associated with the Daoist tradition for over two millennia. This term "inner cultivation" is taken from the text that I have argued is the oldest extant source of that tradition, *Guǎnzǐ*'s "Inward Training" (Nèiyè). A further general term used by this tradition to refer to its apophatic psychological practices, the "Techniques of the Mind" (Xīnshù), probably derives at least in part from the two texts of the same name that are companion texts to "Inward Training" (Xīnshù shàng, xià). In the philosophical literature, including these *Guǎnzǐ* works, the *Lǎozǐ*, the *Zhuāngzǐ*, and the *Lǚshì chūnqiū*, we find the most details about the theory and practice of these contemplative methods, although there is also important information about them in the medical literature as well.

I will begin by presenting a summary analysis of the basic methods and results of this tradition of what one might call sitting meditation. Specific techniques for moving meditation were known as well, although they are most often found in the context of health and longevity practices, such as the famous painting of the various positions of the "Guiding and Pulling" (of vital energy, *dǎoyǐn tú*) that was found at Mǎwángduī.⁵ The "inner cultivation" tradition, which also referred to its practices as *yǎngshén* "nourishing the inner spirit" or *yǎngxìng* "nourishing the innate nature," while sharing concepts and some practices with these health and longevity practices (often referred to as *yǎngshēng*, "nourishing vitality," or *yǎngxíng*, "nourishing the body"), wished to differentiate itself from them. For example, in *Zhuāngzǐ* 15 we read,

To huff and puff, exhale and inhale, blow out the old [breath] and take in the new, do the [gymnastic positions of the] "Bear Stride" and the "Bird Stretch," and to be interested in nothing more than longevity, these are the methods of those who practice the "guiding and pulling" exercises, those who nourish the body and who try to attain the longevity of Ancestor Péng. . . . But to attain longevity without guiding and pulling, to forget everything and yet possess everything, to be serenely without limit yet have many wonderful things follow you, this is the Way of Heaven and Earth, the Potency of the Sage. Thus it is said that serenity and indifference, stillness and silence, emptiness and nothingness, and Non-Action, these are the even level of Heaven and Earth, the substance of the Way and Potency. Therefore the sage finds rest in them and thereby attains balance and ease.[6]

In addition to contrasting "inner cultivation" with these more common medically linked practices, this passage emphasizes one of the preeminent dimensions of apophatic practice, that of cultivating the related psychological states of serenity, equilibrium, stillness and silence, and nothingness. Simply put, the basic practice of "inner cultivation" is to unify or focus attention on one thing, often the inhalation and exhalation of the breath, for a sustained period of time. Through this one comes to gradually empty out the thoughts, perceptions, and emotions that normally occupy the mind and to develop an awareness of the presence of the Way that resides at the ground of human consciousness. We can analyze these apophatic practices into a number of basic categories: proper posture, breath cultivation, apophatic psychological techniques, resultant states, and resultant traits.[7]

PROPER POSTURE

An aligned sitting position for body and limbs is frequently recommended. While the most famous example of this is the renowned passage in *Zhuāngzǐ* 6 in which the leading disciple of Confucius, Yánhuí, teaches the Master about how to attain the experience of "merging with the Great Pervader" (*tóng yú dàtōng*) through the practice he calls "sitting and forgetting" (*zuòwàng*). It is in this *sitting* posture that Yánhuí is able to accomplish the following: "I let organs and members drop away, dismiss eyesight and hearing, part from the body and expel knowledge, and merge with the Great Pervader. This is what I mean by 'just sit and forget.'"[8] To let "organs and members drop away" (*duò zhī tǐ*) means to lose visceral awareness of the emotions and desires, which, for the early Daoists, have "physiological" bases in the various organs. To "dismiss eyesight and hearing" (*chù cōng míng*) means to deliberately cut off sense perception. To "part from the body and expel knowledge" (*líxíng qūzhī*) means to lose bodily awareness and remove all thoughts from consciousness. These are basic apophatic techniques found throughout the textual sources of this tradition. Notice that the ultimate result of these apophatic practices, to "merge with the Great Pervader," implies that, as a result of sitting in a stable posture and following these practices, Yánhuí has become united with the Dào. In many ways this passage contains a succinct statement of "inner cultivation" practice and its principal goal.

Other important passages detailing posture are found in "Inward Training," in the notions of "aligning the body" (zhèng-xíng) in verse 11; aligning the four limbs (zhèng sìtǐ) in verses 8, 14, and 19; and keeping the body calm and unmoving (xíng'ān ér bùyí) in verse 24.[9] For example,

> When your body is not aligned
> Potency will not come.
> When you are not tranquil within
> Your mind will not be in order.
> Align your body, summon potency
> Then it will come cascading on its own.[10]

> ... When the four limbs are aligned
> And the blood and vital breath are tranquil,
> Unify your awareness, concentrate your mind,
> Then your eyes and ears will not be overstimulated.
> And even the far-off will seem to be close at hand.[11]

BREATH CULTIVATION

Cultivating the breath or vital energy (qì) is a foundational practice in all of the major sources of "Inner Cultivation." It is often spoken of as concentrating or refining the breath (zhuān qì), as in this locus classicus from Lǎozǐ chapter 10, but is given a fuller expression in the "Inward Training" verse 19 that is found in five other early sources:

> Amidst the psychic turmoil (of daily living)
> Can you embrace the One and not let go?
> In concentrating your breath can you become as supple
> As a babe? (Lǎozǐ chapter 10)

> By concentrating your vital breath as if numinous
> The myriad things will all be contained within you.
> Can you concentrate? Can you unify?
> Can you not resort to divining by tortoise or milfoil
> Yet know bad and good fortune?
> Can you stop? Can you cease?
> Can you not seek it in others
> Yet attain it within yourself? ("Inward Training," verse 19)[12]

Thus breath cultivation is essential to all forms of higher cognition and to the attainment of the Way. "Inward Training" contains a variety of phrases dealing with similar aspects of concentrating on one's breathing. In verse 5, we read of having "patterned breathing" (qì lǐ); in verse 8, having guided breathing (qì dǎo); in verse 24, we read about relaxing and expanding the vital breath (kuān qì ér *guǎng*). The famous "fasting of the mind" narrative in *Zhuāngzǐ* 4 gives the following advice involving breathing:

> Unify your attention
> Don't listen with your ears, listen with your mind;
> Don't listen with your mind, listen with your breathing.
> Listening stops at the ears; the mind stops at what it can objectify
> As for your breathing, it becomes empty and waits to respond to things.
> The Way gathers in emptiness.
> Emptiness is attained through the fasting of the mind.[13]

The *Zhuangzǐ* also contrasts the deep breathing ("from their heals") of the Genuine (*zhēnrén*) with that of the common people, who breathe from their throats.[14] All of the passages affirm the importance of concentrated breathing in the "Inner Cultivation" tradition.

These passages also affirm that another dimension of breath cultivation is to unify or focus one's attention. As we see above in "Inward Training," verse 19, "Can you concentrate? Can you unify?" (Néng zhuān hū? Néng yī hū?). Elsewhere, in "Inward Training," verse 24, we read of the advice to "focus on one thing and discard myriad disturbances" (*shǒuyī ér qì wànkē*). While it is difficult to say if all subsequent uses refer to precisely the same practice, this is the oldest extant example of this phrase that refers to a contemplative technique that became so important in later Daoist and Buddhist meditative practice.[15] In classical Daoist sources it seems to refer to concentrating attention on one thing: the cycle of inhalation and exhalation that is natural to all human beings. We read in "Inward Training,"

> For all [to practice] this Way
> You must coil, you must contract,
> You must uncoil, you must expand,
> You must be firm, you must be regular [in the practice].
> Hold fast to this to this excellent [practice]; do not let go of it.
> Chase away the excessive [perception]; abandon trivial [thoughts].
> And when you reach its ultimate limit
> You will return to the Way and its potency.[16]

These passages discuss concentrating or cultivating the *qì*, which is often translated as "vital energy" in some contexts, but is best rendered as "vital breath" or "breath" in those most relevant to meditation. Any doubt that *qì* means "breath" in these key passages is dispelled by clear references in some of the less philosophical and more practical works that have been unearthed by archaeologists at sites such as Mǎwángduī in Húnán Province. For example, in a medical text discovered in a tomb that was closed in 168 BCE, the *Shíwèn* (Ten Questions) we read, "The way to inhale *qì*: it must be made to reach the extremities so that essence is generated and not deficient.... Breathing must be deep and long, so that new *qì* is easy to hold. The old *qì* is that of agedness; the new *qì* that of longevity. One who is skilled at cultivating *qì* lets the old *qì* disperse at night and the new *qì* gather at dawn."[17] Furthermore, in the entry in a work on demonography unearthed in the tomb at Shuìhǔdì, on the ominous circumstances when the members of the household cannot breathe, we read, "when the people in a household all do not have *qì* to breathe." (*yí shì rén jiē wú qì yǐ xí*).[18] There are many more examples in this excavated literature of *qì* meaning "breath," and these serve to support the numerous references in the extant classical Daoist literature in which *qì* clearly means "breath" as well.

APOPHATIC PSYCHOLOGICAL TECHNIQUES

In addition to proper posture and concentration of breath and attention, these "inner cultivation" texts also present a wide variety of techniques that have the effect of emptying out the normal contents of consciousness and hence approaching the Dào by apophatic means. Principal among these is the very frequent admonition in "Inward Training" to restrict or eliminate desires (*jìng yù, jiéyù*; e.g., verses 25 and 26), which occurs in similar form in the *Lǎozǐ* as "to minimize or be without desires" (*guǎyù, wúyù*; chapters 1, 19, 37, and 57). The *Zhuāngzǐ*, the *Guǎnzǐ* ("Techniques of the Mind" 1), and the *Lǚshì chūnqiū* also contain similar and identical phrases.[19] Other related apophatic techniques include restricting or eliminating emotions, a staple of "Inward Training" (see verses 3, 7, 20, and 21), as in verse 25: "When you are anxious or sad, pleased or angry, the Way has no place to settle within you."[20] Discussion of the deleterious effects of the emotions are absent from the *Lǎozǐ* but present in the *Zhuāngzǐ* in such well-known passages as the dialogue between Zhuāngzǐ and his Logician foil, Huìshī, about how sages (*shèngrén*) do not have the essential responses of human beings (*rén zhī qíng*): "These people inwardly do not wound their being by likes and dislikes but they constantly go by the spontaneous and do not add anything to the process of life."[21] Restricting or eliminating thought and knowledge is also commended in "inner cultivation" texts. This is prevalent in "Inward Training" (e.g., verses 5, 8, 20, and 23): "Whenever your states of the mind have excessive knowledge, you have lost your vitality."[22] It occurs as well in more general phrases in the *Lǎozǐ*, such as "exterminate sageliness, discard wisdom [*juéshèng qìzhì*], then the people will benefit a hundred fold" (chapter 19), and in the contrast in chapter 48 between the daily increase in knowledge during the pursuit of learning and the daily decrease in knowledge during the pursuit of the Way. Finally, in the *Zhuāngzǐ*, we find the phrase "part from the body and expel knowledge" in the "sitting and forgetting" passage already discussed. This indicates that both sense perception and knowledge are to be abjured. The admonition against sageliness and wisdom from *Lǎozǐ* 19 is repeated in *Zhuāngzǐ* chapters 10 and 11 and in several other related references, such as "excessive knowledge is ruinous" (*duōzhī wéibài*) from Guǎng Chéngzǐ's teaching in chapter 11, and the advice to "discard knowledge and precedent" (*qù zhī yǔ gù*) in chapter 15.[23]

Finally, "inner cultivation" texts recommend in some cases restricting or completely eliminating sense perception. "Inward Training," in verses 13, 19, and 24, recommends avoiding the overstimulation of the senses. *Lǎozǐ* chapters 52 and 56 give the advice to "block the openings and shut the doors [of the senses]" (*sāiqídui bìqímén*), and chapter 12 warns against the deleterious effects of the five colors, tones, and tastes. *Zhuāngzǐ* 6 has Confucius singing the praises of those perfected people who "roam beyond the boundaries of the world" to his disciple Zǐgòng, and describes them as having "left behind hearing and seeing" (*yí qí ěrmù*); later the famous "sitting and forgetting" dialogue has Yánhuí teach Confucius about "Inner Cultivation" practices to "dismiss eyesight and hearing" (*chū cōng míng*).[24]

Taken together these passages recommend an apophatic regimen that develops concentration by focusing on the breathing and stripping away the common cognitive activities of daily life, something that must, of practical necessity, be done when not engaged in these activities, hence while sitting unmoving in one position. There are a wide variety of metaphorical descriptions of these apophatic regimens. These include the idea that following the Way involves "daily relinquishing" (*rìsǔn*) in *Lǎozǐ* 48, the *Zhuāngzǐ*'s famous phrases of the "fasting of the mind" (*xīnzhāi*) in chapter 4 and "sitting and forgetting" (*zuòwàng*) in chapter 6. Both *Zhuāngzǐ* 23 and *Lǚshì chūnqiū* 25.3 talk of "casting off the fetters of the mind" (*jiě xīn miù*). Another common phrase with a few close variations is "to discard (*chú*) / reject (*qù/qì*) / relinquish (*shì*) wisdom (*zhì*) / knowledge (*zhī*) / cleverness (*qiǎo*) and precedent (*gù/gù*) / scheming (*móu*)."[25] Finally, who can forget the beautifully evocative parallel metaphors for these apophatic mental processes as "diligently cleaning out the abode of the vital essence" (*jìng chú jīng shè*), "sweeping clean the abode of the spirit" (*sǎo chú shénshè*), in "Techniques of the Mind" 1, and "washing clean the profound mirror" (*dí chú xuánjiàn*) from *Lǎozǐ* 10, a metaphor echoed in *Zhuāngzǐ* 5: "None of us finds our mirror in flowing water, we find it in still water. . . . If your mirror is clear, dust will not settle. If dust settles, then your mirror is not clear."[26]

RESULTANT STATES

The direct results of following these apophatic psychological practices are remarkably similar across many early texts of the "inner cultivation" tradition, thus indicating a consistency of actual methods and some sharing of ideas and texts. It is useful to borrow an important contrast from cognitive psychologists and talk about these results in terms of "states," which pertain to the inner experience of individual practitioners and tend to be transient, and in terms of "traits," which pertain to more stable character qualities developed in interactions in the phenomenal world.[27]

Probably the two most common resultant states of "inner cultivation" practices are "tranquility" (*jìng*), the mental and physical experience of complete calm and stillness, and "emptiness" (*xū*), the mental condition of having no thoughts, feelings, or perceptions yet still being intensely aware. These are both prioritized in such well-known passages as this from *Lǎozǐ* 16: "Attaining emptiness is the ultimate result; focusing on tranquility is its central practice" (*zhì xū jí, shǒu jìng dū*). Tranquility is prized in "Inward Training" in verses 11, 16, 19, 22, and 25, and in these lines from verse 26:

When the mind can hold on to tranquility
The Way will become naturally stable.[28]

Tranquility is quite common to the *Zhuāngzǐ*, although the specific term is absent from the "Inner Chapters."[29] There are, however, a number of close synonyms for tranquility that do occur in them and in other "inner cultivation" texts that differentiate subtle dimensions of it, including "calmness" (*ān*),[30] "equanimity" (*qí*),[31] "balance" or "evenness" (*píng*), "repose" (*níng*), "stillness" (*jì*), and "silence" (*mò*).[32]

"Emptiness" as a specific term is absent from "Inward Training," although it is certainly implied as the result of many of its apophatic practices. It is fairly common in both the *Lǎozǐ* and the *Zhuāngzǐ*. In the latter we find assertions such as this famous one from chapter 4: "The Way coalesces in emptiness [*Dào jí xū*]; Emptiness is attained through the fasting of the mind."[33] In chapter 15 we read these ideas linking emptiness with various aspects of tranquility: "Thus it is said that serenity and detachment [*tián dàn*], stillness and silence [*jì mò*], emptiness and nothingness, and Non-Action, these are the even level of Heaven and Earth, the substance of the Way and Potency. Therefore the sage finds rest in them and thereby attains balance and ease."[34] As these passages clearly demonstrate, states of tranquility and emptiness are both closely associated with a direct experience of the Way, perhaps the penultimate result of apophatic "Inner Cultivation" practices. There are a number of striking metaphors for this experience of unification of individual consciousness with the Way; three use the concept of merging to express it. Chapter 56 of the *Lǎozǐ* contains advice on apophatic practice (e.g., "block the openings and shut the doors [of the senses]") and identifies the ultimate result as "profound merging" (*xuántóng*). *Zhuāngzǐ* 6 parallels *Lǎozǐ* 56; therein Yánhuí teaches Confucius about the apophatic practice of "sitting and forgetting," the penultimate result of which is "merging with the Great Pervader" (*tóng yú dàtōng*).[35] Chapter 2 also engages this metaphor for the Way, stating that the Way "pervades and unifies" (Dào *tōng wéi yī*) phenomena as different from one another as a stalk from a pillar, a leper from the beauty Xīshī.[36]

Other early "inner cultivation" sources contain similar descriptions of the direct experience of the Way. *Lǚshì chūnqiū* 3.4 links this experience directly to emptiness and speaks of "attaining the One"; *Lǚshì chūnqiū* 25.3 and its parallel passage in *Zhuāngzǐ* 23 talk of attaining emptiness as the penultimate result of correct sitting and attaining tranquility.[37] *Guǎnzǐ*'s "Techniques of the Mind" 1 also describes aphophatic practices that lead to "attaining the empty Way" (*dé xū* Dào).[38] "Inward Training" verse 5 speaks of using tranquility to "halt the Way" (*zhǐ* Dào): "When the mind is tranquil and the Vital Breath is regular, the Way can thereby be halted."[39] Here halting the Way is a metaphor that means stabilizing one's awareness of it; obviously the Dào cannot literally be stopped, because it has the characteristic of being elusive to attempts to dualistically perceive it. Finally, there are a series of similar locutions in "Inward Training" and the *Lǎozǐ* that evoke this experience of the merging of individual consciousness with the Way through the following pattern:[40]

Verb	*Object*
hold fast to / embrace / focus on	the One, the Way
zhí / bào / bǎo / shǒu	

The conceptualizations of the Way in these various sources are quite consistent. As the major force or power that underlies the cosmos, it is responsible for the self-generation of all of its animate and inanimate constituents. It is this activity that leads to some famous metaphors for the Way in the *Lǎozǐ* and the *Zhuāngzǐ*, such as the "mother" (*mǔ*) and the ancestor (*zōng*).[41] Because the Way can only be directly experienced but never completely understood as an object of perception or thought, its qualities can only be evoked. Verse 6 of "Inward Training" accurately captures the concept of the Way for all of the major pre-Hàn "inner cultivation" sources:

> As for the Way:
> It is what the mouth cannot speak of,
> The eyes cannot look at,
> And the ears cannot listen to.
> It is that by which we cultivate the mind and align the physical form.
> When people lose it they die;
> When people gain it they flourish.
> When endeavors lose it they fail;
> When they gain it they succeed.
> The Way never has a root or trunk,
> It never has leaves or flowers.
> The myriad things are generated by it;
> The myriad things are completed by it.
> We designate it "the Way."[42]

It is important to also note that these profound states of experience of the Way are quite often linked with preserving the spirit internally or becoming spirit-like (*shén / rú shén*) in "Inward Training" (see, for example, verses 9, 12, and 13), "Techniques of the Mind," *Lǚshì chūnqiū* 3.4, and the *Huáng Lǎo bóshū* (*Jīngfǎ* 6). They are further associated with a highly refined and concentrated form of vital energy called the Vital Essence (*jīng*) in "Inward Training" verses 5 and 19, and these latter three sources.[43]

RESULTANT TRAITS

As the direct result of the experience of these various dimensions of union with the Way—which, if we understand them correctly, are internal experiences attained in isolation from all interactions with the phenomenal world—adepts develop a series of what are best thought of as traits, more or less continuing alterations in one's cognitive and performative abilities that were highly prized by rulers and literati subjects alike for obvious reasons.

Perhaps the most famous of these is the idea that one can take no deliberate or willful action from the standpoint of one's separate and individual self, and yet nothing is left undone (*wúwéi ér wúbùwéi*). This works because adepts have so embraced and embodied the Way that their actions are the actions that are perfectly harmonious expressions of the Way itself in a given situation. As one of the most famous phrases in the *Lǎozǐ*, we find it in many of the other early sources of "Inner Cultivation," including the Outer Chapters and Miscellaneous Chapters of the *Zhuāngzǐ* and in the *Lǚshì chūnqiū* 25.3.[44] While the specific phrase is absent from "Inward Training," Edward Slingerlands argues that this text shows a definite awareness of the idea: "We see all of the standard metaphors of *wu-wei* in the short text of the 'Inner Training.'"[45] A very similar idea to efficacious nonaction is the concept of being able to respond spontaneously and harmoniously to whatever situation arises. We find this discussed in several sources, but none as directly as this passage from "Techniques of the Mind" 1:

> The cultivated [*jūnzǐ*] are not enticed by likes
> Nor oppressed by dislikes.
> Calm and tranquil, they act without effort,
> And they discard wisdom and precedent.
> Their responses are not contrived.
> Their movements are not chosen.
> The mistake lies in intervening directly oneself.
> The fault lies in altering and transforming things.
> Therefore the ruler who has the Way
> At rest seems to be without knowledge,
> In response to things seems to fit together with them.
> This is the Way of tranquility and adaptation [*jìng yīn zhī Dào*].[46]

The commentary to this includes mention of the important concept of resonance (*gǎnyìng*), a cosmic principle that the cultivated are able to manifest in their interactions:

> "Their responses are not contrived,
> Their movements are not chosen."
> This says that they are adaptable [*yīn*]. To be adaptable is to relinquish the self and take other things as standards. To respond only when stimulated [*gǎn ér hòu yìng*] is not something you contrive to do. To move according to inherent patterns [*lǐ*] is not something you [deliberately] choose to do.[47]

These traits of immediate and uncontrived responsiveness describe well one of the ideas for which the *Lǎozǐ* is famous: spontaneity (*zìrán*). A quality of the Way, the phenomenal world, and the cultivated sage in chapters 17, 23, 25, 51, it refers to their natural, instantaneous and nonreflective responses.

In a fundamental fashion, this almost magical ability to spontaneously accomplish all without seeming to exert any deliberate action is frequently associated with a great deal of potency (dé), an idea often associated with charisma. Potency is a kind of aura of spontaneous efficacy that develops in a person and is visible for all to see through repeated experiences of tranquility, emptiness, and merging with the Way. We find it in all of the early sources of "inner cultivation" theory, often in conjunction with apophatic techniques. For example, in "Inward Training," verse 11, we have:

> When your body is not aligned
> Potency will not come.
> When you are not tranquil within
> Your mind will not be in order.
> Align your body, summon your potency
> Then it will come cascading on its own.[48]

Among the significant traits that result from apophatic practice is dramatically improved cognitive abilities. In "Inward Training," verse 16, we read,

> If people can be aligned and tranquil
> Their skin will be ample and smooth
> Their hearing and vision will be acute,
> Their muscles will be elastic and the bones strong . . .
> They will mirror things with great purity
> And will see things with great clarity.
> Diligently attend and do not waver,
> And you will everyday renew your potency.[49]

Perceptual acuity and general cognitive accuracy are two main results of apophatic practice. Notice the phrase "mirror things with great purity" (jiàn yú dà qīng), which uses the metaphor of the mirror found in Lǎozǐ 10 and Zhuāngzǐ 4, indicating a special kind of unerring cognition of the world. It is the kind of instantaneous knowledge of the world that we find in the Jīngfǎ of the Huáng Lǎo bóshū as the direct result of being aligned, tranquil, even, serene, pure, and numinous: "Seeing and knowing are never deluded" (jiàn zhī bú huò). The more physical of the resulting traits that the cultivated develop in "Inward Training" are reminiscent of the qualities of the sage in the Lǎozǐ: being supple (ruò) and pliant (róu).[50]

Each of the main "inner cultivation" tradition sources details additional cognitive and personality traits that derive from apophatic practices. "Inward Training" says such practices create mental stability and psychic order (dìngxīn in verse 8; zhìxīn in verse 10). The Lǎozǐ speaks of becoming impartial (gōng) in chapters 16 and 42; selfless (wúsī) in chapters 7 and 19; and simple (sù) and whole (pú) in chapters 19 and 38. These qualities are a direct result of experiencing a reduction or elimination of desires that were listed above. Zhuāngzǐ 3 and 19 detail a number of different knacks or skills that derive from "inner cultivation" practice: Cook Dīng trusts the numinous within, does not look with his eyes, and realizes the limits of perception as he relies on the patterns of Heaven to guide him through the interstices of the ox.[51] The bell-stand carver must first make his mind tranquil until he eventually reaches a point where he forgets he has four limbs and a body (*wàng wú yǒu sìzhī xíngtǐ*).[52] Then he can go into the forest to choose a tree to carve. Finally, the *Zhuāngzǐ* collection is, in many ways, devoted to the cultivation of perhaps the most comprehensive of all of these character traits, one that encompasses all of the others discussed to this point: a mode of cognition called *yīnshì*. Angus C. Graham translates this in a very literal fashion: "The 'That's it' which goes by circumstance."[53] The concept is really that of flowing cognition, totally changing and transforming to whatever the situation, and it is exemplified in many of the narratives of the *Zhuāngzǐ*, the "free and easy wandering" of chapter 1, the monkey keeper handing out nuts in chapter 2, Cook Dīng in chapter 3, Cripple Shū in chapter 4, Wáng Tái in chapter 5, Master Lái in chapter 6, Húzǐ in chapter 7, and many other examples in the rest of the text. All of these respond without egotism, without selfishness, without insisting on any one fixed point of view: that is how they survive and flourish. This kind of indifference to fortune or misfortune and creative spontaneous responsiveness to all situations is characteristic of people "in whom potency is at its utmost."[54]

So the basic contours of "inner cultivation" are these: apophatic practices of sitting still and concentrating on, and paying attention to, one's breathing lead to gradual reductions in desires, emotions, thoughts, and perceptions. States of experience result from these reductions that make one feel tranquil, calm, still, and serene, states in which one's consciousness is empty of its usual contents, and in which one feels unified with the Way. These states lead to a series of beneficial cognitive changes and the development of new traits, such as acute perception, accurate cognition, selflessness and impartiality, the ability to spontaneously be in harmony with one's surroundings no matter what the situation, and the ability to be flexible and adjust to whatever changes may come one's way. Table 10.1 summarizes these practices and results.

Despite the lack of precise identities among the specific terms assembled and discussed here, there is a remarkable consistency in their basic interrelationships and relatively focused range of meanings.[55] This indicates the presence of a distinctive intellectual tradition. The lack of identical terms being used for similar ideas across this wide body of texts supports the notion that the early Daoists were a tradition of practice, first and foremost, and secondarily a tradition of texts. If there were an explicit core text or texts, then one would expect a lesser variety in the technical terms used and the appearance of identical phrasing, which is rare in this "Inner Cultivation" material until the *Lǎozǐ*.

In his pioneering study of the stability of a Chinese medical lineage over a period of more than 350 years, Volker Scheid finds an analytical framework for his data of seemingly disparate texts and practices in the writings of the philosopher Alistair MacIntyre on the nature of traditions: "A tradition is constituted by a set of practices and is a mode of understanding their importance and worth; it is the medium by which such practices are shaped and transmitted across gen-

Table 10.1. Summary of "Inner Cultivation" Ideas

Cultivation practices	Posture	aligning the body (*zhèng-xíng, zhèng sìtǐ*) keeping body still (*xíng'ān ér bùyí*)
	Breathing	concentrate (*zhuān qì*) order (*qì lǐ*) guide (*qì dǎo*)
	Attention	focus on one (*shǒuyī*) focus on center (*shǒuzhōng*)
	Apophatic techniques	restricting desires (*guǎyù, jiéyù, wúyù*) restricting thoughts (*chū cōng míng, qūzhī, qìzhī, qùzhī*) restricting perceptions (*sāi qí duì bì qí mén, yí qí ěrmù, duò zhī tǐ, lí xíng*)
	Apophatic metaphors	mind fasting (*xīnzhāi*) sitting and forgetting (*zuòwàng*) casting off mental fetters (*jiě xīnmiù*) sweeping clean numinous lodge (*sǎo chú shénshè*) cleaning off the profound mirror (*dí chú xuánjiàn*) the Way of stillness and adapting (*jìng yīn zhī dào*)
Cultivation results	States	tranquility (*jìng*) emptiness (*xū*) calmness (*ān*) equanimity (*qí*) repose (*níng*) stillness (*jì*) silence (*mò*) serenity (*tián*) detachment (*dàn*) refined/concentrated (*jīng*) spirit-like (*shén*) hold fast to the One (*zhíyī*) attain empty Way (*dé xū dào*) halting the Way (*zhǐ dào*) guarding / returning to the ancestor (*shǒu zōng / fǎn zōng*)

(*continued*)

Table 10.1. (*continued*)

Traits	
	nonaction (*wúwéi*)
	nothing unaccomplished (*wúbùwéi*)
	potency (*dé*)
	resonance (*gǎnyìng*)
	spontaneity (*zìrán*)
	perceptual acuity (*jiàn yú dà qīng*)
	instant knowledge (*jiàn zhī bú huò*)
	suppleness (*ruò*)
	pliancy (*róu*)
	psychological order (*dìngxīn, zhìxīn*)
	selflessness (*wúsī*)
	impartiality (*gōng*)
	simplicity (*sù*)
	wholeness (*pú*)
	flowing cognition (*yīnshì*)

erations."[56] When we see an intellectual tradition based on practice first and foremost and not only on ideas, the types of terminological variation among the core ideas of the "inner cultivation" tradition starts to make sense. Scheid explains,

> A practice relies on the transmission of skills and expertise between masters and novices. As novices develop into masters themselves, they change who they are but also earn a say in defining the goods that the practice embodies and seeks to realize. To accomplish these tasks human beings need narratives: stories about who they are, what they do, and why they do it. Traditions provide these narratives. They allow people to discover problems and methods for their solution, frame questions and possible answers, and develop institutions that facilitate cooperative action. But because people occupy changing positions vis-a-vis these narratives, traditions are also always open to change.[57]

This then allows for the possibility that the relatively rare use of meditation practices in political contexts that we find in early China is simply a natural development within the early Daoist intellectual tradition, not an incursion of ideas from without.

Political Applications of Inner Cultivation

One of the primary areas of change in the "inner cultivation" tradition is the application of its practices to the fundamental concern of the late Warring States Chinese thinkers: rulership. The *Lǎozǐ* (e.g., chapters 37 and 46) begins to address how some of the traits derived from "inner cultivation" practice are beneficial for rulership. For one, they give sage rulers a distinct lack of attachment to themselves and their own desires that leads to making better decisions in governing (e.g., chapters 22 and 49). Later texts, such as "Techniques of the Mind" 2 and *Zhuāngzǐ* 13 and 33, demonstrate thinking aimed at applying the techniques, states, and traits of "inner cultivation" to governing. They developed catchphrases for these applications: for example, "the Way of tranquility and adaptation" (*jìng yīn zhī* Dào) in the former; "tranquil and sagely, active and kingly" (*jìng ér shèng, dòng ér wáng*) and "internally a sage, externally a king" (*nèi shèng wài wáng*) in the latter.[58] This trend continues into the *Huáinánzǐ*, which embellished this unlikely mix of apophatic "Inner Cultivation" practices and results and political thought into a sophisticated new synthesis.

While the *Huáinánzǐ*'s ideas on governing can be found in many of its twenty-one chapters, its most explicit advice to the ruler of how to incorporate the meditative tradition of "inner cultivation" into the practice of governing are found in chapter 9, "The Techniques of the Ruler" (Zhǔshù). This chapter outlines the essentials of governing through nonaction and discusses the need for the ruler to attain states of experience that can be derived only from "inner cultivation" practices. It opens with the following passage:

The ruler's techniques [consist of]
  Establishing non-active management
  And carrying out wordless instructions.
  Quiet and tranquil, he does not move;
  By [even] one degree he does not waver;
  Adaptive and compliant, he relies on his underlings;
  Dutiful and accomplished, he does not labor.

Therefore,

  Though his mind knows the norms, his savants transmit the discourses of the Way;
  Though his mouth can speak, his entourage proclaims his words;
  Though his feet can move forward, his master of ceremonies leads;
  Though his ears can hear, his officials offer their admonitions.

Therefore,

  His considerations are without mistaken schemes,
  His undertakings are without erroneous content.
  His words [are taken as] scripture and verse;
  His conduct is [taken as] a model and gnomon for the world.
  His advancing and withdrawing respond to the seasons;
  His movement and rest comply with [proper] patterns [*xúnlǐ*].[59]

The remainder of *Huáinánzǐ* 9 lays out in considerable detail the philosophy of government by the enlightened Daoist ruler and is the single longest chapter in the entire book, an indication of its significance. Its theory of rulership is completely reliant on the personal development of the ruler, which is the direct result of the apophatic "inner cultivation" practices outlined in chapters 1 and 2 and in the earlier sources of this tradition. According to this work, the ruler must cultivate himself through apophatic inner cultivation techniques. These include the reduction of thoughts, desires, and emotions and the gradual development of emptiness and tranquility. The ruler able to accomplish this is able to develop his potency and perfect his vital essence (*zhì jīng*), and through this to penetrate through and directly apprehend the essences of Heaven and Grand Unity (Tàiyī), another metaphor for the Way.

This connects the ruler directly to the invisible cosmic web of the correlative cosmology of *qì*, and its various types (yin and yang) and phases (*wŭxíng*) and refinements (*jīng*). With this connection, the enlightened ruler can invisibly influence the course of events in the world and affairs among his subjects through the types of resonance (*gănyìng*) detailed in chapter 6, which we also saw as developing in the later works of "Inner Cultivation," such as "Techniques of the Mind" 2. Experiencing the most profound states of inner cultivation also enables the ruler to develop many of the traits envisioned in earlier sources, such as reducing desires to a minimum, impartially designating responsibilities within the government hierarchy, having a cognition devoid of emotions, and being able to spontaneously adapt to whatever situations arise, without hesitation:

> Sages internally cultivate the root [of the Way within them]
> and do not externally adorn themselves with its branches.
> They protect their Quintessential Spirit
> and dispense with wisdom and precedent.
> In stillness they take no deliberate action, yet there is nothing left undone.
> In tranquility they do not try to govern, but nothing is left ungoverned.
> What we call "no deliberate action" is to not anticipate the activity of things.
> What we call "nothing left undone" means to adapt to what things have
>   [already] done.
> What we call "to not govern" means to not change how things are naturally so.
> What we call "nothing left ungoverned" means to adapt to how things are
>   mutually so.[60]

This is a perfect expression for a government of nonaction and hence the application of classical Daoist meditation to politics. During the long later history of Daoism, this interesting combination led to several major political upheavals in which charismatic Daoist adept-politicians led rebellions against the central government. The most famous of these was the Yellow Turban Revolt, which was crushed by the Hàn dynasty central government in 184 CE, but which required such a large expenditure of capital and blood that it hastened the demise of this mighty dynasty, the longest-lasting one in all of Chinese history.[61]

Notes

1. For a synthetic overview of this research, see Roth, *Original Tao*, 173–203. "Techniques of the Mind" is the title of two short texts in the seventy-six-text *Guănzĭ* compendium. Together with "Inward Training" and "The Purified Mind," they constitute a group that in modern

scholarship is referred to as the four "Techniques of Mind" works. The relevant chapters of the *Lǚshì chūnqiū* are 3, 5, 17, and 25.

2. Lewis, *Writing and Authority*, 5.

3. See, for example, Csíkszentmihályi, "Mysticism and Apophatic Discourse," 33–58.

4. These categories are initially presented in Roth, "Who Compiled the *Chuang Tzu?*," 78–128.

5. For an analysis of early archaeological and textual evidence to this tradition of contemplative movement for health and macrobiotic hygiene, see Lǐ, *Zhōngguó fāngshù kǎo*, 346–354.

6. *Zhuāngzǐ, 15/41/19–24*; translation adapted from Graham, *Chuang Tzu*, 265. Unless otherwise noted, all textual references are to the editions in the Chinese University of Hong Kong Institute of Chinese Studies *Ancient Chinese Texts Concordance Series*, D. C. Lau and and Chen Fong Ching, series editors. Their edition of the *Zhuāngzǐ* was published in 2000. They are in the format: chapter (+section where relevant) of original text/page (in this edition) / line (in this edition).

7. The term "apophatic" is an adjective that is often used in Christian mystical contexts, where it refers to approaching the Divine through a *via negativa* of self-negation and using negative metaphors. I use it here to refer to the variety of practices in which the contents of the self are systematically emptied out until only an awareness of the Way remains. This is a common trope throughout classical Daoist texts.

8. *Zhuāngzǐ*, 6/19/20–21. From Graham, *Chuang Tzu*, 92 (modified).

9. Roth, *Original Tao*, 66–67, 60–61, 72–73, 82–83, 92–93.

10. Verse 11. Roth, *Original Tao*, 66; *SBCK*, 16/2b6–8. References to the original Chinese text for all *Guǎnzǐ* passages are to the edition in the massive collection the *Sìbùcóngkān* (*SBCK*), published in 1920 by the Commercial Press in Shanghai. The editors attempted to collect the oldest and rarest extant editions of all works published therein and then reproduced them by photolithography. This is the best of the many collectanea in which the "Great Books" of Chinese culture were published together in one comprehensive edition.

11. Verse 19. Roth, *Original Tao*, 82–83; *SBCK*, 16/4a2–7.

12. Roth *Original Tao*, 82–83; *SBCK*, 16/4a2–7.

13. *Zhuāngzǐ*, 4/10/1–3.

14. Ibid., 6/16/2.

15. For details, see Kohn, "Shouyi," 902–903.

16. Verse 17. Roth, *Original Tao*, 78; *SBCK*, 16/3b6–8.

17. Harper, *Early Chinese Medical Literature*, 394–396.

18. Harper, "Spellbinding," 247. I wish to thank Professor Harper for this and the previous reference.

19. See, for example, *Zhuāngzǐ*, 9/23/29, 12/29/16, 20/53/24+25, 23/65/6, and 25/76/17.

20. Roth, *Original Tao*, 94; *SBCK*, 16/5a4–5.

21. For example, *Zhuāngzǐ*, 5/15/22–24.

22. Roth, *Original Tao*, 60 (verse 8); *SBCK*, 16/2b/1.

23. *Zhuāngzǐ*, 6/19/21, 10/25/13, 11/27/13, 11/27/26, 15/41/27.

24. Ibid., 6/18/28 and 6/19/21.

25. Such phrases are widespread in early "Inner Cultivation" texts. See, for example *Lǚshì chūnqiū*, 3.4/15/1, 25.3/162/19–23; *Zhuāngzǐ*, 15/41/27, 23; and my analysis in Roth, "Evidence."

26. *Guǎnzǐ*, 13.1/95/29l; *Lǎozǐ*, chapter 10; *Zhuāngzǐ*, 5/13/18, 27.

27. See, for example, Cahn and Polich, "Meditation States and Traits."

28. Roth, *Original Tao*, 94; *SBCK*, 16/5a1–3.

29. See, for example, *Zhuāngzǐ*, 11/27/24; 13/34/16, 18, 19, 22; 15/42; and 23/67/11.

30. "Inward Training," 24.

31. Ibid., 3.

32. See, in order, *Zhuāngzǐ*, 5/15/6, 6/17/16, and 13/34/16+15/41/24.

33. Ibid., 4/10/2.

34. Ibid., 15/41/24.

35. Ibid., 6/19/21.

36. Ibid., 2/5/1.

37. *Lǚshì chūnqiū*, 3.4/15/1, 25.3/162/19–23; *Zhuāngzǐ*, 23/67/8–11.

38. *Guǎnzǐ*, 13/96/24.

39. Roth, *Original Tao*, 54–55; *SBCK*, 16/1b10–11.

40. See "Inward Training," verses 9 and 24; *Lǎozǐ* chapters 5, 10, 14, 22, 32, and 52. For details, see Roth, *Original Tao*, 147–150.

41. For the former, see *Lǎozǐ* chapters 1, 20, and 52; for the latter, see *Lǎozǐ* chapters 4 and 70; and *Zhuāngzǐ*, 5/13/13, 7/21/15, 13/35/17, 21/57/26, 22/61/20, and 33/97/15.

42. Roth, *Original Tao*, 56; *SBCK*, 16/2a2–4.

43. See Roth, "Psychology and Self-Cultivation."

44. Roth, "Evidence," 295–314.

45. Slingerlands, *Effortless Action*, 124–125. In this insightful work, Slingerlands applies the "metaphor theory" of George Lakoff and Mark Johnson to this key idea in early Chinese thought.

46. *Guǎnzǐ*, 13.1/96/12–14.

47. Ibid., 13.1/97/23–24.

48. Roth, *Original Tao*, 66–67; *SBCK*, 2b6–8.

49. Roth, *Original Tao*, 76–77; *SBCK*, 16/3b1–5.

50. *Lǎozǐ* chapters 3, 36, 55, and 76.

51. *Zhuāngzǐ*, 3/8/5–6.

52. Ibid., 19/52/7–8.

53. Graham, *Chuang Tzu*, 33 ff.

54. Paraphrased from *Zhuāngzǐ*, 9/23/27.

55. In an earlier work, I have presented evidence for a remarkable consistency across texts as early as the *Huáng Lǎo bóshū* (ca. 300 BCE) and as late as the *Huáinánzǐ* (139 BCE) in terms used for stages of meditation. See Roth, "Evidence."

56. Scheid, *Currents of Tradition*, 9.

57. Ibid.

58. *Guǎnzǐ*, 13.1/96/14; *Zhuāngzǐ*, 13/34/22 and 33/98/1.

59. *Huáinánzǐ* 9/67/3–6. Major et al., *Huainanzi*, 295–296.

60. *Huáinánzǐ* 1/4/22–23; Major et al., *Huainanzi*, 59.

61. For a short summary, see Benjamin Penny, "Yellow Turbans."

Glossary

ān 安
bǎo 保
bào 抱
chú 除
chū cōng míng 出聰明
dàn 淡
Dào 道
Dào jí xū 道集虛
Dào tōng wéi yī 道通為一
dǎoyǐn tú 導引圖

dé 德
dé xū Dào 得虛道
dí chú xuánjiàn 滌去玄覽
Dīng 丁
dìngxīn 定心
duò zhī tǐ 墮支體
duōzhī wéibài 多知為敗
fǎn zōng 反宗
gǎn ér hòu yìng 感而后應
gǎnyìng 感應
gōng 公
gù 故
gù 固
Guǎng Chéngzǐ 廣成子
Guǎnzǐ 管子
guǎyù 寡欲
Hàn 漢
Huáinánzǐ 淮南子
Huáng Lǎo bóshū 黃老帛書
Huìshī 惠施
Húnán 湖南
Húzǐ 壺子
jì 寂
jiàn yú dà qīng 鑑於大清
jiàn zhī bú huò 見知不惑
jiě xīn miù 解心繆 (or 謬)
jiéyù 節欲
jì mò 寂漠
jīng 精
jìng 靜
jìng chú jīng shè 敬除精舍
jìng ér shèng, dòng ér wáng 靜而聖，動而王
Jīngfǎ 經法
jìng yīn zhī Dào 靜因之道
jìng yù 靜慾
juéshèng qìzhì 絕聖棄知
jūnzǐ 君子
kuān qì ér guǎng 寬氣而廣
Lái 來
Lǎozǐ 老子
lǐ 理
líxíng 離形
líxíng qūzhī 離形屈知
Lǚshì chūnqiū 呂氏春秋
Mǎwángduī 馬王堆
mò 漠
móu 謀
Mòzǐ 墨子
mǔ 母

nèi shèng wài wáng 內聖外王

Nèiyè 內業

"Néng zhuān hū? Néng yī hū?" 能專乎？能一乎？

níng 寧

Péng 彭

píng 平

pú 樸

qì 氣

qì 棄

qí 齊

qiǎo 巧

qì dǎo 氣導

qì lǐ 氣理

qìzhī 棄知

qù 去

qūzhī 屈知

qùzhī 去知

qù zhī yǔ gù 去知與故

rén zhī qíng 人之情

rìsǔn 日損

róu 柔

ruò 弱

rú shén 如神

sāiqíduì bìqímén 塞其兌閉其門

sǎo chú shénshè 掃除神舍

shén 神

shèngrén 聖人

shì 釋

Shíwèn 十問

shǒu 守

shǒuyī 守一

shǒuyī ér qì wànkē 守一而棄萬苛

shǒuzhōng 守中

shǒu zōng 守宗

Shū 疏

Shuìhǔdì 睡虎地

Sìbùcóngkān 四部叢刊

Sīmǎ Tán 司馬談

sù 素

Tàiyī 太一

tián 恬

tián dàn 恬淡

tóng yú dàtōng 同於大通

Wáng Tái 王駘

wàng wú yǒu sìzhī xíngtǐ 忘吾有四枝形體

wúbùwéi 無不為

wúsī 無私

wúwéi 無為

wúwéi ér wúbùwéi 無為而無不為

wúxíng 無形
wǔxíng 五行
wúyù 無欲
xíng'ān ér bùyí 形安而不移
Xīnshù 心術
Xīnshù shàng, xià 心術; 上，下
xīnzhāi 心齋
Xīshī 西施
xū 虛
xuántóng 玄同
xúnlǐ 循理
yǎngshén 養神
yǎngshēng 養生
yǎngxíng 養形
yǎngxìng 養性
Yánhuí 顏回
yīn 因
yīnshì 因是
yí qí ěrmù 遺其耳目
yí shì rén jiē wú qì yǐ xí 一室人皆毋氣以息
zhèng sìtǐ 正四體
zhèng-xíng 正形
zhēnrén 真人
zhī 知
zhí 執
zhì 智
zhǐ Dào 止道
zhì jīng 至精
zhìxīn 治心
zhì xū jí, shǒu jìng dū 致虛極，守靜督
zhíyī 執一
Zhuāngzǐ 莊子
zhuān qì 專氣
Zhǔshù 主術
Zǐgòng 子貢
zìrán 自然
zōng 宗
zuòwàng 坐忘

Bibliography

Cahn, B. Rael, and John Polich. "Meditation States and Traits: EEG, ERP, and Neuroimaging Studies." *Psychological Bulletin* 132, no. 2 (2006): 180–211.
Csíkszentmihályi, Mark. "Mysticism and Apophatic Discourse in the *Laozi*." In *Essays on Religious and Philosophical Aspects of the Laozi*, edited by P. J. Ivanhoe and Mark Csíkszentmihályi, 33–58. New York: SUNY Press, 1999.
Graham, A. C. *Chuang Tzu: The Inner Chapters.* London: Allen and Unwin, 1981.
Harper, Donald J. "Spellbinding." In *The Religions of China in Practice*, edited by Donald Lopez and Stephen Teiser, 241–250. Princeton: Princeton University Press, 1996.

Harper, Donald J., *Early Chinese Medical Literature: The Mawangdui Medical Manuscript.* London: Kegan Paul, 1998.

Kohn, Livia. "Shouyi: Guarding the One; Maintaining Oneness." In *The Encyclopedia of Taoism*, edited by Fabrizio Pregadio, 902–903. Oxford: Routledge, 2008.

Lewis, Mark Edward. *Writing and Authority in Early China.* Albany, NY: SUNY Press, 1999.

Lǐ, Líng 李零. *Zhōngguó fāngshù kǎo* 中國方術考. Beijing: Rénmín Zhōngguó chūbǎnshè, 1993.

Major, John S., Sarah Queen, Andrew S. Meyer, and Harold D. Roth. *The Huainanzi: A Guide to the Theory and Practice of Government in Early Han China.* New York: Columbia University Press, 2010.

Penny, Benjamin. "Yellow Turbans." In *The Encyclopedia of Taoism*, edited by Fabrizio Pregadio, 1156–1157. Oxford: Routledge, 2008.

Roth, Harold D. "Evidence for Stages of Meditation in Early Taoism." *Bulletin of the School of Oriental and African Studies* 60, no. 2 (1997): 295–314.

———. *Original Tao: Inward Training and the Foundations of Taoist Mysticism.* New York: Columbia University Press, 1999.

———. "Psychology and Self-Cultivation in Early Taoistic Thought." *Harvard Journal of Asiatic Studies* 51, no. 2 (1991): 599–650.

———. "Who Compiled the *Chuang Tzu*?" In *Chinese Texts and Philosophical Contexts: Essays Dedicated to Angus C. Graham*, edited by Henry Rosemont, Jr., 79–128. LaSalle, IL: Open Court Press, 1991.

Scheid, Volker. *Currents of Tradition in Chinese Medicine, 1626–2006.* Seattle: Eastland Press, 2007.

Slingerland, Edward. *Effortless Action: Wu-Wei as Conceptual Metaphor and Spiritual Ideal in Early China.* Oxford: Oxford University Press, 2003.

"Quiet Sitting" in Neo-Confucianism

I
n the Neo-Confucianism of the eleventh- through seventeenth-century China, Confucian scholars used the term *jìngzuò*, or "quiet sitting," for "meditation."[1] Many of them practiced quiet sitting. They believed that, according to the philosophical framework of contemporary Confucianism, the unique psychological changes obtained through quiet sitting were a meaningful and effective means of grasping the perfect "original nature" (*běnxìng*) that was inherent in each individual from birth. Needless to say, Confucians of this period did not depend solely on quiet sitting to grasp the "original nature" that was believed to inhere in one's mind. However, the experience of the psychological transformations induced by quiet sitting was continuously adopted as an effective way of bringing individuals closer to their "nature."

At the same time, there was an inherent danger in the psychological transformation produced by quiet sitting: it could undermine the absoluteness of the teachings of the Confucian classics, or the Confucian social norms centering on kinship relationships, which constituted the Golden Rule of Confucian philosophy. That is, the search for an "original nature" that could not be explained by Confucian discourses could lead to a relativization of the abstract principles and concrete moral norms of the Confucian classics. At times, it was even said that Buddhist or Daoist scriptures described man's "original nature" more explicitly than Confucian classics. Additionally, absorption in quiet sitting could reduce the social motivation of Confucian scholars, who were expected to fulfill certain roles in society.

For this reason, while Confucian scholars were aware of the effectiveness of quiet sitting, they were also cautious. Among these figures were Zhū Xī (1130–1200), a great master of the school of principle, and Wáng Shǒurén (1472–1528), founder of the famous Yángmíng school of mind, both of whom warned against the dangers of quiet sitting. Caution toward these dangers became even stronger during the Qīng dynasty (1644–1911), when the fundamental framework of Neo-Confucianism was relativized with respect to other schools of thought. However, while in the early period the methods for quiet sitting were never clearly explained, during the late Míng dynasty (late sixteenty century–early seventeenth century), Confucian scholars began to provide simplified manuals on quiet sitting. This is a phenomenon worth paying attention to, as it marks an important watershed in the history of Confucian quiet sitting. This chapter largely confirms, by way of a general discussion, the ambivalent relation between quiet sitting and Neo-Confucianism.[2]

Psychological Transformations Brought about by Quiet Sitting

Chinese Confucian scholars of this period did practice quiet sitting, and this did bring about certain unique psychological changes in their state of mind. Concerning such changes, professor Chén Lái has collected a number of examples from the perspective of "mystical experience," including experiences obtained both by quiet sitting and by other methods.[3] Here, I will quote some of the best-known examples of quiet sitting in order to explore the psychological transformations that it brought about.

From the southern Sòng dynasty (1127–1279), we must first discuss Zhān Fùmín, a disciple of Lù Jiǔyuān (1139–1192), a prominent master of the school of mind in the Southern Sòng. In the Analects of Lù Jiǔyuān, we find a paragraph written by Zhān. In this paragraph, Zhān speaks about his practice of "quietly sitting with eyes closed while consciously arousing one's awareness." He continued this practice for half a month. Then suddenly one day, when he was climbing down the stairs of a pavilion, he felt the true nature of his mind rising up with total clarity. Hearing this, Lù Jiǔyuān said, "The universal principle [lǐ] has manifested itself."[4] Later, in the fourteenth century, a similar episode is recorded by Zhào Xié (?–1365), who is said to have attained some level of enlightenment after reading a text written by Yáng Jiǎn (1141–1225), a famous disciple of Lù Jiǔyuān. In this episode, Zhào talked about his disciple, Lǐ Kědào. During the daytime, Lǐ was able to see the state of his mind being clear and free of any thoughts by quietly sitting and observing his inner self. However, at night, or when he closed his eyes, Lǐ could not help separating his subjective from his objective existence. Then one evening he suddenly experienced frogs' voices echoing into eternity in his eyes. After this unique experience, he was able to experience a state of continuous clear emptiness in his mind.[5]

From the Míng dynasty (1368–1644), the first case that comes to anyone's mind is that of an influential mid-Míng advocate of the school of mind, Chén Xiànzhāng (1428–1500). Chén tried to attain a state of unity between the universal principle and his own mind by following the self-cultivation theory of the school of principle. However, being unable to achieve such unity, Chén engaged in quiet sitting. As a result, the "embodiment of his true mind" appeared before him, as though it were manifesting its physical existence constantly. After that experience, Chén was able to establish his true self, which presided over all of his actions without contradicting any ethical rules or the philosophy of the Confucian classics. Therefore, he decided to instruct his disciples in the practice of quiet sitting.[6] There is also a famous case involving Luó Hóngxiān (1504–1564), one of the main figures of the Yángmíng school in the sixteenth century. Leaving behind earthly matters, Luó Hóngxiān practiced quiet sitting in the mountains for over three months. He claimed that when his quietude reached its culmination, he felt his mind traveling beyond the restrictions of time and space and experienced unity with the entire world. He commented that his physical self felt like a volcanic crater of the "substance of mind" that prevailed in the universe.[7]

Thus, the experience obtained through quiet sitting, that is, the manifestation of one's substance of mind, unrestricted by time or space—a state in which one feels as though one's mind is the pivot and source of the energy that embraces and flows through the entire universe—was continuously discussed by Confucian scholars in premodern China. This kind of experience must therefore have been accepted as a reality by the scholars of the time. Needless to say, as we can see from the examples collected by Chén Lái, such experiences can also be attained by methods other than quiet sitting. Nonetheless, it was widely recognized that quiet sitting was one means of experiencing such psychological transformations.

Furthermore, within the theoretical framework of the Confucian philosophy of the time, this kind of psychological transformation was viewed as the attainment of one's original nature (xìng) and the universal principle (lǐ) inherent in the mind of all human beings. There was a widely shared idea among Confucians that "Heaven is the universal principle [Tiān jí lǐ]," and that "man's original nature is the universal principle [xìng jí lǐ]." Based on this, Confucians thought that one could become a sage by revealing one's original nature, which is also the heavenly principle, through certain kinds of cultivation practice. As a result, a notable number of Confucian scholars practiced quiet sitting repeatedly and confirmed it as an effective method for directly grasping the original nature inherent in one's mind, and for the complete manifestation of one's original nature.

Chén Xiànzhāng, as mentioned, attempted to realize the perfect unity of universal principle and mind according to the method prescribed by a respected master of the school of principle, Zhū Xī. But having failed in this attempt, Chén practiced quiet sitting instead. This proved effective, and he was able to attain his goal. This case clearly shows what quiet sitting meant to many scholars of this period. In that era, a significant number of Confucian scholars were interested in becoming a "sage." However, many were frustrated in their attempts at achieving this goal even when they diligently followed the course set by former great masters. For example, around the turn of the sixteenth century, Huáng Wǎn (1480–1554), a peer of Wáng Shǒurén when both were students, also faithfully practiced the approach advocated by Zhū Xī, but with no effect. As a consequence, he tried quiet sitting.[8]

People like Chén and Huáng regarded as valuable guidelines accounts of those who had successfully used quiet sitting to reveal their original nature. Accounts of such episodes had accumulated since the Southern Sòng dynasty, and Chén and Huáng, too, had attempted to attain such experiences, though without success. Thus, Confucian elites repeatedly practiced quiet sitting.

However, there were those who recognized the unique experience resulting from quiet sitting but considered it to be a dangerous method that could lead to erroneous thinking. These figures did not view such experiences as manifestations of the universal principle or of one's original nature. For this reason, they attempted to prevent others from focusing exclusively on quiet sitting as a way of experiencing the universal principle and their original nature.

Zhū Xī on the Problems of Quiet Sitting

It is a well known fact that Zhū Xī, after years of exploring various schools of philosophy, developed the philosophy of "reverence" (jìng) by integrating the philosophies of quietude (jìng) and awareness-in-action. After learning various schools of philosophy in his search for the truth, Zhū focused on quietude stimulated by his master, Lǐ Tóng (1093–1163), who emphasized the significance of "observing emotions before they have germinated" (guān xǐ-nù-āi-lè wèi fā zhī zhōng). Then Zhū found true awareness-in-action, stimulated by his friend Zhāng Shì (1133–1180). Finally, by integrating these two approaches, Zhū developed the philosophy of "reverence."[9] Zhū's view on "reverence" has been analyzed and discussed in detail by Araki Kengo and others.[10] Here I would like to note that although Zhū Xī discussed the effectiveness of quiet sitting and integrated it into his practice of self-cultivation, he also avoided excessive devotion to it, because of the inherent danger he felt it presented. This is the origin of later controversies surrounding the effects of quiet sitting.[11]

Zhū assumed that our perfect original nature, that is, the universal principle, is inherent in our mind, and he believed that to become a sage is to regain the ability to fully realize this original nature in our personality. However, he also believed that, for various reasons, in reality we are able to realize only a portion of that nature.[12] In order to experience the perfected state of our original nature, it is necessary to focus our mind, through quiet sitting, on this original nature. At the same time, Zhū saw the investigation of the nature or principle of all external things as absolutely indispensable, since their nature is essentially identical to the original nature of our own mind.

Zhū claimed that quiet sitting is necessary for establishing a foundation in our mind for the process of self-cultivation. At the same time, however, he also saw the need to pursue the natures or principles of all external things. He warned against the danger of focusing exclusively on quiet sitting and claimed that our innate knowledge (liángzhī) has been corrupted by the impurity of our constitution and the temptations of our desires, and that we cannot attain the correct awareness of the universal principle solely by relying on innate knowledge. Consequently, he thought that the investigation of external things, which were seen as concrete revelations of the universal principle, was indispensable in the process of regaining the true state of this principle. In other words, we cannot grasp the universal principle correctly only by seeking it in our mind through quiet sitting.[13]

The psychological state generated by quiet sitting, as one focuses on one's inner self, could be viewed as similar to the type of meditation practiced by Chán monks. As such, the practice might result in ignoring the Confucian moral principles that were recognized by Chinese intellectuals as manifestations of the universal principle. Therefore, Zhū Xī replaced quiet sitting with the practice of "reverence," a concept that encompasses awareness both in quietude and in action.[14] At times, Zhū Xī even said that the effect of quiet sitting was to better prepare oneself for external investigation and other practices by bringing focus to the otherwise scattered mind.[15] In general, Zhū Xī felt it was dangerous to be absorbed in quietude. Although he was aware of its value, which he had learned from his teacher Lǐ Tóng, he saw only a limited effect from quiet sitting.

Wáng Shǒurén on the Problems of Quiet Sitting

According to the chronological table edited by his disciples, Wáng Shǒurén first developed his own unique views at Lóngchǎng in Guìzhōu province in 1508. When he preached his idea of "the unity of knowledge and action" (zhī xíng héyī), it caused confusion among his followers, so Wáng decided to lecture on quiet sitting and achieved substantial results.[16] However, he later came to the conclusion that quiet sitting had had undesirable results. When a person practices quiet sitting, according to Wáng, he tends to be absorbed by and to indulge in the realm of quietude, distancing himself from social relationships. Or he may be totally consumed by the unique experience obtained through quiet sitting and begin to talk about strange ideas that would take others by surprise. Wáng concluded that only his theory of innate knowledge of the good (liángzhī) would not lead to such problems.[17]

In short, Wáng admitted the effectiveness of quiet sitting to a certain degree, but he was cautious about focusing on it specifically.[18] He believed that by focusing on quiet sitting, one would tend to become distant from reality and overestimate the value of the experience resulting from quiet sitting. Thus, his support of quiet sitting was qualified. Wáng Shǒurén's view of one's ability to recognize the universal principle was quite different from that of Zhū Xī. Wáng believed that even an ordinary person has the ability to identify accurately the individualized expression of the universal principle in his own mind, although an ordinary person may not be aware of it. Therefore, although their opinions greatly differed, both Zhū and Wáng had a qualified view of the effects of quiet sitting. There were also discussions of the efficacy of quiet sitting among scholars of the later Yángmíng school, and Niè Bào, Luó Hóngxiān, Zōu Shǒuyì and Wáng Jī seriously engaged themselves in the development of this argument.

Zhū Xī and Wáng Shǒurén thought that the universal principle as original nature existed inherently in each person's mind, and they believed that regaining the complete manifestation of this original nature is the basis of sagehood. They also thought that concentrating on one's inner self through quiet sitting could help to awaken one's original nature. This focus on the inner self is completely lacking in daily life, when one's attention is spread out among a variety of external matters. Quiet sitting, therefore, can lead to the experience of certain psychological transformations. Nonetheless, from the perspective of Confucian principles, such practice could also lead in a dangerous direction. Therefore, Confucian scholars often took the stance of "not too close, not too distant" regarding quiet sitting.

Xuē Huì and the Relativization of Confucian Values

Zhū Xī and Wáng Shǒurén were concerned that the unique state of mind obtained by quiet sitting could bring the practitioner away from the realization resulting from the full consciousness of daily life. In fact, there are cases in which this happened. Confucian practitioners of quiet sitting were at times led to the philosophy of Chán Buddhism and the state of "flowing into languor" (liúrù kūgǎo) or "esoteric awareness and subtle enlightenment" (xuánjiě miàojué),[19] thus devaluing the concrete universal principle of Confucianism and the teachings of the Classics. Xuē Huì (1489–1541), who was slightly younger than Wáng Shǒurén, is a clear example of this. On the one hand, as a Confucian scholar, he stressed the importance of not losing engagement with the affairs of the world; on the other, he claimed that the universal principle and the original nature attained at the culmination of quietude is shared by Confucianism, Lǎozǐ, and Buddhism. He even claimed that the more suitable expressions about the universal principle and the original nature are found in Buddhist scriptures and in Lǎozǐ. Thus, Xuē was heading in the direction that Zhū Xī avoided, and was also stepping further into the realm that Wáng Shǒurén was cautious about.

Táng Shùnzhī (1507–1560) wrote a tombstone epitaph for Xuē. According to this epitaph, Xuē first devoted himself to the "learning of inner alchemy." He put down his books and engaged in quiet sitting but was unable to achieve any state of enlightenment. Then he attempted to "converge ears and eyes and clear his mind and sit quietly," according to the teachings of Lǎozǐ, Buddhism, or the Golden Mean. Several years later, he was able to achieve a satisfactory level of understanding, and he published texts describing his experiences, in spite of the criticism he knew this would incite.[20]

By engaging in quiet sitting, Xuē found that he was able to experience the original nature that exists in the deepest layers of one's mind. This original nature is the universal principle and the root of all teachings, and transcends the dogmatic framework of the three teachings (Confucianism, Daoism, and Buddhism). As a result, Xuē came to emphasize how meaningless it was to focus on the differences between these schools. In other words, he claimed that the three teachings are integrated in one's mind, and that in its truly natural state, the mind is completely free and transcends any linguistic framework.[21]

According to Xuē, man's fundamental nature is the same in both Confucianism and Daoism, but while Confucian philosophy revolves around the surface of one's mind and fails to grasp the issues of fundamental existence, Daoism focuses too much on one's free nature and fails to expand adherents' views on more practical matters of life. In essence, however, these two schools of thought share the same principle.[22]

Xuē developed his point further by saying that Buddhism and Daoism provide more convincing arguments, as their expressions of original nature are closer to its real state. In other words, Buddhists and Daoists go to the root of "the internal learning of self-cultivation and the ultimate discourse on the original nature" in a way that "Confucians have never heard before"; Buddhism and

Daoism discuss the universal principle and the original nature more explicitly than Confucianism.[23] Xuē said that Confucian schools rarely talk about the original nature, and that the six Confucian Classics contained no satisfactory descriptions of these issues. He also said that "mundane affairs and human ethics" cannot fulfill the Way of Heaven or lead to man's original nature.[24] As a practical approach to one's true nature, Xuē stresses the necessity of emphasizing quietude as a way of experiencing and affirming the true nature of one's mind, a reality that transcends any linguistic framework and thus cannot be molded into any form.[25]

Xuē's claims devalued the Confucian Classics—the bedrock of Confucian orthodoxy—and the Confucian norms underlying the social order. His insistence that Buddhism and Daoism gave a more direct expression of man's original nature as experienced through quiet sitting than the six Confucian classics explicitly degraded the theories and discussions of Confucian scholars. His claim that earthly affairs and human ethics cannot perfect one's original nature challenged the absolute value attributed to the Confucian social norms, which were seen as a temporary form of the formless original nature. Needless to say, he was not in favor of turning one's back on social activity by devoting oneself entirely to the world of absolute quietude, but rather looked upon daily practice of ethical values as essential manifestations of one's nature.[26] However, Xuē described man's original nature as the source of individual ethical norms. The former could encompass the latter, but not vice versa, implying a devaluation of the absoluteness of the individual ethical norms. Thus, his theory clearly displays the devaluation of both Confucian classics and the practical norms of human ethics. Naturally, then, as Táng Shùnzhī predicted, this incurred criticism from other Confucian scholars. Regarding this, Xuē said, "My theories have been criticized as being totally absurd."[27]

Within the theoretical framework of "sagehood," based on the theory that "Heaven is the universal principle, and original nature is also the universal principle" (tiān jí lǐ, xìng jí lǐ), no matter what form of enlightenment one may experience, it can easily lead to the syncretic theory of "the unity of the three teachings," in the sense that both the universal principle and the original nature are experienced in one's mind. In other words, all three teachings allow us to experience the true existence of our self, an existence that transcends all language and actions as we enter the realm of undifferentiated principle and nature. The linguistic discourse of the Confucian classics can capture only the "substance of mind" as it has been congealed in a specific rhetoric, so its linguistic expression is not absolute. In the state of the undifferentiated mind, the Confucian "principle" can be identified with the "principle" or the "way" of Buddhism or Daoism.[28] But according to Xuē, Buddhism and Daoism discuss the undifferentiated "substance of mind" more explicitly than Confucian texts, because Confucian discourse involves only surface consciousness and daily matters.

As mentioned above, many Confucian scholars had had the positive experience of quiet sitting being an effective and convenient method for attaining a direct experience of the universal principle and the original nature. Stories about the convenience of quiet sitting and its effects were widely circulated. However, quiet sitting was also practiced by Buddhists and Daoists, and Confucian scholars were highly aware of its origin in these two schools of thought. There was always a danger, therefore, that practitioners of quiet sitting would be drawn to Buddhism and Daoism,[29] and that Confucian scholars would begin advocating the philosophy of "the unity of the three teachings," or even put Buddhism and Daoism above Confucianism, as Xuē Huì did. All of this intensified the anxieties of Neo-Confucian scholars who were concerned about the dangers of excessive quiet sitting.

Gāo Pānlóng and Lù Lǒngqí's Contrasting Views of Quiet Sitting

Among later scholars of the Zhū Xī school of Neo-Confucianism, there were differences of opinion regarding quiet sitting. To demonstrate such differences, I will discuss Gāo Pānlóng (1562–1626) and the criticism of Gāo by Lù Lǒngqí (1630–1692). Put simply, Gāo Pānlóng placed importance on quiet sitting as a way to experience the original nature, a position quite similar to what had been advocated by Zhū Xī's master Lǐ Tóng in the twelfth century, though Gāo presumed to follow Zhū Xī's philosophy faithfully.[30] Lù Lǒngqí criticized Gāo and attempted to limit the importance of quiet sitting to merely function as a means of bringing focus to mind and body in order to pursue the universal principle in external affairs. In this sense, Lù, like Zhū Xī, attached less importance to quiet sitting.

The idea of directly bringing oneself closer to the true substance of the original nature through quiet sitting was formed during the time of Yáng Shí (1053–1135), so it had existed even before the time of Lǐ Tóng.[31] As mentioned, Zhū Xī tried to keep his distance from this approach, while still being influenced by the practice of quiet sitting. In the late Míng dynasty, Gāo Pānlóng proactively accepted Zhū Xī's theory of investigating things and exploring principles, while placing significant emphasis on quiet sitting. For this reason, like Lǐ Tóng, he also advocated the necessity of quiet sitting. However, Lù Lǒngqí cautioned about the danger that Gāo's theory of quiet sitting could bring about. The two directions of thought that had not yet been clearly organized and that remained ambiguous in Zhū Xī's mind were manifested in the opinions of Gāo and Lù, after having been filtered by the passage of time.

After long years of engaging in a variety of practices, including quiet sitting, Gāo Pānlóng experienced a unique psychological transformation. His experiences are recorded in detail in the *Kùnxuéjì*.[32] Based on personal experience, he emphasized the necessity of reading and claimed that it is indispensable and important to investigate things and explore principles externally. However, he also underlined the importance of quiet sitting. As recorded in *Kùnxuéjì*, he practiced Zhū Xī's motto, "Quiet sitting for half a day, and reading for half a day," and also recommended it to others.[33]

Further, the nature of Gāo's quiet sitting was similar to Lǐ Tóng's idea of "observing emotions before they have germinated." Thus, Gāo aimed at grasping his true nature through quiet sitting.[34] He did not practice quiet sitting simply to draw the mind away from petty matters and focus on the exploration of principles. At times, Gāo quoted the words of Chén Xiànzhāng, who had made quiet sitting a central part of his theory of self-cultivation.[35]

Other scholars were sometimes led to think that Gāo attempted to first grasp the original nature through quiet sitting, and then to explore the principles of things, which were thought to be essentially identical with the original nature, through extensive reading.[36] This was how Lù Lǒngqí interpreted Gāo's approach, and he criticized him for placing excessive importance on quiet sitting as a way of approaching the substance of mind.

Lù Lǒngqí criticized both Gāo and his close friend Gù Xiànchéng (1550–1612) for distorting Zhū Xī's Confucianism by focusing too much on "quietude." According to Lù, both Gāo and Gù claimed that to restore one's original nature, the principles of things should be pursued externally. In this sense, Lù admitted that both Gāo and Gù were in agreement with Zhū Xī's Confucianism. However, since they placed too much emphasis on quietude, they were inclined to think that the universal principle could be found directly within one's mind through contemplation. According to Lù, Gāo and Gù expanded the realm of mind—the subjective realm—to a level of illusory significance. For this reason, Lù claimed that Gāo and Gù's way of pursuing the universal principle was problematic.[37]

Lù traced the long-term process of Gāo's practice by examining the *Kùnxuéjì*, concluding that Gāo depended too much on the effects of quietude, and that his approach to quietude sought to manifest the original nature that is inherently in one's mind. Therefore, Lù characterized Gāo's approach as the philosophy of Chán Buddhism. Further, Lù said that all of Gāo's other writings on the practice of quiet sitting centered on the experience of manifesting one's original nature, and that although Gāo also underlined the importance of reading, he emphasized quiet sitting even more. Lù pointed out that this resulted from Gāo's misinterpretation of Lǐ Tóng's philosophy of "observing emotions before they have germinated."[38]

Disagreement with Gāo's emphasis on quiet sitting is seen in other sections of his text as well, indicating that this was not an issue that Lù Lǒngqí felt he could ignore. In Lù's opinion, Gāo deviated from the correct path as a result of misinterpreting Zhū Xī's Neo-Confucianism. Therefore, Lù attempted to correct the deviation and lighten the emphasis on quiet sitting. He also disagreed with the idea of "quiet sitting for half a day, and reading for half a day" that formed the basis for Gāo's notions. Lù even attempted to devalue Gāo's text by claiming that the disciple who recorded it was a student of Chán Buddhism.[39] Wáng Shǒurén's school of mind was the direct target of Lù's criticism and the school he wished to defeat. At the same time, Lù also found elements of "pseudo-Confucianism" in the philosophy of Gāo Pānlóng and others, and tried to defeat them as well.

Late Míng Manuals for Quiet Sitting

Starting in the late Míng (sixteenth century), there was a trend toward regulating the practice of quiet sitting by means of comparably clear manuals for Confucian elites. Since early times, Buddhists and Daoists had practiced concentrating on the inner self by sitting quietly and calming the mind. From the twelfth century onward, Neo-Confucian scholars also began to use this method, under the name "quiet sitting," as an effective way to experience the original nature. However, concrete methods of quiet sitting were not much discussed. Despite all of the discussion of quiet sitting during the late imperial period, the concrete form of practice was never clearly indicated.[40] However, beginning in the late Míng, Confucian elites began to provide clear and concise methods of practicing quiet sitting.

Pioneering this new trend was "the way of regulated breathing" propagated by Wáng Jī (1498–1583), one of the most influential disciples of Wáng Shǒurén.[41] Although Wáng Jī asserted that the real state of the original nature is "beyond good and evil" and could be attained only after abandoning all intentional moral efforts, as if being pushed off a cliff,[42] he adopted the concrete practice of "regulated breathing" to make up for the lack of guidance in accessing the original nature. In discussing these points, Wáng Jī used mostly Daoist terms of inner alchemy (nèidān). However, in his manual for regulated breathing, he discussed the method based on the four phases of breathing according to the "Gradual Practice of Dhyāna" (Cìdì chánmén) and "A Little Primer of Concentration and Insight" (Xiǎo Zhǐguān) by the founder of Tiāntái Buddhism, Zhìyǐ (538–597).[43]

Like his teacher Wáng Shǒurén, Wáng Jī did not fully support quiet sitting but recognized its effectiveness as an "expedient way" and advocated "regulated breathing" as a concrete method. With him, we can see the implementation of methods taken from Buddhist and Daoist practices, as well as, for the first time, the use of a simple manual for quiet sitting. This represented an important new trend that continued after Wáng. For example, Yán Jūn (1504–1596), who belonged to the most radical school among the followers of Wáng Shǒurén, talked about the method of "seven-day confinement" (qī rì bìguān) as a practice to uncover one's original nature. This method consists of practices similar to those of Daoism, including swallowing saliva or circulating energy throughout the body while concentrating on the "cinnabar field" (dāntián, the area a little below the navel). The number of days required for this practice is specified as seven, and the practitioner is required to cover his eyes and ears. No matter how painful it might be, the practitioner must look into his inner self in complete silence, sitting in the lotus position. When the practice period is completed, the practitioner takes another seven days off to confirm his original nature while listening to his master's guidance.[44] Listening to the teaching of one's master reminds us of the "mind control" used in modern cult religions. Here, however, I would like to focus on the fact that the technique of quiet sitting to grasp one's original nature is described in an unprecedentedly concrete manner.

Another example of a Confucian scholar borrowing from Buddhist and Daoist meditative traditions is Yuán Huáng (best known by his style name Liǎofán, 1533–1606), who is known for his use of ledgers of merit and demerit in a famous pamphlet titled "On Establishing the Mandate" (Lìmìng piān). In this text, he discusses the way of "establishing one's mandate" and passing the civil service examination by doing good deeds. However, although he succeeded in the civil service examination and became a Confucian official, he also became a disciple of Chán master Yúngǔ, and he even published a short work titled "Critical Points of Quiet Sitting" (Jìngzuò yàojué) based on the Tiāntāi Buddhist text "Gradual Practice of Dhyāna."[45]

In the preface, it is explicitly stated that Yuán wrote his text based on the teachings of the Tiāntāi Buddhism that he learned from Master Yúngǔ. In the twelfth century, Zhū Xī had already been clearly aware that quiet sitting was originally not a Confucian tradition.[46] Likewise, Yuán Huáng explicitly asserted that quiet sitting had been adopted from Chán Buddhism by early founders of Neo-Confucianism. Yuán also said that other Confucian scholars had mistakenly thought that their quiet sitting had allowed them to reach the "ultimate level," when in reality they were still at the elementary level of spiritual realization. As a result, Yuán came to believe that the theories of quiet sitting introduced to him by Master Yúngǔ and his fellow monk, Master Miàofǎ, were the only genuine ones, based on the real highest level of spiritual accomplishment. Yuán Huáng said that he wrote "Critical Points of Quiet Sitting" with reference to the works of Zhìyǐ, while taking the ideas about quiet sitting from the teachings of the above two Chán masters.[47]

Yuán's text consists of six chapters. These chapters merge Buddhist theories of practice with Confucian philosophies of moral virtue. Both the structure and the content of the work are unique. For example, while Zhìyǐ's "Gradual Practice of Dhyāna" underlies the entire work, Yuán's text is easier to refer to, because of the chapter divisions, which Zhìyǐ's text does not have. The highly complex teachings in Zhìyǐ's "Gradual Practice of Dhyāna" are strongly simplified. Furthermore, the first chapter of Yuán's work establishes the Confucian idea that "all things are essentially one" (wànwù yì tǐ) and the crucial Confucian notion of "benevolence" (rén) as basic principles of his own theory. But then he links Confucian "benevolence" to the Buddhist concept of the "four immeasurable frames of mind" (sì wúliàngxīn) extracted from the beginning of the "Gradual Practice of Dhyāna" and includes the latter in his last chapter under the heading "On Enlarging One's Love" (Guǎng'ài piān). In addition, Yuán's text includes explicit criticism of Daoist theories. Yuán also criticized the theories of quiet sitting by previous Confucian scholars, on the grounds that they were quite shallow—comparable only to the introductory level of Chán Buddhism—even though the scholars in question mistakenly believed that they had attained the ultimate state of mind. Yuán explicitly mentions Chén Xiànzhāng and criticizes him by name.[48]

Yuán holds that the state of initial Chán awakening is not a satisfactory level and needs to be overcome in order for a person to attain the second level of Chán awakening, in contrast to what Confucian scholars of the past had mistakenly thought. Thus, experiences of quiet sitting by former Confucian scholars came to occupy a certain place in Yuán's system of thought. Yuán also criticizes Daoists for mistaking the initial Chán awakening for the ultimate one. He guides his readers toward the route he is advocating, urging them on to a higher level of enlightenment.[49]

Yuán Huáng's text must be considered an important benchmark for the movement toward regulating the method of quiet sitting. It explains the method for quiet sitting in a clear and concise manner, while still exhibiting a certain complexity and massiveness, based on the voluminous and extremely complicated theories of Zhìyǐ.

Among the series of regulative manuals for quiet sitting, the work of Gāo Pān-lóng deserves special attention. Gāo's manual for quiet sitting, titled "Recovering [the Original State of Mind] in Seven Days" (Fù qī guī), teaches its readers to concentrate their minds in seven days of continuous quiet sitting:

On the first day, relax and walk slowly. Sleep when you feel tired, and make yourself content. When your tiredness has been swept away, enter your room, burn incense, and sit down with your legs crossed. All methods of quiet sitting simply aim at awakening [the original state of] the mind and making it forever eminently bright, leaving your surface mind with nowhere to go. When your surface mind has nowhere to go, your spirit naturally gains focus and returns to its origin, with no need for you to make particular arrangements. Don't be concerned with any particular location, and don't be concerned with any particular effects. When you first enter quietude and don't yet know how to regulate your mind, just pay attention to the important sayings of past sages, and you will naturally find your way in. After three days of quietude, you will most certainly reach a wonderful realm. But after four or five days, you must take particular care to avoid laxness. Take a brief and slow walk after each meal. Keep your consumption of wine and meat low, to avoid drowsiness. Don't take off your clothes when you lie down to sleep. Just lie down when you feel tired, and get up as soon as you awake. After seven days, your spirit will be replete, and no afflictions will bother you anymore.[50]

As we have seen, this work was later criticized by Lù Lǒngqí. However, its appearance was very important in the development of quiet sitting in the history of Neo-Confucianism. Gāo's work was the first genuinely Confucian manual of quiet sitting that did not include elements of Buddhism or Daoism.

Gāo provided a concrete Confucian method of practice, excluding any elements that referred to Buddhist or Daoist practices. In this sense, his attempt marks an important milestone in the tradition of quiet sitting as interpreted by Confucian schools of philosophy. We should also note that, as with Yán Jūn, Gāo too takes seven days as the period of practice, most likely based on the cycles of seven days (qī rì lái-fù) in the Book of Changes.

In fact, the reason that eminent Confucians of the time, such as Gāo Pānlóng, Chén Lóngzhèng, and Liú Zōngzhōu, accepted Zhū Xī's "quiet sitting for half a day, and reading for half a day" as a guideline for quiet sitting must have been the need to clearly stress the *Confucian* way of quiet sitting, since Zhū Xī himself did not intend to emphasize the practice. The tradition of quiet sitting underwent a qualitative change in the sixteenth and seventeenth centuries, when manuals by Confucian elites began to be written and published. For the first time in history, there appeared a unique way of Confucian quiet sitting. This new tradition is probably related to a similar trend taking place in Buddhism and Daoism at that time.[51]

Conclusion

Based on the ideal of "realizing sagehood" that was so central to Confucians of these periods, quiet sitting was often considered to be a practice with assured efficacy, helping practitioners to gain a direct experience of their original nature that is identical to the universal principle, and that inherently exists in the mind. Indeed, Confucian scholars never ceased to practice quiet sitting.

However, many Confucians also saw a danger in the emphasis on quiet sitting. The concept of original nature might easily merge and become identified with the fundamental existence proclaimed by Buddhism and Daoism. If so, the absolute value of Confucian norms might be undermined. Instead of focusing on correct moral norms as manifested in one's interactions with society—which was essential to Confucian norms—some Confucians became more engaged in the internal observation of the undistinguished essence of mind. In this way, quiet sitting might be identified with the fundamental "emptiness" or "way" advocated by Buddhism and Daoism. Since quiet sitting originated in Buddhism and Daoism, its practitioners, while quietly sitting and contemplating the original human nature that existed before different schools of philosophy were established, could easily be led to the idea of the unity of the three teachings. Indeed, in advocating this syncretist philosophy, Xuē Huì, a Confucian scholar, greatly devalued the efficacy of the Confucian classics and Confucian social norms by claiming that the discourses and nomenclature of Buddhism and Daoism provided a more profound description of the real state of one's original nature. Confucian scholars were continuously torn between the effectiveness and the dangers of quiet sitting. For those who tried to remain Confucian scholars rather than entirely converting to the philosophies of Buddhism or Daoism, quiet sitting became a problematic approach that was both attractive and innately dangerous.

In the seventeenth century, more concrete and clear manuals for quiet sitting began to appear, supplementing the earlier ambiguous statements about such practice. They were all relatively short and described the actual practice and knowledge of quiet sitting in a manner that was easy to understand. As part of this trend, Buddhist and Daoist practices began to be incorporated in such manuals more frequently. However, Confucian manuals for quiet sitting also appeared, marking a unique change that took place in seventeenth-century China.

After the disastrous collapse of the Míng dynasty and the establishment of the Qīng dynasty in the mid-sixteenth century, a significant change occurred in the traditional Confucian paradigm. The Yángmíng school of mind associated with Wáng Shǒurén lost popularity, and Zhū Xī's school of principle began to regain the support of Confucian elites. A new intellectual trend resulted in numerous bibliographical studies of the classics. At the same time, strong emphasis was placed on the daily practice of Confucian moral norms and statecraft. As a result, some Confucian scholars gave up the ideal of sagehood.

Under these circumstances, the effects of quiet sitting came to be criticized more often than before, and, unlike their predecessors during previous dynasties, Confucian scholars of the eighteenth century onward did not actively engage in such practice, except under certain limited circumstances. Thus, in the late seventeenth century, discussions of the use of quiet sitting almost came to an end. The view prevailed that since quiet sitting was a dangerous approach, it should be used only sparingly.

Notes

1. Here I use the term "Neo-Confucianism" in a broad sense, referring not only to the school of principle (*lǐxué*) but also to another main stream of Confucianism during this period, the school of mind (*xīnxué*). For problems related to the usage of this terminology, see Tillman, "New Direction"; de Bary, "Uses of Neo-Confucianism"; and Tillman, "Uses of Neo-Confucianism." Mayumi Yoshida translated my Japanese draft into English. This chapter is closely related to an article in Chinese on the same topic (Mabuchi, "Sòng-Míng shíqí Rúxué").

2. Taylor, "Sudden/Gradual Paradigm," discusses extensively the view of quiet sitting held by Confucian scholars from the Sòng through Míng dynasties (11th–17th century). Inspired by the Japanese scholar Okada Takehiko, Taylor has conducted extensive research on quiet sitting in premodern Chinese Confucianism, and he is considered the leading authority on this topic. However, the framework of sudden (*dùn*) and gradual (*jiàn*) used by Taylor does not fit quiet sitting well. Also, Taylor considers quiet sitting to be strongly related to the school of principle, but this is problematic.

3. Chén Lái, "Shénmì zhǔyì wèntí," 359–84.

4. *Lù Jiǔyuān jí*, 471.

5. *Zhào Bǎofēng jí*, 19.

6. *Chén Xiànzhāng jí*, 145.

7. *Luó Hóngxiān jí*, 298.

8. See Mabuchi, "Kō Wan no shisō." Huáng, however, later had a keen realization of the practice's deficiency, and became critical of quiet sitting.

9. See Tomoeda, *Shushi no shisō keisei*, especially chapter 1, 1.

10. See Araki, *Bukkyō to jukyō*, 323–340.

11. On Zhū Xī and the issue of quiet sitting, see Róngjié Chén, "Zhūzǐ yǔ jìngzuò"; Azuma, "Seiza towa nanika"; Nakajima, "Shushi no seiza"; Taylor, "Chu Hsi and Meditation"; Yáng, "Sòngrú de jìngzuò shuō"; and Yáng, "Zhū jìng yǔ zhǔ jìng." Azuma distinguishes Zhū Xī's quiet sitting from that practiced by his master Lǐ Tóng and others to "seek inner awareness and self-awakening." Azuma argues that Zhū Xī practiced quiet sitting only as a preparatory activity, to calm his mind before pursuing external issues. I am inclined to agree with Azuma, but I also believe that Zhū Xī was in an ambivalent position, in which he still retained some reminis-

cent influence of his master, and therefore also considered quiet sitting as nourishment of one's true self. Tomoeda makes similar observations about the influence of Lǐ Tóng on Zhū Xī's view of quiet sitting even during the later years of his life; cf. Tomoeda, *Shushi no shisō keisei*, 95ff.

12. Araki Kengo calls such a position as that taken by Zhū Xī "intermediary," which I think is a precise description. Refer to Araki, *Bukkyō to jukyō*, 378–382.

13. *Zhū Wéngōng wénjí*, 24:3800.

14. Ibid., 23:2988.

15. See Azuma, "Seiza towa nanika."

16. *Wáng Yángmíng quánjí*, 1230.

17. Ibid., 104f.

18. See Chén Lái, "Shénmì zhǔyì wèntí," 272ff., for a summary of Wáng Shǒurén's views on quiet sitting. See also Liú, "Wáng Yángmíng"; and Taylor, "Sudden/Gradual Paradigm."

19. *Wáng Yángmíng quánjí*, 104f.

20. Appendix to *Kǎogōng jí*.

21. *Xīyuán yíshū*, 1:48.

22. *Kǎogōng jí*, 10:2.

23. Ibid., 9:20.

24. *Xīyuán yíshū*, 2:9f.

25. Ibid., 2:8, 11.

26. In *Kǎogōng jí*, 9:20, he explicitly states that he does not intend to ignore ordinary Confucian moral and ethics.

27. *Xīyuán yíshū*, 2:11.

28. It is well known that Wáng Shǒurén already had such tendencies. Araki Kengo has emphasized the importance of such views among late Míng intellectuals; cf. Araki, "Dèng Huòqú de chūxiàn."

29. See Tomoeda, *Shushi no shisō keisei*, 59f.; and Azuma, "Shushigaku no shin kenkyū," 438. According to Nakajima ("Shushi no seiza") the term "quiet sitting" is found in the important sixth-century Chinese Buddhist text *Móhē zhǐguān*, and is given an important meaning in an official Confucian commentary to the *Book of Changes*, the *Zhōuyì zhèngyì*, in the seventh century. According to Nakajima, however, the term "quiet sitting" was not considered important in any of the three teachings until the eleventh century. Before the Táng period, however, both Daoists and Buddhists had often practiced sitting quietly to calm the mind while focusing on the inner self.

30. For Gāo Pānlóng's opinion on quiet sitting, see Okada, *Ō Yōmei*, 426–430. See also Taylor, "Meditation in Ming Neo-Orthodoxy"; and Taylor, *Cultivation of Sagehood*.

31. Azuma, *Shushigaku no shin kenkyū*, 434ff.

32. *Gāozǐ yíshū*, 3:13–18. The original account is also quoted in Chén Lái, "Shénmì zhǔyì wèntí."

33. Ibid., 8a:26.

34. Ibid., 8a:67f.

35. Ibid., 8a:30.

36. Tsurunari, "Kō Hanryō no kakubutsusetsu ni tsuite," claims that the "investigation of things" (*gé wù*) practiced by Gāo Pānlóng was completely directed inward. However, this claim conflicts with Gāo's emphasis on reading. I believe that in Gāo's view, pursuing the principles of things by studying the classics should be seen as a process to confirm the concrete forms of the universal principle. See relevant discussions in Okada, *Ō Yōmei*, 416, 419f., 425, and 436.

37. *Sānyútáng wénjí*, 2:5f.

38. See *Sōngyáng cháocún*, 2:8–11.

39. See *Sānyútáng shèngyán*, 8:4. On this topic, see Chén Róngjié, "Bàn rì jìngzuò"; Qián Mù, "Zhūzǐ lùn jìng"; and Chén Jiànhuáng, "Bàn rì jìngzuò."

40. We can say that "Tiáoxī zhēn" (Instructions for breathing regulation), written by Zhū Xī in the twelfth century, was the early onset of this later trend. See Miura Kunio, *Shushi to ki to shintai*, chapter 5.

41. I have discussed Wáng Jī's use of regulated breathing in the context of inner alchemy in Mabuchi, "Jugaku no dokyō sesshu."

42. Regarding Wáng Jī's notion of "beyond good and evil," see Shibata, "Ō Ryūkei no shisō." On the philosophy of Wáng Jī, also see Péng, *Liángzhīxué de zhǎnkāi*.

43. Regarding these writings by Zhìyǐ, see Satō, *Tendai daishi no kenkyū*; and Ōno Hideto, *Tendai shikan seiritsushi*. For more details on Wáng Jī's method, see his "Tiáoxīfǎ."

44. *Yán Jūn jí*, 37. On the philosophy of Yán Jūn, see Zhōng Cǎijūn, "Yán Shānnóng."

45. Yuán Huáng's text is easily accessible, because a photocopy of its 1929 edition is included in the *Dàozàng Jīnghuá*, vol. 2, chap. 9. This version of the text must be a relatively faithful reproduction of the original work, since it is identical to the contents referred to in a correspondence between Yuán and a certain Mǎ Ruìhé regarding the text (included in *Liǎngxíngzhāi jí*, vol. 10). My examination of the text here is preliminary, leaving a detailed examination as a topic for future research. For a detailed account of the life, writings, and philosophy of Yuán Huáng, see Sakai, *Chūgoku zensho no kenkyū*; and Okuzaki, *Chūgoku kyōshin jinushi no kenkyū*.

46. See Nakajima, "Shushi no seiza."

47. *Jìngzuò yàojué*, 1f.

48. Ibid., 20–23.

49. Ibid.

50. *Gāozǐ yíshū*, vol. 3.

51. Wǔ Shǒuyáng, who was known as an accomplished practitioner of inner alchemy, considered himself to belong to the Lóngmén school of Daoism and developed clear and detailed descriptions of the skills of inner alchemy. His work is a clear expression of the trend for creating clearly written quiet sitting manuals, which became popular among members of the elite. A similar trend must have taken place in the world of Buddhism at the time.

Glossary

běnxìng 本性
Chán 禪
Chén Lái 陳來
Chén Lóngzhèng 陳龍正
Chén Xiànzhāng 陳獻章
Cìdì chánmén 次第禅門
dāntián 丹田
dùn 頓
Fù qī guī 復七規
Gāo Pānlóng 高攀龍
gé wù 格物
Guǎng'ài piān 廣愛篇
guān xǐ-nù-āi-lè wèi fā zhī zhōng 觀喜怒哀樂未發之中
Gù Xiànchéng 顧憲成
Huáng Wǎn 黃綰

jiàn 漸
jìng 靜
jìng 敬
jìngzuò 靜坐
Kùnxuéjì 困学記
Lǎozǐ 老子
lǐ 理
Liǎngxíngzhāi jí 兩行齋集
liángzhī 良知
Liǎofán 了凡
Lǐ Kědào 李可道
Lǐ Tóng 李侗
liúrù kūgǎo 流入枯槁
Liú Zōngzhōu 劉宗周
lǐxué 理學
Lóngmén 龍門
Lù Jiǔyuān 陸九淵
Lù Lǒngqí 陸隴其
Luó Hóngxiān 羅洪先
Miàofǎ 妙法
Míng 明 (dynasty)
Móhē zhǐguān 摩訶止観
nèidān 內丹
Niè Bào 聶豹
Okada Takehiko 岡田武彦
Qīng 清 (dynasty)
qī rì bìguān 七日閉關
qī rì lái-fù 七日來復
rén 仁
sì wúliàngxīn 四無量心
Sòng 宋 (dynasty)
Táng Shùnzhī 唐順之
tiān jí lǐ 天即理
Tiāntāi 天台
Tiáoxī zhēn 調息箴
Wáng Jī 王畿
Wáng Shǒurén 王守仁
wànwù yì tǐ 萬無一體
Wǔ Shǒuyáng 伍守陽
Xiǎo zhǐguān 小止観
xìng 性
xìng jí lǐ 性即理
xīnxué 心學
xuánjiě miàojué 玄解妙覺
Xuē Huì 薛蕙
Yán Jūn 顏鈞
Yáng Jiǎn 楊簡
Yángmíng 陽明

Yáng Shí 楊時
Yuán Huáng 袁黃
Yúngǔ 雲谷
Zhān Fùmín 詹阜民
Zhāng Shì 張栻
Zhào Xié 趙偕
Zhìyǐ 智顗
zhī xíng héyī 知行合一
Zhōuyì zhèngyì 周易正義
Zhū Xī 朱熹
Zōu Shǒuyì 鄒守益

Bibliography

Araki, Kengo 荒木見悟. *Bukkyō to jukyō* 仏教と儒教. Heirakuji shoten, 1972.

———. "Dèng Huòqú de chūxiàn jí qí bèijǐng" 鄧豁渠的出現及其背景. *Zhōngguó zhéxué* 中國哲學 19 (1998): 1–21.

Azuma, Jūji 吾妻重二. "Seiza towa nanika" 静坐とはなにか. In Azuma, Jyūji 吾妻重二, *Shushigaku no shin kenkyū* 朱子学の新研究. Tokyo: Sōbunsha, 2004.

———. *Shushigaku no shin kenkyū* 朱子學の新研究. Tokyo: Sōbunsha, 2004.

de Bary, William Theodore. "The Uses of Neo-Confucianism: A Response to Professor Tillman." *Philosophy East and West*, 43, no. 3 (1993): 541–555.

Chén, Jiànhuáng 陳劍鍠. "Míng-Qīng lǐxuéjiā duì 'bàn rì jìngzuò, bàn rì dú shū' de zhēngyì jí qí yùnyòng" 明清理学家对"半日靜坐半日讀書"的争議及其運用. *Éhú zázhì* 鵝湖雜誌 327 (2002).

Chén, Lái 陳来. "Xīnxué chuántǒng zhōng de shénmìzhǔyì wèntí" 心學傳統中的神秘主義問題. In Chén Lái, *Yǒu-wú zhī jìng: Wáng Yángmíng zhéxué de jīngshén* 有無之境— 王陽明哲學的精神. Beijing: Peking University Press, 2006.

Chén, Róngjié 陳榮捷. "Bàn rì jìngzuò, bàn rì dú shū" 半日静坐半日読書. In Chén Róngjié 陳榮捷, *Zhūzǐ xīn tànsuǒ* 朱子新探索. Shanghai: Huádōng shīfàn dàxué chūbǎnshè, 2007.

———. "Zhūzǐ yǔ jìngzuò" 朱子與静坐. In Chén Róngjié 陳榮捷, *Zhūzǐ xīn tànsuǒ* 朱子新探索. Shanghai: Huádōng shīfàn dàxué chūbǎnshè, 2007.

Chén Xiànzhāng jí 陳獻章集. Beijing: Zhōnghuá shūjú, 1987.

Gāozǐ yíshū 高子遺書. Wényuāngé sìkù quánshū 文淵閣四庫全書.

Huìān xiānshēng Zhū Wéngōng wénjí 晦庵先生朱文公文集. Zhūzi quánshū 朱子全書 24. Shanghai: Shànghǎi gǔjí chūbǎnshè, 2002.

Jìngzuò yàojué 静坐要訣, by Yuán Huáng 袁黃. Dàozàng Jīnghuá 道藏精華. Vol. 2, chap. 9.

Kǎogōng jí 考功集. Wényuāngé sìkù quánshū 文淵閣四庫全書.

Kùnxuéjì 困學記. Gāozǐ yíshū 高子遺書 Vol. 3. Wényuāngé sìkù quánshū 文淵閣四庫全書.

Liǔ, Cúnrén 柳存仁. "Wáng Yángmíng yǔ Dào-Fó èr jiào" 王陽明與道佛二教. *Qīnghuá xuébào* 清華學報 13, no. 1 (1981), 27–52.

Lù Jiǔyuān jí 陸九淵集. Beijing: Zhōnghuá Shūjú, 1980.

Luó Hóngxiān jí 羅洪先集. Nanjing: Fènghuáng chūbǎnshè, 2007.

Mabuchi, Masaya 馬淵昌也. "Kō Wan no shisō ni tsuite: 16 seiki zenhan no shisō hendō kaimei no tame no 1 case study" 黃綰の思想について— 十六世紀前半の思想変動解明の為の1ケーススタディー. *Chūgoku—shakai to bunka* 中国—社会と文化, no. 3 (1988), 133–157.

———. "Mindai kōki jugaku no dōkyō sesshu no ichi yōsō—Ō Ki no shisō ni okeru dōkyō naitan jissenron no ichizuke o megutte" 明代後期儒学の道教摂取の一様相— 王畿の思

想における道教内丹実践論の位置づけをめぐって. In *Dōkyō bunka eno tenbō* 道教文化へ
の展望, edited by Dōkyō bunka kenkyūkai 道教文化研究会. Tokyo: Hirakawa shuppansha,
1994.

———. "Sòng-Míng shíqí Rúxué duì jìngzuò de kànfǎ yǐjí sān jiào hé yī sīxiǎng de xīngqǐ"
宋明時期儒學對靜坐的看法以及三教合一思想的興起. In *Dōngyǎ de jìngzuò chuántǒng*
東亞的靜坐傳統, edited by Yáng Rúbīn 楊儒賓, Masaya Mabuchi 馬淵昌也 and Halvor
Eifring 艾皓德, 63–102. Taipei: National Taiwan University Press, 2012.

Miura, Kunio 三浦國雄. *Shushi to ki to shintai* 朱子と気と身体. Tokyo: Heibonsha, 1997.

Nakajima, Ryūzō 中嶋隆藏. "Shushi no seiza to sono shūhen" 朱子の静坐とその周辺. *Toyō
kotengaku kenkyū* 東洋古典学研究, no. 25 (2008), 9–32.

Okada, Takehiko 岡田武彦. *Ō Yōmei to minmatsu no jugaku* 王陽明と明末の儒学. Tokyo:
Meitoku shuppansha, 1975.

Okuzaki, Yuji 奥崎裕司. *Chūgoku Kyōshin jinushi no kenkyū* 中国郷紳地主の研究. Tokyo:
Kyūko shoin, 1978.

Ōno, Hideto 大野栄人. *Tendai shikan seiritsushi no kenkyū* 天台止観成立史の研究. Kyoto:
Hozokan, 1994.

Péng, Guóxiáng 彭國翔. *Liángzhīxué de zhǎnkāi: Wáng Lóngxī yǔ zhōngwǎn Míng de yáng-
míngxué* 良知學的展開— 王龍溪與中晚明的陽明學. Taipei: Xuéshēng shūjú, 2003.

Qián, Mù 錢穆. "Zhūzǐ lùn jìng" 朱子論靜. In Qián Mù 錢穆, *Zhūzǐ xīn xuéàn* 朱子新学案.
Vol. 1. Chengdu: Bāshǔ shūshè, 1986.

Sakai, Tadao 酒井忠夫. *Chūgoku zensho no kenkyū* 中国善書の研究. Tokyo: Kōbundō, 1960.

Sānyútáng shèngyán 三魚堂賸言. Wényuāngé sìkù quánshū 文淵閣四庫全書.

Sānyútáng wénjí 三魚堂文集. Wényuāngé sìkù quánshū 文淵閣四庫全書.

Satō, Tetsuei 佐藤哲英. *Tendai daishi no kenkyū* 天台大師の研究. Tokyo: Hyakkaen, 1961.

Shibata, Atushi 柴田篤. "Ō Ryūkei no shisō—ryōchisetsu no ichi tenkai" 王龍溪の思想 —
良知説の一展開. *Chūgoku tetsugaku ronshū* 中国哲学論集 1 (1975).

Sōngyáng cháocún 松陽鈔存. Wényuāngé sìkù quánshū 文淵閣四庫全書.

Taylor, Rodney L. "Chu Hsi and Meditation." In *Meeting of Minds: Intellectual and Religious Interaction in East Asian Tradition of Thought: Essays in Honor of Wing-tsit Chan
and William Theodore de Bary.* edited by Irene Bloom and Joshua A. Fogel, 43–74. New
York: Columbia University, 1997.

———. *The Cultivation of Sagehood as a Religious Goal in Neo-Confucianism: A Study of
Selected Writings of Kao P'an-lung, 1562–1626.* Missoula, MT: Scholars Press, 1978.

———. "Meditation in Ming Neo-Orthodoxy: Kao P'an-lung's Writings on Quiet-Sitting."
Journal of Chinese Philosophy 6 (1979): 142–182.

———. "The Sudden/Gradual Paradigm and Neo-Confucian Mind-cultivation." *Philosophy
East and West* 33 (1983): 17–34.

Tiáoxī fǎ 調息法. Wáng Jī jí 王畿集. Vol. 15. Nanjing: Fènghuáng chūbǎnshè, 2007.

Tillman, Hoyt. "A New Direction in Confucian Scholarship: Approaches to Examining the
Differences Between Neo-Confucianism and *Daoxue*." *Philosophy East and West* 42, no.
3 (1992): 455–474.

———. "The Uses of Neo-Confucianism Revisited: A Reply to Professor de Bary." *Philosophy
East and West* 44, no. 1 (1994): 135–42.

Tomoeda, Ryūtarō 友枝龍太郎. *Shushi no shisō keisei* 朱子の思想形成. Tokyo: Shunjyūsha,
1969.

Tsurunari, Hisāki 鶴成久章. "Kō Hanryō no kakubutsusetsu ni tsuite" 高攀龍の「格物」説
について. *Shūkan Tōyōgaku* 集刊東洋学 68 (1992), 76–93.

Wáng Yángmíng quánjí 王陽明全集. Shanghai: Shànghǎi gǔjí chūbǎnshè, 1992.

Xīyuán yíshū 西原遺書. Taiwan National Library.

Yáng, Rúbīn 楊儒賓. "Sòngrú de jìngzuòshuō" 宋儒的靜坐說. In Yáng Rúbīn 楊儒賓, *Rújiā zhéxué* 儒家哲学. Taipei: Guìguān túshū gǔfèn yǒuxiàn gōngsī, 2004.

———. "Zhǔ jìng yǔ zhǔ jìng" 主敬與主靜. In *Dōngyǎ de jìngzuò chuántǒng*, edited by Yáng Rúbīn 楊儒賓, Mabuchi Masaya 馬淵昌也, and Halvor Eifring 艾皓德, 129–159. Taipei: National Taiwan University Press, 2012.

Yán Jūn jí 顏鈞集. Beijing: Zhōngguó shèhuì kēxué chūbǎnshè, 1996.

Zhào Bǎofēng jí 趙寶峰集. Universal Library online edition.

Zhōng, Cǎijūn 鍾彩鈞. "Tàizhōu xuézhě Yán Shānnóng de sīxiǎng yǔ jiǎngxué: Rúxué mínjiānhuà yǔ zōngjiàohuà" 泰州學者顏山農的思想與講學－儒學民間化與宗教化. *Zhōngguó zhéxué* 中國哲學 19 (1998).

The Science of Meditation

I n contrast to the rest of the volume, this chapter is devoted to popular meditation practices rather than to traditional meditations; its textual sources
are mostly in English rather than in Asian languages. Nevertheless, the
forms of meditation discussed originate from Asian traditions, though the
practices may have been significantly transformed by their entry into Western
modernity. In a sense, therefore, this chapter serves as a natural last chapter of
a volume on Asian traditions of meditation.

Like most of the volume, this chapter is mainly concerned with cultural history. Its focus involves scientific studies, but not to assess the strength of the
measurable outcome and methodology. Rather, it deals with the scientific studies as a source of inspiration for the emerging meditative cultures. It takes the
stance that the shifting foci of meditation research during half a century have
been swayed by three major factors: the larger sociocultural context or societal
orientation, the availability of advanced scientific methodology, and, finally, the
inherent qualities of the various meditation practices.

Modern Meditation Cultures

Modern cultures of meditation, widely popularized and partly or fully dislodged from their traditional contexts, have emerged in several parts of the
world. In Europe and America, the most famous examples are the Transcendental Meditation (TM) movement with its many offshoots, as well as the different versions of Zen and Mindfulness. In Asia, several modernized forms of
meditation have also emerged, but quite independently of the Euro-American
development; we are referring to the Vipassana movement in Sri Lanka and
Burma,[1] Quiet Sitting in Japan and China,[2] and Subud and Sumarah in Indo-
nesia.[3]

Scientific and pseudoscientific rhetoric has gradually become central in many
such movements. Placing meditation outside its traditional contexts has often
replaced the religious content and aims with the technical aspects of the
practice and its utility in coping with modern life. Several movements have
underscored the health and stress-reduction effects of meditation rather than
the traditional religious and spiritual goals. Moreover, the authority of science
has often been used to validate the traditional teaching. Some movements regard scientific findings as supporting their traditional religious tenets and practices embodying deep truths. Positions of this kind have often been couched in

pseudoscientific language and argue that the traditions represent a different kind of science, of equal or even superior validity.

When it comes to the actual publication of meditation studies in recognized scientific journals, Anglo-American scientists have dominated the arena, as they do in many other fields. However, in these various waves of meditation research, the kinds of meditation investigated have been almost exclusively of Asian origin. The largest review to date on the health effects of meditation is from 2007 and refers exclusively to methods of Asian origin.[4] Thus, although the word "meditation" comes from European contexts, meditative practices of Christian, Judaic, or Islamic backgrounds have generally not found their way into scientific studies. The cultural history of meditation science, therefore, displays an extraordinary fusion of Asian and Western concerns.

In most cases, the dominance of Asian practices in scientific studies is probably due to some common characteristics; these practices are effective even without their religious content. Christian, Judaic, and Islamic meditative practices, however, are strongly content-oriented—whether devotional, scriptural, or thematic—and are thus confined to the religious contexts in which they are embedded; they cannot easily be decontextualized or recontextualized in new environments. In contrast, many Asian forms of meditation have a stronger generic and technical element; their effects often instigate psychophysiological mechanisms in the body and in the central nervous system that are relatively independent of their religious or cultural context. Therefore, they are also more readily transferred from one context to another. Tellingly, Asian meditative traditions may also include a large number of content-oriented practices, but it is worth noting that these have seldom been the objects of scientific investigation or transcultural dissemination. Hard-core science prefers common techniques to cultural or religious content.

A Brief History

According to Web of Science, an online scientific citation indexing service,[5] scholarly interest in the psychological aspects of meditation can be traced back to the 1930s, and if Yoga is included, back to the 1920s. However, for a long time the only place this interest showed up was in book reviews, and usually reviews of books that were of popular rather than of scholarly interest. The reviews appeared mostly in scholarly journals devoted to psychology or psychiatry, and were usually concerned with Buddhist meditation or, less often, with the Yoga tradition. Not a single scientific journal publication on meditation was cited before the 1960s.

In the counterculture of the 1960s, meditation suddenly gained enormous popularity in Europe and in the English-speaking world. Initially, this had a limited visible impact on the science of meditation. A rather popular book on meditation, by Mahesh Yogi, appeared in 1963 and was titled *The Science of Being and Art of Living*. However, the use of the word "science" in the title was rhetorical; it was hardly meant to reflect scientific substance. The 1960s saw a few scientific publications on meditation, but not many, and these mainly pursued an interest in the psychological aspects of Buddhist meditation. Some of the articles, however, presaged a more experimental and physiological trend. In the first half of the decade, Arthur Deikman, who later wrote a popular book on the psychology of Buddhist meditation, *The Observing Self*, published two meditation studies, one of them titled "Experimental Meditation."[6] Two Japanese scholars published the first study of meditation using EEG (electroencephalography), which focused on Zen meditation.[7]

Beyond such scattered papers, the first big wave of scientific interest in meditation started with Robert Keith Wallace and Herbert Benson's influential studies from the early 1970s, which were published in scientific journals, conference proceedings, and popular magazines.[8] The number of meditation studies increased quickly, until it reached a first peak in 1977–1978. Popular and scientific interest in meditation was reinforced in 1975 with the appearance of Benson's book *The Relaxation Response*, which topped the *New York Times* bestseller list for nonfiction just before Christmas that year.[9] Nearly all of the meditation studies that were frequently cited during this decade focused on Transcendental Meditation.[10] Research interest in Buddhist methods and psychological issues continued to some extent; the field also included a few studies of other methods, from Ananda Marga to Yoga. The dominant trend clearly involved physiological and clinical studies of TM and related practices. A variety of results of meditation were explored, from antidrug effects to brain physiology, but the main focus was on effects that could be subsumed under Benson's notion of the "relaxation response," an array of measurable stress-reducing physiological changes in the body signifying changes in the central nervous system; the relaxation response was conceived as the opposite of the fight-or-flight response that is linked to stress.

In the mid-1970s, the general popularity of TM began to decline, partly due to its strong association with the waning counterculture, but also due to its claims of being able to teach people how to levitate and other such extraordinary assertions. The effect of this decline on the rate of scientific publications was not immediate. Near the end of the 1970s, however, the number of meditation studies began to decrease and continued to do so for about a decade.[11] Rather critical voices also emerged that argued against some of the studies—in particular against their promotional nature, low data quality, and poor research designs—but also against the TM movement's use of them. In 1984, David S. Holmes published a negative review of meditation studies that was followed by a number of papers contesting some of his critical views.[12] Scientific articles on the relaxation-related effects of TM continued to appear, but the upward trend had peaked, and studies of other types of meditation and effects gradually increased in number and importance.

The latter half of the 1970s saw the appearance of articles by scholars who would become central to the scientific study and popular dissemination of Buddhist-inspired forms of meditation, including Richard Davidson and Daniel Goleman.[13] In the early 1980s, two articles by Jon Kabat-Zinn mentioned

Mindfulness Meditation for the first time in the research literature.[14] Stress reduction, chronic pain, and a number of other clinical issues continued to be central concerns in the studies of the 1980s and 1990s. At this point, the basis for the effects of meditation was linked less to the physiological aspects of relaxation, and more to attentional, belief-related, and emotional changes.

In 1989, the number of scientific meditation studies began to rise again.[15] This reflected a new upswing in popular interest, as meditation began to break out of its counterculture image. In the 1990s, several best-selling books contributed to this popularization of meditation. Most notably, two books by Jon Kabat-Zinn, *Full Catastrophe Living* and *Wherever You Go, There You Are*, paved the way for what would become the mindfulness movement. These books were not primarily concerned with scientific research, but the author's background as a successful American researcher defused the public perception of meditation as deriving from Indian gurus of the counterculture of the 1960s and 1970s. Daniel Goleman's main claim to fame, his book *Emotional Intelligence*, did not mention meditation, but both his earlier and his later books did.[16] James H. Austin, a neurologist and prolific popularizer of Zen, published his first and most famous book, *Zen and the Brain*, in 1998.

After 2000, the scientific study of Mindfulness became a clear trend. Among the fifty most-cited meditation studies at that time, twenty-seven had "mindfulness" in the title, while no other single technique appeared in more than one or two titles. Undoubtedly, several studies discussed Mindfulness without including it in the title. At least seven studies discussed other forms of Buddhist-inspired meditation. Not a single one of those top fifty publications had TM in the title.

The Mindfulness trend went hand in hand with a renewed interest in the brain triggered by the novel technologies of neuroimaging, the fMRI and the PET scan. Among the fifty most-cited meditation studies after 2000, at least fourteen studied the impact of meditation on the brain. The appearance in the year 2000 of a study on functional brain mapping and the relaxation response represents an almost symbolic step from the first to the second phase of meditation research.[17] This study, undertaken by Sara W. Lazar and her co-workers, stands at the end of a long trend of exploring the effects of meditation in terms of the relaxation response. At the same time, it introduces a new and still ongoing trend of using neuroimaging techniques in the study of meditation, in particular Mindfulness, and, to a much lesser extent, other forms of Buddhist-inspired practices.

Lately, meditation studies have entered what has been termed "the era of the wandering mind,"[18] reflecting the discovery that mind wandering or stimulus-independent thought is linked to the so-called default-mode network of the brain.

While the study of Mindfulness practices is a clear trend in terms of sheer numbers, other methods continue to be studied, including loving-kindness meditation, insight meditation, Tibetan Buddhist meditation, TM, Yoga, Qigong, Acem Meditation, and others.[19] The use of neuroimaging techniques has shed light on many new issues, and other approaches continue to be explored, including a large number of clinical studies and a moderate number of physiological studies. Although the relaxation response no longer is the main focus of research, this does not mean that relaxation is not an issue. On the contrary, it is still one of the key issues regarding the effects of meditation.

In the following, we shall look at several trends within the scientific research on meditation. These trends may be seen as different meditative cultures that exist not in isolation but in constant interaction with other cultures, both meditative and nonmeditative, scientific and nonscientific.

From Psychodynamic to Cognitive Therapy

To the extent that we can speak of trends in the rather limited scientific interest in meditation before 1970, it must be in reference to its psychotherapeutic orientation, which reflects a strong interest in psychoanalysis and its later psychodynamic forms during much of the twentieth century.

According to Web of Science, the first two scientific journal items on "meditation" appeared in 1936, as already mentioned. Both were reviews of a popular book on Buddhist meditation that itself revealed no particular interest in science.[20] One of the reviews was rather brief, and simply concluded, "I do not think many will follow the author on this path."[21] The other reviewer, however, was concerned with "the psychotherapeutic implications of Buddhist practice." The issue raised was whether replacing thoughts of ill will with thoughts of benevolence, as recommended by a Buddhist master, would easily become "the pathway to a reaction formation." "Reaction formation" is one of the traditional Freudian defense mechanisms; it is seen as a way of restricting unacceptable desires and instead developing exaggerated behaviors of the opposite kind. In the review, the suggestion was made that the Buddhist notion of *tanha*, "desire," could be restated in Freudian terms as "faultily attached libido." Despite such objections to Buddhist ideals, it argues also that Buddhist meditation "creates a situation rather like free association," in line with psychoanalysis.[22]

A similar interest in the psychotherapeutic implications of Yoga has been around for some time, starting with an article, "Psychoanalysis and Yoga," that appeared in 1925.[23] One of the issues discussed was whether or not Yoga could be seen as a form of self-hypnosis. In the context of Indian philosophy, a discourse on this matter had resolved the question in the negative almost a millennium earlier.[24]

In the 1950s, a number of leading psychoanalysts often referred to as the neo-Freudians, most notably Karen Horney and Erich Fromm, showed a strong interest in Zen meditation.[25] Both Horney and Fromm became personally acquainted with the leading transmitter of Japanese Zen to the West, Daisetz T. Suzuki, whom Horney had quoted in one of her earlier books.[26] The collection of essays on Zen Buddhism and psychoanalysis published by Fromm in collaboration with Suzuki and Robert De Martino in 1960, *Zen Buddhism*, became a classic in its field. In the book, Fromm argues that psychoanalysis may lead to the same kind of maturation and enlightenment as Zen meditation. The general trend, both in the book and in the period as a whole, was to seek in Zen what psychoanalysis and Western thought in general were believed to be missing: a way for ordinary people to deepen their life experience, rather than just a way for the neurotic mind to get rid of its symptoms.

In the 1970s, studies of the psychotherapeutic effects of meditation were far outnumbered by the new wave of physiological studies. At the same time, however, studies of psychotherapeutic effects also increased, with more stringent methods, including behavioral self-control,[27] empathy in counselors,[28] measures of self-actualization,[29] anxiety reduction,[30] and a number of other issues.[31] It is worth noting that studies of psychotherapeutic effects more often involved Buddhist techniques, perhaps due to the strong skepticism in, for example, the TM movement, of psychology and its ways of working. The initiators of the TM movement were for a long time forbidden to teach TM to psychoanalysts.

In the 1970s, psychoanalytic thinking was less dominant yet still influential. A new field, cognitive psychology, was beginning to make its mark. The scholarly interest in Mindfulness and other Buddhist-inspired practices that started in the 1980s and gained momentum in the twenty-first century brought with it a stronger cognitive orientation. This reflected a general shift in the focus on meditation in academic psychology and in clinical psychotherapy, and also in the types of meditation techniques that were investigated. Compared to the physiological focus of the relaxation-oriented practices that dominated the 1970s, the Buddhist-inspired methods were often more concerned with the regulation and monitoring of the attention and the emotions, which fits well with the more openly persuasive and manipulative methods of cognitive therapy. In the past decade or two, this cognitive orientation has frequently been combined with brain studies, to which we shall return shortly.

In 1979, Kabat-Zinn began teaching his patients what he called Mindfulness-Based Stress Reduction (MBSR), a combination of Mindfulness meditation, Yoga, and other mental and physical exercises. The program was primarily designed not to cure illness but to teach patients how to live with it. In the 1990s, Zindel Segal, Mark Williams, and John Teasdale developed a related approach called Mindfulness-Based Cognitive Therapy (MBCT) specifically to aid patients in their recovery from depression. A number of scientific studies have investigated the influence of these programs on patients' mood disorders, stress symptoms, and fatigue.

The Relaxation Response

The first big wave of scientific interest in meditation that began in 1970 arose directly from the popularity of meditation in the counterculture of the 1960s. The main emphasis of this research was on the physiological changes associated with what Herbert Benson termed the "relaxation response." This response is regarded as the opposite of the fight-or-flight response associated with stress and involving the activation of the sympathetic part of the autonomous nervous system. Nowadays, the relaxation response is often explained by changes in the HPA axis (HPA refers to the hypothalamus and pituitary gland in the brain, and the adrenal gland on top of the kidneys).

In working in the opposite direction of the fight-or-flight response, the relaxation response involves the lowering of the heart rate, the reduction of oxygen consumption, and the frequency of breath. A modest decline in blood pressure, the lowering of the skin conductance, and the muscular tone were later also included. These changes were considered to be the physiological basis of the positive effects that meditation had on things such as musculoskeletal pain, headaches, the cardio-vascular system, anxiety, sleep disturbances, and asthma, as well as on creativity and productivity. In general, the relaxation response involves a decline in the stress hormones as well as an increase in alpha activity in the brain. In clinical studies, the relaxation response has been linked to the treatment of several conditions, as well as substance addictions and the rehabilitation of prisoners.

Kovoor Behanan, an Indian graduate student in psychology at Yale, undertook quantitative studies of his own yogic breathing and published the results in a widely reviewed book in 1937.[32] Since the 1930s, there has been a focus on the physiological effects of the postures and breathing exercises of Yoga and Pranayama. In spite of this, when the relaxation effects of meditation were made the subject of physiological studies in the 1970s, they were conceived of as being quite new.

In the 1970s, most of the technology used in exploring the physiological changes of meditation had been around for decades. The blood pressure meter (sphygmomanometer) had been widely used within the medical community since 1901, electrocardiography (ECG) was invented in 1903, skin conductance was measured scientifically in the early 1900s, and electroencephalography (EEG) was invented in 1924 and popularized in the 1930s. The radioimmunoassay that measured hormone levels in the blood, however, and the measurement of oxygen uptake in the body relied on more recent inventions, the former being developed in the 1950s, and the latter in the late 1960s. Apart from these two instruments, the new wave of meditation research was not primarily technology-driven.

The focus on the physiological aspects of relaxation came partly from the general biological orientation of the medical community, in particular its interest in hypertension. The fact that even mild hypertension could in the long run lead to cardiovascular disease and eventually death had been known since the 1950s. The links between hypertension and the various forms of stress was a highly debated topic. Before Benson began exploring meditation, he studied blood pressure in monkeys.

An extra impetus for the scientific study of meditation came from an interest in biofeedback that was at the outskirts of the medical establishment. A famous conference on biofeedback held in 1969 supported the idea that even the autonomic nervous system could be influenced by volitional activity. In the 1970s, several scientific studies focused on both meditation and biofeedback.

However, the focus on the physiology of relaxation was not just a product of trends in the medical community. Both the TM movement and its many off-shoots are what later have been termed "nondirective" techniques. Nondirective techniques emphasize nonconcentration and the acceptance of thoughts as important elements of the practice, and relaxation as the most immediate effect of meditation.[33] Similar ideas were also present in a few other schools of meditation, but much less consistently. When the TM movement began to advocate nonconcentration as a meditation principle at the beginning of the 1960s, this was in opposition to the prevalent yogic emphasis on concentration and directed attention. Buddhist practices usually emphasize concentration rather than effortlessness, though some seek to combine the two. Both Yoga and Buddhism often look upon stray thoughts as a disturbance rather than as part of the process. The emphasis on bodily and mental relaxation as a prerequisite for progress is a characteristic of several practices.

Two features of the TM movement may also have facilitated the focus on the physiology of relaxation. First, the emphasis on the automatic generation of effects, from the most basic form of relaxation to the highest levels of consciousness, seemed to fit well with the mechanistic approach of modern science. Second, in the majority of the TM studies, a critical attitude toward psychological views of meditation has underlain a clear focus on physiology rather than psychology.

The Brain and the Wandering Mind

The brain has been of central interest in meditation research since the first electroencephalographic (EEG) study of Zen meditation in 1966.[34] The investigation of alpha waves and, to a lesser extent, theta waves during meditation was a prominent issue in the relaxation-oriented physiological research on TM and other techniques in the 1970s. Alpha waves are believed to reflect relaxed wakefulness, while the slower theta waves are associated with drowsiness and shallow sleep but also with emotional processing and personality development.[35] In addition to showing these brain waves, EEG also helped to some extent in identifying the location of the brain activity during meditation.

In the twenty-first century, EEG technology has retained much of its importance. In addition to studying alpha and the theta waves, some focus has also been directed toward the much faster gamma waves,[36] though their relevance has been controversial. Gamma waves have been associated with the management of emotions linked to Buddhist and Buddhist-inspired techniques.[37]

The emergence in the twenty-first century of new technologies within the field of neuroimaging has had considerable relevance for meditation research, in particular functional magnetic resonance imaging (fMRI), but also single-photon emission computed tomography (SPECT) and positron emission tomography (PET). In contrast to EEG, fMRI can produce images of any active brain area, not just in relation to the cortex but also deeper inside the brain. The high resolution and great accuracy of fMRI images makes it easier to interpret more of what is going on in the brain. For meditation research, one downside is that the subjects must lie in a large noisy machine—hardly conducive to any meditative practice.

As mentioned, the first fMRI study of meditation made by Lazar and co-workers came in the year 2000; it is still one of the most-cited articles on the topic. In general, the frequently cited fMRI-based studies have explored issues such as brain plasticity, brain networks, neural circuitry, neural connectivity, and cortical thickness. They are typically concerned with the use of attention, as well as with the clinical effects of meditation on emotional disturbances. This is a part of the general orientation of Mindfulness studies, which by the turn of the century had begun to dominate the scientific study of meditation.

Some years into the century, many brain studies of meditation began to focus on the "default-mode network" and its psychological correlate, mind wandering. The default-mode network includes parts of the brain where activity goes up rather than down during rest. This network has plausibly been linked to the kind of spontaneous, stimulus-independent thought that is often referred to as "mind wandering" and the brain "at rest."

At first, the focus on this network was almost completely on the negative effects of such mental activity, as reflected in the title of a frequently quoted article: "A Wandering Mind Is an Unhappy Mind."[38] Mind wandering was linked to depressive rumination. However, the psychological literature gradually also included more favorable views. Focusing on the "emotional cost" of mind wandering, the article cited above also called mind wandering "a remarkable evolutionary achievement that allows people to learn, reason, and plan." An even more recent article, "Ode to Positive Constructive Daydreaming,"[39] argues that the positive aspects of mind wandering have been underreported, and quotes several studies to this effect, suggesting that mind wandering may be beneficial for creativity, memory, planning, adaptation, empathy, and problem solving. Gradually, an increasing number of neuroscientists have taken for granted that the default-mode network and its corresponding mental activities also have positive functions, otherwise these cerebral activities would not have survived evolutionary selection.[40]

The negative view of mind wandering fits well with the strong skepticism toward digressive thoughts that characterizes Buddhism and many other meditative traditions. It also tallies well with the idea that meditative absorption, presumably the opposite of mind wandering, leads to happiness or even "bliss." For a long time, therefore, studies of meditation focused almost exclusively on the negative aspects of mind wandering and disregarded its positive effects. In this light, research suggesting that Mindfulness meditation reduces mind wandering has been favorably interpreted.[41]

Of the few studies reporting higher default mode network activity during meditation than during rest with the eyes closed, one has attributed it to "the experience of contentless thought with continued self-awareness during TM practice,"[42] and not to mind wandering. The notion of "contentless thought" may be inspired by concerns within the TM movement about differentiating TM from the "concentration meditation techniques." Seeing mind wandering as negative seems to reflect a bias prevalent among researchers attracted to the schools related to Mindfulness meditation.

A more recent fMRI study suggests that Acem Meditation and other forms of nondirective meditation differ from Mindfulness and most other Buddhist practices in increasing rather than decreasing the activity in the default-mode network, when compared both to simple rest and to concentrative practice.[43] The increased activity takes place in areas linked to episodic memory and emotional processing. The study speculates that the activation "might be associated with emotional processing related to mind wandering" and that it "may possibly serve to modify stressful emotional memories." Such an interpretation is in line with the psychological focus on Acem Meditation as a method for working through unresolved personality issues. In contrast to TM and other forms of counter-culture spirituality, the Acem technique had already been placed in a psychological framework in the early 1970s.[44]

Conclusion

Several factors have been shaping the meditation cultures linked to the scientific studies that have emerged since the 1970s. Broadly, these factors may be divided into three: the focus of popular culture, the scientific orientation and the available technology at the time, and the meditative traditions and the features of meditation practices.

When the scientific study of meditation rose to prominence in the 1970s, this was a delayed response to the widespread general interest in meditation of the previous decade. Similarly, the downward trend for meditation research from 1979 to 1989 was also a delayed response to the popular disillusionment with the counterculture in general and with the TM movement in particular of the 1970s. When the second wave of meditation research began, the link between popular and scientific interest went both ways. Not only did the new rise in interest in meditation spark an increase in scientific writings on the subject, but this scientific activity in turn also contributed to a more positive image of meditation in the mainstream culture. The focus in the second wave of meditation research has primarily been on Buddhist techniques, in particular the diverse methods referred to as Mindfulness meditation.

Developments within general scientific methodology and thinking have affected scientists' choice of research topics. First, the strong focus in the 1970s on physiology and relaxation partly reflected a long-term scientific interest in the relationship between mind and body, for example, stress, blood pressure, cardiovascular disease, and mortality. Second, the changing orientation of the academic psychology from psychodynamics to cognitive psychology triggered a similar change in the research focus of the study of meditation. And third, the focus on the default-mode network in the early 2000s stimulated interest in the brain's response to meditative practices. Equally important was the availability of new neuroimaging technologies, in particular fMRI. Technology-driven trends within the field of meditation research also included the use of the radioimmunoassay to measure the levels of stress hormones in the blood.

A bias from the classical meditative traditions on research orientation is most clearly seen in the attitude toward mind wandering. The widespread skepticism toward stray thoughts in Buddhism and related meditative traditions has stimulated an almost exclusively negative view of mind wandering. This tendency filtered into the general psychological and neuroscientific literature. However, the larger field also recognizes a number of beneficial functions of mind wandering that are not frequently mentioned in the Mindfulness chapters of meditation research.

It is worth noting that the two above-mentioned meditation studies reporting an increase rather than a decrease of the default-mode activity both focus on techniques that are explicitly nonconcentrative and relaxation-oriented: TM and Acem Meditation. Together with many Mindfulness techniques, these nondirective methods have in common an accepting attitude toward random thoughts during the practice. However, they go further than most schools of Mindfulness in accepting even drowsiness, dozing off, and a naturally slumped body posture as aspects of meditation. Furthermore, in contrast to many Mindfulness practices, they instruct meditators not to actively "let go" of thoughts but to simply gently return to the meditation object. These techniques' emphasis on relaxation and a free mental attitude contrasts with the focus on alertness or mindfulness in most Buddhist practices.

This difference may also underlie the shift in orientation between the first and the second wave of meditation research. As we have seen, the first wave focused on the relaxation response, while the second wave has been more concerned with mindfulness and the management of attention and emotions. Part of the reason for this shift may lie in the differences between the nature of the meditation techniques that have been studied the most: TM during the first wave, and Mindfulness during the second.

It is sometimes difficult to distinguish between the effects of the meditation technique and the effects of the framework surrounding meditation. As mentioned, the skepticism toward psychology in TM may be why so few of the psychological studies from the 1970s involved TM, despite its central position at the time. That this was an effect of the TM teachings rather than of the practice itself becomes clear when comparing TM to Acem Meditation, which is technically similar to TM but is regularly understood in a psychological context.

This chapter has focused on the various elements that have shaped the cultures surrounding the scientific studies of meditation. Many of the elements involved have come from society at large, but also from scientific environments, and from the movements and traditions engaged in meditative practice, and include cultural attitudes, technological innovations, and aspects of technical practice.

However, influence has also run in the opposite direction. The scientific focus surrounding meditation has itself been an important contributor to the development of modern meditation cultures. By encouraging a technical view of meditation, science has stimulated decontextualization and the subsequent re-contextualization of meditative practices. The physiological and psychological focus of scientific research has linked meditation more to the effects of general popular interest than to traditional spiritual goals. Finally, the prestige of science has contributed to a positive image of meditation and thus to the popular dissemination of such practices. In these ways, science has played an important part in creating space for and showing the relevance of meditation in a modern cultural context.

Notes

1. Sharf, "Buddhist Modernism"; Houtman, "Vipassanā in Burma."

2. Taylor, *Confucian Way of Contemplation*; Kohn, "Quiet Sitting with Master Yinshi"; Kohn, *Taoist Experience*, 135–141.

3. Stange, "Inner Islamization in Java."

4. Ospina, "Meditation Practices for Health."

5. Based on searches done in February 2014. See http://apps.webofknowledge.com. In most of these searches, the main search word was "meditation," which was sometimes combined with other terms. Terms such as "yoga" and "biofeedback" were searched separately. The following periods were searched separately as well: 1900–1959, 1960–1969, 1970–1979, 1980–1989, 1990–1999, 2000–2009, and 2010–2014. To decide which articles were most influential, results were sorted according to "times cited—highest to lowest." For some periods, particularly 1970–1979, the results were analyzed further using citation reports showing which of the citations actually occurred in that particular decade.

6. Cf. also Deikman, "Implications."

7. Kasamatsu and Hirai, "Electroencephalographic Study."

8. Wallace, "Physiological Effects"; Wallace and Benson, "Physiology of Meditation"; Wallace et al., "Decreased Blood Lactate"; Wallace et al., "Wakeful Hypometabolic Physiologic State"; Benson, "Decreased Alcohol Intake"; Benson, "Transcendental Meditation"; Benson and Wallace, "Decreased Blood-Pressure"; Benson et al., "Physiologic Correlates of Meditation."

9. Another best-selling book on meditation in the same year was Bloomfield et al., *TM: Discovering Inner Energy*.

10. Eight meditation studies were cited more than thirty times in this decade, and all of them focused on TM.

11. Cf. Davanger, "Natural Science of Meditation."

12. Holmes, "Meditation and Somatic Arousal Reduction"; Holmes, "To Meditate or to Simply Rest"; Holmes, "To Meditate or Rest?"; Suler, "Meditation and Somatic Arousal"; West, "Meditation and Somatic Arousal Reduction"; Shapiro, "Clinical Use of Meditation"; Benson and Friedman, "Rebuttal"; Smith "Meditation, Biofeedback."

13. Goleman and Schwartz, "Meditation as an Intervention"; Davidson and Goleman, "Attentional and Affective Concomitants"; Schwartz et al., "Patterning."

14. Kabat-Zinn, "Outpatient Program"; Kabat-Zinn et al., "Clinical Use of Mindfulness."

15. Davanger, "Natural Science of Meditation."

16. See, for example, Goleman, *Varieties of Meditative Experience*; Goleman, *Healing Emotions*.

17. Lazar et al., "Functional Brain Mapping."

18. Callard et al., "Era of the Wandering Mind?"

19. Sometimes loving-kindness meditation, insight meditation, and Tibetan Buddhist meditation are subsumed under the broader category of Mindfulness practices.

20. Lounsbery, *Méditation bouddhique*; Lounsbery, *Buddhist Meditation*.

21. "Ich glaube nicht, daß viele dem Verfasser auf diesem Wege folgen werden"; Vroklage, "Buddhist Meditation."

22. Anonymous, "Buddhist Meditation."

23. Winterstein, "Psychoanalysis and Yoga."

24. Eliade, *Yoga*, 78–79.

25. See DeMartino, "Karen Horney."

26. Horney, *Our Inner Conflicts*, 163.

27. Shapiro and Giber, "Meditation and Psychotherapeutic Effects"; Shapiro and Zifferblatt, "Zen Meditation."

28. Lesh, "Zen Meditation."

29. Seeman et al., "Influence of Transcendental Meditation."

30. Schwartz et al., "Patterning"; Bahrke and Morgan, "Anxiety Reduction."

31. Cf. Smith, "Meditation as Psychotherapy."

32. Behanan, "Yoga." Cf. Murphy and Donovan, *Physical and Psychological Effects*, 33.

33. Lagopoulos et al., "Increased EEG Activity"; Nesvold et al., "Increased Heart Rate Variability"; Xu et al., "Nondirective Meditation"; Davanger et al., "Meditation-Specific Prefrontal Cortical Activation."

34. Kasamatsu and Hirai, "Electroencephalographic Study."

35. The frequency of alpha waves is 7.5–12.5 Hz, and that of theta waves, 4–7 Hz.

36. The frequency of gamma waves is 25–90 Hz, usually hovering around 40 Hz.

37. Cf. Lutz et al., "Long-Term Meditators"; Fell et al., "From Alpha to Gamma."

38. Killingsworth and Gilbert, "Wandering Mind."

39. McMillan et al., "Ode to Positive Constructive Daydreaming."

40. Buckner et al., "Brain's Default Network."

41. Sood and Jones, "On Mind Wandering."

42. Travis et al., "Self-Referential Default Brain State," 28. The study uses EEG rather than fMRI. Other studies showing increased default-mode network activity during meditation include Holzel et al., "Differential Engagement" (Vipassana); Jang et al., "Increased Default Mode Network Connectivity" ("brain-wave vibration meditation"); and Xu et al., "Nondirective Meditation" (Acem Meditation).

43. Xu et al., "Nondirective Meditation."

44. Hersoug, "Battle for Realism."

Bibliography

Anonymous. "Buddhist Meditation in the Southern School: Theory and Practice for Westerners." *Psychiatric Quarterly* 10 (1936): 524–525.

Austin, James H. *Zen and the Brain: Toward an Understanding of Meditation and Consciousness.* Cambridge, MA: MIT Press, 1998.

Bahrke, M. S., and W. P. Morgan. "Anxiety Reduction Following Exercise and Meditation." *Cognitive Therapy and Research* 2 (1978): 323–333.

Behanan, Kovoor T. *Yoga: A Scientific Evaluation.* New York: Macmillan, 1937.

Benson, Herbert. "Decreased Alcohol Intake Associated with Practice of Meditation: Retrospective Investigation." *Annals of the New York Academy of Sciences* 233 (1974): 174–177.

———. *The Relaxation Response.* New York: Morrow, 1975.

————. "Transcendental Meditation: Science or Cult?" *Journal of the American Medical Association* 227 (1974): 807.

Benson, H., B. A. Rosner, B. R. Marzetta, and H. P. Klemchuk. "Decreased Blood-Pressure in Borderline Hypertensive Subjects Who Practiced Meditation." *Journal of Chronic Diseases* 27 (1974): 163–169.

Benson, H., B. P. Malvea, and J. R. Graham. "Physiologic Correlates of Meditation and Their Clinical Effects in Headache: Ongoing Investigation." *Headache* 13 (1973): 23–24.

Benson, Herbert, and Richard Friedman. "A Rebuttal to the Conclusions of David S. Holmes's Article 'Meditation and Somatic Arousal Reduction.'" *American Psychologist* 40 (1985): 725–728.

Benson, H., and R. K. Wallace. "Decreased Blood-Pressure in Hypertensive Subjects Who Practiced Meditation." *Circulation* 46 (1972): 130.

Bloomfield, Harold H., Michael Peter Cain, and Dennis T. Jaffe. *TM: Discovering Inner Energy and Overcoming Stress.* New York: Delacorte Press, 1975.

Buckner, Randy L., Jessica R. Andrews-Hanna, and Daniel L. Schacter. "The Brain's Default Network: Anatomy, Function, and Relevance to Disease." *Annals of the New York Academy of Sciences* 1124 (2008): 1–38.

Callard, F., J. Smallwood, J. Golchert, and D. S. Margulies. "The Era of the Wandering Mind? Twenty-First Century Research on Self-Generated Mental Activity." *Frontiers in Psychology* 4 (2013): 891.

Davanger, Svend. "The Natural Science of Meditation: A 'Black Box' Perspective." In *Meditation in Judaism, Christianity and Islam: Cultural Histories,* edited by Halvor Eifring, 227–236. London: Bloomsbury Academic, 2013.

Davanger, Svend, Anne Grete Hersoug, and Halvor Eifring, eds. *Fighting Stress: Reviews of Meditation Research.* Oslo: Acem Publishing, 2008.

Davanger, Svend, Are Holen, Øyvind Ellingsen, and Kenneth Hugdahl. "Meditation-Specific Prefrontal Cortical Activation during Acem Meditation: An fMRI Study." *Perceptual and Motor Skills* 111 (2010): 291–306.

Davidson, R. J., and D. J. Goleman. "Attentional and Affective Concomitants of Meditation: Cross-Sectional Study." *Journal of Abnormal Psychology* 85 (1976): 235–238.

Deikman, Arthur J. "Experimental Meditation." *Journal of Nervous and Mental Disease* 136 (1963): 329–342.

————. "Implications of Experimentally Induced Contemplative Meditation." *Journal of Nervous and Mental Disease* 142 (1966): 101.

————. *The Observing Self: Mysticism and Psychotherapy.* Boston: Beacon Press, 1982.

DeMartino, Richard J. "Karen Horney, Daisetz T. Suzuki, and Zen Buddhism." *American Journal of Psychoanalysis* 51 (1991): 267–283.

Eliade, Mircea. *Yoga: Immortality and Freedom.* Translated by Willard R. Task. 2nd ed. 1954; repr., Princeton, NJ: Princeton University Press, 1990.

Fell, Juergen, Nikolai Axmacher, and Sven Haupt. "From Alpha to Gamma: Electrophysiological Correlates of Meditation-Related States of Consciousness." *Medical Hypotheses* 75 (2010): 218–224.

Fromm, Erich, D. T. Suzuki, and Richard De Martino. *Zen Buddhism and Psychoanalysis.* New York: Harper, 1960.

Goleman, Daniel. *Emotional Intelligence: Why It Can Matter More than IQ.* New York: Bantam Books, 1995.

————, ed. *Healing Emotions: Conversations with the Dalai Lama on Mindfulness, Emotions, and Health.* Boston: Shambhala, 1997.

————. *The Varieties of the Meditative Experience.* Manchester, NH: Irvington, 1977.

Goleman, D. J., and G. E. Schwartz. "Meditation as an Intervention in Stress Reactivity." *Journal of Consulting and Clinical Psychology* 44 (1976): 456–466.

Hersoug, Anne Grete, Nina Aarhus Smeby, Morten Wærsted, and Are Holen. "Stress Management with Acem Meditation." In Davanger et al., *Fighting Stress*, 139–145.

Hersoug, Tor. "The Battle for Realism: Schisms in the Early Meditation Movement." *The Meditation Blog*, August 21, 2010. http://themeditationblog.com/the-battle-for-realism-schisms-in-the-early-meditation-movement/#more-105 (accessed May 1, 2014).

Holmes, David S. "Meditation and Somatic Arousal Reduction: A Review of the Experimental Evidence." *American Psychologist* 39 (1984): 1–10.

———. "To Meditate or Rest? The Answer Is Rest." *American Psychologist* 40 (1985): 728–731.

———. "To Meditate or to Simply Rest, That Is the Question: A Response to the Comments of Shapiro." *American Psychologist* 40 (1985): 722–725.

Holzel, B. K., U. Ott, H. Hempel, A. Hackl, K. Wolf, and R. Stark. "Differential Engagement of Anterior Cingulate and Adjacent Medial Frontal Cortex in Adept Meditators and Non-Meditators." *Neuroscience Letters* 421 (2007): 16–21.

Horney, Karen. *Our Inner Conflicts*. New York: W. W. Norton, 1945.

Houtman, Gustaaf. "Vipassanā in Burma: Self-Government and the Ledi Ānāpāna Tradition." In *Hindu, Buddhist and Daoist Meditation: Cultural Histories*, edited by Halvor Eifring, 91–115. Oslo: Hermes, 2014.

Jang, J. H., W. H. Jung, D. H. Kang, M. S. Byun, S. J. Kwon, and C. H. Choi. "Increased Default Mode Network Connectivity Associated with Meditation." *Neuroscience Letters* 487 (2011): 358–362.

Kabat-Zinn, Jon. *Full Catastrophe Living: Using the Wisdom of Your Body and Mind to Face Stress, Pain, and Illness*. New York: Delacorte Press, 1990.

———. "An Outpatient Program in Behavioral Medicine for Chronic Pain Patients Based on the Practice of Mindfulness Meditation: Theoretical Considerations and Preliminary Results." *General Hospital Psychiatry* 4, no. 1 (April 1982): 33–47.

———. *Wherever You Go, There You Are: Mindfulness Meditation in Everyday Life*. New York: Hyperion, 1994.

Kabat-Zinn, J., L. Lipworth, and R. Burney. "The Clinical Use of Mindfulness Meditation for the Self-Regulation of Chronic Pain." *Journal of Behavioral Medicine* 8 (1985): 163–190.

Kasamatsu, Akira, and Tomio Hirai. "An Electroencephalographic Study on the Zen Meditation (Zazen)." *Folia Psychiatrica et Neurologica Japonica* 20 (1966): 315–336.

Killingsworth, Matthew A., and Daniel T. Gilbert. "A Wandering Mind Is an Unhappy Mind." *Science* 330 (2010): 932.

Kohn, Livia. "Quiet Sitting with Master Yinshi: Medicine and Religion in Modern China." *Zen Buddhism Today* 10 (1993): 79–95.

———. *The Taoist Experience: An Anthology*. Albany: State University of New York Press.

Lagopoulos, Jim, Jian Xu, Inge Rasmussen, Alexandra Vik, Gin S. Malhi, Carl F. Eliassen, Ingrid E. Arntsen, Jardar G. Sæther, Stig Hollup, Are Holen, Svend Davanger, and Øyvind Ellingsen. "Increased Theta and Alpha EEG Activity during Nondirective Meditation." *Journal of Alternative and Complementary Medicine* 15 (2009): 1187–1192.

Lazar, Sara W., George Bush, Randy L. Gollub, Gregory L. Fricchione, Gurucharan Khalsa, and Herbert Benson. "Functional Brain Mapping of the Relaxation Response and Meditation." *Neuroreport* 11 (2000): 1581–1585.

Lesh, T. V. "Zen Meditation and Development of Empathy in Counselors." *Journal of Humanistic Psychology* 10 (1970): 39–74.

Lounsbery, G. Constant. *Buddhist Meditation in the Southern School: Theory and Practice For Westerners*. London: Kegan Paul, Trench, Trubner and Co., 1935.

———. *La méditation bouddhique: Etude de sa théorie, et de sa pratique selon l'Ecole du Sud.* Paris: Adrian-Maisonneuve, 1935.

Lutz, A., L. L. Greischar, N. B. Rawlings, M. Ricard, and R. J. Davidson. "Long-Term Meditators Self-Induce High-Amplitude Gamma Synchrony during Mental Practice." *Proceedings of the National Academy of Sciences of the United States of America* 101 (2004): 16369–16373.

Mahesh Yogi, His Holiness Maharishi. *The Science of Being and Art of Living.* New Delhi: Allied Publishers, 1963.

McMillan, Rebecca L., Scott Barry Kaufman, and Jerome L. Singer. "Ode to Positive Constructive Daydreaming." *Frontiers in Psychology* 4 (2013): 626.

Murphy, Michael, and Steven Donovan. *The Physical and Psychological Effects of Meditation: A Review of Contemporary Research with a Comprehensive Bibliography 1931–1996.* 2nd ed. Sausalito, CA: Institute of Noetic Sciences, 1997.

Nesvold, Anders, Morten W. Fagerland, Svend Davanger, Øyvind Ellingsen, Erik E. Solberg, Are Holen, Knut Sevre, and Dan Atar. "Increased Heart Rate Variability during Nondirective Meditation." *European Journal of Preventive Cardiology* 19 (2012): 773.

Ospina, Maria B., Kenneth Bond, Mohammad Karkhaneh, Lisa Tjosvold, Ben Vandermeer, Yuanyuan Liang, Liza Bialy, Nicola Hooton, Nina Buscemi, Donna M. Dryden, and Terry P. Klassen. "Meditation Practices for Health: State of the Research." *Evidence Report / Technology Assessment* no. 155. Rockville, MD: Agency for Healthcare Research and Quality.

Schwartz, G. E., R. J. Davidson, and D. J. Goleman. "Patterning of Cognitive and Somatic Processes in Self-Regulation of Anxiety: Effects of Meditation versus Exercise." *Psychosomatic Medicine* 40 (1978): 321–328.

Seeman, W., S. Nidich, and T. Banta. "Influence of Transcendental Meditation on a Measure of Self-Actualization." *Journal of Counseling Psychology* 19 (1972): 184.

Shapiro, Deane H. "Clinical Use of Meditation as a Self-Regulation Strategy: Comments on Holmes's (1984) Conclusions and Implications." *American Psychologist* 40 (1985): 719–722.

Shapiro, D. H., and D. Giber. "Meditation and Psychotherapeutic Effects: Self-Regulation Strategy and Altered State of Consciousness." *Archives of General Psychiatry* 35 (1978): 294–302.

Shapiro, D. H., and S. M. Zifferblatt. "Zen Meditation and Behavioral Self-Control: Similarities, Differences, and Clinical Applications." *American Psychologist* 31 (1976): 519–532.

Sharf, R. H. "Buddhist Modernism and the Rhetoric of Meditative Experience." *Numen* 42 (1995): 228–283.

Smith, Jonathan C. "Meditation as Psychotherapy: A Review of the Literature." *Psychological Bulletin* 82 (1975): 558–564.

———. "Meditation, Biofeedback, and the Relaxation Controversy: A Cognitive-Behavioral Perspective." *American Psychologist* 41 (1986): 1007–1009.

Sood, Amit, and David T. Jones. "On Mind Wandering, Attention, Brain Networks, and Meditation." *Explore* 9 (2013): 136–141.

Stange, Paul. "Inner Islamization in Java." In *Meditation and Culture: The Interplay of Practice and Context,* edited by Halvor Eifring, 147–161. London: Bloomsbury Academic, 2015.

Suler, John R. "Meditation and Somatic Arousal Reduction." *American Psychologist* 40 (1985): 717.

Taylor, Rodney L., *The Confucian Way of Contemplation: Okada Takehiko and the Tradition of Quiet-Sitting.* Columbia: University of South Carolina Press, 1988.

Travis, Fred, David A. F. Haaga, John Hagelin, Melissa Tanner, Alaric Arenander, Sanford Nidich, Carolyn Gaylord-King, Sarina Grosswald, Maxwell Rainforth, and Robert H. Schneider. "A Self-Referential Default Brain State: Patterns of Coherence, Power, and eLORETA Sources during Eyes-Closed Rest and Transcendental Meditation Practice." *Cognitive Processing* 11 (2010): 21–30.

Vroklage, B. "Buddhist Meditation: Study on Its Theory and Practice According to the Southern School." *Anthropos* 31, nos. 1–2 (1936): 317.

Wallace, R. K. "Physiological Effects of Transcendental Meditation." *Science* 167 (1970): 1751.

Wallace, R. K., and H. Benson. "Physiology of Meditation." *Scientific American*, 226, no. 2 (1972): 84.

Wallace, Robert Keith, Herbert Benson, and Archie F. Wilson. "A Wakeful Hypometabolic Physiologic State." *American Journal of Physiology* 221 (1971): 795–799.

Wallace, R. K., H. Benson, A. F. Wilson, and M. D. Garrett. "Decreased Blood Lactate during Transcendental Meditation." *Federation Proceedings* 30 (1971): A376.

West, Michael A. "Meditation and Somatic Arousal Reduction: A Comment on Holmes's Review." *American Psychologist* 40 (1985): 717–719.

Winterstein, A. "Psychoanalysis and Yoga." *Imago*, 11, nos. 1–2 (1925): 204–205.

Xu, Jian, Alexandra Vik, Inge R. Groote, Jim Lagopoulos, Are Holen, Øyvind Ellingsen, Asta K. Håberg, and Svend Davanger. "Nondirective Meditation Activates Default Mode Network and Areas Associated with Memory Retrieval and Emotional Processing." *Frontiers in Human Neuroscience* 8 (2014): article 86.

Johannes Bronkhorst, PhD, is professor emeritus of Sanskrit and Indian studies at the University of Lausanne, Switzerland.

Edwin F. Bryant, PhD, is professor of Hindu religion and philosophy in the Department of Religion, Rutgers University, United States.

Halvor Eifring, PhD, is professor of Chinese in the Department of Culture Studies and Oriental Languages at University of Oslo, Norway.

Are Holen, MD, PhD, is professor of behavioral medicine in the Department of Neuroscience, Norwegian University of Science and Technology, Norway.

Madhu Khanna, PhD, is professor of Indic religion at the Centre for the Study of Comparative Religion and Civilizations, Jamia Millia Islamia, India.

Masaya Mabuchi, PhD, is professor of Chinese philosophy at the Foreign Language Teaching and Research Centre, Gakushūin University, Japan.

Kristina Myrvold, PhD, is associate professor of religious studies at Linnaeus University, Sweden.

Harold D. Roth, PhD, is professor of religious studies and director of Contemplative Studies Initiative at Brown University, United States.

Geoffrey Samuel, PhD, is emeritus professor at the School of History, Archaeology, and Religion at Cardiff University, UK, and an honorary associate in the Department of Indian Subcontinental Studies at the University of Sydney, Australia.

Morten Schlütter, PhD, is associate professor of Chinese religions in the Department of Religious Studies at the University of Iowa, United States.

Sarah Shaw, PhD, is a member of the Faculty of Oriental Studies at Oxford University, United Kingdom.

Page numbers in boldface type refer to illustrations.

abhidhamma, 66n.13, 123, 129–130
Abhinavagupta, 97
absorption, 14–17, 29, 31–32, 48, 53–56, 59,
    62, 64, 67nn.19,21, 83, 90, 235. See also
    samādhi; vicāra; vitarka
Acem Meditation, 14, 16, 35, 40n, 230,
    236–237, 239n.42
Ādi Granth, 105. See also Gurū Granth
    Sāhib
afflictions, 115, 218. See also *dhyān(a):*
    afflicted (*ārta*)
agency, 6–7, 10–11, 18, 41n.7
agni, 82–83
ahaṁkāra, **51**, 52, **58**, 59, 61–63
ahwāl, 13
akhaṇḍ jāp, 113
ālambana, 54–56, 62, 65, 67n.19, 96
Allah (*or* Allāh), 37, 106
Amitābha, 33, 37, 175–177
Amitāyus, 151, 153, 155–157, 159
ānanda, 53–54, **58,** 61–62, 64, 66n.13,
    68n.29
Ananda Marga, 229
ānāpānasati, 40, 134
an-ātman, 38. See also *anattā;* no(n)-self;
    self-negation
anattā, 122. See also *an-ātman;* no(n)-self;
    self-negation
anicca. See impermanence
aniconic symbols (or *yantras*), 11, 71–72
antaryāga, 76–77
anuprekṣā. See four reflections
anussati. See recollection
apophatic practices, 5, 38, 186–187, 190–192,
    195–197, 199–200, 201n.7
ar(a)hat, 96, 122, 126–128, 130
arousal reduction, 14–17
asaṁprajñāta samādhi, 64–66, 69n.38
ascesis (*or* asceticism), 10, 48, 94, 104, 115
asmitā, 51, 53–54, **58,** 61–64, 66n.12, 68n.34

asubha, 99n.9, 124, 130–131, 140n.21. *See*
    also foulness (*or* the foul)
ātma(n), 9, 62, 68n.30
attention, xi–xii, 5–8, 18, 20nn.31–32,
    21n.43, 28, 40, 125, 127, 131, 181n.42, 190,
    197, 211, 230, 232, 234–235, 237; focus of,
    8, 19n.3, 28; mindful, 42n.16; mode of, 8,
    44; unified, 187, 189. *See also* awareness;
    focused attention
attention-based technique, 1–2, 4, 17
attention training, 11. *See also* awareness
    training
awareness, 35, 51–53, 55–58, 60–65, 67n.17,
    68n.32, 69n.34, 75–76, 78, 83, 90, 123, 129,
    132, 134–135, 187–188, 208, 211–212;
    open (*or* inclusive, choiceless), 16–17,
    29–31, 41n.11; physical, 48, 53, 55. *See*
    also attention; mindful awareness (*or*
    presence); *puruṣa:* awareness of; subtle
    awareness; *śūnyatā:* awareness of;
    universal principle: awareness of; Way
    (Dào): awareness of the
awareness-in-action, 210
awareness training, x, 8, 20n.32. *See also*
    attention training
Āyāraṅga, 93

bahiryāga, 76–77
Benson, Herbert, 229, 232–233
Bhai Gurdas, 109, 118n.22
bhakti, 49, 103–104, 106. *See also* devotion
Bhaskararāya Makhin, 71, 77
bhāv(a)nā, 39, 75–77, 96, 115, 134, 138
Bhāvanopaniṣad Bhāṣya, 77
Bhoja Rāja, 62–63
bīja, 64. See also *nirbīja; sabīja*
bindu, 72–73, 78–79, 85–86, 88–90
biofeedback, 233, 238n.5
birth and death: beyond, 107; breaking one's
    mind of, 14, 169; liberation from, 104, 150

bla, 152
body and breath practices (*or* techniques), x, 11, 132
body practices, 18. *See also* mindfulness of body
brahman, 9, 62, 68nn.30,33, 88, 90
brahmavihāra, 129, 135
Brahm Bunga Trust, 112, 119n.32
brain waves, 30, 40, 234, 239n.42
breath, 6, 35–37, 109–110, 133–134, 138–139, 140n.21, 141n.26, 142n.42, 187–190, 233; counting of, 31; natural, 30. *See also* body and breath practices (*or* techniques); *dbugs; prāṇa; qì*
breath cultivation, 187–188
breathing, 93, 110, 160, 188, 191, 196–197. *See also* mindfulness of breathing
breathing meditation, 16, 18, 31, 35
breathing regulation, 112, 216, 222nn.40–41
breathing techniques (*or* practices), 6, 18, 49, 104, 109–110, 160
Buddha, 7, 11, 33, 66n.13, 99n.12, 122, 127–128, 130, 132, 135, 140n.6, 141n.28, 142n.43, 145–146, 148, 150–151, 170, 177
Buddhaghosa, 34, 124–127, 129, 131–134, 138, 140n.8, 141n.29, 142nn.40,42
Buddhahood, 145–147, 150–151, 160–161, 175–176
Buddha invocation, 170, 174–176, 178, 181n.34. *See also nen butsu; niàn(-)fó*
Buddha nature, 9, 37, 146, 166–167, 169–170, 172–173
buddhi, **51,** 52, **58,** 59, 61–63, 67n.28, 68n.31

cakra, xii–xiii, 9, 37, 71, 78–88, 161n.2. *See also* Śrīcakra
calm(ness), xii, 14, 79, 83, 122–123, 126, 130–131, 136, 140n.13, 141n.37, 172–173, 179, 191–192, 197. See also *samatha*
calming the mind, 136–137, 172–173, 179, 216, 221
Cáodòng tradition, 165–166, 171–175
Centering Prayer, 35
Chán, 13, 165–179
chanting, 5, 36–37, 85, 104, 110–114, 123, 134, 136, 175, 181n.34
'*Chi med Srog Thig,* 147, 149–157, **155,** 160
citta, **51, 52**–54, 56, **58,** 59, 61–65
clarity, 14–17, 195, 208

Cloud of Unknowing, 14, 27, 32–33, 36
compassion, 135, 142n.39, 145
concentration, xi, 15, 27–30, 32–33, 35, 40n.1, 41n.11, 42n.16, 48–49, 54, 60, 62, 64, 67n.17, 72, 74, 89, 110–112, 114–115, 117n.1, 128–129, 133, 174, 176, 188–191, 196–197, 211, 216, 218, 234, 236. *See also* absorption; *dhāraṇā; dhyān(a);* meditation: concentrative vs. nonconcentrative; *samatha; savicāra*
Confucius, 187, 191–192
consciousness, 64, 81, 86, 90, 97, 108, 112, 125, 129, 146, 187, 190; center of, 78, 85; divine, 15, 19n.1, 86; energy of, 76; fire of, 89; full, xi, 212; individual, 192–193; light of, 75; objective, 73 (see also *śakti*); pure, 52, 63, 65, 71–73 (see also *puruṣa; śakti*); sense, 80; states (*or* levels, planes, spheres) of, 21n.60, 46, 53, 69n.37, 73, 78, 83, 129; stream of, 40; subjective, 73 (*see also* Śiva); surface, 213; transformation of, 49, 77, 83
consciousness-as-power, 87
constructivism, ix, 11, 37–38, 41n.7
context, 7, 28, 41n.7, 104, 136, 147; American, 152; Asian, 152; Buddhist, 6, 34, 136; Chinese, 33, 180n.13; Christian, 5–6; Confucian, xiv; contemporary, 9; cultural, 9, 11–12, 160, 228; Daoist, 6; European, 228; Indian, 53, 231; Jain, 98; medical, 152; modern, 14, 17, 29, 33, 130, 135, 238; monastic, 135; mystical, 201; phenomenal, 73; post-Vedic, 49; political, 198; premodern, 10, 153; psychological, 237; public vs. private, 135; religious, 11–12, 228; ritual, 152; scientific, xi, 33; secular, xi; social, 12, 117; sociocultural, xiii, xiv, 11, 227; suggestive vs. nonsuggestive, 28, 37, 39; symbolic, xiii; Tibetan, 153; traditional, 17, 112, 227; Yogic, 6
correlative cosmology, 200
cosmic energy, 6, 37, 71
cosmic principle, 85, 89, 194

Dàhuì Zōnggǎo, 14, 165–175, 179; critique of seated meditation, 166–169; and doubt, 170–171; enlightenment and, 167, 170–171
dāntián, 37, 216

Dào. *See* Way (Dào)
Daoist rulership, 198–199
dbugs, 152
death, 63n.31, 93–94, 131; averting, 147, 157; fearless of, 114; initiatory, 86; meditation on, xi, 38, 43; mindfulness of, 132–133, 137, 141n.31; surmounting, 114
decontextualization, 228, 238
default mode network, 40, 230, 235–237, 239n.42
deity, 28, 35, 37, 71–73, 75–78, 80, 85–86, 88–89, 109, 132, 146–148, 151–160
devotion, x–xi, 2, 5–6, 18, 35, 38, 49, 103–116, 117n.1, 122, 128, 210, 228. *See also bhakti*
Dhammapada, 122–128, 133, 138, 139nn.1–2
dhāraṇā, 48, 75
dhikr, x, 4, 12, 18, 36, 118n.18
dhyān(a), 4, 7, 13, 15, 49, 74–76, 99nn. 4–5, 115; afflicted (*ārta*), 94, 96; four (in Buddhism), 66n.13; four (in Jainism), 94–97; pious (*dharmya*), 94–96; pure (*śukla*), 94–96; wrathful (*raudra*), 94, 96
dhyāna śloka, 72, 75
doubt, 16, 37, 170–179, 180n.22
drowsiness, 15–16, 112, 125, 218, 234, 237
duān-zuò, 5, 13
Dudjom Rinpoche, 147, 149–150, 156
Dusenbery, Verne, 116

ecstasy, 14, 16, 21n.47, 40, 90, 136
effortlessness, 8, 30, 32–33, 114, 169
ekaggatā (or *ekāgrata*), 33–34, 126, 136. *See also* one-pointedness
ekatānatā, 33. *See also* one-pointedness
Eliade, Mircea, 16, 39–40
emotion, 7, 16, 28–29, 31, 38, 51–52, 80, 107, 115, 138, 145, 187, 235, 237; observing, 210, 115; positive vs. negative, 9, 83; reducing (*or* eliminating, regulating, restricting), 190, 196, 200, 232
emotional change, 230
emotional pattern, 9, 17, 41n.11
emotional processing, 40, 234, 236
emotional unification (*or* integration), 122, 136
emptiness, 9, 15, 85, 156, 186–187, 189, 191–192, 195, 197, 200, 208, 219. *See also śūnyatā;* void; *xū*
encounter dialogue, 165, 168, 179n.3

energy, 76, 83, 86–87, 209, 216; cosmic, 6, 71 (see also *śakti*); vital, 82, 87, 186, 188–189, 193 (see also *prāṇa; qì*); life, 152, 160 (see also *bla*)
energy center. See *cakra*
energy manipulation, 8
enlightened Buddha (*or* guru, master, ruler), 94, 96, 107, 145, 150–151, 199, 200
enlightenment, xii, 95, 114, 138, 146, 150–151, 165, 167, 170–174, 177–179, 208, 212–213, 218, 232
enstasis (*or* enstasy), 16, 40, 78
Epistle of Prayer, 5, 10, 14

focus: forceful vs. effortless, 32–33; meditative, 48, 59, 61, 165; mental (*or* inward), 19n.3, 34–35, 63, 79; narrow (*or* exclusive) vs. open, 17, 29, 31–33, 56, 129, 210
focused attention, 27, 30, 41n.11, 187, 189
formless spheres, 124, 128–130, 135. *See also* meditation: formless
foulness (*or* the foul), 122, 130–131, 142n.42
four reflections, 94–96
fundamental aspects of reality (*or* existence), 9–10, 12, 14–15, 17–18, 212, 219

Gāo Pānlóng, 214–215, 218, 221nn.30,36
Gītā, 62–63, 65–66
God, 5–6, 9, 33, 36, 57, 103–117. *See also* Allah (*or* Allāh); Īśvara
god, 15, 18, 103–117, 132, 145, 148, 153, 158
goddess, 37, 71, 75–78, 83, 85, 153, 159–160. *See also* Tripurasundarī
Goenka, S. N., 98
gōng'àn, 20n.18, 165–179. *See also* keyword; *kōan; niànfó gōng'àn*
gross element, 51–52, 55, 58–64, 68, 85–86. See also *mahābhūta*
gross form, 50, 76–78, 84
gter-ma, 148–150, 153, 155–156, 159, 161n.8
gter-ston, 147–149, 161n.8, 161nn.10–11
guṇa, 50, **51,** 54, **58,** 61–62, 67n.26, 68n.28
gurdwārā, 105, 110–113
gurmantra, 108–111, 113, 119n.34
gurmukhi script, 105
guru, 10, 57, 76, 88–89, 103–116, 118n.20, 230
Gurū Arjan, 105, 113
Gurū Gobind Singh, 105, 108

Gurū Granth Sāhib, 103, 105–109, 112–113, 116, 117n.6, 118n.15, 119n.34. *See also* Ādi Granth

Gurū Nānak, 104–107, 115, 118n.18

Hānshān Déqīng (1546–1623), 16, 27, 32–35, 37, 178

Haribhadra, 97

Hatha Yoga, 5, 18

health, 17, 19, 122, 127, 133, 146–147, 150–153, 158–160, 186, 201n.5, 227–228

Hemacandra, 95, 97–98

huàtóu, 33, 166–179, 180n.10. See also *kànhuà*; keyword

Huìnéng, 5, 166, 168

hypnosis, 7, 11, 29, 39–40, 231

image, 5, 7, 19n.3, 29, 34–36, 54–55, 75–76, 88, 122, 125–127, 130, 154, 160. See also *nimitta*; *pratyaya*

impermanence, 122, 127–128, 131, 134

inner cultivation, 186–188, 190–200, 201n.25

inner transformation, xi–xii, 2, 4, 8–9, 12, 14, 17–18, 107, 111, 138

inside-out changes (*or* processes), 12, 29

insight, 12, 54–57, 62, 71–72, 127–131; calm and, 122–123, 126, 134, 140n.13, 141n.37; concentration and, 27, 29, 40n.1, 41n.11; discriminating, 94. See also *vipassanā* (or *vipaśyanā*, Vipassana)

insight meditation, 16, 42n.41, 230, 239n.19

Inward Training, 186, 188–190, 192–195, 200n.1

Īśvara, 9, 54, 65, 69n.39

janam-sākhī, 107, 118n.20

jap(a), 18, 117n.1, 118n.15; *akhaṇḍ*, 113, 119n.34

Japjī Sāhib, 106, 108, 117n.5

Jesus Prayer, x, 18, 20n.15

jhāna (or *jhāṇa*). See *dhyāna śloka*

Jina, 94, 96

jìng(-)zuò, 4, 13, 166, 207. *See also* quiet sitting

jñāna, 49, 73–74, 76, 78

Jñānārṇava, 97

Kabat-Zinn, Jon, 14, 229–230, 232

kaivalya, 52, 69n.38

kammaṭṭhāna, 124, 138

kànhuà, xii, 165–179; calmness and, 171–173; doubt and, 170–171, 173–175; enlightenment and, 167. See also *huàtóu*; keyword

karma, 65, 93, 95, 105, 138, 142n.45; positive (*or* good) vs. negative, 114, 147, 156

kasiṇa, 124–126, 128–129, 131, 140n.14, 140nn.15–16, 140nn.21,23, 141n.26, 142n.42

Kaulāvalīnirṇaya, 89

keyword, xii, 20n.15, 32–33, 37, 165–168, 174, 177. See also *gōng'àn*; *huàtóu*; *kànhuà*; *kōan*

khālsā, 103, 105, 108, 110

kīrtan, 105, 109, 112

kōan, 7, 12, 20n.18, 31, 37, 138. See also *gōng'àn*

Kulārṇava, 72

Kuṇḍalinī yoga, 81, 86–89

kusala-citta, 127–128, 135

Lakṣmīdhara, 85

Lǎozǐ, 37, 185–200

liṅga, 67n.28, 86–88

Línjì tradition, 165–166, 171–172

logismoí, 34

loving-kindness, 16, 135, 141n.30, 142n.38, 230, 239n.19

Lù Lóngqí, 214–215, 218

Lǚshì chūnqiū, 185–186, 190–194

macrocosm, 78, 86, 88

madness, 12

Mahābhārata, 53, 66n.13

mahābhūta, **51**, 52, **58**, 59, 61

Mahāprajña, 98, 100n.22

Mahāvīra, 93, 96

Mahesh Yogi, 228

manas, **51**, 52, **58**, 62

maṇḍala, 72, 78, 118n.20, 125, 148, 153, **155,** 158–160

mantra, 28, 42, 71–74, 77, 90, 97, 109, 118n.20, 140n.11; meaningless, 11, 37; repetition (*or* chanting, recitation) of, x, 30, 77, 85, 159, 160, 179; seed, 73, 86–87, 159

mantra (*or* mantric) meditation, 29, 36, 140n.11. See also *gurmantra* manuals, 106, 108, 124, 131, 139n.3, 207, 216–219, 222n.51

maqāmāt, 13

martial arts, 18, 22

māyā, 73, 105

McLeod, W. H., 107

medicine, x, 2, 11–12, 17, 124, 147, 152, 157–158, 186, 189, 196, 233–234

meditātiō, 1, 35

meditation: Asian, ix–xi, 1, 29, 35–36, 227–228; Buddhist, xi–xiii, 1, 6, 15–16, 40n.1, 66n.13, 98, 122–139, 145–161, 165–179, 189, 214, 216, 228–232, 234–237; canonical vs. noncanonical, 93–99; Chán, 166, 210, 217; Christian, x, 1, 35–36, 228; classification of, 8, 27–40, 93, 96; communal (*or* collective) vs. individual, 7, 10–11, 18, 132; concentrative vs. nonconcentrative, 16–17, 28, 30–32, 35, 39–40, 49, 54, 60, 234, 236; Confucian, ix, xii, xiv, 9, 132, 192, 207–220; Daoist, ix, xii–xiii, 9, 33, 38, 185–186, 189, 200, 216; definition of, xii, 1–19, 111, 168; directive vs. nondirective, 27–40, 234, 236–237; discursive vs. nondiscursive, 1, 35–36; effect of, 6, 11, 15, 27, 38–40, 227–235, 237; European, x, 2, 29, 34, 227–228; formless, 76, 129, 133–134; Greco-Roman, x–xi; guided vs. self-administered, 7, 11, 39; Hindu, 9, 18, 48, 71, 97; Indian (*or* Indic), 39, 110, 114, 138; Islamic, x, 36, 228; Jain(a), xii–xiii, 93–99, 137; Judaic, x, 36, 228; lying, 13, 31, 141n.29, 166–168, modern, xii, 9, 27, 36, 227, 237–238; moving, 186; Neo-Confucian, xii, xiv, 9, 132, 207–220; recitative, x, xii, 8, 12, 35, 103, 106, 109–111, 114–116; seated, 168–170, 180n.17; sitting, 127, 132–135, 141nn.28,37, 166–170, 186; stages of, 13, 30, 48–66, 71–91, 95–99, 108, 118n.18, 122–139, 202n.55; standing, 13, 31, 128, 132, 141n.29, 166–168; study of, ix–x, xiii–xiv, 3–4, 36, 227–231, 233–237; Sufi, x, 4, 10, 12–13, 18, 36, 118n.18; Tantric, 4, 39, 71–91, 145–161; the term, xi, 1, 4, 7, 13, 15, 18, 35, 39, 66n.13, 93–94, 99n.4, 134, 168, 223; thematic vs. nonthematic, x–xi, 28, 31, 36–39, 228; Tibetan, xii–xiii, 9, 17, 132–133, 145, 161, 230, 239n.19; walking, 13, 31, 125, 132, 135, 141n.29, 166–168;

Zen, xii–xiii, 8, 31, 165–179, 229, 231–232, 234. *See also* breathing meditation; *dhyāna śloka; duān-zuò; jìng(-)zuò; muraqaba;* quiet sitting; *samādhi;* yoga

meditation object, xi, 5, 7–13, 21n.43, 28–39, 41n.11, 42n.41, 54–65, 67n.19, 68n.29, 72, 93, 97, 122–139, 237; thematic vs. nonthematic, 28, 31, 35–39. See also *kammaṭṭhāna*

mental attitude, 8, 14, 28–31, 237

microcosm, 77–78, 86, 88

mindful awareness (*or* presence), 15, 33–34

mindfulness, 35, 76, 122, 126–127, 132–133, 142n.42, 227, 230, 232, 235–237, 239n.19; concentration and, 35, 40n.1, 42n.16, 128; *vipassanā* and, 27, 31, 40n.1, 41n.11

mindfulness meditation, 14, 230, 232, 235–236

mindfulness of body, 123, 132–133, 141n.26

mindfulness of breathing, 40n.1, 132–134, 141n.26

mind wandering, 15–16, 34, 40, 140n.14, 230, 234–237

mokṣa, 52, 114

monothetic definition, 3–4

mu'āyana, 13

mudrā, 71, 74, 80, 158, 180

mukti, 52, 114

muraqaba, 13, 118n.18

mushāhada, 13

mystical experience, ix, 10, 104, 107–108, 114, 185, 208

mysticism, 9, 12, 18, 20n.36, 38, 43n.46, 66n.10

nāḍī, 81, 161n.2

nām, 106–108, 113–114, 117n.6, 118n.22

name of the Buddha (*or* Buddha['s] name), x, 33, 36–37, 174–178, 181n.34

nām simran, x, xii, 9, 103–117

Nèiyè. *See* Inward Training

nen butsu, x, 18. *See also* Buddha invocation; *niàn(-)fó*

neuroimaging, 40, 230, 234

neuroscience, 235, 237

niàn(-)fó, x, 18, 170, 175–179, 181n.34. *See also* Buddha invocation; *nen butsu*

niànfó gōng'àn, 177, 178, 179, 181n.52

nibbāna, 127, 129, 137. *See also* nirvana
nimitta, 125–127, 130, 134, 141n.26
nirbīja, 64–65, 90
nirguṇa, 104
nirodhaḥ, 53
nirvana, 159. See also *nibbāna*
nirvicāra, **58,** 59–62, 94
nirvikalpa, 57, 58
nirvitarka, 55–57, **58,** 60–61, 64
no(n)-self, 38, 131. See also *an-ātman; anattā;* self-negation
nonaction, 186, 194, 198–200
nyāsa, 76, 85

obstacle, 15, 32, 34–35, 68n.34, 80, 127, 146–147
one-pointedness, 8, 31, 33–34, 54, 122, 126. See also *ekaggatā* (or *ekāgrata*); *ekatānatā*
open monitoring, 27, 30, 41n.11
original nature, xii, 177, 207, 209–216, 219
outside-in changes (*or* processes), 11–12, 28–29

Padmasambhava, 148, 150, 153, 158–160
Patañjali, 48–49, 52–55, 57–59, 61–65, 66n.13, 68nn.29–30, 69n.39, 97
perennialism, ix, 9, 12, 15, 20n.36
posture (*or* position), 5, 8, 17–18, 76, 110, 132–135, 141, 176, 187–188, 197, 237; cross-legged, 13; lying, 13, 141n.29, 168; *samādhi*, 131–132; seated, 4, 13, 17, 168–169; sitting, 110, 132, 134–135, 168–169, 187; standing, 13, 112, 132, 141n.29, 168; walking, 13, 132, 135, 141n.29, 168
prakṛti, 49–50, **51, 58,** 59, 61–65, 67nn.26,28, 68n.31
prāṇa, 37, 82–83, 87. *See also* vital energy
pratyaya, 54–55, 67n.18
prayer, xivn.3, 1, 5–6, 17–19, 34–36, 106, 111–113, 117n.1, 119n.34, 157. *See also* Centering Prayer; Jesus Prayer
prekṣā-dhyāna, 98
psycho-cosmos, 73–74, 78, 86, 88
psychotherapy, x, 7, 18–19, 29, 41n.10, 231–232
pūjā, 78, 90
Pure Land, 172, 175–177

puruṣa, 9, 49, **51,** 52, 54–55, **58,** 62–65, 66n.13, 68nn.30,32, 68n.34, 69n.39; awareness of, 63–65

qì, 37, 188–190, 197, 200. *See also* vital energy
Qì-gōng (*or* Qigong), 8, 18, 230
quiet sitting, xii, 166, 169, 180n.17, 207–220, 227. See also *jìng(-)zuò*
quietude, xii, 13–14, 19n.3, 169, 172, 208, 210–213, 215, 218

rahit-nāmā, 108
rajas, 50, **51, 58,** 67n.26, 83
recitation, x, 4, 36–37, 94; buddha-name (Chinese Zen), 175–178, 181n.34; divine name (Sikh), 103–105, 107, 112, 115, 118n.29, 119n.34; mantra (Tantra), 77, 159–160
recollection, 117n.1, 123–124, 126, 131–134, 141n.30
recontextualization, 228, 238
recorded sayings, 11, 166–167, 180n.29
relaxation, xii, 14–15, 17, 229, 231–234, 236–237; logic, 21n.57, 36
relaxation response, 29, 229–233, 237
relaxation techniques, 1, 17
religious conversion, 10–12
remembrance, 103–104, 107–108, 113–114, 116, 117n.1
repetition, 5, 17–19, 29, 37, 94, 103, 107–116, 119n.34; inner (*or* mental), 139, 174. See also *mantra:* repetition (*or* chanting, recitation) of
Rinzai. See Línjì tradition
ritual, x–xi, 1, 5, 18–19, 71–78, 85, 89–90, 91n.5

śābda (or *śabad*), 37, 105, 107, 114
sabīja, 64, 67n.17
sādh sangat, 111–112
śakti, 9, 61, 71–73, 76, 80–81, 85, 87–88, 90
Śākyamuni, 146
samādhi, xii, 13, 15, 34, 40, 48–66, 78, 90. *See also* posture (*or* position): *samādhi; samāpatti*
samāpatti, 54–58, 60–61, 64, 67nn.19,21. See also *samādhi*
sāmarasya, 77

samatha, 27, 29–31, 122, 126–128, 130–132, 134–135
Sāṁkhya, 49, 51–52, 54, 57–59, 62, 66n.10
saṁprajñāta, 53–54, 62–65, 67n.19
saṁskāra, 52, 55–57, 64–65, 66n.12, 67nn.17–18
sangha, 132
sànluàn, 20n.31, 35
Sant tradition, 104, 107, 118n.18
sat-tarka, 77
sattva, 50, **51, 58,** 61, 62, 67n.26, 68n.29, 83
savicāra, **58,** 60, 64
savikalpa, 57, 58
savitarka, 55–57, **58,** 60, 64
seed. See bīja
self, 9–11, 15, 38, 49, 62–63, 66n.13, 68nn.31,33, 69n.38, 76, 97, 122, 161, 194, 201n.7, 209, 213, 216, 221nn.11,29; inner, **85,** 89, 108, 208, 210, 211, 216, 221n.29; physical, 82, 209; psychic, 82; sense of, 51; true, 39, 64, 76, 208, 221n.11. See also an-ātman; anattā; ātma(n); no(n)-self; puruṣa
self-awareness, 51, 56, 65, 235
self-centeredness, 103, 105, 114, 116
self-cultivation, 111, 186, 208, 210, 212, 215
self-negation, 186, 201n.7. See also an-ātman; anattā; no(n)-self
self-transformation, 10, 12, 18
sēvā, 116
shamanism, 14, 18, 147–148, 152, 160
Sheng Yen, 6, 35
shi-kan ta-za, 6, 8
siddhi, 59, 67n.21, 79, 97, 147, 150, 153, **159**
silence, 14, 90, 122, 179, 186–187, 192, 216
silent illumination, 166, 167, 168, 169, 171, 172, 175
sitting in oblivion, 38
Śiva, 9, 72–73, 76, 85, 87–88, 90
sleep, 15–16, 21n.60, 50, 66n.11, 69n.37, 170, 218, 233–234
Sōtō. See Cáodòng tradition
spiritual exercise, xi, 36
Śrīcakra, 71–72, 74, 76–79
Śrīvidyā, 71–72, 76–77, 80
Śrīyantra, 71–73, **75,** 77–78, 80, 82, 85, 88, **89,** 91
state (of mind [or consciousness, awareness]), xiii, 1–2, 4, 13–18, 28, 31, 39, 48, 50–69, 73, 78–79, 83, 90, 96–97, 122, 126, 142n.42, 190, 196–197, 208–210, 212–213, 216–219; emotional and cognitive, 115; enlightened, 128, 150, 161n.13; meditative (or meditation[al]), 13–14, 16, 21n.60, 50, 53, 60, 130, 161n.13; mental, 137; natural, 79, 94, 212; psychological, 187, 210; resultant, 187, 191–193, 197; self-induced, 11; short-term (or passing, transient, transitory), 4, 13, 21n.47, 40, 129; skillful, 135; technique vs., 4, 18, 32, 130; trait vs., 13, 40, 187, 196–200; trance-like, 112; vacuous, 167
stillness, 14, 29, 67n.26, 169, 172, 187, 191–192, 197, 200
Śubhacandra, 97–98
subtle awareness, 15, 48, 53, 58
subtle body, 37, 71–72, 77–78, 80–82, 87–88, 151, 161n.2
subtle element, 54, 59–61, 63, 68nn.29,31, 85
subtle essence, **51,** 52, **58,** 59–61
Sukhmani Sāhib, 113
śūnyatā, awareness of, 156. See also emptiness; void; xū
sūtra, chanting (or reading) of, 5, 36, 170
syncretism, 213, 219

Tài-jí, 8, 18
tamas, 50, **51, 58,** 67n.26, 83
tanmātra, **51,** 52, **58,** 59–61, 68n.31
Tantra, ix, xii, 4, 39, 49, 71–91, 97, 141n.34, 145–161, 179
technical differences, 40
technical element (or feature, tool), xi, xiii, 6, 7, 29, 31, 36–38, 227–228
technique, 1–19, 72, 87, 89, 104, 106, 110, 126, 138, 158; ambivalence toward, 5–6; apophatic, 186–187, 190–191, 195, 197, 200; attention-based, 2, 8, 17; state vs. 4, 18, 32, 130; (thematic) content vs., x–xi, 1, 11–12, 36–39, 42n.41, 228
thought control, 96
thought process, 140n.17
thoughts, 7, 19n.3, 29, 34, 41n.11, 52, 54, 65, 67n.18, 83, 109; accepting (or allowing), 28, 30–32, 35, 42n.11, 234; beyond, 35, 65; contentless, 235; deluded, 32, 34–35, 37, 166, 178; digressive, 28, 31, 33–35, 235; discursive, 55; distractive, 8, 32–34;

thoughts (cont.)
exploring, 34–35; flow of, 34; freedom
from (or lack of, no), 34, 191, 208; letting
go of, 237; logical, 36; peripheral, 28,
31–34; random, 5, 15–16, 28, 30, 32–34,
172–173, 237; reducing (or chopping off,
blocking out, abandoning, stilling,
terminating, emptying of, quietening,
not giving rise to, stopping, calming
down, ridding the mind of, excluding,
avoiding, suppressing, keeping away,
eliminating, restricting, removing,
emptying out), 15–16, 28, 31–35, 53, 65,
128, 165, 173, 187, 189–190, 196–197, 200;
replacing, 231; stimulus-independent,
230, 235; stray, 234, 237; trivial, 189
TM. See Transcendental Meditation
trait, 13, 40, 73, 83, 84, 187, 193–196,
198–200. See also state (of mind [or
consciousness, awareness])
tranquility, 14, 50–51, 83, 134, 186, 191–192,
194–197, 199–200
Transcendental Meditation (or TM), 30, 35,
227, 229–230, 232, 234–237, 238n.10
Transformation. See inner transformation;
self-transformation
Tripurasundarī, 71–73, 76, 84–85

ultimate reality, 9, 15, 38, 146–147
universal mechanism, 5–6, 17, 27, 35–37
universal principle, xii, 146, 208–215, 219,
221n.36; awareness of, 210
Upaniṣads, 48, 62–63, 65, 68n.30
Upatissa, 124–126, 139n.3
Uttarajjhayaṇa, 93

Vācaspati Miśra, 55–57, 59, 61–63, 67nn.
23–24, 68n.29, 69n.36
vāhigurū, 103–104, 108–113, 115–116,
118n.29
via negativa, 38, 201
vicāra, 48, 53–54, 58–59, 61, 64, 66n.13, 126,
136. See also nirvicāra; savicāra
Vimuttimagga, 124, 139n.3, 141n.26
vipassanā (or vipaśyanā, Vipassana), 16, 27,
29–31, 35, 40, 98, 122, 127–128, 134, 141n.33,
227, 239n.42

visualization, x, xii, 1, 5–8, 18, 36–37, 49, 71,
76–77, 84–87, 89, 97, 124–126, 131, 136,
145–147, 158–160
Visuddhimagga, 124, 139n.3, 141n.26
vitakka, 126, 136, 141n.24. See also vitarka
vital energy, 82, 87, 186, 188–189, 193. See
also prāṇa; qì
vitality, 82, 152, 157, 160–161, 186, 190
vitarka, 48, 53–55, 58–59, 61, 64, 66nn.12–13.
See also nirvitarka; savitarka; vitakka
void, 39, 85–86, 90, 173. See also emptiness;
śūnyatā; xū
vṛtti, 53–55, 65, 67nn.18–19
Vyāsa, 53–58, 64–65

Wáng Jī, 216, 222nn.41–43
Wáng Shǒurén, 207, 209, 211–212, 215–216,
220, 221nn.18,28
watchfulness, 15, 34–35, 114
Way (Dào), xii, 9, 169, 173, 186–197, 199–200,
201n.7, 213, 219; awareness of the, 187, 192,
201n.7
wisdom, 29, 39, 50, 67n.26, 136, 145, 190–191,
194, 200
worship, 71–77, 86, 88–90, 91n.5, 103, 105,
108, 114–115, 117n.1, 170

xū, 186, 191–192, 197. See also emptiness;
śūnyatā; void
Xuē Huì, 212, 214, 219
Xuěyán Zǔqīn, 172, 174

yantra, x, xii–xiii, 8–9, 11, 37, 71–91, 136,
137, 142n.40. See also Śrīyantra
yoga, ix, xii–xiii, 8, 13, 16, 48–66, 138,
228–234, 238n.5. See also Hatha Yoga;
Kuṇḍalinī yoga
Yoga Nidra, 16
Yogaśāstra, 95, 97–98, 99n.6
Yoga Sūtras, 48–66, 133
Yuán Huáng, 217–218, 222n.45
Yúnqī Zhūhóng, 177–178

Zhìchè Duànyún, 174–175, 177–178
Zhuāngzǐ, 185–187, 189–196, 199, 201n.6
Zhū Xī, 207, 209–212, 214–215, 217–220,
221n.11, 222n.40

About the Editor

HALVOR EIFRING is professor of Chinese at the University of Oslo, where he teaches Chinese language, literature, and culture and currently directs the international research project "Two Thousand Years of Mind Wandering." He is general secretary of the Acem International School of Meditation.